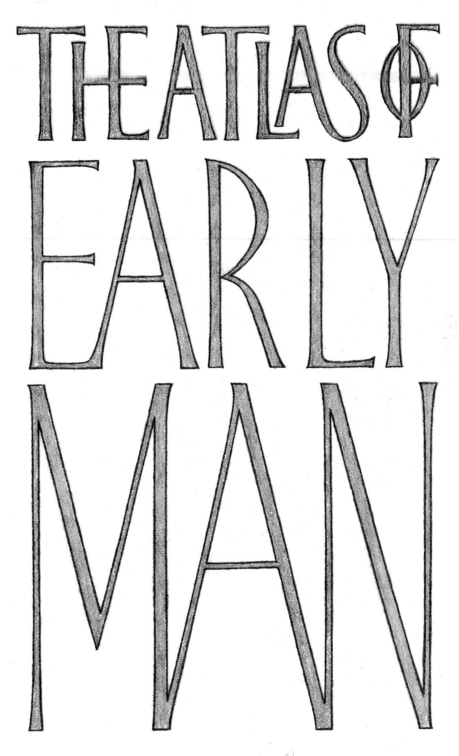

THE ATLAS OF EARLY MAN

Jacquetta Hawkes

Assisted by David Trump

M

To BARBARA WYKEHAM
who first convinced me that people want
a history designed to show
"What Happened at the Same Time as What".

Edited and designed by
Dorling Kindersley Limited
29 King Street, London WC2E 8JD

SBN 333 19897 2

First published 1976 by
MACMILLAN LONDON LIMITED
London and Basingstoke
Associated companies in New York
Dublin Melbourne Johannesburg and Delhi

Made and printed in Great Britain

HALF TITLE PAGE: *Ivory relief of a warrior in ceremonial
dress. From the palace of Shalmaneser III, Nimrud.
Ninth century BC.*

TITLE PAGE: *Bronze head of Aphrodite. Praxiteles.
Fourth century BC.*

Contents

Introduction 7

35,000–8000 BC

Period I 13
Advanced Hunting cultures –
Cromagnons – flint and bone tools –
cave paintings – peopling of
Americas and Australia – end of Ice
Age – Late Hunting cultures

Technology 24   *Architecture* 28
Art 32   *Summary chart* 36

8000–5000 BC

Period II 39
First farmers – domestication of
plants and animals – New Stone
Age – first pottery – villages and
towns – Mother Goddess worship
– rock paintings

Technology 46   *Architecture* 50
Art 54   *Summary chart* 58

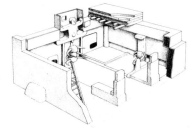

5000–3000 BC

Period III 61
Literate civilization – cities –
Copper Age – unification of Upper
and Lower Egypt – kilns – seagoing
sailing ships – megalithic tombs –
wheeled vehicles

Technology 72   *Architecture* 76
Art 80   *Summary chart* 84

3000–2000BC

Period IV 87
River valley civilizations – Ur –
pyramids – ziggurats – Maltese
temples – lake dwellings –
Gilgamesh – Sargon – Imhotep –
bronze technology

Technology 98 *Architecture* 102
Art 106 *Summary chart* 110

2000–1000BC

Period V 113
Minoan Crete – Mycenaean
civilization – rise of Assyria – New
Kingdom in Egypt – Hammurabi –
Ramesses II – Shang Dynasty –
Stonehenge – alphabetic writing

Technology 124 *Architecture* 128
Art 132 *Summary chart* 136

1000–500BC

Period VI 139
Assyrian Empire – Medes and
Persians – Phoenicians – Greek city
states – Olmecs – Etruscans –
Homer – Solomon – Buddha –
Confucius – coinage

Technology 152 *Architecture* 156
Art 160 *Summary chart* 164

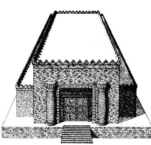

500BC–AD1

Period VII 167
Persian Empire – Roman conquest
of Europe – Alexander the Great –
Darius – Persepolis – Great Wall
of China – Parthenon – stupas –
hill forts – Greek drama

Technology 184 *Architecture* 188
Art 192 *Summary chart* 196

AD1–500

Period VIII 199
Imperial Rome – Christianity –
Mayas – Gupta Dynasty – Jesus of
Nazareth – Hadrian – King Arthur –
Constantine – fall of Rome –
beginnings of Byzantium

Technology 216 *Architecture* 220
Art 224 *Summary chart* 228

Atlas of Archaeological Sites 230

Gazetteer 246

Index 248

Acknowledgments 254

Introduction

This book has a very definite purpose. For several decades I have been writing for readers with a general interest in prehistory and early history. The experience has convinced me that they feel one great need. How often has a person come up to me and said "It's all very well, but can't you make me understand 'what happened at the same time as what'?" – or words to that effect.

I sympathise with them very much. Even for the nearer and more familiar periods of our past the recognition of contemporaries of all kinds is hard enough. Who can readily link in time, say, kings and inventions, statesmen and artists, wars and architectural style? Who would be happy if given a particular date and asked to say who was living and what was happening in France, Turkey, India, China, Mexico and North America? There has been an abundance of linear histories pursuing from first to last the history of a people or land or of any of the innumerable special themes that concern students of the past. There have been few that move sideways, as it were, rather than on and on, few concerned to show what happened at the same time rather than what followed.

This is why I determined to produce a book that would answer the question "what happened at the same time as what?" For the purpose I have divided the 40,000 or so years from the full emergence of Homo sapiens down to AD 500 into eight time steps, each one of them taken right round the globe to display what was happening in many fields of human activity and what famous men and women were living.

In some ways it would have been good to have more steps to secure more precise contemporaneity, but it was evident that this would make the work dauntingly elaborate – and far too bulky. So they are limited to eight, representing progressively shorter time spans as events and individuals crowd on to the stage of our knowledge.

In writing the main texts, I found it impossible to keep to a standard form, since the nature of the information available is so very different as between one period and another. As soon as the material allows, however, I have begun each section with a rapid global survey of the main points of interest, then sketched in a more coherent outline of its history.

As for the selection of the pictures, I make no apology for including as many as possible of the most familiar treasures from the past, for it would have gone against my whole intention to do otherwise. Readers and viewers want to know the comparative ages of the Lascaux and Altamira cave paintings, the pyramids of Giza, Stonehenge, the head of Nefertiti, the gold mask of Agamemnon, Shang bronzes, the Parthenon and the Pantheon, the temple pyramids of Mexico, to pick a few items at random. So these famous pieces appear in the period spreads, although less familiar subjects have been chosen for the text pages.

In both text and illustrations most attention is focused on the centres of innovation and achievement, while at the same time the lack of change in other regions is recorded. In this way it can be seen how regions that have been backward may quicken and lead a new advance, while the early homelands of progressive change grow sluggish. I hope I have now explained my purpose.

In trying to achieve it I have encountered two main difficulties. The first, which I must feel more as the author, is the hard intractability

The boy pharaoh Tutankhamun depicted with his wife (daughter of Akhenaten) on the back of one of his thrones. The throne is of wood, overlaid with gold.

7

of words, their cumbersomeness, the amount of space they take to express even a simple meaning. Sentences cannot skip quickly enough from place to place to give a picture of all that is happening at one time. To get as near as possible to achieving this I have sometimes cut in disconnected references to some contemporary event or life – but plainly to do this very often would lead to chaos – or at the very least to irritation. Happily, however, this difficulty can be overcome by using other forms of expression. For each section the chart, the world map and the pictures illustrating art, architecture and technology convey what was happening at the same time as what almost in a glance. That has been our intention in planning the volume.

The second difficulty is of a totally different kind. It is caused by present uncertainties about the best known of all scientific aids to archaeology – the method of dating that is often summarily called Carbon 14, but for which I have preferred the term radiocarbon dating. When it was first introduced, soon after the war, it was hoped that this way of obtaining dates by analysing the breakdown of radioactive isotopes of carbon in various organic substances, such as charcoal and bone, was going to give us fairly exact dates back to about 30,000 years ago. Much work was done to perfect the technique and it seemed it must become more and more accurate. Then it began to appear through testing Egyptian antiquities of historically know age that something was wrong with radiocarbon dates before about 1000 BC. They were, in fact, too late, and increasingly so as one went further back in time. For example, an Egyptian object known to have been made in c.2500 BC would be dated by radiocarbon analysis to c.2100 BC.

Evidently the intake of Carbon 14 has not been constant. Almost as soon as the trouble had been recognized a possible remedy was forthcoming. The ingenious yet technically simple method of dating timber by counting annual tree rings had already been carried quite far into the past and now it was found that with the use of the long-lived bristlecone pines of California it could be pushed back much further. Their rings could be directly tested by radiocarbon methods and in this way the degree of error fixed back to about 4500 BC. Once this had been done – and of course what I have made to sound simple was a very laborious business – it became possible to make the necessary correction to the radiocarbon dates, although it was complicated by the fact that there were wobbles in the curve that made precision even more elusive.

For some years now it has been the custom among archaeologists to use two dates, one according to radiocarbon age (which gives correct relative dates as between one antiquity and another) and the other with the bristlecone correction that is as near as possible to the real age according to our calendar. The first form was written as b.c., the second as B.C. It was obvious that this was a temporary expedient and that as confidence in the bristlecone figures grew firmer a shift to the calendrical B.C. figures must be made.

Although minor adjustments are still going on, and perhaps there is still an undertow of uneasiness about the corrected dates, we decided that confidence in their reliability is now so general that they must be adopted for this book. It might well be said that it is madness to produce a book so largely dependent on a chronological framework at a moment of such uncertainty and change. However, I can say from experience that there has never been a moment when it has not appeared rash to produce any wide-ranging archaeological work, when the cautious have not counselled delay.

The most conspicuous alteration in the historical picture caused

The Great Sphinx at Giza

by radiocarbon dating in general and heightened by the recent correction is to push back the dates of prehistoric Europe in relation to those of the orient. Indeed, rather exaggerated claims have been made for the revolutionary effects entailed. The public has been encouraged to suppose that instead of the West usually being indebted to Asia and the eastern Mediterranean for progressive innovation, Europe was often in the van. Anyone using this book with that idea in mind must see how false it is. The only adjustment of much interest to the general reader is that megalithic tomb building seems to have owed nothing to Mediterranean influences but to have been native to Europe. Also that it is possible to claim the Maltese temples as the earliest monumental architecture in stone, older by several centuries than the step pyramid and its associated buildings in Egypt. They are, however, relatively crude and modest in scale.

This question of cultural changes brought about by migration, trade, war, the travels of individuals or direct borrowing from individuals brings me to the only theoretical matter I need to raise. I have generally avoided bringing any personal view of history into the text, but there is one exception. I have revealed myself as a diffusionist – although a moderate one. Although every case must be judged on its merits, I believe that technical inventions, or peculiarities in art styles or crafts-manship are somewhat more likely to be due to one of the above means of learning from others than to independent origins. I probably would not have thought of raising this issue had there not been a strong wave of anti-diffusionisms in archaeology. I believe it to be dictated by a wish to make the flowing movements of existence more amenable to "scientific" analysis. It is clearly against most of the manifestations of recorded history. Readers will, I think, be able to see why work on this volume has only strengthened my preference for a rational diffusionism.

A few more explanations need to be made in this Introduction. First as to the use of archaeological terms. I have as far as possible shunned them. I have usually translated Palaeolithic as Old Stone Age and Neolithic as New Stone Age. The last, highly progressive phase of the Old Stone Age (the Upper or Late Palaeolithic) is referred to as the Advanced Hunting period, and the Mesolithic which followed as the Late Hunting period. Particularly in Period I it proved impossible not to use the term "culture" in the specialized sense of a grouping of distinctive ways of making and doing things which in the remote prehistoric past is all we have to identify a coherent people or society.

Then there is that troublesome conflict in geographical usage between those who bring the Middle East right to the Mediterranean, seemingly leaving only Anatolia (Asia Minor) for the Near East, and those who keep to earlier custom in extending the Near East as far as Iraq. I have followed the latter school.

No one, I think, can disagree if I say that the plan of this book is a very ambitious one. I have been most ably assisted in carrying it out by David Trump and the picture-seekers of Dorling Kindersley, but we know that with so vast an undertaking faults will be found even in our best endeavour. All the same, when next I am asked what happened at the same time as what, I shall be able with some confidence to refer the questioner to this Atlas of Early Man.

King Arcesilas of Cyrene supervises the weighing, recording and storing of a commodity – probably wool, for which his country was famous. Laconian kylix, sixth century BC.

35,000–8,000 BC

I am beginning this series of time steps through history at 35,000 BC because that was when, within a few thousand years, modern man was established as the sole human species on earth. It was also the dawn of an age of rapid cultural advance. Tools became more exactly designed for specialized uses, hunting and fighting weapons became more effective, skin clothing and shelter afforded better protection against the cold. Far more important for any true evaluation of human advancement, it was not long before these advanced hunting peoples began to create works of art of high imaginative quality, executed in an amazingly wide range of techniques. Their fine sculpture, modelling, painting, and engraving put us in touch with them on fully human terms. We can see them as already our brothers, with the same creative urge, the same gift for image making; they are already feeling their way towards religious symbolism.

This must be the right date at which to begin even if only because any earlier one would leave us very little to record in our various categories beyond simple stone tools and a few almost featureless settlement sites. I think, though, that I should give an outline of what went before in order to answer some questions very relevant to the purpose of this book.

First of all, at the risk of irritating readers who already know the answer, I must deal with the question of prehistoric men and the giant reptiles. In spite of all efforts to dispel the idea that they were contemporaries, it is still quite common to see drawings of hairy men dressed in even hairier skins shaking clubs at dinosaurs or ducking to avoid the gaping beaks of pterodactyls. The fact is, of course, that the reptiles evolved their vast bulk and strange forms and excrescences during those unimaginably long spans of time known to geologists as the Jurassic and Cretacious periods, which lasted from 180 to 70 million years ago. Even with the great lengthening of the time span of human evolution that has recently been accepted, the earliest tool-making humans did not appear on earth much before two million years ago. It was, therefore, impossible by many tens of millions of years for even very apish-looking forebears to have confronted even the latest generations of huge reptiles.

Newspapers so often announce that another fossil "man" has been unearthed and our ancestry pushed back another million or so years that many people must read these accounts with either scepticism or amusement. One reason for this apparently elastic ancestral line is that it is extremely difficult to decide what features should be accepted as the criteria for humanity. One possible definition is cultural: that beings known to have been capable of making tools should qualify as men. The troublesome word in this definition is "known", for very early tools have often been found without human fossils, and we can never be sure that human fossils found with no tools nearby are not the remains of tool-making men.

In general, physical characteristics are now preferred as criteria. Brain size is important, and human evolution has in fact involved a fairly steady increase in the number of "little grey cells" up to the emergence of modern man. On the other hand, brain size is not a reliable guide for judging which species were on the direct line of our ancestry and which were on side branches that were to die out. Oddly enough, the exact pattern of teeth and their cusps is one of the most useful indications of which fossil beings could or could not have had us as their descendants.

Inevitably there is much that is uncertain about the emergence and development of our kind on earth, but in spite of this, enough of humanity's true story is now known for it to satisfy our present purposes. First of all, it can be said that the evolutionary emergence of

OPPOSITE: *Olduvai Gorge, Tanzania.*

OVERLEAF: *The rotunda, or "Hall of Bulls", at Lascaux Cave in the Dordogne, France.*

humans, that is to say of the genus *Homo*, took place during the period known to geologists as the Pleistocene. This seems to have begun something like two million years ago and to have lasted until it was succeeded by the Holocene (or Recent) period after the retreat of the last glaciation some 10,000 years ago.

The Pleistocene is sometimes popularly called the Great Ice Age, and it was indeed distinguished by being colder than the preceding Pliocene. But the cold was not continuous. The long earlier part of the period is still wrapped in a fog of ignorance, but from about 600,000 years ago the Northern Hemisphere (with some local variation) was subject to four phases of extreme cold when ice covered about one-quarter of the land surface. Of the warmer intervals between these glaciations, the second was the longest and warmest. The final glaciation, although it had minor fluctuations in cold and humidity, was perhaps the most intense. Its onset was about 70,000 years ago, and the ice sheets and glaciers had retreated to roughly their present positions by 8000 BC; so the Pleistocene includes the whole of the period to be covered in this section.

As well as blanketing vast areas with ice, the glaciations had powerful effects on the rest of the planet. They probably often coincided with periods of much greater rainfall farther south, particularly in Africa. In many regions beyond the edges of the ice, finely pulverized rock dust was carried by the wind to form thick deposits of fertile soil (loess). These supported good pasture for the great herds of animals to be hunted by Old Stone Age peoples, and they later provided a soil easily and rewardingly cultivated by the primitive tools of early farmers. Some of the widest spreads of loess can be found in China and in the lands stretching from south Russia (the "black earth" of the Ukraine) across much of the north European plain. Another very significant effect of the glaciations was to lock up huge quantities of water and so to lower sea levels all over the globe. Such low sea levels made it possible for people to enter the Americas by a land bridge between Siberia and Alaska; they joined Britain with the continent and Denmark with Sweden. In southern Asia, by exposing the Sunda Shelf, they linked Java with the mainland and made it easier for human beings to reach Australia.

This, then, was the shifting background against which ancient man evolved, developing his brain and its cultural capacities. It may well be, indeed, that the changes, demanding movement and adaptation, stimulated both mental and physical evolution. The Pleistocene of geology coincides with the Palaeolithic, or Old Stone Age, of human history.

ICE AGE LAND BRIDGES
The conditions created by the glaciations of the last Ice Age allowed the Cromagnons to reach every continent. The water held in ice sheets lowered sea levels and thus created greater land masses. Not only were the distances between continents shortened, but actual land bridges were formed between certain areas. The accompanying map shows the greatest extent of the glaciation as well as the maximum amount of land exposed about 18,000 years ago. Present-day geographical boundaries have been outlined for comparison purposes.

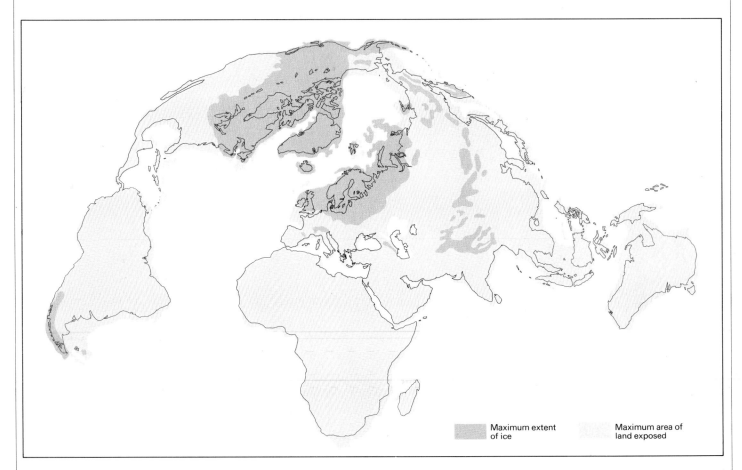

Maximum extent of ice   Maximum area of land exposed

Among all that we do not know, or dispute, about our origins, two important facts now look well established. One is that our genus of *Homo* originated in the African continent, perhaps something like two million years ago. The second is that for a very long time two distinct groups of the hominid family were contemporaries, and indeed lived side by side in some regions. One group, with many variants, known as the Australopithecines ("Southern Apes") had relatively small brains (about 600 cc, much the same as those of the great apes), heavy brow ridges, and massive, prominent teeth. They are fairly well known from the works of Raymond Dart and Robert Ardrey, who studied the remains of some of the last survivors in South Africa, and through the well publicized representative skull found by Mary Leakey in the Olduvai Gorge in Tanzania. Her discovery has become known as Nutcracker Man because of the huge size of his molar teeth. The second group, recognized only in recent years through further discoveries of the Leakey family, were the intellectuals of that remote age; they had a rather higher brow and larger brain (about 700 cc), were almost certainly the first stone tool makers, and were very small, averaging about four feet in height. These beings have been judged already worthy of admission to the genus *Homo* and are very probably our direct ancestors. The name of *Homo habilis* (or Skilful Man) has been granted to them in recognition of their status as pioneer tool makers.

Any imaginative visitor to Olduvai can feel some contact with these inhabitants of over one and a half million years ago. Most important, there on the edge of the Serengeti Plain one can get an idea of the wonderful abundance of animal life which, though with changing species, supplied the needs and excited the emotions of human hunters throughout the Old Stone Age. Then down on the floor of the gorge, enclosed by its coloured walls, there are squatting places, one with a semicircle of stones suggesting a windbreak. There food bones and stone tools, rough yet effective for jabbing, cutting, and scraping, lie thickly scattered. It is easy to imagine family groups of these little people crouched devouring their meat, fish, or birds. How far could they communicate with one another by sounds or words? And did Nutcracker Man, whose skull lay on one of these sites, serve *Homo habilis* for food or in some domestic capacity? Those are questions I would very much like to have answered.

This first stage in human evolution took place in Africa. It is not at present known how soon men began to spread out of the continent into Asia and Europe. It can only be said with confidence that by the time of the first interglacial about half a million years ago they were becoming widespread. Now for the first time questions of global contemporaneity arise. There have also been changes in the names and status that we ascribe to the fossil men concerned, and these need some explanation.

Two of the earliest discoveries of men of this period were made in Java and in the Chou-Kou-Tien caves near Peking, and as a result those two characters, Java Man and Peking Man, were familiar to most informed adults before the Second World War. There was also a third more shadowy figure, represented only by his lower jaw, known as Heidelberg Man. Since the war several more fossils of broadly the same kind of being have been found and once it was decided that all be assigned to the same genus, the name *Pithecanthropus erectus* – the Upright Apeman – was given to the genus. This title is still often used, but with the adjustment in classification caused by the discovery of *Homo habilis* and other factors, it has been decided to promote the whole breed to the rank of *Homo*. So the Java, Peking, and Heidelberg men, with all their approximate contemporaries, are now most properly referred to as *Homo erectus*. We know from their skeletal remains that they lived and hunted in suitable areas throughout the Old World from China to Germany and in North and East Africa, while tool finds suggest an even wider range. Most can be dated from about 500,000 years ago and on into the second glaciation some 50,000-100,000 years later.

It is now thought most probable that *Homo erectus* was descended from the stock of *Homo habilis*. He seems usually to have been taller – about five feet in height – and had a larger brain, averaging 1000 cc, but with wide variation. Yet he still showed the primitive features of a low forehead, a massive ridge of bone above the eyes, massive and prominent teeth, and a lack of chin.

Of even more significance for the purposes of this book is the cultural advance that went with the physical evolution of these ancient beings. We know from the Chou-Kou-Tien cave dwellings that they controlled fire even if they could not kindle it. Then in Africa and Europe, but not in eastern Asia, *Homo erectus* seems to have been the maker of the first shapely and standardized tool. This was the handaxe, a weighty, all-purpose implement, which in this period was rather roughly flaked but in time assumed perfectly proportioned forms combining an effective point with cutting edges.

What makes the handaxe of particular interest here is that by the time of its perfection

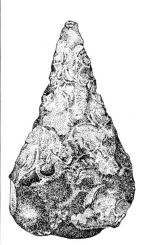

The first standardized tool was the handaxe, a weighty, all-purpose implement.

during the second interglacial, it was being manufactured over a truly vast area: from South Africa to southern England and from England across the southern half of Europe and the Near East to India. Here, surely, is the earliest argument for diffusion, for an implement as distinctive as the handaxe would not have been created independently in many different places by similarity of need. This view is supported by the fact that the area of its distribution is coherent, whereas the form was unknown in eastern Asia, where stone-working was to remain rather crude and backward throughout the Old Stone Age. There was, of course, a very long time for the diffusion to take place, but it is nevertheless astonishing, for one would not expect these still primitive people to be either mobile (outside their own hunting grounds) or communicative.

The handaxe makers seem generally to have lived in open encampments beside rivers and lakes. Although their tools (and there were others in the kit besides the handaxe) are usually found caught up in the river gravels, camp sites are known as far apart as Kenya, Spain, and eastern England. They show the men to have been great hunters, capable of killing even elephants.

By chances of preservation and discovery, fossil remains of the more advanced handaxe-makers of the second interglacial and third glacial phases are scanty, and the few that we have come from Europe. Two of them, from Steinheim in Germany and Swanscombe on the Thames estuary, show that by about a quarter of a million years ago, the presumed descendants of the more progressive branches of *Homo erectus* were already considerably nearer to modern man, with a much slighter brow ridge, less prominent teeth, and a brain capacity reaching up to the lower limit of *Homo sapiens*. On the other hand, the forehead was still low and the skull plates very thick.

These beings are usually referred to as Neanderthaloids, a projection backward in time from the familiar Neanderthal Man who became the dominant breed of the third interglacial age and the earlier part of the final glaciation. Remains of the earliest true Neanderthals, those of third interglacial times, have been found in Germany, eastern Europe, and Israel. Then, for the period after the onset of the last glaciation, the number of known fossil Neanderthals shoots up to something like a hundred individuals. They have been found right across Europe, in North Africa, the Near East, and Iran, with one outlier in Uzbekistan.

The popular image of Neanderthal Man tends too far towards the apish. Although his

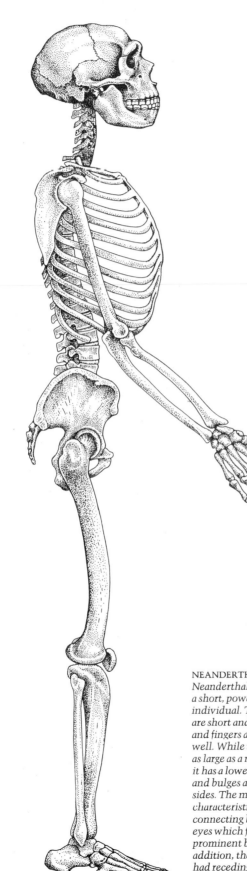

NEANDERTHAL MAN *The Neanderthal skeleton shows a short, powerfully built individual. The extremities are short and the feet, hands and fingers are stubby as well. While the cranium is as large as a modern man's it has a lower, flatter crown and bulges at the back and sides. The most well-known characteristic is the heavy connecting bone above the eyes which forms a prominent brow ridge. In addition, the Neanderthals had receding chins and larger cheeks.*

limb bones were rather heavy and his head set far forward on the neck, he certainly did not shamble along with bent knees, and there is no reason to believe that he had much body hair. Although he was still somewhat beetle-browed and the vault of the skull was low, its capacity was large, allowing a brain size often above the modern average. Surprisingly, it has turned out that the Neanderthal fossils with the less primitive features are the more ancient. The explanation seems to be that one of the more rugged strains of Neanderthaler occupied western Europe during brutally harsh glacial conditions, and under this climatic influence such primitive features as heavy brow ridges and jaws were increased. This extreme type then died out before the advance of the more intelligent, graceful, and well-armed *Homo sapiens* –much as the native Tasmanian, the most primitive of modern races, succumbed within 75 years of the first European settlement of his island.

In their culture the Neanderthals made some striking advances towards full humanity. Their tools and weapons, which had much in common throughout all their territories, were, like their persons, strong and a little clumsy. The implements were made of thick flakes of flint or other stone, but neatly finished with fine chipping. Among them were stout scrapers, presumably used to prepare skins for garments. Warm clothing, together with a hardy physique, enabled them to live farther north than the handaxe makers. The great advance, however, was spiritual: they buried at least some of their dead with ceremony. Stone slabs or animal horns might be used to demarcate graves, and food and implements were laid beside the body. So far as we know, this was the first time that such rites had been practised, and it can hardly be doubted that they manifest a belief in some kind of after-life, perhaps springing from a heightened sense of individuality.

Now we have reached our opening date of 35,000 BC. By this time, with the last glaciation still at its height, the Neanderthalers had been dispossessed of their main hunting grounds (although a scattering of beetle-browed descendants seem to have survived for a while in outlying regions such as Java and parts of Africa). The successful groups of modern human beings who supplanted them were the creators of highly efficient hunting cultures of a distinctive style. They are collectively known to archaeology as Upper Palaeolithic cultures, but so as to avoid the use of too many specialist names they will be referred to as Advanced Hunting cultures. One of their most characteristic features was the production of thin,

CROMAGNON MAN *The Cromagnon skeleton shows a tall, strong person with a large head. The wide face encloses a prominent chin, a high-bridged nose and big eyes. Except for the fact that the head is slightly longer and that the brow ridges are more apparent, he could be taken for a present-day individual.*

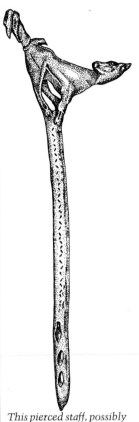

This pierced staff, possibly a spear-thrower, was made from reindeer antler. It was only one of numerous fine carvings found at Mas d'Azil, France.

narrow, parallel-sided "blades" of flint or other fine stone as blanks for working up into a variety of implements. A second vital innovation was the manufacture of chisels and gravers with sharp, strong cutting edges intended for working in bone, antler, and ivory. Increasingly, these burins, as they are often called, were used not only for shaping specialized tools and weapons in organic substances, but also for carving and engraving works of art. They are the first tools of any complexity designed not for direct use but to make other implements; they were, in fact, the forerunners of machine tools. Because of the outstanding technical importance of these two innovations, the cultures of the Advanced Hunters are sometimes labelled "blade and burin".

We have to approach such gifted and dynamic ancestors through their implements because in many regions this is all that is left to judge them by. But the people who in the favourable conditions of southwestern Europe were able to create superb works of art must have had many other skills and endowments. We can be sure that they spoke fluent and well-developed languages and probably had more advanced social systems than any that had gone before. We know that they danced and had simple flutes, and there can be little doubt that they sang and told tribal stories.

We identify these hunters as belonging to a race that is called Cromagnon, after the French cave in which their remains were first discovered. If ever there was a noble savage, Cromagnon Man was physically endowed for the role. He was tall and well built, with a full, smooth forehead and a long skull that gave him a brain capacity much above the present-day average; his face was strong, with a narrow nose and prominent chin. There could hardly be a greater contrast with the more extreme breeds of Neanderthaler who not long before had been masters of many of the same hunting grounds.

Where did the Cromagnons and their Advanced Hunting tradition originate? There is evidence in Africa, the Near East, and Europe that men very close to *Homo sapiens* and presumably descended from the more progressive Neanderthaloids were already present early in the last interglacial age, roughly 120,000 years ago. Thus, for a long span of time they were living contemporaneously with the early Neanderthalers and indeed may have borrowed cultural ideas from them and perhaps sometimes interbred with them (though this is by no means certain). It seems that with the onset of the last glaciation the progressive stock of *Homo sapiens* that was to emerge as Cromagnon Man was hunting over some genial region not adversely affected by the glacial conditions of northern latitudes, and was advancing there in social and cultural life.

Where these cradlelands were is still only vaguely known. Archaeologists can hardly commit themselves beyond "somewhere in southwest Asia" or "somewhere between the east end of the Mediterranean and the mountains of inner Asia." Among the many pieces of evidence that point in that direction, perhaps the most important are that primitive items from the blade and burin equipment have been found in early contexts in the Near East, and moreover that radiocarbon dating shows that at least two of the true Advanced Hunting cultures made an earlier appearance in western Asia, the Levant, and central Europe than in western Europe, where they arrived fully formed. This order of events can be seen in the chart on page 36. There seems little doubt, then, that groups of Cromagnons with their progressive traditions were spreading from orient to occident in the opening millennia of the period from 35,000 to 8000 BC.

This reference to a plurality of "groups" needs explanation. In the early days of archaeology, when the existence of this late Old Stone Age world was first being revealed in the cave dwellings of France and Spain, the excavators observed that various groups of distinctive flints and bone tools invariably appeared in the same relative order in the layers of occupation rubbish on the cave floors. They were recognized as specialized cultural divisions within the blade and burin tradition and named after the French sites where they were best represented. When very similar remains were found throughout much of Europe and into Asia, the French names were extended to them. Although later generations of archaeologists have preferred to name many more localized cultures of the period and have questioned whether the extension of French nomenclature is valid, there still seems good reason to believe that widespread similarities of culture do in historical truth indicate movements of people or contacts among them. Radiocarbon dating supported this view when it proved that the succession of cultures corresponded to successive periods of time (though with some overlapping), and that in some instances the succession indicated a consistent spread from east to west.

Here I want to say a few words about the more important of these Advanced Hunting cultures. The cultural pioneers who began to spread through Asia and Europe, encountering and perhaps borrowing from the Neanderthalers in the process, remain such shadowy figures that no more need be said of them. It

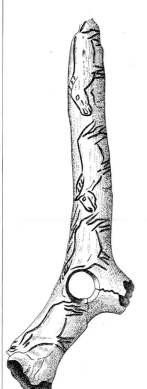

Carved batons were made by the Cromagnons from antler or bone. They were T or Y-shaped with a hole bored into their widest point and were often highly ornamented. No one function has been proved for them; they may have served as thong-softeners, arrow-straighteners or for some ritual purpose.

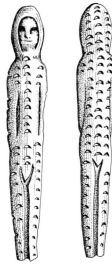

A Gravettian carved ivory figurine found at Buret', Siberia, shows how the hunters clothed themselves in the arctic cold. The individual wears a tailored single piece hooded garment made from skins, the fur turned to the outside.

was their immediate successors, whom we call the Aurignacians, who were the first dynamic innovators and almost surely the first artists. They appear early in Afghanistan, Iran, and the Levant and are thought to have spread westward by way of the Balkans and central Europe. But they did not cross the Pyrenees.

The Aurignacians were followed by the Gravettians, who made further advances in specialized hunting gear and in the arts. Their cultural traditions were eventually centred in central and eastern Europe, particularly in the loess lands of the Moravian region and southern Russia, where they became great mammoth hunters. Their spread to the west seems to have been in the main by a southerly route, for they were strongly established in Greece and Italy and it may have been from there that they reached southern France and became the earliest of the Advanced Hunters in Spain and Portugal. Other such hunters with a culture akin to the Gravettian also reached the British region at about this time.

The Gravettian thrust to the east was even more remarkable. They reached the southern Urals, where they introduced not only the blade and burin technology but also cave painting in a style comparable to that practised by their contemporaries in the Dordogne 2500 miles away. This Gravettian penetration of Asia can probably be connected with the later arrival of more Advanced Hunters who appeared in some numbers in Siberia, round Lake Baikal. These people, too, preyed on mammoth and other big game, made small carvings, and in general lived in much the same way as their precursors to the west.

It seems to have been the dynamic Gravettian tradition that gave rise to the most brilliant and successful of all Advanced Hunting cultures, that of the Magdalenians. This was a west European group, chiefly at home in the territories between the Alps and the Cantabrian mountains of Spain, where the finest art of the period is found. But the Magdalenians also reached Valencian Spain and Britain, and they went eastward as far as Moravia. As tool makers they were highly inventive, but, above all, they developed their art to an extraordinary height of feeling and execution.

The sudden emergence of full human creativity among the Advanced Hunters of this period at the end of the Old Stone Age is surely one of the most astonishing chapters in all our history. The Neanderthalers had taken a tentative step, but the Cromagnons made a graceful leap forward. There are, I think, two explanations, one material and one mental. The material one is simple: the open steppe and

tundra of glacial times supported great herds of game – bison, reindeer, horse, and mammoth – that could be killed by trapping as well as by pursuit, thus offering an easy supply of meat, and with it abundant leisure. And in southwest Europe where the climate was rather less harsh, conditions were ideal for the hunter-artists. As for the mental explanation, it is evident that after hundreds of thousands of years during which the people of each generation normally did exactly what their parents had done and cultural improvement was extremely slow, the Cromagnons began to think in terms of solving problems. With this new sense of challenge, they invented within a relatively short time the spear-thrower and thong-softener, composite hafting of flint, a variety of specialized barbed spears and harpoons, the eyed needle, a fat-burning lamp, and probably the bow and arrow.

For their dwellings the hunters favoured a seasonal use of caves, living at the mouth and on terraces just outside. There fires were maintained, and further protection was probably secured by rough walls and skin hangings. We assume that each cave housed a family group, and in ravines where several were within sight of one another, there must have been a sense of tribal community. One can imagine the scene after nightfall when points of firelight glowed in the vast, frosty dark. In the lighted circle the humans ate, talked, mended gear, and told stories, while in the outer darkness their animal neighbours slept or prowled.

In the absence of caves, the hunters were capable of building snug huts. Those that we know most about belonged to the mammoth hunters of Moravia and Russia. They were roundish or oval, with hearths on sunken floors. Sometimes they had low walls built of stones or mammoth bones, along with a tented roof of skins. Encampments might consist of at least half a dozen of these huts, and again we assume that each belonged to a family group.

They dressed well, too. In addition to the evidence of a neatly fur-clad figure from Siberia, a painting from France shows a man wearing a high fur collar with a red garment below. Their bone needles also suggest that the hunters' clothes were cut and stitched; they perhaps approached those of the modern Eskimo in excellence. Men even more than women loved to ornament themselves with necklaces and bracelets of shells, teeth, beads of ivory, mother of pearl, and stone.

Much of this personal finery has been found in graves. The Neanderthals' tentative care for the dead was intensified among the Advanced Hunters. There was still no wish to separate the dead from the living, for most

One of a pair of limestone reliefs, the Venus of Laussel represented an inner vision of fertility and motherhood.

graves were dug in the cave or hut floor. The bodies, evidently dressed and ornamented, were most commonly placed in a crouched position, and often covered with red ochre as a symbol of life-giving blood. A woman of forty (a ripe old age for those days) found in a grave in a Moravian hut had been strewn with ochre; her body was facing westward, and it was covered by two shoulder blades of a dead mammoth.

All such details of life and death bring the hunters closer to us, but it is their art that stirs and unites us. On a subject that has already filled scores of books, what should I say in a single page? First of all I must point out that this was essentially a European art, and I hope I shall not be accused of racism if I find it remarkable that there was nothing savage about it, but that it reflected a heightened realism that was truly humane. Historically, it seems that although the Aurignacians had no art in their Asiatic cradlelands, in the west they were the first to make simple animal drawings and carvings that included some human subjects. These first essays at representation can be dated to 25,000 BC or even earlier. With the Gravettians, accomplishment, particularly in sculpture, became much greater. They made some delightful animal figures in realistic style, but their most characteristic products were female figurines in bone, ivory or stone, showing enormous breasts, bellies, buttocks and thighs. These little carvings were made over most of the Gravettian range from Italy and the Pyrenees to the Don. Some strike us as grotesque; others have beauty. Essentially, unlike the animal portraits, they came from an inner vision of fertility and motherhood. In this sense, they can be said to be the first evolved religious symbols; it might not be wrong to call them idols. Their religious meaning is well brought out in a pair of Gravettian relief carvings (found at Laussel in the Dordogne), one of which portrays a slender young man, the other an opulent but faceless female holding a bison horn. The continuity of meaning and emotion between these works and the "Mother Goddess" figures of New Stone Age and even historic times can hardly be denied.

Sculpture and engraving among the Advanced Hunters were raised to their greatest heights by the Magdalenians. They were equally masters whether working on a large scale or small, on engravings, reliefs, or in the round. Some of their most exquisite carving was on their implements, where it must have been done mainly for aesthetic pleasure.

The cave paintings for which the Advanced Hunters are most famous are very largely concentrated in southwest France, the French Pyrenees, and the Cantabrian mountains of Spain. They are difficult to date precisely. Not long ago, there was a shift of opinion from the original view that there was a Gravettian and a Magdalenian cycle, and now almost all cave paintings are attributed to the Magdalenians. The recent discovery, however, of an outlying group of paintings in Gravettian territory in the south Urals seems to prove that the earlier hunters did in fact use pigments with some skill. There is still no question that it was the Magdalenians who painted the great masterpieces, including those in the two supreme sanctuaries of Lascaux and Spanish Altamira. The art seems to extend over the five thousand years of their prosperity (c.15,000-10,000 BC), with a growing technical mastery that culminated in the polychrome style of Altamira.

The Advanced Hunting Age of Europe came to a glorious end in this earliest outburst of artistic creation. There was to be no other to approach it before the Old Kingdom art of Egypt some seven thousand years later.

I must now show how the Advanced Hunting cultures of Eurasia relate in time to the first human penetration of the Americas and Australia. Both events almost certainly took place within this early period. It has recently been established that there were men in Australia by 20,000 BC, contemporary with late Gravettian times in Eurasia. This has aroused general surprise, for even at the height of glaciation it would have been necessary to make a sea crossing between Borneo and the Celebes. Wherever they came from, having made the passage these hunters held to a Stone Age type of culture until European settlement and in a few areas until today. The indigenous Australians also retain such archaic physical features as long skulls, strongly marked brow ridges and large, often prominent teeth.

The problem of the peopling of America is both more difficult and more significant. I will set it out as simply as I can. No fossil remains of Neanderthal or earlier beings have come to light anywhere in the continent. The descendants of the pre-Columbian peoples, despite local variation, are predominantly of a mongoloid racial type. The fact that their blood groups show virtually none of B, and in some regions 100% O, strongly suggests that they derive from a small, homogeneous ancestral group likely to have entered America at only one time. It is generally agreed that the pioneers would have crossed from Siberia to Alaska, and most probably during a period when there was an ice-free land bridge uniting them. These ideal conditions probably prevailed twice during the final glaciation: between 24,000 and

18,000 BC and again from 10,000-9000 BC. The earliest reliably established remains of human beings and their cultures date from 10,000, corresponding to the last phase of the Magdalenian in Europe. These people were big-game hunters, and are mainly identified for us by various types of well-made stone spearheads, "projectile points." (American archaeology classifies these cultures after the characteristics of the projectile points – e.g. Clovis, Sandia and Folsom.)

From all the above facts, it would seem nearly certain that the first immigrants crossed the land bridge either towards the end of its earlier existence or immediately it opened for the second time. Unfortunately (if I may be allowed unscientific sentiments), in many places in both North and South America crudely flaked tools have been found that have an earlier "look" than the projectile-point cultures. Most of these are scattered surface finds, but here and there people have claimed to find hearths or other signs of human occupation in the vicinity and have dated their finds as contemporary with Old World Aurignacians or even before. No single "pre-projectile" site has stood up to careful testing, but the cumulative effect has been enough to convince some reasonable people that the first Americans had arrived by the beginning of the long period I have been discussing (i.e. 35,000 BC).

As for the spread of these big-game hunters of late glacial times, they seem to have peopled the vast continent with remarkable speed. The main corridor, after a swift traverse of Alaska, was by way of the High Plains, then through Mesoamerica (where in Mexico, as in the north, slaughtered mammoths have been found, together with the spearheads that killed them), on through the tropics to reach the southern cold of the Strait of Magellan by 9000-8000 BC. It is a truly remarkable story, for the impetus that drove a tiny population of hunters from arctic to antarctic verge can only have been the curiosity, the irresistible urge to find out what lay beyond that range, that jungle, that great river. Surely, too, it is another proof of the possibilities of diffusion, and a justification for believing in the reality of the wide spread of the Advanced Hunting groups of Eurasia.

The last two thousand years of the Ice Age were the end of one epoch, but they also saw the first stirrings of another. Over much of Europe the melting of the ice and the invasion of open pasture by forest and by water were to force big changes upon the descendants of the Advanced Hunters. These climatic changes also enabled some to move northward with the reindeer and occupy new hunting grounds in Denmark and northern Germany.

In the Mediterranean lands of southern Europe and in the Near East, changes in climate were less extreme, allowing a gradual evolution of Gravettian and other Advanced Hunting traditions. Yet in spite of such regional differences, the late glacial and post-glacial phase of our history has enough coherence to be treated as a more or less distinct cultural period. This cultural period has been called the Middle Stone Age (Mesolithic) as coming between the Old Stone Age (Palaeolithic) and the New Stone Age (Neolithic).

The coherence appears mainly in a shift from dependence on big game to the hunting of many smaller animals, fishing, fowling, and an increased consumption of wild vegetable foods. With this came a common trend in the way the hunters made their tools and weapons. Small flints had already been made by Gravettians and others for multiple hafting, but now the knappers contrived to make most of their flints so minute that one marvels at their skill. Why men made this change to the use of "microliths" at approximately the same time over many regions of Eurasia and Africa is a puzzling question. As usual, some of us prefer a diffusionist explanation, while others find the answer in their belief that similar responses are independently produced by similar needs.

The Mesolithic or Late Hunting cultures began early in the Near East (including the western slopes of the Zagros range). Here microliths and grinders for wild cereals were in use by about 13,000 BC. It was in the Levant that beginnings such as these led to a full Late Hunting culture, the Natufian, which provides a perfect example of a way of life intermediate between that of the hunter and the farmer. It almost exactly coincides with the two millennia that ended the Ice Age, 10,000-8000 BC, and therefore with the decline of the Magdalenians in the west and the spread of the projectile-point hunters through the Americas.

The Natufians chose to live where the ancestors of wheat and barley grew wild, and their equipment of reaping knives, querns, pestles, and mortars proves that they harvested the grain in quantity. It is also possible that they added to their meat supply by herding gazelles. Population grew with food supplies, and so did a more settled way of life. We know of Natufian villages with up to fifty huts; large cemeteries tell the same story. Yet they had no domesticated plants or animals, no pottery or weaving, and they still relied on hunting small game for much of their diet. The old tradition of realistic animal art and personal finery lingered on among them.

Technology 35,000 – 8000 BC

In the thousands of years before the opening of this period, people had exploited a wide range of natural materials. Stone, bone, antler, shell, ivory and wood were utilized as well as more perishable sources such as bark, vegetable fibres, animal hair and tendons. But it was the Advanced Hunters who might be said to have developed the first "toolkit".

Among their implements were knives for general cutting, scrapers for cleaning hides, burins or gravers for working bone, and projectile points for arrows or lances. Throughout most of the world these tools were skilfully shaped by fine flaking on flint blades which had been struck from carefully prepared cores. Various techniques involved blunting sharp edges to prevent unintentional injury, edge-trimming and shallow surface flaking. Surprisingly, grinding was first used in Australia where the earlier technique of crude flaking of core nodules was retained. Later on, throughout many areas of the world, the development of microliths coupled with the technique of hafting for composite tools added yet more variety and flexibility to implements.

The Advanced Hunters worked antler, bone and ivory systematically for the first time. Flaking, splintering, polishing and perforation were used to make a variety of weapon-heads, ornaments, awls, batons, harpoons, toggles, spear-throwers, needles and other skin-working tools. Bone and ivory objects were occasionally decorated with incised geometrical patterns.

The appearance of several items such as the spear-thrower and bow (implied by the arrow-heads) show that early man made use of simple scientific principles to increase his effectiveness as a hunter. These long-distance weapons were among the most significant material achievements of the time.

Fire had been known since much earlier for warmth, light, cooking and as a weapon against animals. In this period its ability to transform certain materials became apparent. Figurines of baked clay have been discovered in Czechoslovakia along with evidence of the first use of coal as a fuel.

Most travel was by foot but boats of a sort were certainly in use before 8000 BC as there are proven contacts with offshore islands.

Although this initial technology was certainly limited, it did allow societies to develop and prosper to the point where at least a few of them could produce masterpieces of cave art.

What is so striking about this technology is its comparative uniformity and slow rate of progress over the greater part of the world.

	Areas of major interest
•	Centres

The Americas
Skilfully flaked flint projectile points which tipped hunting spears and darts were characteristic of the Advanced Hunters of the New World. The use of traps and nets was already known in this period.

Cody knife

Scraper

Clovis point *Folsom point* *Fish tail point*

Folsom
Clovis

El Inga

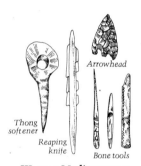

Arrowhead

Thong softener

Reaping knife

Bone tools

Western Mediterranean
Fine and varied work in flint as well as bone was common to parts of this area. Perforated implements for working thongs to suppleness show that organic materials were also exploited at this time.

COMPARISON OF MATERIALS IN USE

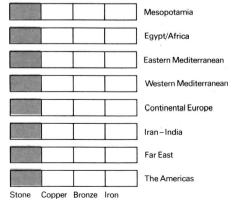

				Mesopotamia
				Egypt/Africa
				Eastern Mediterranean
				Western Mediterranean
				Continental Europe
				Iran – India
				Far East
				The Americas

Stone Copper Bronze Iron

Continental Europe
Advanced hunting and fishing
equipment of stone, bone and
antler such as the spear-
thrower and fowling fork
were widespread in central and
eastern Europe. Lamps and
palettes were used in France to
assist in cave decoration.

*Stone
lamps*

*Palette, grinding stone,
pigments*

Fish hook

*Spear-
thrower*

*Fowling
fork*

Harpoon

La Gravette
• Lascaux
Altamira • •
Aurignac • • Solutré
• La Madeleine
• Grimaldi
Parpallo •

• Addaura   • Romanelli

Eastern Mediterranean
As well as the more common
hunting tools of the period,
reaping knives and sickle flints
for intensive collection of wild
grain have been found. Bone
was skilfully employed for
ornaments and tools.

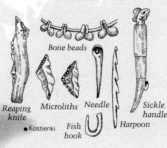

Bone beads

*Reaping
knife*

Microliths

Needle

*Fish
hook*

Harpoon

*Sickle
handle*

• Kostienki

Belbusi • • Mureybet
Zawi Chemi
• Shanidar
• Zarzi
Kebara • • Eynam   • Ali Kosh
• Wadi-en-Natuf
• Haua Fteah

Far East
Crudely flaked hunting and
food gathering equipment
persisted throughout further
Asia. The crudeness is more
marked through the islands
and into the Australian
continent.

*Stone
blade*

Chipping tool

Burin

• Shirataki

• Mal'ta

• Chou-Kou-Tien

• Shi-Tung-Kou

Iran – India
The sickle handle, reaping
knife and whetstone indicate
the presence of Late Hunters.

*Reaping
knife*

Whetstone

Microliths

*Sickle
handle*

• Bandera Wela

Scraper

*Bone
tools*

Blade

Microliths

*Reaping
knife*

Egypt/Africa
Competent flintwork and
some use of bone was widespread throughout this area.

• Kom Ombo

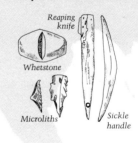

Stone bowl

Comb

Needle

Mortar

Axe

Quern

Mesopotamia
Stone querns and mortars
indicate that wild grain on the
hill slopes was harvested. A
highly competent use of bone
is indicated by the comb and
pierced needle.

• Kalambo Falls
LUPEMBA

• Bambata Cave

Flake tool

Mesopotamia

The comb from Mureybet shows that Advanced Hunting peoples were skilled in the art of bone carving. The stone mortar, found together with carbonized grain not native to this lowland area, suggests that Mureybet at least was very close to food production by 8000 BC – well in advance of the people of the flood plain further downstream. They still relied on hunting, however, for most of their food supplies.

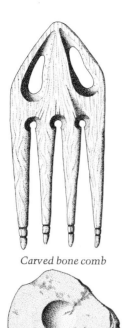

Carved bone comb

Stone mortar

Egypt/Africa

Progressively smaller tools, including composite ones such as the projectile, have been found on the Mediterranean coast. But beyond the Sahara a heavier flint industry as evidenced by the blade continued until much later.

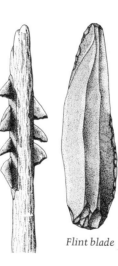

Flint blade

Eastern Mediterranean

Evidence left by the Natufians who settled in this area suggests that they made use of natural grains although no remains have been found. Sickle blades were usually set in bone handles. Naturalistic portraits of animals were carved occasionally on these implements.

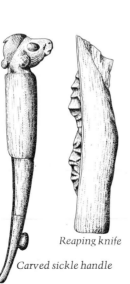

Reaping knife

Carved sickle handle

Western Mediterranean

In this area, as in many others, composite tools containing a number of flint blades (or microliths) variously set into a wooden or bone haft, became a feature after the great game herds of the last Ice Age dwindled. Among them was the reaping knife used for harvesting wild grains. Other tools were used in smaller game hunting. Bone was employed for such tools as needles and points.

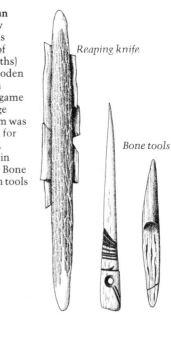

Reaping knife

Bone tools

Spear-thrower

Continental Europe

The cave art of France and Spain brought with it technological advances suggested by the palette and stone lamps. The pictures themselves may have been regarded as necessary for the fertility of the game and for the success of the hunters in bringing it down. The bone spear-thrower undoubtedly helped too. It worked on the lever principle and increased the throwing range of the hunter.

Palette, grinding stone and pigments

Iran – India

Advanced Hunters along the Zagros and Elburz ranges shared with their western neighbours the technique of intensive exploitation of the wild food resources as illustrated by the reaping knife and whetstone.

Whetstone

Reaping knife

Far East

A competent but unexciting technology is evident in the stone blade. Even the greater emphasis on shell-fish as a major food resource called for no special advances in material equipment, though it allowed the early development of permanent settlements.

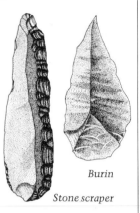

Burin

Stone scraper

The Americas

The hunting equipment of the early settlers, although lacking in variety, was skilfully and efficiently made. The pressure-flaked projectile points, mostly surface finds, have been classified according to their method of production, such as the Clovis and Folsom points below.

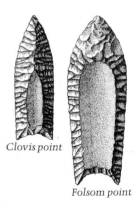

Clovis point

Folsom point

Flint technology

Flint has two distinctive characteristics compared with most other stones. The in its microcrystalline structure it has no "grain" and so can split in any direction, and it fractures to a very sharp edge. These properties were recognized very early, making it the preferred stone wherever it was available for flaked tools. Blows from a tougher hammerstone detached flakes which were themselves used to make tools, or fashioned the core to some desired tool form. To control the process, the knapper used hammers of different weight or material, altered the strength and direction of his blows, and applied pressure to the core to control the run of the cleavage. In some areas the flint was baked to improve its flaking qualities. Trimming, or secondary working, was often carried out by pressure, using a bone or stone point to push off small spalls of flint to give a finished shape and surface to the tool.

Bone, antler, ivory

These materials are less hard than stone but more resilient, and require different techniques for working. Doubtless the earliest techniques involved the splintering of the bone refuse of meals. Later a flint graver or burin (a tool with a stout chisel-like working edge) was used to separate a sliver of bone or antler by grooving and levering. The principal technique, however, was grinding. The splinter was worked up and down against a block of abrasive sandstone or similar material until all irregularities had been smoothed away. Needles as well as harpoons and mattocks were made this way.

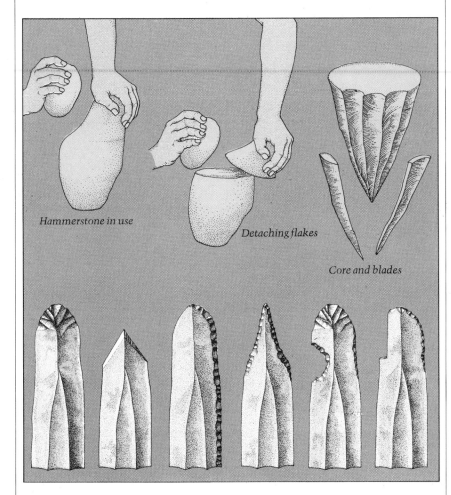

Hammerstone in use

Detaching flakes

Core and blades

Microliths

A later development was to divide the blades into smaller segments or microliths. Notches were chipped in the sides of blades facilitating their removal by twisting. These microliths could then be trimmed to simple, often geometric shapes. The main advantage was that these could be mounted more adaptably in bone or wooden hafts, and replaced individually whenever they became worn or damaged. By this means, arrows and harpoons could be given a wide range of barbed shapes; sickles and reaping knives could have easily renewable cutting edges.

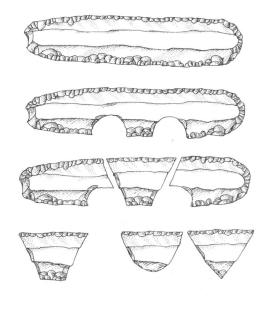

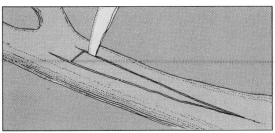

MAKING A NEEDLE FROM ANTLER *Two grooves are cut along the shaft with a flint graver.*

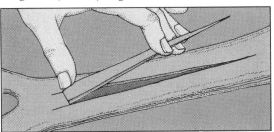

The resulting sliver is levered until it snaps off at the base and can be lifted out.

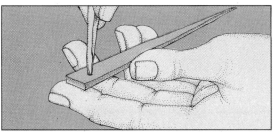

The eye is drilled by to-and-fro rotation of a fine flint point, as with a modern bradawl.

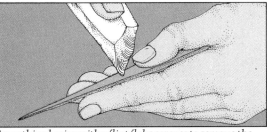

Smoothing begins with a flint flake scraper to remove the worst of the irregularities.

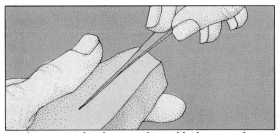

Finishing is completed on a sandstone block; a smooth polish can be achieved and the tip sharpened.

Architecture *35,000-8000 BC*

Early man's nomadic hunting life did not encourage permanent settlements. People most likely made do with scanty shelters which they constructed for protection against rain and sun. Rock shelters with overhanging ledges and caves were utilized but probably formed only a very small proportion of residences. The control of fire was necessary to empty deep caves of predators and in many regions caves were rare or non-existent.

Later, the Advanced Hunters made much greater use of caves. Shelter was necessary for survival in the harsh conditions of the last Ice Age and caves were a convenient source. Surprisingly, their use was only seasonal even at this time. However, we know more about cave dwellings than any contemporaneous hut because they are so easily found. While their inhabitants might have made only minimal structural changes (such as the addition of hearths and wind-breaks), the food refuse, discarded tools and by-products of flint and bone working found on cave floors furnish us with most of our archaeological evidence in this early period.

Few of the earliest man-made structures have survived. But some early buildings have been uncovered, notably in Eastern Europe and Palestine. The hide and bone huts of the mammoth hunters and the twig and daub ones in the more temperate climates exhibit a surprising sophistication. On their evidence we would probably be safe in assuming that huts were built in all inhabited areas.

It is difficult, however, to evaluate these buildings as architecture. Until more have been discovered and investigated we are unable to speculate accurately on the relationship of these structures to their surroundings. Were those buildings the end products of long development within their respective societies or was each a response to the immediate problems of the community, the site, and the available raw materials? Whatever the answer, these huts, poor though their remains are, were the true beginnings of architecture.

▨	Areas of major interest
●	Centres
▲	Sites

The Americas
Natural caves are the only known dwelling sites in the New World at this time. Though there must have been temporary camps in the open, they have yet to be found.

Cave

Western Mediterranean
Caves were used extensively, being widely distributed in the limestones of the area.

Cave

COMPARISON OF MATERIALS IN USE

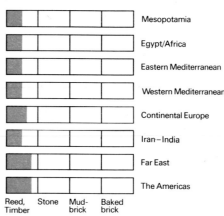

	Reed, Timber	Stone	Mud-brick	Baked brick
Mesopotamia				
Egypt/Africa				
Eastern Mediterranean				
Western Mediterranean				
Continental Europe				
Iran–India				
Far East				
The Americas				

Continental Europe
Some examples of tent-like huts have been found in central and eastern Europe and similar structures must have been much more widely distributed than the few excavated examples suggest. There is evidence for this in the huts occasionally depicted in cave paintings.

Skin tents, Pushkari

Mammoth bone hut, Mezhirich

▲ Pushkari

▲ Mezhirich

Far East
Scattered examples of elaborate tent-like huts have been found as far as central Asia. There must have been others, perhaps of different materials throughout the region. A few occupied caves are known from Australia.

Skin tents

SIBERIA

Eastern Mediterranean
Natural caves are quite common here, and built huts are also known in the Natufian area of Palestine and Syria. These huts had circular stone footings with light superstructures, probably of twigs and daub.

Stone and mud huts

Cave

Egypt/Africa
Good examples of occupied caves are known from the Mediterranean coastlands, but they occur much less widely south of the Sahara. As no buildings survive, we can only guess at huts.

Cave

Mesopotamia
No caves are present in the plains and the scanty evidence that exists suggests light shelters of reeds as the likeliest housing.

Stone and mud dwellings

Cave

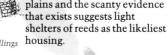
Reed shelter

Iran – India
Both caves and huts are known along the line of the Zagros between Iran and Iraq. The huts were probably of stone with a perishable covering as in the Eastern Mediterranean.

Cave

Mesopotamia
Little trace of dwellings has been found, but flimsy structures of reeds and mud were possibly erected in the lower valley.

Mud and reed hut

Egypt/Africa
We have no evidence of man-made buildings in the African continent at this early period.

Eastern Mediterranean
More permanent dwellings became general as intensive food collection and game herding made food supplies more reliable. At Natufian sites in Palestine like Eynan (Ain Mallaha) circular huts 26ft. (8m.) across were dug 3½ft. (1m.) deep and faced with rubble. The floor was at least occasionally stone-paved and the walls coated with plaster. The form of the roof is largely guess-work.

Natufian huts

Western Mediterranean
Caves were widely used but built huts of this period have yet to be identified in the area. Certain cave paintings strongly imply their existence.

Continental Europe
In the arctic conditions of the time, timber was very scarce and the excavated huts of Moravia and southern Russia were constructed mainly of skins. Oval hollows were dug into the ground and many large bones and teeth, usually of mammoth, were used to weight down the hide roof. A central hearth served for cooking and heating. Some of the investigated examples are up to 98ft. (30m.) long, with a row of hearths down the centre. This suggests that a number of individual families lived as a community under a single roof, each family having its own fireplace.

Iran – India
Scanty traces remain of earlier huts but after 8000 BC oval and circular stone structures with coverings of wattle and daub, reeds or matting were found in Zawi Chemi. The earlier huts are assumed to have been similar.

Far East
The only known buildings of this date are in Siberia, particularly Mal'ta and Buret' near Lake Baikal. Their similarity to the huts of European Russia clearly indicates some kind of link or diffusion.

The Americas
There is no evidence of man-made buildings in this period.

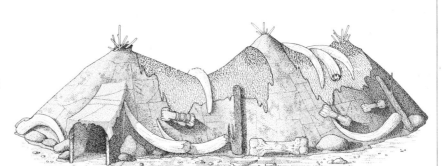

Mammoth hunters' dwelling, Pushkari, Russia

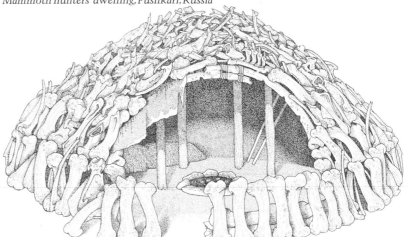

Mammoth bone hut, Mezhirich, Russia

Wattle and daub huts

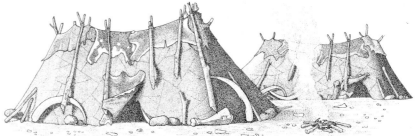

Skin and bone houses, Siberia

CAVE DWELLING *Natural caves held obvious attractions for early peoples. Hearths of loose stones were constructed on the outside terrace for cooking and the fire also served to guard against predators. Simple wind-breaks of branches and skins could be built near the entrance for further protection in inclement weather.*

Danger Cave, Utah, USA

31

Art 35,000 – 8000 BC

Of all the outbursts of artistic genius that have enlivened the course of human history, this first one is surely the most astonishing. The Advanced Hunters of the late Old Stone Age were the originators of representational art. Before them some early tools, notably the handaxe, show a sense of form, and the Neanderthals made circular hollows on stone surfaces. That, so far as we know, was all.

About ten thousand years after modern peoples *(Homo sapiens)* had displaced the Neanderthalers and spread through habitable parts of Asia and Europe they began their careers as artists. It is possible that the Aurignacian people in western Europe led the way with some simple works, but this is very doubtful. The earliest more surely dated representations were made by the Advanced Hunting people known as the Gravettians. What are probably the oldest examples, 25,000 BC or earlier, come from eastern and central Europe.

The Gravettians made some lively animal carvings, but their speciality was small figurines of women in stone, ivory, bone or clay. Often they have very full thighs, buttocks, breasts and bellies, while faces, arms and feet are sketchy or lacking. The "Venuses" as they have been called, can be seen as the earliest religious symbols, since they seem to express a timeless sense of motherhood and fecundity.

The Gravettians introduced their art into western Europe, where the true flowering came with their probable descendants, the Magdalenians, principally in southwest France, the French Pyrenees and Cantabrian Spain. Although they were gifted sculptors and small carvers, their great achievement was in the development of painting between 15,000 and 10,000 BC. They kept powdered ochre, haematite and manganese in bone tubes and applied it moist with brush, pad or blowpipe.

Most of the paintings were made in the depths of caves, far from the hearth and living place. They served for hunting magic, but also manifested a reverence for the game animals – and surely gave pleasure to the artists.

Towards the end of the period this art of the Advanced Hunters declined, then almost entirely disappeared, although here and there faint traces of it survived among the Late Hunting (Mesolithic) peoples.

Areas of major interest

● Centres

▲ Sites

The Americas
There is no evidence that the big game hunters of the period practised any art.

Western Mediterranean
The cave art of the French Pyrenees, Cantabria and southern Spain is assigned to this region but in general differs little from that of southwest France and the Rhône. Nearly all the fine paintings and engravings were made by Magdalenians, 15,000 – 10,000 BC. The Spanish cave of Altamira is Lascaux's only rival; its magnificent polychrome paintings are later, c. 12,000 BC. There is an outlying group of engravings in Sicily and Apulian Italy.

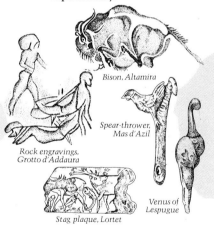

Bison, Altamira

Spear-thrower, Mas d'Azil

Rock engravings, Grotto d'Addaura

Venus of Lespugue

Stag plaque, Lortet

Continental Europe
The Dordogne region of France
has Gravettian sculpture and
engravings dating from after
about 20,000 BC, but is mainly
famous for its superb painting
and relief sculpture in caves
and engravings on small
objects. Most of these were
Magdalenian work, 15,000 –
10,000 BC. Lascaux contains
the finest paintings of all.
These date from soon after
15,000. In central and east
Europe, including south
Russia, Gravettian female and
animal figurines predominate.

Far East
The most easterly known cave
paintings of the period are in
the Kapova cave in the
southern Ural mountains. In
the region of Siberian Lake
Baikal, Advanced Hunters
with a culture akin to the
Gravettian carved slender
figures, mostly female, and
bird forms. These may
be relatively late, however.

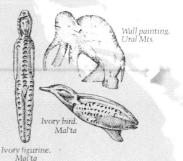

*Wall painting,
Ural Mts.*

*Venus of
Laussel*

*Venus of
Willendorf*

Mammoth, Dordogne

Horse, Vogelherd

*Ivory bird,
Mal'ta*

*Ivory figurine,
Mal'ta*

• Mal'ta

URAL MTS.

Eastern Mediterranean
The art of the Advanced
Hunters is represented only by
a few animal engravings on
rocks and pebbles in south
Anatolia. In the Levant,
particularly Palestine, the Late
Hunters of the Natufian culture
made excellent carvings of
animals on the handles of
implements and shaped
decorative beads.

Laussel
Lascaux
Altamira ● ▲▲ Pech Merle ▲ Vogelherd
Lortet ▲▲   ▲ Willendorf
Lespugue Mas d'Azil

● Addaura

Iran-India
Although Advanced Hunters
were present in Iran from early
times, there is no evidence that
they created works of art.

Egypt/Africa
Rather rough engravings of
game animals are found on
exposed rocks, mostly in
Upper Egypt, and some may
well date from this period.

Mesopotamia
This region was outside the area
of the Advanced Hunting
cultures and their art.

Mesopotamia
No Advanced Hunters
inhabited this area.

Egypt/Africa
Except for questionable
rough rock engravings,
there is no recognizable
art in this area.

Eastern Mediterranean
The Late Hunters of the
Natufian culture decorated
their implement handles
with animal carvings as
can be seen on page 26.

Western Mediterranean
Among the many caves in
Cantabria with paintings
and engravings, that of
Altamira is by far the finest.
The roof is crowded with
paintings of bison and other
animals in the polychrome
style that was the culmination of Magdalenian art
(c. 12,000 BC). In the
southern French group
the Venus of Lespugue is
one of the most highly
stylized and beautiful of the
Gravettian figurines. There
are many engravings on
implements and plaques:
the composition of stags
and salmon on bone from
Lortet is deep-cut, the
turning of the stag's head
well conveyed.

Painted deer, Altamira, Spain

*Venus of Lespugue, carved
ivory, France*

Painted standing bison, Altamira, Spain

Engraving of stags and salmon, Lortet, Hautes-Pyrénées, France

Continental Europe

Among the many fine relief carvings on cave walls or stones in the Dordogne group, the woman holding a bison horn (Gravettian) is of greatest interest. An associated relief portrays a youth, and the two together suggest the beginning of a long-lived fertility cult. The yellow paint on the Lascaux horse may have been sprayed on. The feathered dots suggest hunting magic c. 15,000 BC. The horses of Pech-Merle show an experiment in the decorative use of dabs of colour. The silhouettes of hands were made by spraying paint round a hand held on the cave wall. The important group of Gravettian figurines from central and eastern Europe is represented by the famous Venus of Willendorf; the concentration on material symbolism at the expense of face, arms and feet is typical. The vigorous little horse and mammoth from Vogelherd are good examples of east Gravettian animal sculpture, perhaps before 20,000.

Carved ivory horse and mammoth (actual size), Vogelherd, Germany

Venus of Laussel, limestone, Dordogne, France

Venus of Willendorf, stone, Austria.

Yellow Horse, Lascaux Cave, Dordogne, France

Painted horses with negatives of hands, Pech-Merle, France

Iran-India

No works of art from this area have been found.

Far East

The Urals mark the boundary between Europe and Asia. Since the Kapova cave is in this range and to the east of the nearest east European Gravettian art, it can be included in this region. The paintings are large, rough monochrome paintings of mammoths, a horse and a rhinoceros. The lean figurines and bird sculpture from the Lake Baikal area complete all the known art of this region.

Painted mammoth Ural Mts., USSR

The Americas

No works of art from this area have been discovered.

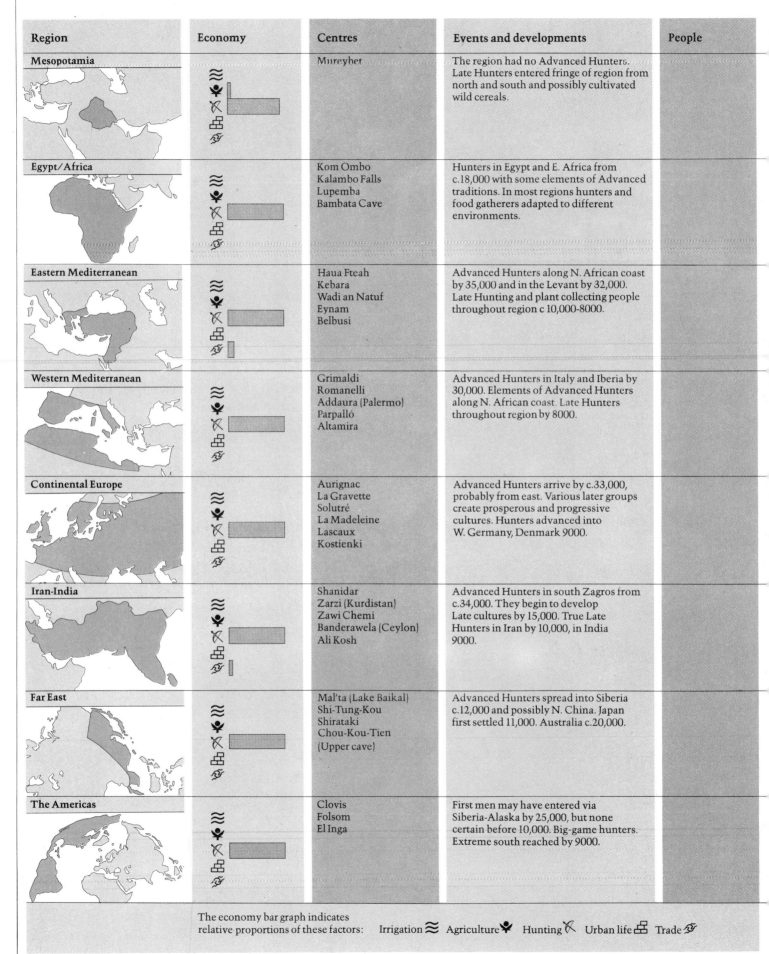

Region	Economy	Centres	Events and developments	People
Mesopotamia		Mureybet	The region had no Advanced Hunters. Late Hunters entered fringe of region from north and south and possibly cultivated wild cereals.	
Egypt/Africa		Kom Ombo Kalambo Falls Lupemba Bambata Cave	Hunters in Egypt and E. Africa from c.18,000 with some elements of Advanced traditions. In most regions hunters and food gatherers adapted to different environments.	
Eastern Mediterranean		Haua Fteah Kebara Wadi an Natuf Eynam Belbasi	Advanced Hunters along N. African coast by 35,000 and in the Levant by 32,000. Late Hunting and plant collecting people throughout region c 10,000-8000.	
Western Mediterranean		Grimaldi Romanelli Addaura (Palermo) Parpalló Altamira	Advanced Hunters in Italy and Iberia by 30,000. Elements of Advanced Hunters along N. African coast. Late Hunters throughout region by 8000.	
Continental Europe		Aurignac La Gravette Solutré La Madeleine Lascaux Kostienki	Advanced Hunters arrive by c.33,000, probably from east. Various later groups create prosperous and progressive cultures. Hunters advanced into W. Germany, Denmark 9000.	
Iran-India		Shanidar Zarzi (Kurdistan) Zawi Chemi Banderawela (Ceylon) Ali Kosh	Advanced Hunters in south Zagros from c.34,000. They begin to develop Late cultures by 15,000. True Late Hunters in Iran by 10,000, in India 9000.	
Far East		Mal'ta (Lake Baikal) Shi-Tung-Kou Shirataki Chou-Kou-Tien (Upper cave)	Advanced Hunters spread into Siberia c.12,000 and possibly N. China. Japan first settled 11,000. Australia c.20,000.	
The Americas		Clovis Folsom El Inga	First men may have entered via Siberia-Alaska by 25,000, but none certain before 10,000. Big-game hunters. Extreme south reached by 9000.	

The economy bar graph indicates relative proportions of these factors: Irrigation ≈ Agriculture ☙ Hunting ⚔ Urban life ⌂ Trade ⤳

Religion	Technology and inventions	Architecture	Art
	Late Hunting equipment with microliths and polished bone tools. Fishing; heavy picks and axes. Ovens, mortars. Bone needles and combs.	Circular mud-brick huts. Clusters of round huts of rammed mud. Rectangular houses before 8000?	Rare figurines. Some Late Hunting period cave art by Upper Euphrates?
	Chipped flake tools and weapons with Advanced blade types in East. Late Hunting equipment with microliths widespread after c.10,000.	Some cave dwellings. Transient camps.	Hunters' rock engravings.
Dead buried with ornaments, head-dresses, beads, etc. in Late period.	Advanced Hunting equipment with blades. Wild grain collecting with microliths and grinders by 13,000. Late Hunting and fishing. Very progressive. Mortars, querns, reaping knives, ornaments.	Caves with outside terraces. Round or oval huts with hearths and paving mortar in groups of up to fifty from end of Advanced through Late periods.	Naturalistic small sculpture in the round and on implement handles. Rock engravings in S.E. Anatolia.
For Advanced period probably veneration of animals. Hunting magic as in Europe. Ceremonial burial.	Advanced Hunting equipment and bone tools. Bow and arrow in Spain by 15,000. Late Hunting equipment with microliths.	Only cave dwellings as yet known for Advanced period. Windbreak in Iberia during Late period.	Cave engravings in S. Italy and Sicily. Animal cave paintings and engravings in N. Iberia. Engravings and painting on plaques.
Fertility cult with "goddess" figures. Veneration of animals with rites suggesting totemism. Shamans? Hunting magic. Ceremonial burial.	Advanced Hunting equipment with a great variety of bone implements. Harpoons, spear-throwers, thong-softeners. Lamps, paint cases.	Cave dwellings. Oblong, skin-covered huts with sunken floors, hearths, and stone or mammoth bone walling in E. Europe.	Cave painting, engraving and relief carving. Modelled sculpture in round and engraved implements in S. Central and S. France. Female statuettes in E. Europe.
	Advanced Hunting equipment with blades. Microlithic tools plentiful by 15,000. Late cultures in Central India with some microliths in semi-precious stones.	Cave dwellings and transient encampments. Round huts with stone foundations by 9000.	By Late period cave paintings in Central India.
In Siberia probably much as in Europe.	Chipped flake implements of older tradition with some intrusion of Advanced equipment. Fur clothing with leggings, tunic and caps.	Oblong skin-covered huts with sunken floors, hearths and a walling of stones and mammoth bones in Siberia. China, Japan unknown.	Human and bird figurines. Animal cave paintings in Urals.
	Early rough flake tools? Finely flaked spearheads of various types from 10,000. Spear-throwers. Little use of bone and no microliths.	Cave dwellings. Transient encampments.	

Religion	Technology and inventions	Architecture	Art

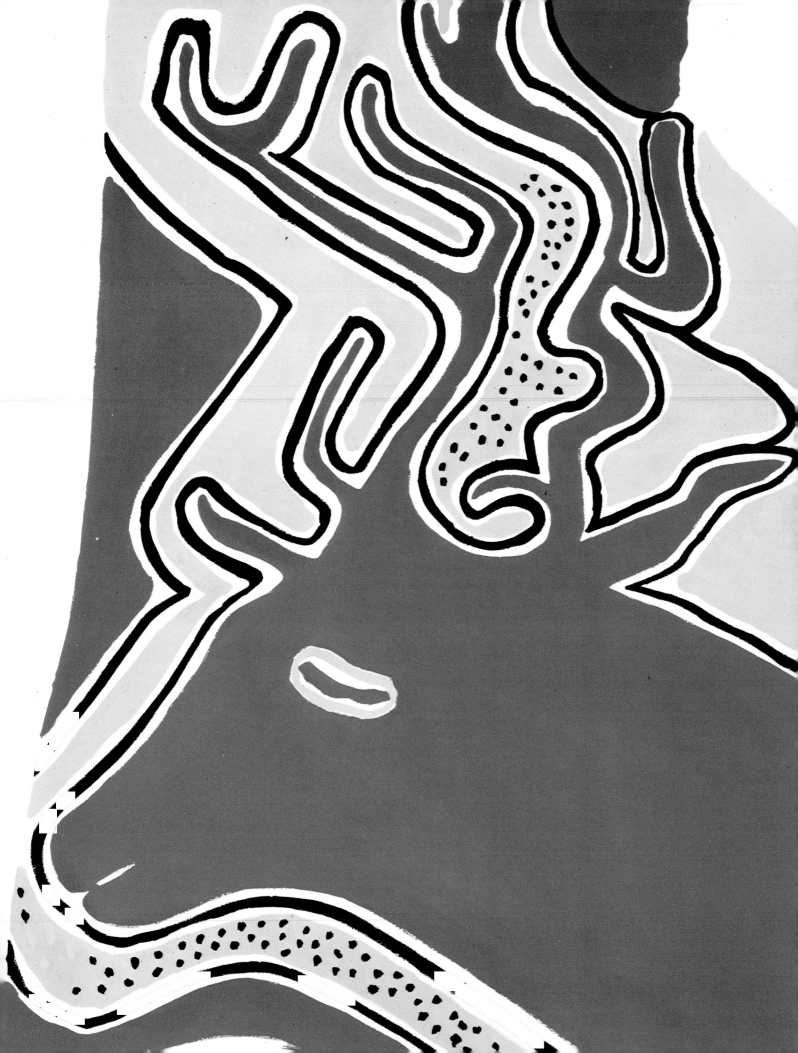

8000– 5000BC

The leading events of this period concern the domestication of plants and animals in the Near East, followed by the further elaboration of mixed farming, its gradual spread westward and the development of crafts such as potting and spinning for woven textiles that accompanied the more settled agricultural life. Together these changes comprise what has been called the Neolithic Revolution, a gradual revolution to be sure, but one of great importance for it provided the necessary foundation for the growth of civilization. This present period in fact covers the greater part of the New Stone Age or Neolithic culture. Stone, bone and wood remain the only materials for all implements, but the grinding and polishing of new forms, such as hoes and axes, is another technological advance of the time.

From our point of view the period has further significance. Although in the previous period there were progressive areas where Advanced and Late Hunters had a far higher achievement than that of other peoples, all people throughout the then inhabited parts of the world depended upon the hunting and gathering of natural foods – animal and vegetable. In this period that degree of unity was ended for ever. By the sixth millenium BC some men were beginning to control nature, to establish substantial villages and even towns of a sort with their fields and pasture, and to change the characters of the once wild animals and plants. The rest of mankind, however, remained hunters and food gatherers. Ever since this time peoples in different parts of the world have lived on increasingly different material bases, the technological van accelerating, the archaic rear dwindling but little changed. Now we have supersonic flight and the stone-tipped arrow.

I have already described how by the end of glacial times Late Hunting peoples in the Near East (typified by the Natufians), though still relying on natural resources, were already moving towards the new economy. True farming was first to be developed in uplands that on a map look like the profile of an umbrella with the Levant as its handle and the great sweep from southern Anatolia round the head of the Tigris-Euphrates valley and along the southwest flank of the Zagros as its cover.

Over this area descendants of the Late Hunters began to select and control wild cereals and wild sheep and goats in a manner that was to alter their genetic bases and produce true domestic breeds. These processes were subtly complicated, whether intentional or not. For instance, one of the most important changes in cultivated cereal was that the ear retained its grains instead of scattering them as for natural seeding. Wild plants having this mutation would have been more easily gathered, and once carried home, would have inevitably provided a disproportionately larger amount of the seed corn. Furthermore the cultivators (women were traditionally the plant gatherers) learned deliberately to select ears with more numerous or larger grains for seed.

Similarly the early herdsmen who advanced from the loose control of animals towards true stock breeding, at first tended to select the smaller, more docile individuals. The protection of herds from predators allowed mutations to be established that would have been eliminated in the wild. By this means the growth of horns was altered and also in cattle piebald colouring emerged, now so characteristic of many domestic breeds.

The primary reason why domestication began in that umbrella-shaped area is because the wild ancestors of wheat and barley, sheep and goats, were native to that region. Another reason was that, as we have seen, the peoples of the Near East had long maintained progressive cultural traditions. To these explanations can be added the facts that the upland valleys offered good water supplies, often fertile soil and their natural configuration made it easier for men to confine their herds

Reconstruction of a stag's head found in a niche in the wall of a shrine at Çatal Hüyük, Turkey. Such animal paintings were ritualistic, the stag being an attribute of a deity rather than a god itself.

and to move them between summer and winter pastures. So began the more masterful relationship of men with nature which in time brought the conviction that God had granted them "dominion over the cattle and over all the earth...".

The history of domestication was not uniform within the "umbrella" lands of the pioneers. Herding and then breeding sheep and goats began very early in the Zagros, probably even before 8000 BC. By the late eighth millennium crops were also being grown, although hunting and plant gathering still provided a considerable part of the diet. Before very long there were settled village communities in the upland valleys and foothills throughout the range, and in some places villagers had added pigs to their stock.

In Anatolia and the Levant this order of events was reversed: villagers were cultivating plots of wheat (einkorn and emmer) and barley before they had domesticated animals. It seems that here and there, as at Jericho, quite large agricultural communities remained wholly dependent on hunting for their meat. Stock-breeding, now including cattle in Anatolia, began in the later eighth millennium.

The relatively settled life of agricultural villages with its new needs and opportunities had a revolutionary effect on dwellings, domestic equipment and the crafts. Architecture varied with local conditions, but in general houses were built to last and were equipped with fixed corn-grinders, ovens and good provision for storing grain. In the southern Levant, with its strong Natufian tradition, the earliest houses were round. But after 7000 BC rectangular plans were adopted there and elsewhere; they were presumably found to be far better suited to compact building for villages and towns.

Layout differed from region to region, some houses had no more than a living room and storage area while others had several rooms, a courtyard, and even a second storey. Very often amenity and pride of possession was shown in highly polished plaster floors with rush matting, and decorated walls of coloured dadoes and simple painted patterns.

One great craft invention was fired pottery. The earliest certainly known example (c.7000 BC) is from the Zagros region. There was a well-defined phase in the Levant and Anatolia when villagers living in comfortable, well-equipped houses, had not mastered the art of potting. This situation recurred as farming spread more widely. The old view that farming and potting always went together has long been disproved.

Spinning and weaving, usually of wool, was another important invention of the seventh millennium. Weighted spindles were used but nothing is yet known of the looms.

A more significant development than the new crafts was the rise of trade. The hunters of the previous period had exchanged sea shells for ornaments and obsidian, so excellent for fine knapping, in very small quantities and over modest distances. Now the trade in obsidian (originating in the volcanic regions of central Anatolia and round Lake Van) followed many long routes, and there was further trade in the best flints. Trade in luxuries such as rare and attractive substances for adornment and personal possessions flourished at this time. Turquoise and many other semi-precious stones were carried far and wide to satisfy the aesthetic sense and vanity of men and women.

Because of the nature of the archaeological evidence and the undoubted prime importance of farming as a foundation of future civilizations, I have seemed to agree with an economic interpretation of history. Yet just as the Hunters' art with its magico-religious implications was, humanly speaking, their most significant achievement, so nothing was more revealing of the advance of humanity in the earliest farmers than their religious art, ritual and imagery.

Rather than discussing religious forms generally, I have decided to include them in the particular settings of Jericho and Çatal Hüyük. These two extraordinarily interesting places have good claim to be called the oldest towns in the world. Nowhere else can the great creative surge of the first stages of the Neolithic Revolution be better appreciated.

Palestinian Jericho had already enjoyed a considerable history before the beginning of our period. By 8000 BC it had some two thousand inhabitants (of Natufian descent) who led their perennial spring water to their corn fields and vegetable plots. Probably aggressive neighbours or nomads coveted the spring, for after a few centuries the enterprising townsfolk enclosed their settlement within a massive, stone-faced wall at least four metres high. Inside it they built a solid stone tower (or towers) rising to eight metres and containing a well-masoned stairway. The originality, enterprise and energy involved in building these unique defences are astonishing and seem to imply some powerful leadership.

Not much is known of the religious ideas of the inhabitants of Jericho in the eighth millennium but, like their Natufian ancestors, they preferred to bury their dead within or among their houses. Furthermore, this time saw the beginning of the cult of skulls. Towards the end of the millennium the place was deserted for a time, then reoccupied by people who lived in far better houses and kept domestic goats as well as cultivating wheat, barley and legumes.

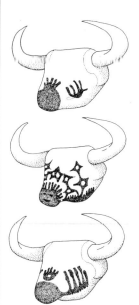

One of the many groups of bulls' heads found in the shrines at Çatal Hüyük, Turkey. It was found below a large plaster statue of the goddess giving birth to a ram.

The dead were still buried under houses, sometimes in large numbers, and many of them decapitated. These headless bodies are the reverse aspect of a strangely developed cult of skulls. Nine skulls were found on which the fleshy parts of the face had been carefully reproduced in tinted plaster, with cowrie and other shells inserted for eyes. The best skulls are so finely modelled and life-like that they are works of art as well as cult objects. The evidence of the headless bodies and the loving care of the plasterwork make it almost certain that the skulls had belonged to men and women of Jericho rather than to enemies, and therefore represent a veneration of ancestors.

The townsfolk of Jericho also practised other forms of worship. A female figurine with hands below breasts, icon of the Mother Goddess, is symbolic of the most widespread and popular cult of the age and one which we shall find at its height at Çatal Hüyük. A small stone pillar set in a niche of a domestic shrine seems to be the earliest known manifestation of the pillar cult familiar in Bronze Age Egypt, Crete and Greece.

This phase of Jericho's history ended about 6000 BC while our knowledge of Çatal Hüyük – a riverside settlement on the Konya plain of Anatolia – begins only in about 6250 BC. By this time it covered over thirty acres, the greater part being furnished with tight-packed houses of mudbrick, entered from above through their flat roofs. Probably at its height there were about a thousand houses and a population of some six thousand which was extraordinarily large for that time.

More strictly than Jericho, Çatal Hüyük deserves the name of town because, as the excavators say, "the economy was based on simple irrigation agriculture and cattle-breeding, trade and industry." Its food supplies showed the rich variety characteristic of early farming when domestic and wild species were exploited simultaneously. The townsfolk cultivated three types of wheat and one barley, and grew or gathered field peas, pistachios, almonds, crab apples, juniper and hackberry. They probably also enjoyed a wide range of green and root vegetables and soft fruits. Cattle provided them with most of their meat and perhaps with dairy produce, but they also kept a few goats and hunted deer and wild pig. They seem to have eaten wild birds and their eggs and to have done a little fishing. They could add to their sense of well-being with hackberry wine and beer.

Along with this abundant food supply the people of Çatal Hüyük won further prosperity through their "trade and industry". From their

town they could see the volcanic cone of Hasan Dag, and it is thought that they not only worked obsidian but controlled a considerable trade in it. On the other hand, they imported Syrian flint for their finest implements. Among the population were highly skilled wood workers, textile and basket weavers, stone polishers and potters. Beads were made from native copper and later there was small-scale smelting, though the metal was still used only for trinkets. Some part of all their products may have been traded, while they in turn had to import all raw materials except wood over lesser or greater distances.

Even more remarkable than the size and economic activity of this community of 8000 years ago was the art and religious life of the town. Scattered among the houses were a number of shrine rooms, built much like the ordinary houses but marvellously distinguished by their decoration and furnishings.

From a bewildering diversity of religious expression I can only evoke some of the most strange and powerful. Of primary importance was a fertility cult concerned equally with people and beasts and centred on different aspects of the supreme Goddess. She appears as the Crone, the Mother and the Maiden. Her male consort is shown as youth and bearded man and is further symbolized by bull, ram, stag and boar. Secondary cults in the shrines are concerned with death and funerary rites and also with wild animals and hunting magic.

Free-standing idols were found which portray the Goddess in all forms from the most stylized to the fully naturalistic. Among the latter she sometimes appears with leopards: in one, magnificently fat, she sits enthroned between two felines as a child is born to her. She is also represented in large wall reliefs of painted plaster. The most awe-inspiring shows her straddled above three horned bulls' heads as she gives birth to a ram.

Statuettes of the divine consort are less common but still varied: as both youth and grown man he sometimes appears riding a leopard or bull. His presence is symbolized again and again in pairs of spreading bull horns found set in double rows along plaster balks or in bucrania and in the huge wall paintings of bulls.

The death cult is most conspicuous in wall paintings, often in deliberate opposition to scenes or symbols of life. Among the most memorable manifestations are painted vultures with vast wings, their hooked and feathered beaks pecking at little headless human bodies. Even more macabre are carefully modelled female breasts within which are hidden the skulls of corpses of scavenging creatures – fox,

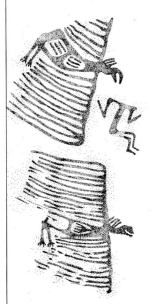

Paintings of enormous vultures attacking headless humans appear in the earliest shrines. As part of a funerary cult the people of Çatal Hüyük exposed their dead to vultures and later buried the bones beneath benches.

weasel and vulture – very barbarous in our eyes yet expressing the concept of the unity of life and death. The funerary cult was also more directly apparent in the shrines. While the bones of the ordinary people of Çatal Hüyük were buried beneath plaster benches in their houses, the flesh having been removed by vultures or exposure, under the similar benches in the shrines there were often much richer burials. These were accompanied not only by beads and other personal ornaments as were some of the ordinary burials, but by stone vessels, ceremonial knives and the most extraordinary of all the Çatal Hüyük products – circular mirrors of obsidian set in neat plaster backs. These graves, the one sign of social distinctions in the town, suggest a priestly or shamanistic elite. While the mirrors could have been ritually used by such people, we can perhaps allow them to symbolize for us a step towards greater self-awareness that must have been taken in the life-experience of the first settled farming communities.

I have given so much space to Çatal Hüyük partly for its richness and intrinsic fascination, but still more because it is the perfect example of man poised between the earlier instinctive hunting life with its elements of savagery and the life of high civilization that was to dawn at around 3000 BC. The continuance of hunting, the animal painting and preoccupation with animal symbolism in religion and the extravagantly experimental cult practices, all look back to the past. But the Mother Goddess of life and death with her consort and bull cult, were images that were to be refined and to flourish in the Bronze Age civilizations of the Old World along with the basic farming economy, the crafts and the crowded towns.

There is substantial evidence that rapid population increases at Çatal Hüyük led many people to emigrate and found new settlements elsewhere in southern Anatolia. This provides a localized example of a process characteristic of the sixth millennium. As the New Stone Age economy and cultures matured they spread outward from their primary centres within the "umbrella". In most of the lands involved in this spread, cattle and cereals appeared abruptly in their domesticated forms and in many places the domestic crafts of potting and weaving also appeared suddenly without any trace of local evolution. There can be no question, therefore, that movements of farming peoples occurred, perhaps often originating in a "population explosion" such as seems to have happened at Çatal Hüyük. On the other hand, native peoples may sometimes have adopted the new way of life through trade and neighbourly contacts. Their traditions then quickly modified those of the newcomers to produce distinctive regional cultures.

I must now give a brief account of this secondary diffusion of the Neolithic Revolution before turning for a final look at the rest of the world, where the revolution was not felt before 5000 BC and men continued to live by hunting and food gathering.

Before and immediately after 6000 BC, simple mixed farming had been carried to the fertile plain of Thessaly and southward to the Peloponnese. Crete was also settled at this time, though perhaps more directly from southwest Anatolia. Crete is of particular interest not only because of its glorious future, but because it is a clear example of farming being spread by the enterprise of families seeking new homes on new land. The sea crossing had apparently been too much for the hunters, so that the settlers brought their boats to a virgin and paradisiacal island. They shipped with them the seed corn and the young animals that were the products of domestication in the Near East. They had bread wheat, emmer and einkorn wheat, six-row barley and lentils; they had sheep, goats, pigs, cattle and dogs. Some of the emigrants chose cave dwellings, others built small villages. One group selected a low hill above a stream in a sheltered valley some three miles from the north coast. There they hastily raised some shelter over their heads – probably flimsy wooden huts. So was Knossos founded! There was to be a village on this hill almost continuously until the first Minoan palace was built there four thousand years later.

By the middle of the sixth millennium farmers had followed the Thracian plain and the valley routes northward from the head of the Aegean to settle in Macedonia (Bulgaria and Yugoslavia) and in southern Hungary and Rumania. There, standards of housing and of farming continued to rise. All communities made pottery, much of it attractively painted, and exchanged the skin dress of hunters for textiles. Obsidian could be obtained from Melos, a source already discovered by the Late Hunters, and female figurines, in many different forms, were made almost everywhere, presumably for cultic use.

Two more steps to the west remain to be chronicled. Well before 5000 BC many little farming settlements were set up along the east coast of Italy by peoples crossing the Adriatic from the Yugoslav coast. These western frontiersmen of the Neolithic Revolution freely supplemented their domestic economy with wild foods. In one village by an estuary the people ate great quantities of cockles, and with pioneering enterprise devised a flint tool expressly for opening them.

Finally, some primitive farming appeared round the coasts of Spain and Portugal. Here, however, cave dwelling was usual and the stone tools were derived from those of the Late Hunters. The New Stone Age way of life was not fully developed in the lands of the western Mediterranean until our next period (page 70).

Having followed the spread of farming to its westernmost limits before 5000 BC, I must now return to the Levant (the "umbrella handle") to see whether there was a contemporary southward expansion from Palestine. Many people still have a vague impression that farming must have begun very early in Egypt, but this was not so. The Nile valley being far from the uplands where the revolution began was not affected by it until about 5500, at least two and a half thousand years after its inception in the Levant. The long delay was probably due not so much to the intervening desert as to the contrast of conditions, and therefore of techniques necessary for farming, between the uplands and the swampy, sun-scorched and rainless valley. Similar factors, though on a vaster scale, delayed the cultivation of Sumeria. Farming apparently arrived at much the same date in Upper and Lower Egypt and was undoubtedly of Asiatic origin. The climate encouraged the use of palm and matting huts rather than mudbrick housing. But since predynastic Egypt falls properly within the next chapter no more need be said here.

At about the time when the first settlers were beginning the tremendous task of clearing and irrigating along the Nile banks, what seems to have been a purely herding life based on cattle and sheep appeared along the North African coast, in the Horn of Africa, and Kenya. Some of the earliest Saharan rock-paintings may date from this phase. It took a long time for any part of the new economy to penetrate south of the Sahara.

Before turning to the great overland expansion of farming towards the east, I must glance at Cyprus. Tucked in between the Levant and Anatolia and visible from their shores, it is not surprising that it was reached quite early, perhaps before 6000 BC. Agriculture and stock-breeding were introduced by settlers who are best known from their curious little town of Khirokitia. They showed conservatism in maintaining the Natufian tradition of round houses, also in their stone tools and in preferring stone vessels to pottery. On the other hand, the houses were snug and well-equipped, the town quite large and well laid out, the vessels of the finest. Cyprus provides an early example

of islanders, in their isolation and security, going their own way.

By far the most historically important movement of this time took place in and around the upper and middle valley of the Tigris-Euphrates. We have seen how by about 7000 BC villages were prospering in the uplands adjoining the great rivers, but there was still no settlement on the valley floor – the plains of Mesopotamia. Now, with well-developed farming skills, men began to move on to this fertile alluvial soil, particularly into that northern part which was to be Assyria where there was enough rainfall to grow crops.

The first people to build villages and lead their flocks on to the plain chose the relatively barren steppe lands of the Jezirek between the Tigris and Euphrates, where they may have settled even a little before 6000 BC. These first true Mesopotamians seem to have had cultural ties with the Levant. Their early presence in the valley has only recently been recognized. Much better known are the peoples who followed them by the middle of the millennium, and who may very well have moved down from the surrounding uplands. This situation would accord with the fact that the most northerly group settled mainly near the well-watered foothills round the head of the rivers, as did their neighbours to the southeast. Further south again, mainly beyond the Little Zab in the middle Tigris area, a third group was somewhat differently placed. A lack of rainfall obliged them to irrigate – and so began the great system of canals that was to make all southern Mesopotamia fertile by 3000 BC.

These three Mesopotamian groups have been named by archaeology after the sites of Tell Halaf, Hassuna and Samarra respectively. All three grew the now familiar cereal crops and while still hunting some wild game, herded sheep and goats and a few cattle. All three developed painted pottery, although in the early days the Samarrans specialized in fine alabaster vessels. All three were well housed, but here there is one sharp distinction: the Halafians, like the people of Khirokitia, showed conservatism in retaining round houses. All three practised the fertility cult associated with the Goddess, although her representations differed widely; all three tended to bury their dead in cemeteries rather than in their houses. The Samarrans placed figurines of the Goddess and phalli in their graves, together with fine beads, alabaster vessels and other possessions. These same people seem to have been the most prosperous; the Hassuna people were perhaps the most rustic. It would be a mistake, however, to think any of them lacked a certain style: figurines suggest flounced skirts and tall hats or hairdos; vase painters loved to show dancing girls; the introduction of flax almost certainly led to linen garments and Halaf pottery was raised to a pitch of aristocratic elegance.

One historical point remains to be made. Before 5000 BC the Halafians spread westward to the Mediterranean (probably again after rapid population growth), covering a vast range from Nineveh (Mosul) to Ugarit on the Syrian coast and reaching Anatolia.

While the population grew on the north Mesopotamian plain and down the Tigris, the lower Euphrates (facing desert instead of fertile uplands) and the great southern plain that was to be Sumeria, remained virtually uninhabited. Although settlement may have begun in the south (notably at Eridu) just before 5000, this history, like that of Egypt, belongs essentially to our next period and until then I shall leave it.

While the settlement of the plains was in progress, peoples of the pioneering Zagros uplands also advanced their agriculture and adopted pottery, including simple painted wares. Yet during the sixth millennium they lost their position in the van of the New Stone Age advance. Upland valleys may be ideal for small scale farming but they handicap expansion into larger units. In any event, the Neolithic Revolution failed to make itself felt in India before 5000 BC.

Yet the new economy was adopted over great expanses of mountain and high plateau to the north and east. In spite of the grim climate, villages sprang up in Transcaucasia between the Black and Caspian seas and on the Iranian plateau. Indeed the spread reached out towards Central Asia, with numbers of mixed farming settlements in Turkmenia, along the southern edge of the Kara Kun desert, and with outliers as far as Afghanistan. In all these regions there were the usual cereals, sheep, goats and occasionally cattle. Potting and weaving were invariably adopted at some stage. But all tended to be on a modest level, with small villages, small houses and few luxuries of any kind. Hunting and gathering were still important for food supplies.

Of all these territories with their general uniformity and local peculiarities of culture, I select the north Iranian plateau between Zagros and Elburz as the most significant. There was some farming here even before 6000 BC but this region prospered with the settlement of Siyalk. Not only was Siyalk itself a relatively large place and well sited for mountain trade routes, but the inhabitants were among the first to work the native copper, plentiful in the eastern desert. They used it not for beads, but for small tools, pins and needles. In this technological enterprise we can see them looking forward to the copper using era of our next period.

I have now given an outline picture of the diffusion of mixed farming from its primary centres in the Near East until it extended from Spain to Afghanistan and from Turkmenia to Upper Egypt. It was a very large area and yet the humanly inhabited lands outside it were very much larger still. In all these vast, still primitive territories, human societies continued to live entirely on what nature had to offer by an infinite variety of hunting, fishing, fowling and plant gathering. There were also within the food-producing regions very many local groups who either preferred or were obliged by the terrain to remain as hunters.

In Europe the Late Hunting peoples showed themselves well able to adjust to the complete change in their surroundings that came with the warmer climate. By 8000 BC birch and pine forests were invading the old open hunting grounds and they were later followed by the far denser mixed oak forests. The principal game were now red deer and wild cattle. In many regions there was an increase in fowling that went with a general use of the bow and arrow, and strand looping as well as fresh water and sea fishing intensified. Paddled boats (dugout or skin-covered) seem to have come into use here at much the same time as in the Mediterranean. While composite tools with microliths were still made, quite heavy chipped flint axes were devised for tree felling and wood working.

A little community with a lakeside encampment in Yorkshire (Star Carr) gives the most exact idea of the social patterns of the time. There were four or five family groups, some two dozen men, women and children in all, who lived in shelters on a platform of branches and brushwood. They remained there only from late autumn to early spring, but returned each year over some twenty seasons. Presumably during the warmer weather they moved about more freely.

A much more lively impression of the Late Hunters' life has been preserved in the rock paintings of eastern Spain. Artists were probably at work there both before and after the small beginnings of farming in the peninsula. Unlike their predecessors of the Old Stone Age these painters loved to show human beings, and human beings involved together in scenes of hunting, fighting and dancing. The men, almost always carrying bows or spears, dash about with enormous energy and zest, pausing only to shoot at ibex deer or boar. The women, though hampered by long skirts, are shown dancing.

In Scandinavia dense forests caused most hunters to live along the coasts where they could not only fish and gather shellfish, but also hunt seals, porpoise and sea birds. They, too, had their artists who engraved animals on rocks in the old naturalistic style and carved them in stone and amber. In some localities such as Denmark, this kind of existence was to persist until 3000 BC, and in a great circumpolar belt from the Baltic to Siberia until recent times. Ways of life in Siberia ranged from settled fishing along the Amur to reindeer-hunting over the tundra.

Hunting and food gathering seem to have persisted throughout the period in southeast Asia as well (including Java, Borneo and Sumatra) and in Japan. Again one must picture most people living along the coasts (where huge middens proclaim their fondness for shellfish) and some in riverside caves, hunting pig for their main meat supply. It has been claimed that there was very early cultivation of such local plants as bean, waterchestnuts and gourds in Thailand, but this is still uncertain. On the other hand, there is no doubt that potting was being practised before 6000 BC, an unusual craft for hunters and fishers.

The rise in sea levels that followed the melting of the ice cut off the Americas from Asia. It is thought that from then until the arrival of the Europeans, cultures and civilizations developed virtually without outside influence. The changes that took place in the Americas in this period were not very different from contemporary events in the still primitive areas of the Old World. In the eastern woodlands of North America the big game hunting tradition was coming to an end by the beginning of the period; the warmer climate brought a greater dependence on plant collecting and fishing. In the central plains, however, old ways could be more nearly maintained, with bison taking the place of mammoth as the chief game animal. In the west and in the uplands of Mexico what has become known as the Desert culture was taking shape. Although deer, mountain sheep and other animals were hunted with spear-throwers, a large part of the diet was supplied by the collection of all kinds of seeds, nuts, berries and roots. These were parched, then ground on the large, flat milling stones that the Spaniards were to call *metates* and which are still to be seen in American Indian houses. The Desert peoples were neither settled nor nomadic, but made regular seasonal shifts seeking out one source of food after another. They often used caves for shelters. Such a life limited them to simple equipment, but they were skilful makers of baskets, mats and netting. In some regions the Desert tradi-

tion persisted until the mid-nineteenth century.

So far as we know, it was only in Mexico that there were the first small signs of food production during this time. In the Valley of Mexico and the Tehuacán valley to the south (both to be centres of civilization), a few plants such as beans, squash and peppers were being cultivated. At the end of this period a very small and primitive maize, the great American cereal of the future, was grown. The contribution these cultivated plants made to the general food supplies, however, was still almost negligible.

Little is known of South America at this time, but the shift from big-game hunting seems to have followed much the same course as in North America, though here the smaller game included llamas. There was one divergence: before 5000 BC people began to form more settled communities along the coasts of Chile and Peru, where, like their contemporaries across the Pacific, they won a good living from the produce of the sea.

From an historical point of view this period (8000-5000) must, I think, be judged as one of promise rather than attainment. It saw a number of inventions and discoveries that have served us well ever since. Most remarkable, of course, was the domestication of all the principal cereals and livestock that were to support not only the Bronze Age civilizations of our next period, but also so large a part of mankind up to the present day. It saw the dawn of the idea of comfortable and serviceable houses. Yet in those mental and creative powers which distinguished mankind, progress was not so great. There was no imaginative art to compare with what had gone before, and the strange, somewhat crude and barbarous manifestations of the Çatal Hüyük shrines were incompatible with the great religious inspiration of art and architecture that was to burst out with civilization.

I must add an envoy to the hunting life. It had been the shaper of all peoples' emotions and enthusiasms until this time, but from now on it was to be pushed further and further into obscure refuges. The conditioning of so many hundreds of thousands of years could not easily be suppressed. Farming meant the imposition of routines on both sexes: men were more tied, with lasting responsibilities rather than sudden excitement; women would have to spend untold hours at the millstone or loom. One has only to look at the Spanish cave paintings to see the *joie de vivre* that came from successful hunting. All through succeeding periods we shall find hunting as the privilege of the elite, with humble people enjoying it when they could. This instinct is with us yet.

Technology *8000-5000 BC*

The mastery of food production, arguably the most important single technological advance made by mankind, belongs to this period. The change was by no means sudden. At 8000 BC a few Near Eastern sites like Jericho, Mureybet, Zawi Chemi and Shanidar already appear to have had herds of sheep, goat and gazelle under conditions closely approximating domestication. Intensive gathering of wild grain had reached an advanced stage too. By 5000, domesticated animals, now including cow and pig, and cultivated crops such as a variety of wheats, barleys and legumes, were staples of the economy from the Adriatic to Central Asia, over areas far wider than the hill districts occupied by their wild ancestors.

This change had many repercussions. It called for new and improved tools; it led immediately to more permanent settlements, allowing a much larger, and so more specialized, range of material equipment; it allowed an increase of population and encouraged trade. It may be no exaggeration to say that by 8000 man was close to the limits of his technical abilities in a hunting/food gathering way of life.

A number of developments followed quite rapidly. In semi-desert regions away from the hills, it had been found that the cultivatable area could be greatly increased by irrigation, which in turn called for advances in social organization. From a surprisingly early date, the properties of native copper were at least occasionally noticed, though it was not until much later that metal was used for more than ornaments or trinkets. The weaving of textiles also began in this period and was a great improvement on hides and pelts for clothing.

A characteristic feature of the Neolithic period was the development of ground stone and pottery although their presence did not necessarily indicate food production. Many early farmers made little use of ground stone and none of pottery while, conversely, some food gatherers used the former and, where their resources allowed permanent settlement, the latter too.

A further notable change of this period was the spread of the miniature flint tools or microliths. Microlithic industries are found at this time from the Atlantic to India, and the spread was probably the result of concentration on small game hunting.

There is much stronger evidence for the use of boats at this time, especially from Europe. A few dug-out canoes preserved in clay were found near Perth and some paddles were unearthed near Scarborough and in Denmark.

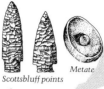

Areas of major interest
• Centres

COCHISE

Coxcatlan • • El Riego

Scottsbluff points   *Metate*

The Americas
Further new forms of projectile point were developed. Querns, known as *metates*, show that in Mexico wild maize had become a food source.

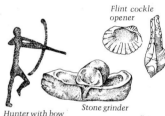

Flint cockle opener

Hunter with bow   *Stone grinder*

Western Mediterranean
The bow and arrow was now certainly part of hunting equipment, being shown in Spanish rock art. At Coppa Nevigata flint awls were devised for opening cockle shells – a major source of food. Crop cultivation around the Mediterranean coast is indicated by the stone grinder.

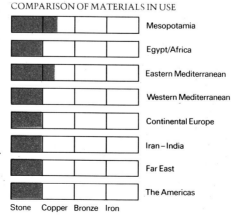

COMPARISON OF MATERIALS IN USE

Mesopotamia

Egypt/Africa

Eastern Mediterranean

Western Mediterranean

Continental Europe

Iran – India

Far East

The Americas

Stone   Copper   Bronze   Iron

Far East
In China and further south, intensive food gathering was approaching full food production. Permanent settlements dependent on the exploitation of shellfish were already present in Japan, but the fairly primitive stone tools such as the axe and spatula show little advancement.

Stone axe

Spatula

Continental Europe
Late Hunting equipment is well represented in the bow, hafted axe, flint knife, barbed harpoon and fish hook.

Harpoon

Axe

Fish hook   *Flint knife*

Bow

Eastern Mediterranean
Mudbrick construction became widespread in permanent settlements here and elsewhere. Storage containers and stamps suggest a growing economy based not only on agriculture but on an increasing trade in obsidian.

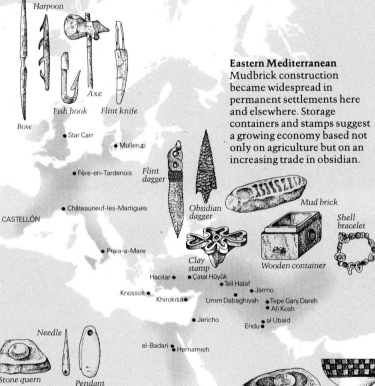

Flint dagger

Obsidian dagger

Mud brick

Shell bracelet

Clay stamp

Wooden container

• Star Carr

• Mullerup

• Fère-en-Tardenois

CASTELLÓN

• Châteauneuf-les-Martigues

• Praia-a-Mare

Hacilar •   • Çatal Hüyük

• Tell Halaf

Knossos •   • Jarmo

Khirokitia •   Umm Dabaghiyah   • Tepe Ganj Dareh
                                • Ali Kosh

• Jericho   • al Ubaid
              Eridu •

el-Badari •   • Hemamieh

Iran – India
A full food producing technology, including irrigation and competent pottery and leading to fully settled villages, spread to the east and north from the Zagros as far as Turkmenia and the Caucasus.

Painted pot

Stone axe

Stone grinder

Egypt/Africa
The stone quern indicates that the techniques of food production may have been known in the Nile Valley, while throughout the rest of Africa bone and flintwork continued earlier traditions.

Needle

Stone quern   *Pendant*

Bone harpoon

Halaf pot

Stone quern

Husking tray

Mesopotamia
Food production became firmly established and began to spread to the much more fertile flood plains of the south with the development of irrigation. One notable result was the early flowering of fine pottery.

Mesopotamia

Equipment was developed for turning grain into edible food. The husking tray, with its grooved bottom, was used for breaking up the ears of corn. The grain was then transferred to the stone quern, where hard work with the rubber reduced it to coarse flour. This would be mixed to a dough (probably without yeast), to make thin wafer-like bread. Baking was carried out on hot plates over an open fire, or, as here, in proper built ovens (partly closed chambers below or above ground).

BREAD OVENS A fire was built in the chamber, which was then cleared, loaded with the bread and covered to retain its heat.

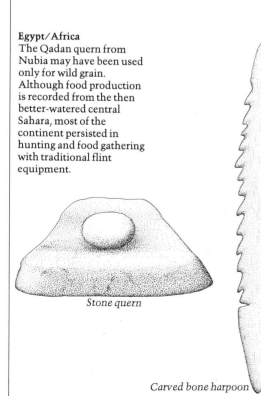

Stone quern and rubber

Ceramic husking tray

Egypt/Africa

The Qadan quern from Nubia may have been used only for wild grain. Although food production is recorded from the then better-watered central Sahara, most of the continent persisted in hunting and food gathering with traditional flint equipment.

Stone quern

Carved bone harpoon

Eastern Mediterranean

The technology of Çatal Hüyük is an outstanding example of the developments in this area in this period. Craftsmanship of the highest order went into the shaping of flint and obsidian which were traded through the Levant and brought wealth to the area. The stamp seals suggest more evolved ideas of property ownership, not surprising in a town of 13 ha. and perhaps 5000 inhabitants. The hand-moulded mudbrick from Jericho is an early example of a building technique that is still used today.

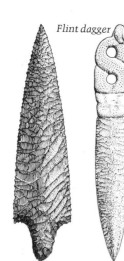

Flint dagger

Obsidian dagger

Stamp seals of baked clay

Hand-made mudbrick

Western Mediterranean

Farming practices were brought by sea round the Mediterranean coasts, though we have no evidence of the boats used. We do know that grain crops were raised in Italy and that domesticated animals had been introduced at least as far as Provence.

Using a stone grinder

Continental Europe

In the north and west, a whole new economy and way of life was devised to suit the post-glacial conditions. The emphasis on hunting smaller animals, fish and fowl led to the wider use of the bow and arrow and barbed harpoon.

Bone harpoon

Wooden bow stave

Iran – India

Though its sites are less dramatic than some farther west, this area played a major part in the mastering of food production. The polished stone axe was a much more efficient tool than its flaked predecessor.

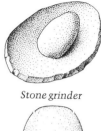

Stone grinder

Polished stone axe head

Far East

In an area tending towards full food production, the polished stone axe was a major weapon for winning cultivatable fields from the jungle. An indigenous food-producing economy may already have been present in Thailand.

Stone axe head

The Americas

Big-game hunting on the Great Plains continued with points of new shapes such as the Scottsbluff and Eden.

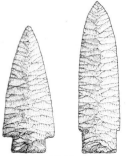

Scottsbluff points

DOMESTICATION OF ANIMALS *The first step towards domestication was the concentration of hunting at certain sites on particular species such as red deer at Franchthi and gazelle at Nahal Oren. As the game came to be herded, husbandry methods began to appear. The culling of young males first, leaving only enough to serve the flock, is clear from the food refuse of sheep bones at Zawi Chemi before 8500 BC. Full domestication followed later and involved selective breeding of such species as wild sheep, wild goat, aurochs and wild pig. At this later stage recognizable changes in the skeleton began to appear–notably the reduction in horn size.*

Maximum extent of wild sheep

Maximum extent of wild cattle

Maximum extent of wild pigs

Maximum extent of wild goats

Oldest known evidence of animal domestication

▲ **Sheep**, Zawi Chemi Shanadar, Iraq. 8650 BC

▼ **Cattle**, Thessaly. Greece; Anatalia, Turkey. 6300 BC

■ **Pigs**, Çayönü, Turkey. 7200 BC

● **Goats**, Ganj-Dareh, Iran. 8200 BC

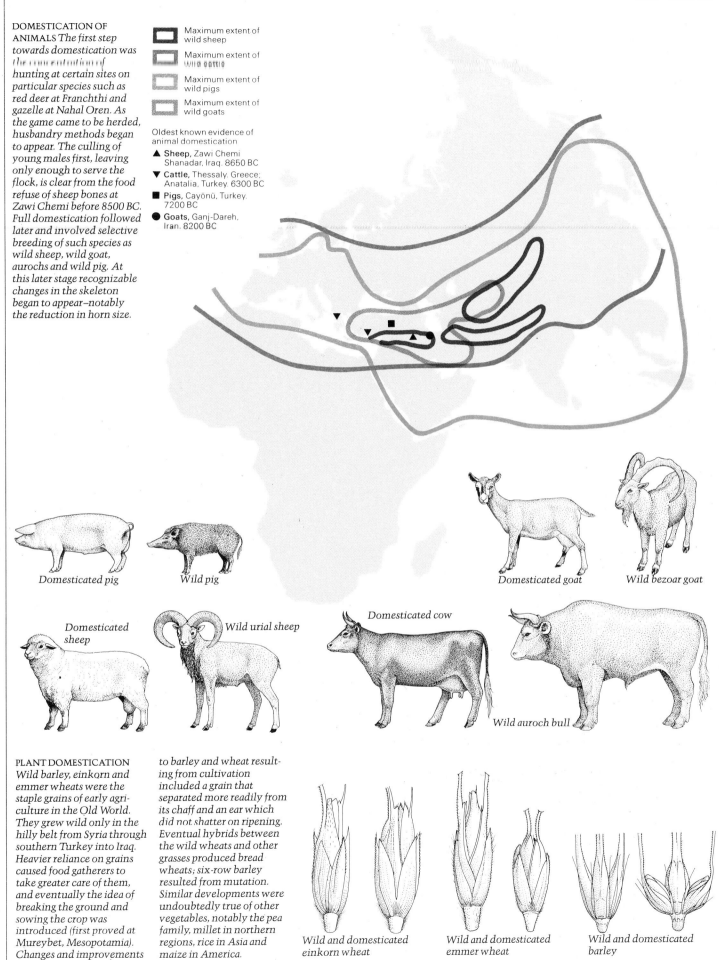

Domesticated pig

Wild pig

Domesticated goat

Wild bezoar goat

Domesticated sheep

Wild urial sheep

Domesticated cow

Wild auroch bull

PLANT DOMESTICATION *Wild barley, einkorn and emmer wheats were the staple grains of early agriculture in the Old World. They grew wild only in the hilly belt from Syria through southern Turkey into Iraq. Heavier reliance on grains caused food gatherers to take greater care of them, and eventually the idea of breaking the ground and sowing the crop was introduced (first proved at Mureybet, Mesopotamia). Changes and improvements* *to barley and wheat resulting from cultivation included a grain that separated more readily from its chaff and an ear which did not shatter on ripening. Eventual hybrids between the wild wheats and other grasses produced bread wheats; six-row barley resulted from mutation. Similar developments were undoubtedly true of other vegetables, notably the pea family, millet in northern regions, rice in Asia and maize in America.*

Wild and domesticated einkorn wheat

Wild and domesticated emmer wheat

Wild and domesticated barley

49

Architecture 8000-5000 BC

Over most of the world, this period saw little change. Many, though not all, caves were abandoned as the climate improved yet there was little advancement in hut construction. Earth houses were not needed in the warmer weather and perishable wooden structures rarely survive. Throughout Europe, Africa, the Far East and the Americas, the most developed architecture consisted of simple stick and thatch huts and shelters.

But in those areas where domestication of animals and crop cultivation were practised – Mesopotamia, eastern Mediterranean and Iran-India – architectural advance is more apparent. The mastery of food production made permanent dwellings a necessity – crops and animals had to be guarded. Once people abandoned the restless hunting life they could afford to spend more time making their homes sturdy and comfortable.

Construction was of stone footings surmounted by sticks and brush, or of clay slabs, later giving way to sun-dried mudbricks. These bricks were first shaped by hand (as at Jericho) but later the mud was rammed into moulds. It was not long too, before rectangular houses almost universally replaced circular ones which had copied earlier tents or bivouacs. Frequently there were internal fittings such as benches for sitting or sleeping, cupboards for storage, a hearth or oven for cooking. Often, however, cooking was done in the open, in attached courtyards, perhaps to combat the smoke and avoid the fire risk. At some sites, notably Çatal Hüyük, some rooms were set aside as shrines for religious or ceremonial purposes.

Considerable variations existed within the general pattern of building. A high quality plaster was used in some areas to coat the inferior mudbrick. Roofs were usually flat, but the circular houses of Khirokitia in Cyprus had fine corbelled vaults. Upper storeys were already present at Hacilar and strangely enough at Çatal Hüyük the roofs were used for all communication, no space being left between houses at ground level at all.

Most settlements were quite small but at least two notable exceptions are known. Çatal Hüyük covered 13 ha., though only a small proportion of this has been excavated. It may have held 5000 people. The extent of Jericho is more clearly defined at 4 ha., since it was surrounded by a massive stone wall with external rock-cut ditch. The circular tower which stands behind the wall can fairly be described as the world's oldest known monument.

	Areas of major interest
●	Centres
▲	Sites

The Americas
Caves and temporary shelters continued as before.

Tents

Western Mediterranean
Natural caves remain the only documented dwellings, though huts were probably erected.

Cave

COMPARISON OF MATERIALS IN USE

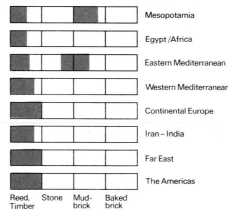

	Mesopotamia
	Egypt /Africa
	Eastern Mediterranean
	Western Mediterranean
	Continental Europe
	Iran – India
	Far East
	The Americas

Reed, Timber   Stone   Mud-brick   Baked brick

Continental Europe
Few traces remain of buildings
of this period but more
substantial evidence of the
huts of Late Hunters and food
gatherers have been found at
Lepenski Vir on the Danube.

Dwelling, Lepenski Vir

Far East
Little is known of dwellings in
this area at this early period.

Eastern Mediterranean
The mastery of food production
led to permanent settlements
throughout the area and
substantial buildings on some
sites. Round houses were
followed by rectangular ones
which were more suited to
town planning.

House, Hacilar

*House group,
Çatal Hüyük*

*Round houses,
Khirokitia*

▲ Lepenski Vir

Hacilar ● ● Çatal Hüyük

● Jarmo

● Khirokitia

Iranian house

Iran – India
Villages of rectangular
mudbrick houses sprang up
over much of western and
northern Iran and on to
Turkmenia, east of the Caspian.

Egyptian huts

Egypt/Africa
Scanty remains of buildings
survive from this area; simple
huts of locally available
materials were probable.

House, Jarmo

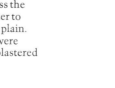

Mesopotamia
Permanent villages spread
along the hills and across the
northern plains, and later to
the rich southern flood plain.
At Jarmo early houses were
built of clay (pisé) and plastered
with mud.

Mesopotamia
The standard building material was mudbrick which is wetted earth moulded into shape and dried in the sun. It was built up into walls using more mud as mortar. The houses of Jarmo, however, were built of clay, known locally as pisé. Floors and roofs were both of mud laid over reeds, supported in the latter case by timber beams. The small rectangular houses contained store-rooms, sleeping quarters and a living room with a hearth. The walled court-yard attached to each obviously played a major part both as a working area and, with its built oven, a cooking area.

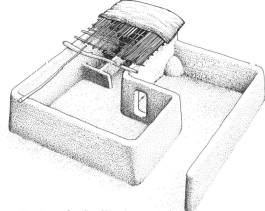

Rectangular dwelling house, Jarmo

Egypt/Africa
Evidence for this period from Egypt is extremely scarce, probably because it is buried deep beneath the Nile silt. Scanty traces of light huts may not be typical.

Simple reed huts

Eastern Mediterranean
This area, which was peopled by many food producing groups, contained the most varied architecture of the period.

JERICHO *Around 8000 BC an open settlement of well-constructed round houses of mudbrick was enclosed in a defensive stone wall 10 ft (3 m.) thick and at least 13 ft. (4 m.) high. Against this a tower 33 ft. (10m.) across and 28 ft. (8·5 m.) high was erected. Later the wall was further heightened and a ditch cut in the rock outside it to enclose an area of 4 ha. After a period of abandonment, Jericho was recolonized about 7000 BC. The town walls were not renewed but rectangular houses of mudbrick with high quality plastered walls and floors spread over the site.*

Stone tower and walls, Jericho, Israel

HACILAR *Similar in style but larger than the buildings at Çatal Hüyük, the dwellings here were rectangular of square bricks with stone foundations. The two-storey buildings were laid out in blocks back-to-back and entered from courtyards or narrow lanes.*

Houses, Hacilar, Turkey

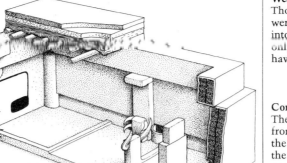

Shrine room, Çatal Hüyük, Turkey

KHIROKITIA *The round houses here belong to a different tradition, being raised on circular footings of stone with domed mudbrick roofs. They had gallery bedrooms and high thresholds to keep out rain and mud.*

ÇATAL HÜYÜK *In the mudbrick rectangular houses was found an extraordinary series of shrines. The sanctuaries were furnished with wall paintings, plaster reliefs, animal heads – real or modelled – and cult statues. These rooms were similar in plan and construction to domestic ones, with hearths, platforms, benches and ovens, but they were elaborately decorated and frequently larger.*

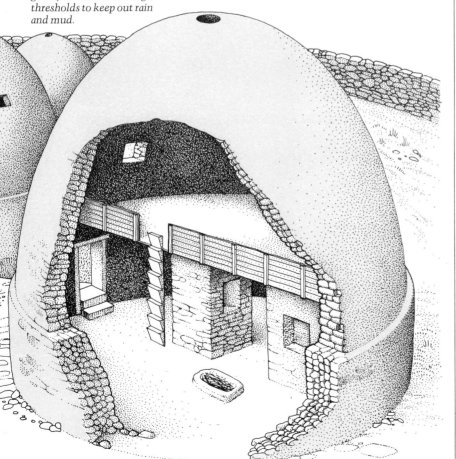

"Beehive" houses, Khirokitia, Cyprus

Western Mediterranean
Though farming people were beginning to move into the area by 5000 BC, only natural cave dwellings have been found.

Continental Europe
The most detailed evidence from this area comes from the site at Lepenski Vir in the gorge at Iron Gates. On a terrace beside the Danube a row of trapezoidal timber-built houses was erected by a community of fishermen. Simple hearths and other domestic fittings were found along with frequent and curiously carved stone heads.

House, Lepenski Vir, Yugoslavia

Iran – India
Small, rectangular and flat-roofed houses were similar throughout the area, although at Ali Kosh slabs of clay were cut direct from the ground for building. Elsewhere, as at Ganj Dareh, the more usual mudbrick was employed.

Mudbrick and straw house

Far East
No evidence of buildings has been found at this time.

The Americas
In the New World no architectural development had taken place. The structure of temporary shelters can only be guessed at.

Bark tent

Art 8000 – 5000 BC

The art of this period falls on either side of the great divide in ways of living and seeing that came with the adoption of farming and the resulting increase in skills and possessions.

On one side the surviving hunting societies here and there continued to portray animals and related subjects with some degree of realism. On the other side, the art of the peoples who adopted farming during this period was mainly decorative. We know it from their pottery, but there is no doubt that all kinds of perishable belongings, particularly textiles and baskets, would also have been enriched by colour and pattern.

In addition to their decorative arts, many of the farming peoples also used their ceramic skills to make small models, most often female figurines symbolizing the Mother Goddess.

The most characteristic and lively of the hunting art still comes from Europe. In eastern Spain, Late Hunters painted on large, exposed rock surfaces, usually in reddish colours that stand out strongly against the grey stone. In subject matter this Mesolithic art contrasts with that of our earlier period, for although both animals and people may be painted individually, they far more often appear in scenes of hunting, dancing and warfare in which there are large numbers of figures all active and frequently running at high speed.

In contrast, the other main centre of Late Hunting art in Europe maintains the isolated figures and relative calm of the Old Stone Age work. This is in Scandinavia. It forms two divisions, the stocky little animal sculptures, mostly from Denmark, and the rock engravings of game animals found up the coasts of Norway.

For hunting art outside Europe, it is very probable that the earlier rock engravings of the central Sahara were made in this period, including the "big-heads" that are thought to represent divinities. Probably some of the Egyptian rock art should also be included.

The decorative art of painted pottery is confined to the Near East where the finest work comes from Anatolia, Syria and northern Mesopotamia. The artists, who may very often have been women, used mainly geometric compositions, often both elaborate and stylish. Formalized animals and motifs such as the rosette and the cross might be added.

The most important and fascinating works of this period are the mural paintings, sculptures and pottery figures from Çatal Hüyük in southern Anatolia.

Areas of major interest

● Centres

▲ Sites

The Americas
There is no evidence of either decorative or representational art at this time.

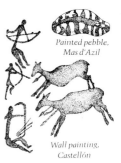

Painted pebble, Mas d'Azil

Wall painting, Castellón

Western Mediterranean
Most of the vital and often well-composed scenes of hunting life painted on cliff and rock faces in eastern Spain are likely to date from this period. The contemporary Mesolithic hunting people who succeeded the earlier inhabitants in the cave of Mas d'Azil painted abstract designs on pebbles.

Continental Europe

Of the animal art that persisted among the Late Hunters of Europe, the outline engravings of elk and other wild animals on coastal rocks of Norway are the most realistic. In Denmark the hunter-fishers made small carvings in the round and also sometimes engraved their possessions with simple geometric patterns. Singular carved stone heads were made in Yugoslavia.

Rock engraving, Klosterfoss

Stone statue, Lepenski Vir

Amber elk's head, Egemarke

▲ Klosterfoss
▲ Egemarke

Mas d'Azil ▲
CASTELLON

▲ Lepenski Vir

Eastern Mediterranean

The people of Jericho created the most interesting art in the Levant when they modelled plaster features on the skulls of their dead. It was sensitively done and may even have an element of portraiture. They also made near life-size stylized human figures in plaster. In Anatolia, in addition to the unique paintings and sculpture of Çatal Hüyük, there is painted and figure-shaped pottery – and voluptuous female figurines from Hacilar.

Leopard relief, Çatal Hüyük

Mother goddess, Çatal Hüyük

Painted pot, Çatal Hüyük

Plastered skull, Jericho

● Çatal Hüyük

▲ Hajji Firuz
▲ Arpachiyah
Samarra ▲   ▲ Tepe Sarab
Tell es-Sawwan ▲

● Jericho

▲ Hôsh

Statuettes, Tell es-Sawwan

Halaf dish

Samarran dish

The Far East

Potting was just beginning in Japan, but the oldest Jōmon wares are hardly works of art.

Mother goddess, Tepe Sarab

Iranian clay figurine

Iran-India

Along the flanks of the Zagros range early farming communities made a wide variety of female figurines and painted pottery in relatively simple styles.

Rock carvings, Hôsh

Egypt/Africa

It is likely that some of the engravings of wild animals on the rock cliffs of the Nile valley were made at this time. Like most such art they are difficult to date.

Mesopotamia

The most accomplished work was that of the pot painters, particularly those of the Hassuna, Samarra and Halaf cultures. The geometric and occasional animal designs are in red, brown or black on a cream or buff background. The finest Halaf ware, some of which dates from after 5000 BC, may be polychrome, red, black and white. These same peoples made a variety of figurines in pottery and stone.

55

Mesopotamia

The villagers of Tell es-Sawwan by the Tigris were active artist-crafts-people. They carved shapely vessels and standing and sitting female figurines in alabaster as well as painting pottery in the classical Samarran style. Of the widespread Halaf painted pottery some of the finest polychrome ware comes from Arpachiyah, near Mosul.

Alabaster statuette with inlays, Tell es-Sawwan

Samarran pot

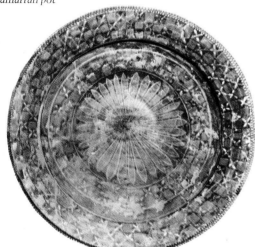

Polychrome pottery plate, Halaf period, Arpachiyah

Egypt

The Late Hunting people were probably responsible for carving elephant, antelope, sheep and many other wild animals on rock surfaces in the upper Nile valley. They are mostly rather crude, some being drawn in outline, others in sunk relief. These drawings were scratched in wadis.

Rock carving of food animals, Hôsh

Eastern Mediterranean

The numerous shrines among the houses of Çatal Hüyük are the oldest religious buildings completely furnished with works of art. The murals include painting and plaster cut-outs. They depict hunting and cultic scenes, including bulls and funerary vultures. A painting of the town with an active volcano behind ranks as the earliest known landscape. Some walls have bulls' heads in which real horns and frontal bones are incorporated. Other plaster reliefs represent the goddess, rows of breasts, and in one instance confronted leopards. Stone and terracotta cult images show the goddess in different aspects, also versions of her male companion (compare Laussel). In the finest of these the goddess is seated between two leopards as she gives birth to a child. In others she is giving birth to a bull or ram. The variety of subjects, styles, techniques in the art of these fertility shrines is extraordinary.

"The Hunter", wall painting, Çatal Hüyük, Turkey

Wall painting of a volcanic eruption, Çatal Hüyük

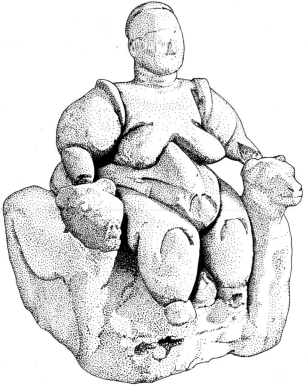

Clay figurine of goddess giving birth, Çatal Hüyük, Turkey

Red deer hunt scene, Çatal Hüyük

Western Mediterranean

The rock paintings of eastern Spain show scenes from the daily life of the hunters and their women. In the frequent hunting scenes the men are often shooting with bow and arrow. As well as deer, the game includes boar, ibex, wild goat and cattle. In style this art has much in common with the far later bushman paintings of Southern Africa

Rock painting of a hunting scene, Castellón, Spain

Continental Europe

Among the animals carved in amber by the hunter-fishers of Mesolithic Denmark are a bird, a bear and an elk's head. The head shows the kind of fine engravings that these people often made on their implements. The fishing community of Lepenski Vir on the Danube carved grotesque human figures and heads in stone. They seem to have been a local creation.

Carved head, Yugoslavia

Carved amber bear and elk's head, Denmark

Iran-India

Among the most striking of many Goddess figurines from the early farming villages along the flanks of the Zagros are two from Tepe Sarab. They have huge breasts and thighs. These same villagers made spirited boar figures which they stabbed, probably as a rite of hunting magic.

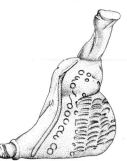

"Mother Goddess" figurine, clay, Tepe Sarab, Iran

Far East

The Japanese were beginning to make simple pottery but its fine plastic decoration develops only after 5000 BC. There is as yet no evidence that the Chinese began painting pottery before that date.

The Americas

Nothing is known for the period that would qualify as a work of art.

Region	Economy	Centres	Events and developments	People
Mesopotamia		Jarmo Umm Dabaghiyah Tell Halaf Al-Ubaid Eridu	Early farming develops and spreads in northern foothills in 7000-6000. First settlement in northern plain 6000. First settlement of lower Sumerian plain during 6th M.	
Egypt/Africa		Hemamieh El-Badari	Small population of hunters and fishers from Delta to 2nd Cataract. First farmers by 5500.	
Eastern Mediterranean		Jericho Hacilar (village) Catal Hüyük Khirokitia Knossos	Levant and Anatolia lead way in mixed farming and rare town life from 8000. Farmers arrive in Greece and Crete c.6000. Trade in obsidian.	
Western Mediterranean		Praia-a-Mare Castellón Châteauneuf-les-Martigues	Hunting and food gathering continues until farmers begin to spread to Italy, south of France and Iberia c.6000. Hunters persist in hinterlands.	
Continental Europe		Tardenois Star Carr Mullerup	Spread of forests. Hunting life continues with increase in fishing and fowling. Sea levels rising: isolation of Britain c.6000.	
Iran-India		Ali Kosh Ganj Dareh	Very early spread of farmers, mainly sheep herders along Zagros. Hunting and food gathering continue in India.	
Far East		Numerous sites but none outstanding	Hunting, fishing and food gathering continue. Strandloopers in Japan. Possibly some farming in N. China before 5000.	
The Americas		El Riego Coxcatlan Cochise	Big-game hunting dies out except on plains of N. America. Small-game hunting and plant gathering. Beginnings of plant growing in Mexico by 6000.	

The economy bar graph indicates relative proportions of these factors: Irrigation ≈ Agriculture ✿ Hunting ⚔ Urban life ⊞ Trade ∽

Religion	Technology and inventions	Architecture	Art
Fertility cults with female figurines and phalli. Dead buried with grave goods and occasionally red ochre.	Domesticated sheep and goats, barley and wheat. Irrigation by late 6th M. Pottery 6000. Kilns and ovens. Mudbrick. Copper beads.	Small rectangular houses of pisé or clay slabs. Interior plaster. Mudbrick after 5500. Shrines.	Painted pottery figurines
Unknown	Flint implements derived from Old Stone Age. Rough pottery from 5500.	Flimsy huts of matting and reed.	Rock engravings of animals?
Cult of heads – ancestor worship? Advanced cult of Mother Goddess, associated with animals. Funerary cult vultures.	Small flint and obsidian tools, including sickle blades. Polished stone axes and drills, stone bowls. Pottery from c.6500. Textiles; obsidian mirrors. Copper beads and smelting.	Stone town walls and towers. Round houses in Levant c.8000 followed by rectangular. Two storey town houses. Large shrines.	Representational wall painting and reliefs. Stone sculptures in round and relief. Ceramic figurines. Painted pottery 6th M.
Continuation of hunting cults and magic. Little evidence for first farmers. Dead buried with grave goods.	Small flint tools and weapons including bow and arrows. Pottery after 6000. Some polished stone. Querns, sickles.	Caves still widely in use as dwellings.	Rock paintings and engravings. Painted pebbles. Impressed pottery.
Continuation of hunting cults? Dead buried with grave goods and occasionally red ochre.	Small flint tools and weapons. Heavy chipped flint tree-felling axes. Antler harpoons; fish hooks, nets and traps. Bows and arrows.	Flimsy huts often with sunken floors. Encampments of four or more.	Earliest Scandinavian animal rock engravings. Animal sculpture in round of amber and stone. Early geometric engravings.
Some evidence for Mother Goddess and animal cults. Pierced boar figurines suggest hunting magic.	Continuation of small flint implements. Some polished stone axes. Mortars and querns. Earliest known pottery 7000. Stone bowls. Mudbrick.	Small rectangular houses of clay-slab. Larger mudbrick houses from 7000.	Female and animal figurines.
Unknown	Small stone tools in China and Japan. Pottery in Japan and Thailand by 6th M?	Unknown	Unknown
Unknown	Chipped flint projectile points. Atlatl. Pestles and mortars. Rough querns. Coiled baskets. Twined fibre blankets.	Transient huts and tents	Unknown

5000–3000BC

The all-important achievement of this period was unquestionably the dawn of literate civilization. A convergence of social, religious, technological and economic advances brought it to pass, creating true city life and various kinds of centralized government. Although substantial towns developed in some of the early centres of mixed farming, notably in the old Zagros territory of southern Iran, it was only in the last two or three centuries of the fourth millennium and only in Mesopotamia and Egypt that the changes were revolutionary enough to represent a difference in kind from anything that had gone before. We shall find that Sumeria led the way in the development of cities and the first essays in literacy, but Egypt caught up with a bound when united by her divine rulers of the First Dynasty. This period therefore closes with the peoples of both the great river valleys entering high civilization together, although with very different social and political forms. In both, however, civilization was shaped and coloured by a totally religious view of life and the cosmos.

Other historical events of this time were in large part an extension of those of the previous period: the further spread of farming to western and northern Europe and eastward to parts of India and China.

In Europe some of the peoples now reached by the Neolithic Revolution came to use their increasing numbers and social organization to create a crude yet monumental form of architecture – that of their large stone, or megalithic, tombs. For simple illiterate societies to devote their spare energies and resources to a creative megalomania has happened at other times and places – the most amazing instance being Easter Island – but it is not very common and this was its first occurrence. If the radiocarbon dating is to be trusted the oldest of these tombs were being built from 4500 BC, when temple-crowned towns were springing up in Sumeria and that country was taking the lead of the ancient world. However, the building of megaliths spread and reached its climax only towards the end of the fourth millennium, contemporary with the unification of Egypt and the rule of the first human being known by name. This was also the time when the very earliest, and still architecturally primitive, temples were under construction in Malta.

The rapid progress towards civilization inevitably involved appropriate technological advance. In the previous period inventions had been of a domestic kind, of advantage to the home life of farmers. Now they were associated mainly with transport, communication and more organized trade, or with increasing production for relatively large populations.

Over the progressive regions of Eurasia this period roughly coincides with the Copper Age, sometimes known as Chalcolithic to emphasize the fact that stone remained in use for many implements. It is not a very well-defined period, yet the name calls attention to the growth of metallurgy which was to be one of the most important of civilized skills and at the same time a great stimulus to trade. The use of native copper for tiny tools, beads and other trinkets among the Anatolians and other early upland farmers was mentioned several times in the last chapter. There were also examples of the small-scale reduction of metal from ores. In the fifth millennium, however, the smelting of ores became common and axes and blades of some size were cast in open moulds. The settlers of the Mesopotamian valley, particularly the Halafians in the north, brought some knowledge of copper working with them and would have maintained contacts with the mountain zones for ore supplies. Probably the evolution of the smelting process was connected with the development of improved kilns for firing fine painted pottery and, more generally, with a new knowledge of the control and purposeful use of heat. By the end of the millennium there must have been specialist coppersmiths who, with

White marble head of a lady from Uruk, Mesopotamia. Originally perhaps attached to a wooden body, the eyes and eyebrows would have had coloured inlays.

Early First Dynasty faience figurines of humans in crouching positions.

their furnaces, crucibles, moulds and ability to produce shining liquid metal from dull ores would already have been invested with something of the awe and mystery that was to surround smiths in later times.

There is no doubt that so far as the two great river valleys were concerned, it was the Mesopotamians who led the way in the production of copper. Although its use seems to have been introduced gradually into Egypt from rather before 4000 BC, Egyptologists agree that the techniques were derived from Asia. While good supplies of copper ore were available in the Sinai desert, Egyptians made little use of it before the beginning of dynastic times, remaining attached to their exquisite flint work. Rather more surprisingly, the Egyptians were also the pupils in the highly skilled art of faience manufacture which involved the synthesizing of glass and copper. This was a Mesopotamian invention dating from about 4500 BC which did not reach the Nile until the very end of our period. The Egyptians came to adopt the turquoise-blue glaze with such enthusiasm that it became known as "Egyptian faience" and was used for the thousands of beads, human figurines, hippos and scarabs that are now scattered throughout the museums and cabinets of the world.

Two related inventions almost certainly made during the fourth millennium were the solid wooden cart wheel and the potter's wheel or turntable. Both seem to have been made in Mesopotamia; the cart wheel is already a pictographic sign by 3400 BC and true wheel-turned pottery dates from about the same time.

Although previously there were boats substantial enough to carry livestock, these were paddle craft; true shipbuilding for oared, sea-going vessels was now developed and a simple square sail invented. These contributions to overseas trade are likely to have been made by the Egyptians together with the Levantines (particularly the people of Byblos who controlled what was to become a widespread trade in cedar and pine timber). The Egyptians had an incentive to harness the winds; the strongly prevailing north wind of their valley enabled them to sail up river against the current. For this simple purpose masts could be fixed even on primitive reed boats.

The greatest contribution the Mesopotamians were to make to the future was an invention of a very different kind and of a more gradual development: the art of writing. By the middle of the fourth millennium the management of the temple estates and their incomes (in the form of grain, cattle and other commodities) had become so complicated that some kind of record was needed. At first simple pictograms of the actual material objects were drawn. The great turning point came when it was realized that a sign could stand for a sound – phonetic writing had begun. At the same time, ideograms were used. For example, a disc which had once meant "sun" now could stand for "time" or "day". As the scribal profession and schools developed, the system of combined phonetics and ideograms became appallingly complicated. The old pictographic element almost entirely disappeared when the signs were made by impressing the stylus into the soft clay tablet to produce the true cuneiform, or wedge-shaped, script. It was not until our next period that this evolved far enough to enable men to write down literary works and to adapt cuneiform to other languages beyond the original Sumerian. The last centuries of the fourth millennium and the first of the third, when writing was being forged into a practical vehicle for language, are often called the Protoliterate Age.

Meanwhile, for our purpose, the relative position of Egypt in the race towards literate civilization is of extraordinary interest. There seems no doubt that the Mesopotamians (led by the Sumerians of the southern plain) were the initiators. Pictographic tablets mostly found in the ancient Sumerian city of Uruk are actually older by perhaps two centuries than any Egyptian writing, moreover they are more primitive in concept. Egyptian hieroglyphic writing when it began in about 3300 BC was already fully developed into a combination of signs for sounds and for ideas. This was attained only by evolution in Sumeria. We know that there were contacts between the two lands at this crucial time and it seems likely that Egyptian intellectuals must have taken the notion of writing from the Sumerians. But the Egyptians deliberately invented an almost totally different form. The Egyptians' own name for their writing meant "speech of the gods" and this is expressive of the fact that Egyptian hieroglyphs were from the first concerned with royal inscriptions for the divine pharaohs rather than with account keeping as in Sumeria.

One of the most marvellous and significant objects ever unearthed by archaeologists is the great carved slate palette from the old southern capital of Hieraconpolis. On it was written the name of King Narmer, the earliest name of an individual we have been able to read. Narmer was probably the first king of Dynasty I. The names of most of the succeeding rulers of this dynasty are recorded in inscriptions, together with references to their activities, so we are at

The electrum wolf's head from Tepe Gawra, Mesopotamia, has gold wire teeth, the inside of the head and the eye sockets being filled with bitumen. Electrum and copper pins attach the separate ears, lower jaw and teeth to the head.

once more in touch with these ancient monarchs than with their contemporaries in Mesopotamia. More remarkable still is the great invention of papyrus paper made by the Egyptians at this time. A simplified, cursive script could be written upon it with brush and ink. Thus, while the Sumerians led off the race, the Egyptians had soon passed them.

In only one other region did writing develop within 5000-3000 BC and this was in Elam. By the time the Egyptians created hieroglyphs, the Elamites had a curious geometric script of their own devising. It was probably inspired by the earliest writing of their Sumerian neighbours and foes.

In later periods we shall see some degree of literacy being achieved in land after land, until at last it reached western Europe with the Romans. Yet all through the Bronze Age of 3000-1000 BC the indefatigable scribes of the two great river valleys remained the true literates, to whose tablets, papyrae and monumental inscriptions we turn for poetry, tales, history, laws, letterwriting and science.

I must also describe one further invention of the period which was closely connected with writing and also with the rise of trade and commerce. This was the cutting of intaglio seals to be used as marks of origin or ownership. Clay stamps with patterns on them were already made by some of the more advanced communities of the previous period but it is not certain that they were employed in this way. At about the time of their first experiments in pictographic writing, the Sumerians began to carve animals and religious scenes on cylinders of lapis or other fine stones. These could then be rolled on tablets, jar sealings or dockets of clay to make single or repetitive positives. Sumerian cylinder seals were actually imported into Egypt where they were widespread until replaced by the scarab stamp seal, more suitable for use on papyrus. From time to time I have commented on signs of growing self-awareness in man: the rapid adoption of seals, often used for registering documents, shows the new sense of property and ownership that came with civilization and the end of kinship communities. There was a continuity of meaning as well as craftsmanship between these seals of over five thousand years ago and those that dangled on the broad fronts of confident Victorians.

I have attempted to outline the principal events and advances made during 5000-3000 BC in the progressive centres. Because most changes occurred after 3500 BC this final half millennium has demanded most attention. Now I must return to the beginning and sketch

in the general history of the entire period both in those centres of progress and outside them.

In fact the events of these two millennia are not easy to interpret in historical terms. While in the northern part of the Tigris-Euphrates valley the Halafians still had another five hundred years of prosperity, villages were springing up on the southern plain round Eridu and Ur. Indeed, the labour of draining the Euphrates swamps and building irrigation canals had probably begun in a small way before 5000 BC. Little is known of these people who first prepared the way for the world's earliest civilization except that they were quite unlike the various peoples in the upper valley, having more in common with their neighbours to the north. Probably they came from that direction, perhaps from the Iranian highlands. If so they had much to endure in adjusting themselves to the pitiless heat and featureless expanse of the alluvial plain. Undoubtedly they must have been farmers, but fishing was also of importance to them. It is due to this interest that we encounter one of the most telling examples of continuity between the villages of the period's beginning and the cities of its end. From the first village shrine at Eridu through to the main temple of the historical city the same sacred site was used, foundations standing above foundations in the accumulating mound. Masses of fishbones were found among the offerings in the early shrines and when the divinity whose house it was emerged into history, it proved to be Enki, god of the sweet waters. He was often to be portrayed with fish swimming in streams falling from his shoulders.

About 4500 BC the region was settled by people who came to be called Ubaidans. They in fact settled most of the sites where the great cities of Sumeria were to grow – including Ur (where Woolley found their remains under the silt of the flood). Later they spread up the valley, succeeding the Halafians and becoming the first people to dominate the whole of Mesopotamia. Moreover, their influence was felt in Syria and Cilician Anatolia. In time they grew prosperous, their villages expanding into towns. They traded with Syria for timber and Iran for copper which they began to employ freely. They also established a sea-faring trade down the Arabian Gulf, where settlements have been found along the coast of Saudi Arabia. Great quantities of oyster shells suggest that these people were not only enjoying shellfish but already seeking pearls.

Another break in cultural tradition and an acceleration in civic advance began around 4000 BC. Some historians believe that these changes were due to the arrival of the

Terracotta male figurine of
the al-Ubaid period found
at Eridu, Mesopotamia.
The figure is decorated with
knobs of clay; some red
paint remains on the face.

Sumerians on the plain, perhaps again coming
from the north. Others do not accept a distinct
immigrant group but see the Sumerians as an
amalgam of all the prehistoric peoples of the
region. The language, however, when it came
to be recorded, does suggest a Sumerian tongue
overlaying a more primitive one that might
well have been that of the Ubaidans. It also
contains some Semitic elements and it is likely
that Semites were already drifting into the
valley from the western deserts.

The fourth millennium in Sumeria is one
of the most remarkable passages in human
history. Already at its beginning old settlements
such as Eridu, Uruk, Ur, Lagash and Nippur had
become substantial towns and from 3500 BC
they waxed into cities. The citizens now included large numbers of specialist artisans –
potters, carpenters, makers of mudbrick,
coppersmiths – and fine sculptors too. There
must have been a growing band of merchants
importing raw materials such as wood, stone
and copper ore as well as luxury goods. With its
rapidly growing population and trade, its
vigorous intellectual and religious life, Sumeria
made its influence felt through much of the
Near East. An early caravan route would have
been established along the Euphrates to bring
close communication with such places as Mari
and Brak in the upper valley, where temple
architecture imitated the Sumerian.

The cities themselves had grown with more
dynamism than plan; mudbrick houses served
by crooked alleys and thoroughfares crowded
the city mound which was dominated by
magnificent temples. The finest known are at
Uruk (biblical Erech). There, in a complex of
huge buildings, perhaps already dedicated to
the city divinity and Sumerian goddess of love,
Inanna, they showed every elaboration of pilas-
ter and colonnade. The facades were enriched
with cone mosaics in geometric patterns of red,
black and white. Some temples stood on massive platforms, prototypes of the ziggurat.

It was at Uruk that thousands of the early
pictographic tablets were found. There is also
a fine, carved alabaster vase with scenes of
naked priests bearing sacrificial animals, fruits,
cereals and wine for the goddess. Standing near
Inanna is a grandee with a train-bearer. These
scenes and these tablets bring us at once to the
heart of the new civilization that owed so much
to centralized government. It is largely by
chance, in contrast with Egypt, that historians
have delayed the beginning of Mesopotamia's
Dynastic period to the third millennium, when
the names of kings were securely recorded. Yet
undoubtedly in this abundantly creative
Protoliterate Age, Sumeria was dividing into the

city-states of historic times, their rulers vaguely remembered in the legendary king-lists. Each city was now ruled in the name of its presiding god or goddess by an individual known as an *ensi* or Great Man. He, in his turn, was served by priestly administrators responsible for the temples' rituals as well as their estates. It was these officials who felt and met the need for writing.

Across the Tigris we have seen how the Elamites were stimulated to produce their own script, while in Susa, their chief city, talented potters turned out some of the most delightful pottery in the world. Trade beyond the mountain routes to the orient brought prosperity to towns such as Siyalk, Hissar and Anau. It has recently come to light that as far east beyond the Zagros as Tepe Yahya in the Soghun Valley, citizens of modest-sized towns were capable of writing in the Elamite script by 3200 BC.

But long before this, farming had been spreading from Iran into northwest India and settled villages grew among the foothills and mountains of Baluchistan, Sind and in the Makran. To the east of the River Zab, villages spilled down from the foothills on to the Indus plain. They were small but enduring places, many of them still thriving when the Indus cities were built during our next period. These villages may have taken their farming from Iran, but local domestication was possible because these first Indian farmers already had the massive, humped zebu breed among their cattle.

It was also at this time that fully developed mixed farming was established in China. Indeed, if the very scanty radiocarbon dates are confirmed, this had happened by the beginning of the period, rather earlier than in India. The first farmers occupied only a limited area, cultivating the fertile loess lands along the Yellow (Huang Ho) and the Wei rivers – although before 3000 BC cultivation had spread down the valley. To the north and south, as well as in Japan, life continued very much as before. The Yang Shao farmers, as they are called, were at a typically New Stone Age or Neolithic stage of development. They had small, self-sufficient villages and were totally dependent on chipped, and a few polished, stone tools. Their huts were neat and sturdy, some round, some rectangular, with thatched roofs supported on stout posts. White clay was used for floors, ovens, cupboards and benches. The villagers grew millet and wheat (but *not* rice as yet), were fond of pork but also had some sheep and cattle. Their settlements must have been noisy with dogs, for they kept many and may have eaten them – like the Chinese of

Painted beaker from Susa, Iran. A frieze of long-necked waterbirds circles the top while further down a decorative motif is enclosed by the sweeping horns of an ibex.

A stand and standard made of copper-arsenic bronze (one of man's earliest alloys) were among the hundreds of items uncovered in a cave near Engedi, Israel. The standard was decorated with ibex heads and the stand supported crude bird figurines and spools.

Small female figurine, perhaps a dancer, of painted clay. A funerary offering found at Mamarija, Libya.

today. Their one artistic outlet was in beautiful painted pottery, including the magnificent full-bellied funerary jars.

Many specialists today maintain that this Yang Shao culture was indigenous, created by the local folk with virtually no outside contacts. Yet wheat and probably sheep must have had western origins and the painted pottery appeared fully perfected from the beginning. The pottery is generally, though not specifically, similar to painted ceramics of western Asia, particularly to those of Turkmenia and Iran. Isolated though Yang Shao appears, as a rational diffusionist I think it is incredible that there was not some significant relation between the two traditions. Painted ceramics of this kind, from eastern Europe to China, fall within the well-defined limits of the sixth to the early fourth millennia. Surely the coincidence is too great?

Having followed the influences of the rising Mesopotamian civilization to their limits and then gone beyond them to observe the continued expansion of simple farming into India and China, I must now return westward to see how the world's first recorded royal dynasty emerged in Egypt late in our period. The land of the Nile, as we have seen, was briefly influenced by Mesopotamia, but because of the opportunities offered by this immense and extraordinary valley, the Egyptians soon caught up with the Sumerians and in some ways surpassed them.

The ancient Egyptians were always to call their country the Kingdom of the Two Lands and to express their sense of the unity of opposites in a rich symbolism. Lower Egypt, the delta, had its red crown, its papyrus and bee, and its protective cobra-goddess Wadjet; Upper Egypt, the six hundred miles of valley to the First Cataract, had its white crown, its sedge and its culture-goddess Nekhbet. The unification of the Two Lands under kings who wore both crowns first took place at this time and became a great recurring theme in both history and mythology. Whenever the pharaohs and central government weakened, the Two Lands were liable to split apart and there would be renewed struggles to join them together again.

The conditions of life in Lower and Upper Egypt in fact differed in a number of ways. The delta had a considerable rainfall, and in early times the Nile branched into a dozen streams dividing the land into sections. Such watery conditions favoured meadows, pastures, gardens and vineyards. Moreover, because it looked out onto the Mediterranean, to some extent it belonged to that world. Upper Egypt was over six hundred miles of almost rainless,

enclosed valley, where the great unifying thoroughfare of the Nile was bordered by narrow strips of alluvial soil. Its high fertility was regularly renewed every year between July and November when the flood deposited mineral-rich silt from the highlands. The early cultivators had only to tread their seed into the mud for bumper crops to grow in the delicious climate of winter and early spring. Two crops were often to be raised in a year.

I have already said that, just as in Sumeria, cultivation had begun in a small way before 5000 BC. Grain, livestock and farming skills were of Asian origin. Little enough is known of these pioneers, but during 4000-3500 BC we can watch them developing their villages and small towns, together with their arts and crafts.

The life of these earlier predynastic Egyptians was essentially similar to what we have seen in many other places. They grew wheat and barley, kept sheep, goats and cattle – and pigs in the north. They also had flocks of geese. Everyone liked to go fishing and fowling among the reed beds or hunting ibex, gazelle and hare in the *wadis*, which at that time had not become desert. Perhaps it was all a little easier thanks to the Nile. Life might have been more peaceful and intimate than on the boundless plain of Sumeria and this contributed to a more relaxed, hopeful and conservative view of the world.

Certainly, despite the simplicity of their huts these Egyptians enjoyed some elegancies: they wove linen, used fine oils for cosmetics and ground malachite on ornamental palettes for eye shadow. Their country was dividing up into districts or *nomes*, and no doubt the chiefs and their wives who controlled them had acquired some dignity. With the extension of irrigation and plentiful food, population and settlement size grew fast.

Yet if one could have travelled from Sumeria to Egypt about the year 3500 BC there is no doubt that Egypt would have seemed very rustic and backward in comparison. In most places there were clusters of huts instead of compact towns, modest shrines in place of monumental temples, very little metallurgy and probably few specialist artisans in general. The social organization was still largely tribal, and perhaps most significantly, no chieftain was big enough to appear with train and train-bearer.

Only a few centuries later all this had changed and Egypt was set to surpass Mesopotamia in grandeur if not in influence. What had caused this great leap forward? Everyone is agreed that it was a sudden, strong stimulus coming directly or indirectly from the

Sumerian civilization. It shows not only in the seals and script, in the style and subject matter of art, but most tellingly, in a monumental architecture with obvious Sumerian features. It is, however, disputed whether these Asian elements were introduced by peaceful infiltration or by "an invading Dynastic race" who made themselves the rulers of the native Egyptians. Burials have shown the influx of a taller, more round-headed race during this late predynastic period, while works of art depict what look like battles of conquest.

Certainly this era must have seen groupings of *nomes* under ambitious rulers until the close of predynastic times when it is thought that Upper and Lower Egypt had been welded into single kingdoms confronting one another in a struggle for supremacy. The southerners were victorious and united valley and delta under their rule. According to later legend the great unifier was called Menes. It seems most likely that this was a title given to Narmer of the famous palette, which portrays the king as ruthless conqueror, wearing the white crown on one side, the red on the other. Suddenly we are in a world of civilized statesmanship. As an act of conciliation, Menes-Narmer founded a new capital city at Memphis near the junction of valley and delta, and there also seem to have been interdynastic marriages and religious changes to cement the union.

Cultural advance was equally rapid. Gold was fashionable, copper was common enough to be used for all kinds of tools –including those needed for fine carpentry and cabinet making. In the elaborate mastaba tombs of the kings and queens of Dynasty I was found a great wealth of exquisite stone and good copper vessels; turquoise, lapis lazuli and gold jewellery; ivory gaming sets and enough wine to last all eternity.

Partly because the kingdom was still less urbanized than Sumeria and trade outside its immediate border smaller, Egypt had less influence on her neighbours. Yet she was to have maritime traffic with the eastern Mediterranean, including, as we have seen, with the Levantine port of Byblos.

At this time, however, Syria and Palestine generally remained more in touch with lands to the north. The geographical position of this region made it inevitable that it should always be one of mixed populations and cultures being subject to nomadic incursions. In the earlier part of the period farmers and herders lived in the Negev on the edge of the Sinai desert. At Beersheba they avoided the heat of day and the cold of night by burrowing into the loess to make a human warren of rooms and passages.

The "Hunter's Palette", Hieraconpolis, Egypt. Kilted hunters carrying an assortment of weapons are shown engaged in a lion hunt.

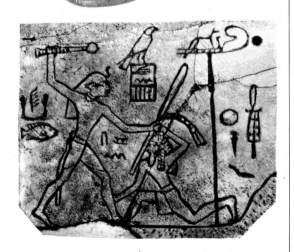

An ivory label found at Abydos, Egypt, shows a king of Dynasty I striking an enemy. Such labels can be used for dating purposes as they are related to annual events within each reign.

One of a pair of clay figurines from a tomb at Cernavoda, Rumania. Both figures were coated with a black-brown slip and were modelled in the same fashion. Both show stumpy feet and tilted heads. The rather obese female shown below is sitting on the ground with her hands resting on a raised knee.

Yet these troglodytes were by no means primitive. They imported turquoise, ivory and shells for ornaments and they were skilled coppersmiths and ivory-carvers. The ivory figurines, probably serving a fertility cult, are among the weirdest and most singular of the age.

Another, rather later, style of living is represented by the Ghassulians who were widespread in Palestine. Their settlements of rectangular mudbrick houses with mural decorations on stone foundations were verging on towns in size. They seem also to have had public halls and temples, though of very modest size in comparison with their contemporaries at Uruk. In some time of trouble the copper treasure belonging to one of these humble-looking temples near the Dead Sea was wrapped in matting and hidden in a cave. The 600 pieces, including a crown and many beautiful ritual sceptres, now make a dazzling display in the national museum in Jerusalem.

During the last centuries of the fourth millennium the Levant could not remain unaffected by the ferments of civilization in the great river valleys. Mesopotamian influences were strong in Syria. There were incursions, possibly of Semites, from both north and east. Towns began to grow. Byblos was probably the richest and most advanced of them, with its material needs served by its perfect little harbour and its spiritual needs by its presiding goddess (patronized by the Egyptians). There were towns at Ugarit, Hama and Megiddo. Jericho, with its strategic command of the pass into Syria was still occupied. In many other places that were to become towns there were settlements at this time, but, as a whole, civilization was static in the Levant.

Anatolia also is undistinguished in this intermediate period between the precocious achievements at Çatal Hüyük and Hacilar and the revived vigour of the Bronze Age. The life of the farmers went on much as before, with copper tools becoming more plentiful. Many communities had their own painted pottery but otherwise the arts were at a low ebb. Only in the southeast, where there were contacts with the Levant and northern Mesopotamia, was there much sign of enterprise. Here the ancient settlement of Mersin had a stormy history and about 4500 BC was strongly fortified, apparently by native Anatolians against their eastern neighbours. The stout walls of mudbrick on stone foundations had slit windows lighting the barrack rooms behind. There was also a house for the chiefly commander. The inhabitants had a plentiful supply of copper for both tools and weapons – but their principal armament was the sling. They are sometimes credited with a minor but useful invention – the attachment of handles to pots. In about 4350 BC this early citadel fell and thereafter the power of the Levant and the Ubaidans of Mesopotamia was paramount for some centuries.

Elsewhere there were settlements in a number of places that were to flourish in the next millennium, including Beycesultan in the Upper Maeander valley. Here there was a sizeable agricultural settlement (of the usual mudbrick houses) that had some added prosperity through commanding a ford on the natural route from inner Anatolia to the Aegean coast. Once again the inhabitants were well supplied with copper and had some silver and probably gold ornaments.

Connections between Anatolia and territories to the west continued, but, particularly in the Balkans, there was much vigorous local initiative leading to prosperous local cultures. Yet the settlement of hitherto uninhabited islands frustrates those who would have us believe that all such progress was due to internal growth and none to movement and diffusion. It seems to have been during the fifth millennium that men first settled a number of Aegean islands, including the delectable Cyclades – though they had earlier visited Melos for its obsidian. The small fortified citadel of Dimini near the coast of Thessaly also suggests an invading force – most likely led by a chiefly family who lived in the megaron type of house of the innermost enclosure. The inhabitants made an outstandingly attractive spiral-painted pottery which spread to other settlements in the region. In general, the village communities of Greece, Crete and the Aegean maintained the New Stone Age way of life much as before. It was not until the very end of our present period that they took a quick step over the threshold into the opening of a wonderfully creative Bronze Age.

It was in the Balkans that the early Neolithic farming peoples, while still having trade and perhaps other contacts with Anatolia and the Mediterranean, produced thriving and progressive communities that seem to have the same dynamism and boldness of invention that had possessed some of the Anatolians over a thousand years before. In the south, in Bulgaria and much of Rumania, they built their houses of mudbrick in the Asiatic style. Further north, where wood was plentiful, the houses were of timber framed with ridge poles and gables, often walled with clay and wattle, a type of construction that was to be favoured in central and eastern Europe. Many of the villages were substantial and permanent enough to form large mounds. One of the largest was at Vinča, on the Middle Danube close to Belgrade, and another at Karanovo in southern Bulgaria.

Their cultural vigour is apparent in both technology and art. From 4500 BC these efficient farming peoples took advantage of the abundant sources of the metal to develop copper working on a large scale. They even had both the material and the skill to cast heavy axes with cylindrical holes to take the haft – almost certainly the earliest metal shaft-hole axes ever to have been made. Their artistic powers showed in ceramics; the Asian tradition of painting was giving way to sterner, stronger forms which the potter created by incising spiral and other bold motifs on dark surfaces. To the northwest of the Black Sea, however, in Rumania and the Ukraine, paint was still pre-

The male figurine of the pair sits on a four-legged stool (both of one piece) with his arms propped on his knees. The folds of his cheeks are pushed up by his hands and the pose reflects a pensive attitude. These figures were certainly religious in meaning.

ferred even in the fourth millennium and some of the most striking of all prehistoric painted pottery was designed there.

The most interesting artistic creation of these Balkan peoples is their modelled figurines. Men and animals appear, but females greatly predominate and there can be little doubt that these figurines are rooted in the old Mediterranean and Asian mother-goddess cults. Some, however, have to our eyes a curiously modern, secular look. The sheer genius of an artist working in eastern Rumania can be seen in the seated figures of a woman and a man. These widely famous figures came from a tomb (Cernavoda) and were certainly religious in meaning. The Vinča people produced many finely stylized cult figures, made pots in human form and gave others weird "owl-faced" lids.

While the Balkans prospered, the exceptional dynamism of the early farmers was even more evident in their immense colonizing spread towards the west. One of the peoples of our previous period had developed their own sturdy tradition centred on Hungary and adjacent loess lands. Their way of life had much in common with their Balkan neighbours, yet their social customs must have been quite different. They lived in spaciously laid out villages of very long solid wooden houses (up to 30 metres) which supposedly sheltered an "extended" family with their several groups of parents and children. These Danubians, as they are conveniently called, spread along the loess lands of central Europe, on into northeast France and the southern Netherlands. Over the whole of that vast area their farming, housing, habits, tools and pottery were all so nearly identical that even the most hardened anti-diffusionists cannot deny that we are encountering here the fairly rapid spread of a people. To grow their wheat, barley and legumes they probably cleared the land of vegetation by burning, the fertility of the soil soon being exhausted. If they had to wait years for its restoration, new land ahead was always attractive. The Danubians probably reached their westernmost limits (well short of the North Sea coast) very early in this period and so were the first to bring a fully-fledged farming life to the fringes of western Europe. Later they split into various groups that remained for many centuries.

It was not very much later, however, that farming with the same basic livestock and cereals was spreading to the west from the early settlements of the Mediterranean coasts. It was probably from them that the hunting peoples of Denmark and south Sweden first learnt and adopted the farming arts.

In the period 8000 – 5000 BC we saw the rather tenuous early settlements on the Mediterranean coasts of Italy, the south of France and eastern Spain. Now with rapidly increasing populations villages multiplied throughout southern Italy and Sicily and round the coasts of the Iberian peninsula – although in the harsh and mountainous hinterland hunting tribes maintained their more exhilarating, more precarious way of life. Farming was also carried northward and westward through France only a few centuries after the earliest settlement of the Danubians. There may have been well-organized communities in Brittany by about 4800 BC and in the British Isles a few centuries later.

This spread of farming from the south and southwest, although well-supported by radiocarbon dating, was of a very different kind from that of the Danubians, and showed an infinite variety of cultural traditions. For example, in southern Italy most people lived in deeply entrenched villages or homesteads, in the south of France and Iberia cave dwelling was still popular, in Switzerland and north Italy there were the lakeside pile dwellings, and in Britain hilltop earthworks. The pottery, flintwork and most other things made by these peoples were equally various. Only in the original Asian foundation of their main foods – wheat, barley, sheep, cattle (some locally domesticated), pigs – and in common use of polished stone implements, was there a clear unity. There may also have been religious and cultic bonds. One explanation would seem to be that in this part of Europe the hunting peoples were well established and played a large part in creating and varying the new farming cultures.

Trade, though of a small and often local kind, was of some importance in the distribution of superior material – obsidian, fine flint, hard igneous stones – for polishing. Here also we encounter the first west European industry: the mining of fresh flint from its native chalk in England and Belgium. It seems to have started by 4000 BC although the largest, most famous example of all, Grimes Graves in East Anglia, may belong to our next period.

I am left with the best known and most extraordinary creations of these New Stone Age communities: the megalithic tombs, menhirs and stone rows formed from massive, normally unhewn blocks. They were widespread where suitable stone was available and even today the tombs can be numbered in the thousands. Virtually all were intended for the same purpose: to bury the dead communally and over several, sometimes very many, generations. Some received as many as a hundred bodies, accompanied only by modest possessions. As many of the finest tombs are on the coasts and as their building spread rapidly not only to Britain and Ireland but to the remote Atlantic isles of the Hebrides and Orkneys, there seems to me no doubt that they were often the mausolea of farming groups who had sought new land by sea routes. Nor do I find it possible to doubt that the tombs – despite the variety from small "dolmen" to awe-inspiring passage grave – represent some community of cult, possibly centred on notions of rebirth through the goddess whose symbols appear occasionally among them. This unity is particularly obvious in such great passage graves as those of Breton Gavr'inis, Hougue Bie in Jersey, the marvellous Irish group round New Grange and Maes Howe in the faraway Orkneys. There is also the potent common symbolism of megalithic art, particularly of the spirals, arcs and serpents carved in Brittany and Ireland.

Radiocarbon dating seems to have shown that the earliest tombs, several of which are in Brittany, were being built from about 4500 BC at the time when the citizens of Eridu and Uruk were beginning to raise their public temples. They therefore represent the oldest monumental stone building in the world. Most, however, date from after 4000 BC and their building as well as use continued into the next millennium. New Grange, at about 3300 BC, is a near contemporary of the great temples of Uruk with their columns and mosaics.

From about 3500 BC copper was coming into use in Italy and Spain. In southern Spain, rich in copper ores, the farming communities prospered and lived in quite large settlements, some of which later came to be fortified. One, Los Millares in Almeria, has a cemetery of passage graves, the first of which may have been built before 3000 BC, but Los Millares and its Portuguese counterparts belong more properly to the next period.

In the Americas progress was slow, but not unimportant for the future. In Mexico, in much the same regions as the earliest experiments in food production, beans and maize were considerably improved in yield; they were now usually cooked instead of being eaten raw. Yet cultivation still produced a very small proportion of the total food supply – in Tehuacán it

has been estimated as about 14 per cent. In the Andean highlands of South America there may have been some cultivation of popcorn as well as of beans, and guinea pigs were now bred to eat. There is evidence that llamas were becoming domesticated as food animals.

Late in the period the craft of pottery made its first appearance in the Americas. Surprisingly, this invention was made not in Mexico or Peru but in coastal settlements in Ecuador.

Over nearly the whole of North America food collecting and hunting prevailed but they were becoming increasingly varied and efficient. The use of polished stone tools, often of fine quality, began in about 5000 BC. Hunters became more fully adjusted to the conditions of the eastern woodlands and population extended into the north. There was also a curious local development showing man's readiness to seize exceptional opportunities. The hunter-fishers round Lake Superior discovered large quantities of native copper on their territories. They mined it and made a great range of tools by hammering it either cold or hot. So in a continent where metal was to be so little used, the Great Lakes had a little Chalcolithic Age in the fourth millennium BC.

In the southwest, in the high country, on the borders of New Mexico and Arizona, the Cochise food gatherers were beginning to grow some maize. It can safely be assumed that it was introduced from Mexico.

Elaborate spiral decoration is found on an entrance stone to the passage grave at New Grange, County Meath, Ireland.

Technology 5000-3000 BC

The world in this period may be divided into three zones of technological competence. Firstly, there were considerable areas – most of the Americas, all Africa beyond the Sahara and the whole of Australia – where hunting and food gathering, with its simple technology, continued unchanged and unchallenged.

Secondly, in three regions – further Asia, from north China to Thailand, and two small areas in Mexico and central Peru – new groups began to master crop cultivation as others had already done in southwest Asia. The plants they chose to domesticate were locally available ones: water chestnut, beans and rice in Asia; various beans, squashes and maize in America. To these regions should be added the greater part of Europe and the Indus, where food production was introduced from outside.

Thirdly and most interestingly, there were the areas in southeast Europe, north Africa and most of southwest Asia where farming had long been established and had already led to notable technological advances. Even here, however, there is an apparent change of emphasis as the early hill villages lagged, to be outstripped to a remarkable extent by new settlements on the plains of Sumer and the Nile. The reason is simple – the exploitation of the plains called for a much higher level of social organization, craft specialization and trade, all of which stimulated technology.

This is most obvious perhaps in the invention of writing, a skill quite unnecessary until society and economics became so complex as to demand an efficient system of recording. More efficient transport was found to be needed too, and wheeled vehicles were developed in Mesopotamia as well as sea-going sailing ships in the eastern Mediterranean and probably in the Persian Gulf. Craft specialization within the larger settlements stimulated advances in pottery making; the potter's kiln and wheel are both found at this time. Less easily studied are techniques of crafts like weaving and carpentry, in which similar improvements must have been appearing.

The most notable advance, and the one with the widest implications for trade, craft specialization, skilled wood working and the economy generally, was in the field of metallurgy. Copper was being worked sporadically for beads, pins and other trinkets even before 5000. But that was only a prelude to the full use of metal, based on smelting and casting in sufficient quantity to produce functional tools and weapons, and leading subsequently to experiments with alloys and the earliest bronze.

	Areas of major interest
●	Centres

The Americas
Hunters continued to develop their flint projectile points, but the food gatherers now produced implements such as the stone muller. Around the Great Lakes the discovery of native copper, which could be shaped by cold hammering led to the production of such tools as the gouge.

● Bat Cave

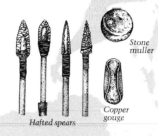

Hafted spears

Stone muller

Copper gouge

Fiorano pottery

Clay ladle

Painted pottery

Western Mediterranean
A simple early farming technology spread through the area. The very high quality of some pottery, however, particularly in the Tavoliere, implies that in some fields specialist craftspeople were already at work.

COMPARISON OF MATERIALS IN USE

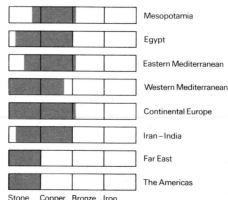

Mesopotamia

Egypt

Eastern Mediterranean

Western Mediterranean

Continental Europe

Iran – India

Far East

The Americas

Stone   Copper   Bronze   Iron

Continental Europe

Farming was spreading over a wide and diverse area, from the Black Sea to the Atlantic. The characteristic artifacts were the polished stone axes, adzes and sickles for clearing and cultivating fields and the pottery for storing and cooking the various grains.

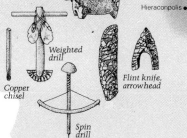

Hafted axe head

Clay lamp

Arrowhead

Cardial pottery

Ladle

MEATH ● New Grange

Stone adze

BRITTANY ● Sittard

● Köln-Lindenthal

Flint sickle

● Camp de Chassey

● ARLES

● Vinča

● El Garcel

Tavoliere ●

Matera ● Molfetta

Stentinello ● Sesklo ● Dimini

Tarxien ●

Far East

In Japan settlements based on food gathering – notably shellfish – continued and in north China early farming spread widely. Pottery and ground stone tools have been found in excavated villages.

Stone adze

Arrowhead

● KANTO PLAIN

Whalebone comb

Storage vessel

● Pan P'o Ts'un

Eastern Mediterranean

Metal working was the main contribution of this area to technological advance, as copper, silver, gold and later experimental bronze alloys were brought into service and gradually improved for use as tools and ornaments.

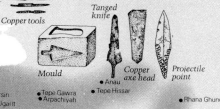

Silver ring

Copper tools

Tanged knife

Mould

Copper axe head

Projectile point

● Anau

● Tepe Hissar

● Mersin

● Tepe Gawra

● Ugarit

● Arpachiyah

● Byblos

● Rhana Ghundai

Uruk ●

● Susa

Ur ● Eridu

● Tepe Yahya

● Kulli

Clay ladle

Siyalk pot

Clay stamp seal

Iran-India

With a less advanced metallurgy, this area's technological achievements are best shown in its wide range of skilled potting. Stamp seals hint at a more advanced economy.

Memphis ● ● Sakkara

● el-Gerza

Abydos ● ● el-Badari

Hieraconpolis ●

Painted pot

Wheel

Cylinder seal

Copper pin

Pictograph

Mesopotamia

The Tigris-Euphrates plain fostered great advances in copper working and skilful pottery along with cylinder seals for protection of property. Writing in the form of pictographs and the development of the wheel were the most impressive achievements.

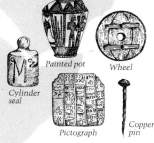

Stone pot

Weighted drill

Copper chisel

Flint knife, arrowhead

Spin drill

Egypt

Progress was made over the whole range of human technology. Copper working, pottery, weaving, carpentry, even the obsolescent crafts of flint flaking and stone vessel grinding, were carried to new and remarkable heights, all based on the efficient exploitation of the Nile valley for arable farming. Hieroglyphs made their first appearance.

Mesopotamia

Writing was devised for a specific purpose – business accounts – when unaided human memory simply could not cope. The earliest known examples date soon after 3500 BC. Numbers probably came first, one dash for 1, four dashes for 4 and so on. Words began with pictographs – standardized and somewhat simplified pictures of concepts. But many concepts cannot be pictured, so where possible something else pronounced the same way, a rebus, had to be drawn instead. A determinative – a symbol to explain the class of concept – might be added. For example,  would mean "son".

Quite soon the limits of what could be achieved by these principles were reached and some phonetic system had to be devised. Though some symbols came to represent pure sounds, pictographs were not entirely discarded. It was in this period also that true pottery kilns became standardized throughout Mesopotamia and the wheel made its first appearance.

Early cuneiform tablet.

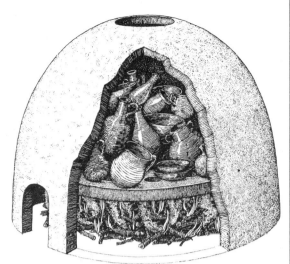

KILNS *Low, domed structures with floors and vented tops were developed to prevent pottery being marred by open firing.*

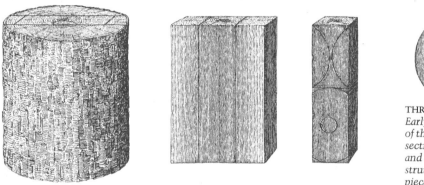

THREE-PIECE WHEEL *Early wheels were made of three solid wood sections cut from a plank and joined by cross struts, the middle piece being the largest.*

Egypt

The invention of the kiln, here as well as in Mesopotamia, allowed higher firing temperatures and greater control of the atmosphere. The potter could oxidize his wares to yellow or red or reduce them to grey and black. A flourishing industry of fine stoneware was helped by the development of the pump drill from the earlier bow drill. It was weighed down with rocks attached to the handle and fitted with a crescent-shaped piece of flint. The vessels were ground with abrasives and polished with sandstone. Writing also developed here at this time, probably due to Mesopotamian influence.

KILNS *Early kilns were tall chimney-like structures. Mud or stone was used to cover the top.*

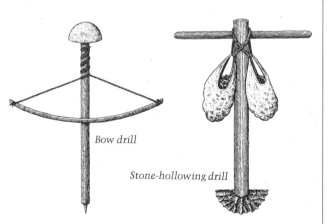

Bow drill

Stone-hollowing drill

HIEROGLYPHICS *This serakh inscribed on top of a palette spells "Narmer." The fish sound is "nar" and the chisel is "mer."*

Eastern Mediterranean

The practical difficulties and intricacies of early copper working led to the rise of specialist craftsman people. Copper first had to be smelted or separated out from the accompanying rock at high temperatures. Blowpipes of rolled hide-strips fitted with ceramic ends were used to raise the temperature in circular, partly sunken, stone fire-places. After purifying the metal and perhaps alloying it, the copper was melted in a crucible. Then an open mould modelled in terra-cotta or carved in a refractory stone like steatite was heated and filled with the liquid metal. Once cooled and hardened, the copper tool was lifted out. It was smoothed by grinding and the cutting edge was toughened by hammering.

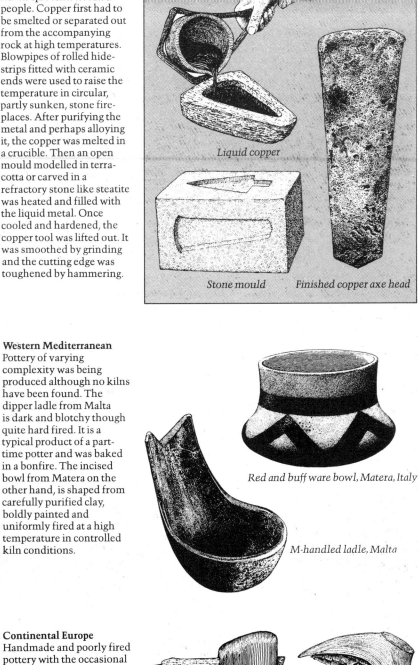

Liquid copper

Stone mould *Finished copper axe head*

Western Mediterranean

Pottery of varying complexity was being produced although no kilns have been found. The dipper ladle from Malta is dark and blotchy though quite hard fired. It is a typical product of a part-time potter and was baked in a bonfire. The incised bowl from Matera on the other hand, is shaped from carefully purified clay, boldly painted and uniformly fired at a high temperature in controlled kiln conditions.

Red and buff ware bowl, Matera, Italy

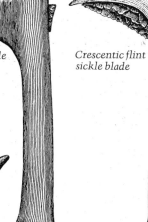

M-handled ladle, Malta

Continental Europe

Handmade and poorly fired pottery with the occasional grain of wheat or barley preserved as an imprint in the clay is evidence for settled farmers penetrating the area. Further support is offered by the sickle for crop gathering and the stone adze which was used perhaps for trimming timber or as a hoe.

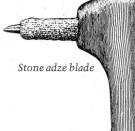

Stone adze blade *Crescentic flint sickle blade*

Clay ladle

Iran-India

The eastward spread of farming communities brought high quality pottery to the hills over looking the Indus. Artistically there is much of new interest here, but technologically it represents the diffusion of techniques developed farther west rather than new advances. The stamp seal shows that economic ideas were also adapted to different areas.

Clay stamp seal, Quetta Valley, India

Painted pot, Quetta Valley, India

Far East

Typical farming equipment like the storage jar for grain has been found in the Yellow River villages. The polished stone adze would have served for either wood carpentry or as a hoe for cultivating the ground.

Storage vessel, Pan P'o Ts'un, China

Polished stone adze, Pan P'o Ts'un, China

The Americas

The early American food producers have left us little illustrative material and while there was a precocious use of copper in the Great Lakes region, the Indian hunters of the Great Plains still depended on their hafted, finely flaked projectile points.

Hafted projectiles

Architecture *5000-3000 BC*

As the change to food production led to the establishment of settled villages, the growth of those villages and towns led to the development of large-scale architecture. The food surplus in the fertile Tigris-Euphrates and Nile valleys meant that labour was available after the primary needs of provision and shelter had been met. Furthermore, community effort had already been utilized for carrying out public works, such as vital irrigation canals and flood control banks.

In Mesopotamia, the natural outlet for this surplus effort was temple building, since it was believed that the good will of the gods was essential to the productivity of the land. To the Sumerians, a temple was as necessary as a canal, and fortunately for posterity a god might appreciate the aesthetics of design where a river flood would not. And so the Sumerians built temples to the best of their abilities, to sweeten their gods but also, one suspects, to test and stretch their own technical skills, to foster their own civic pride, and even perhaps just to outdo the neighbouring city.

In Egypt it was the king who commanded, not the gods. Monumental architecture was therefore directed at building tombs to last through eternity rather than temples. The mastaba combined a number of functions, as grave marker, as storeroom for the offerings to the dead, and as symbolic house for the residence of the soul of the deceased. Later, when the pharaohs themselves came to be worshipped as gods, temples and palaces increased in size and importance.

It would be a mistake, however, to regard a vast and efficient agricultural system as an essential prerequisite of monumental building. Any community with spare time and labour, once its primary needs have been met, may choose to devote the surplus to building. This was true of Malta at this period where an isolated people, technologically backward in other respects, began to build stone temples of surprising sophistication. And it was true along the Atlantic seaboard from Iberia to Scotland, where monumental tombs of impressive dimensions were constructed. These were both firmly community enterprises, not ordered by kings or priests. The tombs and the early Maltese temples are as monumental as the contemporary buildings of the Near East, and in their own contexts even more extraordinary.

Areas of major interest
● Centres
▲ Sites

Tent

The Americas
The hunters and food gatherers, and also the more progressive people who had begun to produce a small proportion of their food supplies, continued to live in natural caves and simple huts.

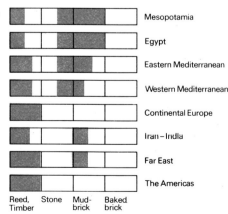

Passage grave. Anta do Silval

Western Mediterranean
Scant evidence remains of the flimsy huts enclosed in multiple rock-cut ditches. Western communities constructed monumental tombs made of large-sized blocks.

COMPARISON OF MATERIALS IN USE

Mesopotamia

Egypt

Eastern Mediterranean

Western Mediterranean

Continental Europe

Iran – India

Far East

The Americas

Reed, Timber   Stone   Mud-brick   Baked brick

Continental Europe
The Danubian longhouse, reconstructed from the post-holes of its decayed timbers, accommodated a community consisting of a number of families. The megalithic tombs which still stand along the Atlantic seaboard were also community buildings, but for the dead.

Danubian long house.
Köln-Lindenthal

Megalithic grave. Essé

Far East
Substantial but still simple buildings of timber and thatch are found in village settings at this time.

Round house.
Pan P'o Ts'un

Rectangular dwelling.
Pan P'o Ts'un

Eastern Mediterranean
Architecturally, the early metal using peoples developed walled townships, often with a "palace" at the centre. Fortified settlements may imply the rise of an aristocracy as well as the need for defences against neighbours.

Fortified settlement. Dimini

● Pan P'o Ts'un

House. Tepe Hissar

Iran – India
The small village communities here produced comfortable and competent domestic building in the style of their western neighbours.

▲ Essé   ● Köln-Lindenthal

▲ Anto do Silval

● Dimini

Tepe Gawra ●   ● Tepe Hissar
Tell Hassuna ▲   ● Arpachiyah

● Sakkara   ● Eridu

Egypt
Monumental architecture was concentrated on tombs. As the country moved towards unity, its ruler became powerful enough to demand a sumptuous resting place for his mortal remains.

Mastaba tombs. Sakkara

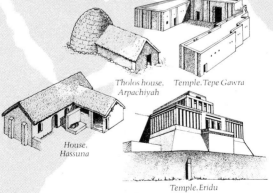

Tholos house.   *Temple. Tepe Gawra*
Arpachiyah

House,
Hassuna

Temple. Eridu

Mesopotamia
Substantial domestic housing was built in various forms, but it was the temples of the city gods which were the most decorated and required the more skilful construction.

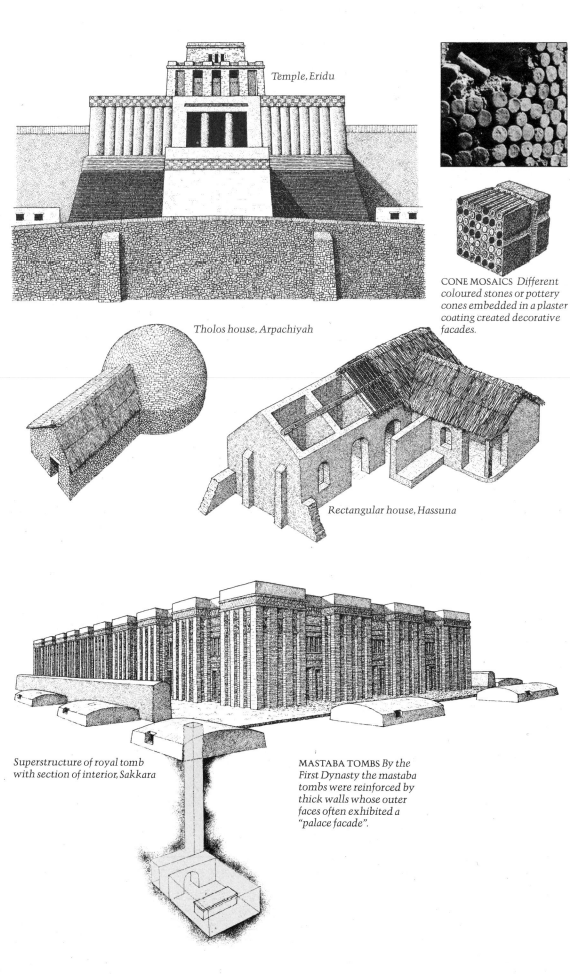

Mesopotamia

With the simplest of raw materials, mudbrick, the early inhabitants of this region achieved extraordinary results. Architectural advances are most evident in temple building, particularly in Sumer; the site of Eridu is the best studied. A simple but effective innovation was the use of an artificial mound to raise the temple above the humbler secular dwellings of the city. It might have been meant as a substitute mountain on the flat plain, or could have been the result of burying the structure of each building in more mudbrick before raising its successor on the same site, in preference to desecrating it by demolition. The temples themselves grew rapidly larger, more complex and more impressive. In domestic architecture, simple rectangular houses with courtyards continued as before throughout the area, a notable departure being the circular houses or "tholoi" of Arpachiyah. In these the main room was roofed with a corbelled vault of mudbrick.

Temple, Eridu

CONE MOSAICS *Different coloured stones or pottery cones embedded in a plaster coating created decorative facades.*

Tholos house, Arpachiyah

Rectangular house, Hassuna

Egypt

The ruins of the royal tombs preserved in the desert allow us to reconstruct them as well as the vanished palaces on which they were modelled. The standard building materials were mudbrick and imported timber. The mudbrick structures which can be traced in plan make it clear that simple mastaba tombs were greatly enlarged and embellished as more powerful rulers increased their territories and wealth. This is evident from the reconstruction of the superstructure of the tomb of Queen Merneith at Sakkara.

Superstructure of royal tomb with section of interior, Sakkara

MASTABA TOMBS *By the First Dynasty the mastaba tombs were reinforced by thick walls whose outer faces often exhibited a "palace facade".*

Eastern Mediterranean
Dimini is one of the earliest towns known in Europe. The dominating "megaron" palace, a rectangular hall with pillared porch, must have been the residence of the ruler and the administrative centre of the community. Several other large houses were found whose main rooms could be entered through an open porch or sometimes an antechamber. The settlement was surrounded by six concentric walls of undressed limestone forming narrow gates and passages which served a defensive purpose.

Fortified settlement, Dimini, Greece

Western Mediterranean
Monumental communal tombs were built of large-sized stone blocks. Orthostat-and-lintel construction was used in the parallel-sided gallery graves. Some passage graves, however, were roofed by corbel vaulting.

Passage Grave, Anto do Silval, Portugal

Continental Europe
The long, rectangular, gabled houses of the Danubians had timber frames and wooden lattice walls coated with clay. Rows of posts supported the thatched roofs and some hearths have been identified.

Danubian long house, Köln-Lindenthal, Germany

Iran-India
The mudbrick rectangular houses of the area were similar to domestic buildings in Mesopotamia.

Far East
Several whole villages of timber, daub and thatch huts have been excavated. As at Pan P'o Ts'un the houses, both rectangular and circular in plan, were of some size and complexity.

In some the roof (either ridged or conical) ran right to the ground, sufficient headroom being provided by recessing the floor into the ground. In others, height was obtained by means of side walls.

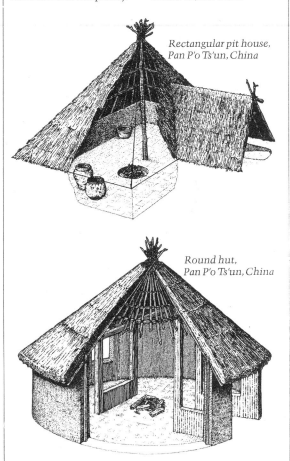

Rectangular pit house, Pan P'o Ts'un, China

Round hut, Pan P'o Ts'un, China

The Americas
There were no noteworthy architectural advances.

Art 5000 – 3000 BC

With its art, as with all other aspects of its history, this period is dominated by the first rise of Sumerian and Egyptian civilization.

Before that late phase there had been few innovations in artistic creativity, although there were fresh centres for some old forms, notably of painted pottery and figurines. Perhaps the most interesting of those few new departures was the decorative carving of the megalithic tombs of western Europe. The finest of this work was done by the New Stone Age farmers of Brittany and Ireland. It consists of geometric patterns engraved on the stones, most often inside the tombs, but occasionally on exterior blocks. Most of the designs are of spirals, concentric circles or other curvilinear forms, but they include some rectilinear motifs such as lozenges and triangles. At New Grange (Meath, Ireland) the relief is deep-cut and strong.

Excellent painted pottery now began to be produced to the west and east of the old centres. The most striking of the European examples of this ceramic art come from Greece and the Balkans, while in the Far East the Yang Shao farmers of northern China began to produce their superbly painted vessels. Among the almost universal output of figurines throughout the Near East and Mediterranean, some of the best are again from Greece and the Balkans, while the carvings of the Beersheba villagers provide a good example of local work.

The spreading mastery of copper technology produced some ornamental work that qualifies as art. The vigorous plastic moulding and animal heads on sceptres and other copper objects from Engedi, Palestine, can be seen as representing more work of this kind that was melted down for later re-use.

The art of all other regions, however, must appear of minor significance when weighed against the great schools of art being founded in Mesopotamia and Egypt. They are of immense significance not so much for the work produced before 3000 BC, remarkable though it was, but because they firmly established characteristic styles that were to inspire the masterpieces of Sumerian and Egyptian art of our next two periods.

It is a paradox of this early phase, that while it saw the clear definition of these styles, it was also the one time in which there was interplay between them. Some of the work of the late predynastic artists in Egypt was undoubtedly influenced by that of their Sumerian contemporaries.

Areas of major interest
● Centres
▲ Sites

The Americas
Pottery was being made in Ecuador by c.3200 BC. Footed bowls are of sound design, if hardly works of art.

Figurine, Malta

Painted pot, Lipari

Western Mediterranean
This region has no very noteworthy art that can with certainty be dated before 3000 BC. In southern Italy and its islands farming communities made simple painted pottery, some with incised geometric patterns.

Continental Europe

The most distinguished earlier works of art are the varied and striking figurines and painted pottery from the Balkans. It is very probable that the best decorative art of the megalithic tombs of Brittany and Ireland dates from the last few centuries before 3000 BC. Hunter-fishers in the northern regions continued to make animal carvings of amber.

New Grange stone

Clay idol, Střelice

Amber horse, Woldenburg

Kettle, Gneiding

Eastern Mediterranean

The Levant has a number of individual and apparently local creations such as polychrome wall paintings in the houses of Tell el Ghassul, the Engedi bronzes (p. 65) and odd Beersheba figurines. Good painted pottery, such as Dimini ware, began to be made in northern Greece, while a variety of figurines, some curvaceous and in free attitudes, were modelled in Crete, the Aegean and Greece.

Torso, Knossos

Torso, Lerna

Painted pot, Dimini

Far East

The art of pottery painting reached its greatest heights in this period in villages such as Pan P'o Ts'un. The magnificent Yang Shao jars painted with spiral and other curvilinear patterns, usually buried with the dead, must largely date from before 3000 BC – though some may be later. In Japan the Jōmon fishing and hunting folk were now making elaborately modelled pots.

Amphora, Pan P'o Ts'un

Jōmon pot, Shimojima

Figurine, Mujinazawa

▲ Shimojima

• Pan P'o Ts'un

• New Grange

▲ Woldenberg

Gneiding ▲   ▲ Střelice

▲ Trușești

▲ Lipari

• Dimini

• MALTA   • Lerna

▲ Knossos

▲ Tell Brak

Uruk •   • Susa
Eridu •

▲ Tepe Siyalk   KANDAHAR

Abydos ▲ Gebel-el-Arak

Hieraconpolis •

Egypt

The artists of late Predynastic and Dynasty I times worked in bone and ivory as well as in stone. They were already carving reliefs on funeral stelae, but much of their work embellishes weapons and stone palettes. The subjects already reflect the supreme importance of pharaoh, but delightfully naturalistic animal studies were also made. The Asian influence appears in the style and even costume of relief carvings.

Flint knife, Gebel-el-Arak

Narmer palette, Hieraconpolis

Thoth as baboon

Mace head, Hieraconpolis

Ivory statuette, Abydos

Mesopotamia

Most of the finest works of art of this founding time of Sumerian art come from the ancient southern city of Uruk. As civilization developed, its artists began to create a humane, hierarchical style of stone carving – both in relief and in animal and human figures in the round.

Statue, Eridu

Alabaster vase, Uruk

Head, Uruk

Eye idol, Tell Brak

Iran-India

Some of the most attractive painted pottery ever known was made in western Iran during this period. The painters used both animal and geometric designs. Some of the best examples come from Susa (in ancient Elam) and Tepe Siyalk. In India the farming villagers were also beginning to make pottery and ornate if rather quaint figurines.

Goddess, Kandahar

Vase, Susa

Beaker, Tepe Siyalk

Mesopotamia
Among much remarkable
sculpture from Uruk (such
as the head shown in
greater detail on p. 60) is a
large pedestal vase in
alabaster carved with
religious scenes. "First
fruits" are being offered to
the Goddess who stands in
the top register receiving a
bowl of fruit from a naked
priest. Behind the priest
stood the king and his train-
bearer. Priests, sheep,
wheat, and palms occupy
the lower zones.

White marble head, Uruk

Egypt
The ivory handle of the
Predynastic Gebel-el-Arak
knife shows a battle scene
on one side and a man
between confronted lions
on the other. Sumerian
influence is obvious. The
"victory palette of Narmer"
(slate, 25 ins [62.5 cms]
long) exemplifies the
unification of Egypt under
Dynasty I. Both style and
subject matter (the king
holding and smiting an
enemy; the horned
goddess, Hathor; the Horus
falcon) are already typically
Egyptian. The grotesque
beasts on the front still
show Asian influence. On
Scorpion's limestone macehead the king, having slain
his enemies, opens an
irrigation channel with
a hoe.

"King Narmer's Palette," Hieraconpolis

*The macehead of King Scorpion,
carved limestone, Hieraconpolis*

Alabaster vase of Jemdet Nasr period, Uruk

Flint knife with carved ivory handle, Gebel-el Arak

Eastern Mediterranean
In later New Stone Age times potters in northern Greece (Thessaly) began to paint pots with bold designs of spirals and meanders, often in black and red on a pale ground. The style is called after the fortress of Dimini.

Painted pottery vase with spiral design, Dimini, Greece

Western Mediterranean
Painted pottery in several different styles was made in southern Italy, Sicily and the Aeolian island (Lipari). Some, like a weaker version of the Greek Dimini ware, had spiral designs, but flame patterns painted in red were a local variant. This is the furthest west to be reached in any force by the spread of painted pottery.

Painted pot, Lipari, Sicily

Continental Europe
In western Europe the great innovation of the period was the use of relief sculptures on megalithic tombs. The spiral and other designs had symbolic meaning. Among the most well-known compositions are those on the passage grave of New Grange. Amber carvings continued earlier traditions.

Spiral decoration on kerbstone, New Grange, Ireland

Carved amber horse, Woldenberg, Germany

Iran-India
In southern Iran, particularly at Susa, the pot-painters made a brilliant adaptation of animal forms into patterns (see p. 65). Further north in the uplands, as at Tepe Siyalk, animals might be shown more realistically. The painting was in dark brown or black on a cream background. The painted beaker shown below was decorated in a typically lively style.

Painted beaker of Siyalk III phase, Tepe Siyalk, Iran

Far East
The finest of the great funerary jars in the Yang-Shao style of the Chinese villagers have a marvellous dynamism and sense of movement. In contrast, the Japanese Jōmon potters were interested in modelled plastic form. Their few figurines were crude.

Archaic Jōmon pottery figurine, Japan

Funerary jar, China

The Americas
Early pottery was practical rather than artistic.

83

Region	Economy	Centres	Events and developments	People
Mesopotamia		Arpachiyah Tepe Gawra Eridu Uruk Ur	Valley cleared and irrigated by peoples from Iran. They push up river and dominate earlier northern farmers. Sumeria now takes lead. Foundations laid for city life and Sumerian civilization.	
Egypt		El-Badari El-Gerza Hieraconpolis Memphis-Sakkara Abydos	Clearance and irrigation of valley and delta by various groups of farmers. Possible invasion by "Dynastic Race." Consolidation of two kingdoms – Upper and Lower Egypt. Upper wins the power struggle. Unification under Menes 3200. Dynasty 1.	Menes (=Narmer?)
Eastern Mediterranean		Mersin Ugarit (Ras Shamra) Byblos Dimini Sesklo	Levant and Anatolia influenced by peoples from Mesopotamia and lose cultural leadership. Cyprus prospers from copper trade. Growth of towns in Cilicia, Syria and Lebanon during 4th M.	
Western Mediterranean		Stentinello Tarxien Arles District El Garcel Camp de Chassey Tavoliere	Mixed farming with villages develops in Italy and spreads westward to islands, south of France and Iberia by 5000-4000 BC.	
Continental Europe		New Grange South Brittany Meath Sittard (Holland) Köln-Lindenthal Vinča	Mixed farming spreads by Atlantic coastal and other overland routes and by Danube to west and north by about 4000 BC.	
Iran-India		Susa Tepe Hissar Tepe Yahya Anau Rhana Ghundai Kulli	Intensification of farming in S. Iran. Area influenced by Mesopotamia; villages growing into towns during 5th-4th M. Susa becomes capital of Elam. Growth of villages in N.W. India.	
Far East		Pan P'o Ts'un Japan: many shell middens, especially Kanto plain.	Further development of farming in N. China. Fishing and hunting in Japan in larger, more settled communities. Farming widespread in Thailand and Indo-China.	
The Americas		Ocampo Bat Cave	Intensive food gathering, hunting and fishing. Cultivation of beans and primitive maize in Mesoamerica and southwest N. America. Experimental cultivation in Peru.	

The economy bar graph indicates relative proportions of these factors: Irrigation ≈ Agriculture ✿ Hunting ⚔ Urban life ⊞ Trade ⏃

Religion	Technology and inventions	Architecture	Art
Fertility cults associated with Mother Goddess and bulls. Establishment of city gods ancestral to Sumerian pantheon.	Copper smelting and casting, faience c.4500. Pottery kilns, wheel, seals 4000. Writing, fired bricks 3500. Experimental bronze 3100.	Temples on platforms. Columns with cone mosaics. Rectangular town houses. Tholos houses.	Painted pottery. Sculpture in relief and in the round. Seals.
Local divinities of *nomes* developing into national pantheon: Horus, Seth, Re, Hathor, etc. in human-animal forms. Divinity of pharaohs.	Early predynastic cultures with flint and polished stone tools. Hand-made pottery. After 3500 rapid developments in linen weaving, goldwork, copper smelting and casting. Potters wheel. Fine carpentry. Spin drill for stone vessels. Hieroglyphic writing.	Mastaba tombs. Palaces. Temples and shrines.	Early predynastic animal figurines, palettes and combs. Painted pottery and figurines. Late Pre-Dynastic and Early Dynastic relief carvings on ivory handles, palettes, maceheads and funerary stelae. Ivory carving in round.
Fertility cult with Mother Goddess.	Stone and flint using during 5th M continuing later in Greece and Balkans. Copper smelting and casting in Anatolia and Levant after 4500. Sea-going sailing ships. Earliest bronze.	Fortress (Mersin). Simple temples. Mudbrick and gabled timber houses. Megaron "halls." Underground dwellings.	Painted pottery. Ceramic and ivory figurines. Copper animal-headed and decorative sceptres (Engedi).
Fertility and Mother Goddess cults. Communal burial. Veneration of ancestors?	Flint and polished stone tools. Hand-made pottery. Drystone and large-stone building. Copper working by late 4th M.	Megalithic dolmens and passage graves. First rock-cut tombs. Earliest Maltese temples. Open village huts and houses.	Engraving on megaliths. Incised pottery figurines.
Communal burial. Veneration of ancestors?	Latest microliths, axes, bone and antler equipment of old hunting and fishing cultures. Gradually superseded from c.4000 by polished stone axes and adzes, farmers' sickles; hand-made pottery.	Dolmens and passage graves. Long barrows. Hilltop earthworks. Gabled timber long houses.	Megalithic carvings. Figurines. Animal rock engravings.
Fertility and Mother Goddess cults.	Stone still dominant but copper for small utensils. Pottery with kilns and wheel by late 4th M. Seals and writing before 3000.	Dams for upland valley irrigation. Pisé and mudbrick houses. Temples on platforms. Occasional use of columns.	Painted pottery. Figurines. Animal moulds. Seal cutting.
Little evidence. Dead buried with grave goods.	Chipped and polished stone tools. Early painted pottery in China. Elaborate, plastically decorated pottery in Japan.	Villages of substantial square and round huts with sunken floors and thatched roofs.	Painted and plastic pottery.
Unknown	Continuation of chipped stone spear heads. Baskets and querns spread to N. America. Native copper in Great Lakes area.	Flimsy huts and tents in shifting camps and villages.	None preserved.

3000–2000BC

This period was one of fulfilment and also of new promise. We have seen how in the last centuries of the fourth millennium the Sumerians led the way towards high civilization and how the Egyptians, after a dawdling start, quickly caught up with them. Now these two civilizations were to ripen simultaneously – though with very different fruits. What they achieved during this millennium represents in many ways the height of the Bronze Age world. By 2500 BC a third powerful, though less creative, civilization had arisen in the Indus valley. If a merchant had set out at this time from the orderly, well laid out southern Indus capital of Mohenjo-Daro, taken ship up the Arabian Sea, stopped at the growing entrepot at Bahrein, he could have landed to do business at the fine city of Ur. There he might have witnessed the solemn procession following the royal hearse to the cemetery, where the ladies with their gorgeous harps and hair sparkling with gold would soon be accepting immolation and burial with their king together with all the rest. Joining a caravan up the Euphrates he could have stopped to deal with the Semites at Mari. From this city he could readily have found fellow merchants travelling to the Mediterranean coast where, taking ship at Byblos, it need not have taken much more than a week to reach the pharaoh's capital of Memphis. He would, of course, have gone out to Giza to see the Sphinx and the pyramids with their vast polished limestone surfaces and golden peaks. They would have appeared so obviously superhuman that the merchant could not have doubted that the pharaohs lying within were divine indeed.

Mesopotamia, Egypt and the Indus manifest fulfilment: it was in the Mediterranean, and particularly in the lands round the Aegean, that the third millennium was a time of new promise. Here from Troy and the offshore islands, through the Cyclades thriving from maritime ventures to Early Minoan Crete, there were already signs of the first European high civilization that was in turn to have its enchanting fulfilment after 2000 BC.

In technology the most important advance of the time was the discovery of alloying – how by adding tin to copper the harder, more manageable bronze could be produced. The Sumerians had been groping towards this process late in our last period, but now the right proportions were discovered and there was rapid advance in both smelting and casting. In progressive areas outside the river valleys, eastward to India and westward to Greece, this millennium roughly coincides with the Early Bronze Age. Further to the west and north a true Bronze Age was not to begin until about 2000 BC, the Chalcolithic or even Neolithic technologies lingering on.

Intellectual innovations were, of course, innumerable: Sumeria's scribal colleges were probably first in the production of poetic literature, scholarship and elementary mathematics, but Egypt had her pyramid texts and abstruse theological literature. The Egyptians also seem to have been first with one practical intellectual achievement: the establishment of a calendar as early as 3000 BC. The Indus people devised their own script, but it was used mainly on their beautiful seals and probably remained primitive.

If the Sumerians led in literature, the Egyptians were supreme in the visual arts and architecture. The truly amazing growth of an elegant monumental architecture in masoned stone, as well as the pyramid (from 2700-2500 BC) is not even approached by the ziggurat temples of Sumeria, remarkable though these were. The local Maltese temple architecture, relatively small in scale, was probably at its height at much the same time. Indus architecture tended to be severe and functional and megalithic building in western and northern Europe continued but without new inspiration.

Detail from the "War" side of the "Standard" of Ur. The opposite side depicts scenes of peace. This oblong wooden box, ornamented with shell and limestone figures on a lapis lazuli background is probably in fact the sounding box of a lyre. It was found in one of the earliest tombs of the Royal Cemetery of Ur, Mesopotamia.

In sculpture and painting Egyptian artists were in a class apart, the Old Kingdom being one of the great epochs of art history. Contemporary sculpture in Sumeria was vigorous but often crude; it was superior however, in Semitic northern Mesopotamia and produced fine works such as the supposed head of Sargon. This was at a time (Dynasty VI) when Old Kingdom art was in some decline. If the Indus people produced much sculpture it must have been in wood and have perished, yet their few little masterpieces show a sophisticated talent. One other school of this third millennium is worthy of a place beside those of the three river valleys: that of the Cyclades. The stylized cult figures, usually of the goddess, and the famous harp and flute players have an assured mastery in astounding contrast with the naturalism of the high civilizations.

I must now fill in the more general historical background of these leading events, this time beginning with Egypt where, for the opening centuries, the historical record is much more firmly established than in Sumeria. Following unification and Dynasty I, Dynasty II began in about 2900 BC. Together these two are usually referred to as the Early Dynastic or Archaic period. During the Second Dynasty progress was held back by renewed fighting between north and south. It was only with Dynasty III, in about 2700 BC, and the beginning of the Old Kingdom, that high civilization can be said to have arrived. But what an arrival it was! Within a few centuries the concentrated wealth and power of the pharaohs were used to create some of the finest art and most extraordinary architecture the world has ever known. Zoser, the second pharaoh of Dynasty III, had as his vizier one Imhotep, the first great man of history whose name is known to us for his personal gifts and not from royal birth or associations. It was his genius that devised the Step Pyramid of Sakkara and the marvellous temples and tombs associated with it. Here all at once was monumental architecture in stone, with fine masonry, fluted columns, elegant stylized motifs on capitals and friezes, and exquisite portrait reliefs. It seems fitting that Zoser should also have had the first known life-size statue in his tomb.

Imhotep's genius having pointed the way, it took less than two centuries for the Old Kingdom to reach its climax under the pharaohs of Dynasty IV: Snefru, who built the first true pyramid and the three following generations of his house, Khufu (Cheops), Khafra (Chephren) and Menkaure (Mycerinus). Their pyramid tombs at Giza have been called the most famous monuments in the world.

In many ways Dynasty IV was the summit of Egyptian kingship. These pharaohs were not stewards of the gods but themselves divine, immortal sons of the sun god, Re. On earth they ruled and taxed a prosperous land through a growing network of officials from chamberlains, viziers and other exalted persons (mainly members of their own family), down to the lesser men who controlled the *nomes.* In the afterlife, they were certain of joining the other gods in an unchanging eternity. Their bodies and the statues within which their spirits dwelt were secure in pyramids and were worshipped in the adjoining temples. Egypt was a theocracy indeed! With it went complete confidence in the rightness of things: it can be seen in the calm nobility of the statue of Khafra, more humanly in those of Menkaure and his wife. There is no need to doubt that it extended to their subjects who were confident that their divine monarchs could keep them in benign harmony with the gods and with nature.

Yet Dynasty IV fell into rapid decline from the reign of Menkaure. With Dynasty V (beginning c.2500 BC) the status of the pharaohs declined. This may have been due to the greater power of the priesthood of Re at Heliopolis. Certainly pharaohs of this house built huge temples to the god instead of huge tombs for themselves. The kingdom, however, was still prosperous and united. There now began a social process that was to recur throughout history, the spread of privilege from a small elite down to the humbler classes. Once immortality had been limited to those of royal blood, now officials, priests, scribes, architects and physicians hoped to attain it and duly had portrait statues made for their tombs.

Dynasty V came to an end in about 2340 BC, at the time when Sargon the Great was winning his empire. With Dynasty VI the great era of the Old Kingdom was cracking. Provincial governors or monarchs were taking wealth and power to themselves and were a growing threat to the crown. Yet pharaohs of this house, particularly the two Pepis (Phiops) did maintain central government and conducted foreign wars and trade. Pepi II was fated to have the longest reign in history, well over 90 years. When at last he died the state was collapsing from internal strains. Egypt was then affected somewhat by the spreading upheavals which we shall find bringing old orders to an end throughout much of the ancient world. So the third millennium which had begun brilliantly with man's first experience of high civilization ended with his first experience of its collapse.

Egyptian culture, already fully recognizable under Menes, attained distinctive form in the Old Kingdom. Its art was marvellously naturalistic – to a degree not to be met again until the days of classical Greece. While the development of writing was ending the anonymity of prehistory through the recording of individual names, Egyptian portrait sculptures were making people visible in all their variety of type and character. This love of realism is shown also in the hieroglyphic writing which was perfected during this period and maintained for three thousand years.

Side by side with what we should now call the fine arts, Egyptian craftsmen in the service of the elite perfected many of the refinements of civilized life: fine linen, jewellery, cosmetics in exquisite vessels, elegant inlaid furniture.

All these manufactures involved trade for raw materials. The timber trade through Byblos greatly increased; there were voyages down the Red Sea to Punt (probably Somalia) for incense, and trade with the Nubians south of the frontier for such luxuries as ivory and ebony. The Egyptians themselves worked copper and turquoise mines in Sinai. As to the principal technological advance of this millennium – metallurgy – the Egyptians having begun strongly with Early Dynastic copper working, now lagged far behind the Sumerians and others in the manufacture of bronze.

These enterprises and the defence of the kingdom involved the pharaohs in foreign relations which followed a similar pattern for many centuries. They kept the "Libyans" of the western desert in check with skirmishes and occasional minor wars; they controlled the nomadic Bedouins in the east to protect their mining interests in Sinai; and to the south, while the frontier was held on the First Cataract, friendly trading expeditions were sent into Nubia and on occasion punitive ones against troublesome chiefs.

Turning now to Mesopotamia we find the history of the first half of the third millennium full of gaps and uncertainties. Many individual names have come down to us but they are entangled with legend. Gilgamesh, for example, the hero of supernatural epic, was he or was he not a flesh and blood king who ruled Uruk at about the time Zoser was building his Step Pyramid in Egypt? Archaeology may confirm that he was – as it has already confirmed the existence of several other semi-legendary figures.

One thing is sure: it was by now established that the pattern of life in Sumeria would be

Terracotta figure of Gilgamesh, the hero of supernatural epic, found at Khorsabad, Mesopotamia.

*Sargon of Akkad, who
established the first great
Empire known to history.
This almost life-sized head
of cast bronze was
discovered at Nineveh,
Mesopotamia.*

*This famous stele of Naram
Sin, grandson of Sargon,
celebrates his victory over
a mountain people of the
Zagros. Carved from sand-
stone it is over 6 ft (2 m)
high and was found at Susa.*

based upon small city-states ruled by kings deputizing for the god or goddess who was the nominal head of state. In early days the temple estates with their lands, workers and tribute were of prime economic importance, but in time the royal power encroached on that of the temple, and palaces were built beside the temples to share in the domination of the crowded cities.

Inevitably the rulers of these city-states fought fiercely against one another over water supply boundaries and other local disputes. More important, ambitious and militaristic individuals among them succeeded in establishing themselves and their descendants as overlords controlling other states as national kings. Then they in their turn were defeated and another city and its dynasty seized the hegemony. Because of their political division, the Mesopotamians lacked the concentrated power of a great national state which was what enabled the pharaohs to create their mighty works. Yet in true urbanization, in technical advance, and above all, in far-flung foreign trade (much of it in the hands of private merchants), they remained in advance of the Egyptians.

Historians allow the "Protoliterate" period to last through the first century or two of this millennium, placing the beginning of the Early Dynastic period at about 2800 BC or a little earlier.

It is not possible to summarize the complicated and only partly known history of the cities and their rulers in the Early Dynastic age. The overlordship seems first to have been held by Kish, then to have been won by the very ancient city of Uruk and later by Ur, Lagash, Umma and others. Nippur, lying at the heart of the vast, flat Sumerian plain and sacred to the great god, Enlil, appears not to have sought supremacy but remained a holy city and centre of learning.

Where do the rulers buried with such extravagance of life and treasure in the Royal Cemetery of Ur fit into the history of the Early Dynastic period? It is difficult to say, since the names recorded in the tombs do not appear among those of the First Dynasty of Ur in the King List. It is probable, however, that they were earlier, dating from the century after 2600 BC – the age of the Giza pyramids.

During all this time the ancient Sumerian cities of the south had dominated the valley, although some of their kings, notably of Kish, had Semitic names. We have seen that there were Semites in the valley in prehistoric times. Now, during the early centuries of the third millennium, more of them entered the

The electrum helmet of
Prince Mes-Kalamshar was
found at Ur's Royal
Cemetery. Made from a
single sheet of metal, it is
decorated with relief and
chased designs. The holes
were used to lace a quilted
lining.

He-goat caught in a thicket
found in the great death pit
at the Royal Cemetery of
Ur. It is made of gold, silver,
lapis lazuli, shell and red
limestone.

valley from the western deserts, took to settled life in the cities, and pushed peacefully southward into ancient Sumeria. These Semites, who had adopted Sumerian culture and adapted cuneiform to the writing of their own language, are known as Akkadians. The mingling of the two peoples and their traditions produced a vigorous civilization, but it was not long before the Semites were to become the dominant partners.

In c.2350 BC a warlike, usurping king of Umma, one Lugalzagesi, having defeated and sacked the city of his traditional rival the king of Lagash, went on to subdue other city-states until he could call himself "King of the Land of of Sumer". It proved, however, that the Ummite was only preparing the way for another conqueror greater than himself. This was Sargon the Great, the first ruler in Mesopotamia whose name is familiar in world history. Sargon was a self-made man of insatiable military ambition, and during a long reign won hegemony over the whole valley and then conquered northward to the Mediterranean,

through Syria (including Lebanon's cedar forest). He also ruled Elam and campaigned and claimed authority southward along the Arabian Gulf. So he established the first great Empire known to history, and brought vast wealth and trade to his capital city of Akkad. Although troubled by revolts and pressure from a fresh influx of Semitic peoples, or Amorites (to use the biblical version of the name), the empire held for 150 years, and Sargon's grandson, Naram-Sin (c.2260 BC) even extended its frontiers. A famous stele celebrates his conquest of a mountain people of the Zagros.

It was in fact another people from these mountains, the Gutians, who largely brought about the collapse of the Semitic empire and took control of northern Sumer. The old Sumerian south, however, regained prosperity, winning back the Gulf trade from Akkad. This was the time of Gudea of Lagash, a peace-loving ruler, proud of his temple-building, whose strong, calm face is known from a number of statues. Then, as Lagash weakened,

A wooden model left as a funerary offering in an Egyptian tomb shows a primitive plough being pulled by oxen. These models as well as the tomb wall paintings were intended to provide the dead man with his needs in the after life.

Ur returned to greatness under the rule of a successful general, Ur-Nammu. The Third Dynasty of Ur which he founded about 2100 BC came to rule the whole valley. Rather on the lines of Sargon, the dynasty imposed a centralized bureaucracy with governors appointed over city-states. The kings themselves claimed a semi-divine power, being celebrated through hymns, shrines and sacrifices.

The Third Dynasty maintained internal peace and foreign trade, but towards the end of the millennium it suffered attacks from Hurrians of the northern mountains and the mounting power of the Amorites, who presently took control of the north. The final blow, however, was struck by a king of Elam who marched into Sumeria and occupied Ur. The Lament for the city written for this sad fall speaks for the end of Sumerian greatness. Although Ur and many of the old cities survived, the real power shifted irrevocably northward and into the hands of the Semites. Sumerian seems soon to have died as a spoken language, though it long remained in use for learning and literature.

The destruction of Ur, when its king and the image of its moon god were carried off to Susa "like a bird that has flown from its nest" was one climax of a thousand years of warfare between Elamites and Sumerians, and was sufficient proof that Elam was still prospering. So, too, were many of the upland towns and settlements, such as Tepe Yahya in southern Iran, providing a link between Mesopotamia and India. Prosperity was increased by trade in precious substances such as lapis lazuli (mainly from Afghanistan), soapstone, carnelian and tin.

While such trade went by packass along the overland routes, there was also a growing trade along the Gulf, the merchants of Sumer and Akkad supplying woollens, hides and oil in exchange for copper from Makran (probably modern Oman) and luxury goods. In the second half of the millennium an important port of call grew up by the freshwater springs of Bahrein. Traders there had contacts with both Sumeria and the Indus valley.

The origins of the Indus civilization are not yet understood, although it must have owed something both to the Iranian settlements and to influences from Mesopotamia. While already mature by 2500 BC, it was at its height at about the time of Sargon's empire and the Fifth Dynasty of Egypt, but was already in decline early in the second millennium. Therefore, it was of much shorter duration than the other two great river valley civilizations

and its culture was less widely influential. Yet it flourished over a larger area than the other two, for while its chief cities lay on the flood plain of the valley, it also extended along the coasts on either side of the delta.

The Indus script is preserved mainly on seals that were probably used as marks of ownership, and on a few copper tablets and potsherds. Unhappily even these brief inscriptions have not been deciphered, so that we are once again in a nameless, wordless realm.

Over all the vast territory of the Indus civilization there was so striking a uniformity in products, buildings and way of life generally that it is thought to have been a unified state tightly controlled from the twin capitals of Mohenjo-Daro and Harappa. These cities, and other lesser ones such as Kalibangan and the port of Lothal (with its fine dock at the head of the Gulf of Cambay), were laid out on a regular grid very unlike the unplanned streets and alleys of Sumerian cities. An efficient system of drains ran under the streets between the blocks of houses and there was a generous provision of wells. In contrast with the sun-dried mudbrick that was the all but universal building material in Sumeria, Indus architecture was characteristically in fired brick.

The cities were centred on strongly fortified citadels which were raised on massive platforms built against flooding. In or near these were workers' hutments, large granaries, and flour mills – evidently centralized municipal food depots. Here great quantities of grain must have been brought in by bullock wagon from the surrounding countryside to feed the citizens. Together with the imposed town planning these arrangements suggest a strong socialized administration. (To some the whole Indus civilization suggests a Bronze Age totalitarianism.)

At Mohenjo-Daro a grandiose stepped bath and surrounding buildings are likely to have served a ritualistic purpose, but no true temple buildings have been found to compare with those of Sumeria and Egypt. Religion is chiefly represented to us by female figurines probably representing a Mother Goddess and by a three-headed horned god probably ancestral to the Hindu Siva. There is evidence for bull and tree cults and a veneration of such wild animals as the rhinoceros and elephant. Fire altars were used at Kalibangan.

Just as in the other river valley civilizations, the Indus economy was based on wheat and barley cultivated by irrigation. Rice was grown on the west coast, cotton was an

A calm nobility is evident in this monumental stone statue of the Pharaoh Khafra. The falcon god Horus stands in a protective pose behind the king and underneath the throne are the heraldic plants symbolizing the union of Upper and Lower Egypt.

Zoser, second pharaoh of Dynasty III. This early life-sized limestone statue was found in a chapel adjoining the Step Pyramid at Sakkara, Egypt.

important cash crop. Cattle included both the Humped Brahmani variety and others; buffalo and pigs were also reared.

The metallurgy of the Indus people was conservative to the point of backwardness and remarkably standardized. In trade, however, they were more enterprising. We have already seen that their merchants traded by land and sea with Sumeria and the lands between. They seem to have set up trading colonies in Bahrein and in Ur and other cities of Sumer and Akkad. This foreign trade was at its height during the time of Sargon and the Third Dynasty of Ur.

The visual arts appear to have been of far less importance in the lives of the Indus people than they were for the Sumerians and Egyptians. This may have been largely because it seems that highly organized religious institutions centred on theocratic rulers were lacking, and hence the patronage of the arts that went with them.

The third millennium did not see any very striking developments in China or Japan. Neolithic village communities with simple agriculture and herding were still the most advanced forms of society, while over much of the territory men continued to live by hunting and fishing.

One technical advance certainly took place, the adoption of the potter's wheel among Neolithic peasant communities living to the east of the Yang Shao homeland, from Honan to the coast. They used it to produce formal and often elegant vessels in a glossy black ware. These people differed also from their western neighbours in enclosing their villages with walls of rammed earth.

In Japan the middle phase of the long-lived Jōmon culture is thought to coincide with the third millennium. The coast-dwellers still depended largely on mussels, oysters and other shellfish for their basic diet, while the mountain-dwellers hunted and gathered berries, nuts and roots. The cultivation of millet and vegetables was beginning. Potters were producing ever larger and more ornate vessels and these were sometimes used for the hearths. There may well have been an increase in population: villages of at least sixty huts are known.

In southern Siberia the last centuries of the millennium were distinguished by the appearance of a copper using culture known as the Afanasyevskaya. Not very much can be said of the life of its creators as they are known chiefly from their tombs, many in the steppes of the Minusinak basin and a lesser number in the Altai Territory. They seem to have been hunter-herders with cattle, sheep and horses.

Wall painting of geese feeding, from the wall of Nefermaat's mastaba at Meidum, Egypt.

Seneb the Dwarf (Chief Steward of the Royal Clothing) and his family, painted limestone, Dynasty VI, Giza, Egypt.

Pharaoh Menkaure and his queen are shown in an affectionate pose in this dark slate unfinished pair sculpture from Giza, Egypt.

*A marble Cycladic "Venus".
These figures were
extremely stylized with
elongated heads, crossed
arms and parallel legs.*

While still depending on stone for their principal tools they used copper for needles, awls and knives and, more plentifully, together with gold and silver, for ornaments. Most effort was lavished on burials, where family groups seem to have been interred together in large rectangular pits, along with food, drink and possessions. These graves were enclosed by a circular stone wall and covered with a mound. The Afanasyevskaya people had probably spread from the west, for they were of European (Caucasoid) stock. Later the area was to be taken over by Mongolian peoples.

The eastern Mediterranean, and particularly the Levant, was inevitably strongly affected by the two great civilizations to the north and south. The headwaters of the Tigris-Euphrates led up into eastern Anatolia where copper and silver were to be had, and from the western bulge of the Euphrates trade routes were open to Cilicia, Syria and Lebanon. Sumerian rulers as well as Egyptian wanted Lebanese timber for their temple-building: Gudea of Lagash records how he "made a path to the Cedar Mountain . . . cut its cedars with great axes" and floated them down the Euphrates.

Town life and the use of bronze which had begun just before 3000 BC now made rapid progress. Walled towns were found throughout the region and were probably the seats of royal chiefly rulers. The Levant, with Palestine lagging somewhat behind Syria and Lebanon, was already falling into the pattern of the small city-states which were to be fought over by the great powers of Egypt and Mesopotamia in the next millennium. There were also kingdoms, perhaps richer but more barbarous, in many parts of Anatolia. The royal graves of Alaca Hüyük were furnished with superb weapons, cult objects, vessels and personal ornaments in bronze, silver and gold. The first settlement at Troy was followed by Troy II, rebuilt with stout walls and a large royal hall. It was here that the Schliemanns found the famous gold treasure which they named after Priam, though in fact it was buried some 1500 years before the Trojan war.

Western Anatolia contributed to the great prosperity of the Aegean world. This was founded on maritime trade, although wealth and well-being might have been enhanced by the cultivation of olives and vines at this time. Substantial towns grew up on Lemnos and Lesbos. The Cycladic Islands, however, were hardly large enough to support towns and most people lived in villages near the coast. The daring of their sailors and notorious pirates carried them throughout the Aegean and far beyond – even as far as the Balearics. Crete,

now in the Early Minoan period, ended the Cycladic ascendancy after 2500 BC. Her foreign trade was growing fast, much of it conducted from ports at the eastern end of the island. Some large mansions and small open towns were built. Bronze working and small-scale urbanization (best represented by the walled town of Lerna) reached mainland Greece a little later than the islands. Towards the end of the period, however, there was rapid progress. Metallurgy became general and the well-to-do could afford gold and silver vessels.

In spite of trade, royal riches and contacts with "the great powers", the lands of the eastern Mediterranean did not achieve high civilization at this time. It is symptomatic that writing was not adopted here before 2000 BC. The physical structure of the territory, the peoples and their cultural traditions, were too various and broken for civil administration and government to develop on a large scale. Nor could the agricultural foundations rival the productivity of the extensive, ever-fertile irrigated field systems of the great valleys.

During the last centuries of the millennium the region was disturbed, in some areas catastrophically, by folk movements such as we have seen causing upheavals simultaneously in Egypt and Mesopotamia. In Greece and Anatolia the immigrants were probably Indo-Europeans, the heralds of the great expansion of these peoples which was to change history. In the Levant the invaders were Semitic peoples, by origin desert nomads. They included Amorites (the same people who destroyed the Third Dynasty of Ur) and the first Canaanites. Other groups infiltrated Egypt and added to the confusion of the internal breakdown of the Old Kingdom.

In the western Mediterranean the Chalcolithic Age lasted much longer than in the east. In Italy bronze working came in from about 2500 BC, but Spain and Portugal remained dependent on stone and copper throughout the period.

The peoples of the western Mediterranean also continued to devote their most concentrated labours on tombs for the communal burial of their dead and other religious building. In Spain and Portugal impressive megalithic tombs were still being built or used during at least the first half of the millennium. At Los Millares, in the southeastern corner of Spain, there grew up a large settlement enclosed within strong, turreted walls. Outside was a cemetery of some 80 carefully built megalithic passage-graves. This must have been the stronghold of an exceptionally important chiefdom. In

Terracotta female figurine or "Mother Goddess" from Mohenjo-Daro, India.

some places, notably in Italy, Sardinia, southern Spain and Portugal, communal burial chambers were cut into the rock.

By far the most spectacular of all these local creations, however, took place in Malta. From modest beginnings in the previous period, the inhabitants of this small island went on to build imposing temples and temple-tombs (hypogea) in a style entirely their own. They employed very large blocks which were not, as in what is usually meant by megalithic architecture, left rough, but carefully shaped and richly embellished with spirals and other sacred motifs. The colossal sculpture of a standing woman at the temple of Tarxien, together with numbers of smaller seated and lying figures of a very ample female, prove beyond reasonable doubt that these temples were devoted to the ancient Mediterranean worship of the Mother Goddess. The earliest of these temples were probably built a few centuries before the time of Zoser. Remarkable though they are, it must be emphasized that they are tiny and primitive when set beside Imhotep's glorious creation.

In central, western and northern Europe the life of the farming communities continued in many regions without very striking change for much of the third millennium. The various peoples, mostly village dwellers, continued to grow their wheat and barley, herd their cattle and sheep. Although copper working was spreading from the Balkans and eastern Europe, the west remained in a stone using, late Neolithic, stage of development. Throughout the regions where megalithic tombs had been built in the last millennium new ones continued to be built and old ones used.

In Britain the Late Stone Age saw a very distinctive form of religious sanctuary, the earliest dating from the very beginning of the period, if not before. These were the "henges" in which a sacred area, sometimes set with circles of wood or standing stones, was enclosed within a more or less substantial earthen bank. Avebury in Wiltshire is a famous example. At Stonehenge itself the little bank and ditch that few people notice as they cross to reach the stones was probably cut before 2500 BC, but as the sanctuary was not brought to its most splendid height until at least five centuries later, it will find its place in our next period.

Towards the end of the third millennium, folk movements affecting the greater part of Europe made profound changes in social and cultural life. If they had come within historical times the names and doings of the people concerned would have been household words. As it is, we can only use such lame archaeological

terms as Beaker folk, Battle Axe people and so forth. Among the fighting groups that were migrating throughout the continent, the Beaker folk were the most widespread and easily identified (from their distinctive pots). Some think that they originated in Iberia as people from the backward interior of this area seem to have destroyed Los Millares and other advanced centres; others would put their cradleland in central Europe. Certainly wherever they and the other related tribesmen went they introduced the burial of individuals under round mounds. Although megalithic tombs might sometimes still be used, they were no longer built and the communal form of burial was at an end. These newcomers probably often imposed themselves as an aristocracy, not mingling with the natives for several generations. They did much to introduce copper and elementary bronze working to western and northern Europe.

The Americas in this period witnessed a gentle advance towards better agriculture and larger and more settled village communities. These advances were still concentrated in the old progressive centres of Mexico, South America and the southwest of the United States; elsewhere tribal life remained based on hunting, food gathering and fishing.

In Mesoamerica this millennium represents the last phase before the step forward of the Pre-classic age. A moister climate and the successful hybridization of maize after 2500 BC brought about a vastly increased yield. Together corn and vegetables now became important parts of the diet instead of insignificant additions to wild food supplies. The cultivators, however, were still without pottery.

In the fertile valleys of coastal Peru such as those of Chicama and Virú, the people grew beans, squash and gourds as well as collecting wild plants. After 2500 BC they seem to have done less hunting in the mountains but greatly increased their fishing. Their houses appear to have been flimsy huts, but the crowded villages might have had as many as a thousand inhabitants. They twined and wove fabrics from native cotton.

There was still no pottery in Peru at this time, although we had seen it beginning in Ecuador at the end of the last millennium. Excellent ceramics were developed there now as well as modelled figurines. In about 3000 BC pottery appeared in Colombia, and there, as in Ecuador, was used for both vessels and grotesque figures (notably the human and animal-headed bowls).

Technology 3000-2000 BC

Mesopotamia and Egypt, which had taken a few steps forward before 3000 BC, began making spectacular progress soon after that date. Most significant was their increasing ability to work with bronze. The manufacture of bronze itself resulted from a process of deliberate research – an unprecedented activity involving experimentation with a variety of alloys. Early artifacts of the period show that experimentation stopped once the blend of 10% tin to 90% copper was discovered.

There was one drawback to the use of bronze: copper is hard to find in its natural state, and tin even more so. Yet the Mesopotamians and Egyptians persevered, and their search for copper and tin to supply the increasing demand spread the news of the recently discovered alloy. The usefulness of bronze as a workable metal led to the creation of better tools with which to work it. Better tools led to better carpentry, and so to better boats and vehicles. The social results of metal as wealth were also enormous.

Communications improved rapidly as wheeled traffic increased throughout the world. By 2000 the wheel had reached eastward to the Indus Valley, northward into the Steppes, and westward to the North Sea – perhaps even beyond. Water traffic too was increasing. Although we know that there were boats that plied the Atlantic, we know little about them. But in two areas, the Mediterranean and the Persian Gulf, there were certainly substantial seagoing ships, which carried on trade between Egypt and the Levant or sometimes Cyprus and Crete, and on the Persian Gulf between Sumer, Bahrein and the Indus Valley.

By the time the spark of the new culture kindled in the Indus Valley, sometime around 2500 BC, it was already sinking to a warm glow in the Near East. In many fields, such as writing, architecture, and metallurgy, the peoples of Egypt and Mesopotamia did not appear to make many new advances. The techniques devised by their ancestors apparently worked well enough to satisfy their needs, and so there were fewer and fewer improvements.

In northern Europe, people continued to grind and flake stone but they did develop some skill at making stone copies of metal weapons and in mining flint. In the Far East and the Americas, the benefits of community life were being experienced in farming settlements like those already established in southwest Asia. Pottery began to be widely used in Mexico, Colombia and Ecuador; the Peruvians were becoming adept at weaving in cotton.

Areas of major interest

• Centres

TEHUACAN VALLEY

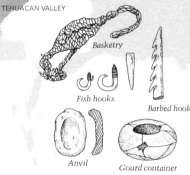

Basketry

Fish hooks

Barbed hook

Anvil

Gourd container

The Americas
Hunting and food gathering equipment was still dominant, although agriculture was playing an increasingly important part in Mexico and Peru. Coiled basketry was widespread.

• Valdivia

VIRU VALLEY

Stone grinder

Beakers

Slate plaque

Stone rollers

Western Mediterranean
Incised slate plaques or cosmetic palettes and very distinctive bell beaker pottery spread widely through the area. The grinder was necessary equipment for an agricultural society and the stone rollers made possible the construction of large-scale architecture.

COMPARISON OF MATERIALS IN USE.

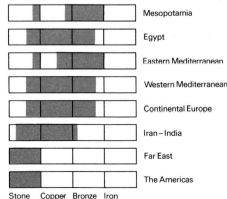

Mesopotamia

Egypt

Eastern Mediterranean

Western Mediterranean

Continental Europe

Iran–India

Far East

The Americas

Stone   Copper   Bronze   Iron

Far East
Stone, bone and wood were still the main materials for tools and weapons. Reaping knives were widely employed in harvesting grain.

Stone implements

Reaping knife

Axe

Sword and bow

Fish spear

Arrowhead

• Togaruishi

• Lung Shan

• Yang Shao

Continental Europe
A highly developed flint mining industry which utilized picks and lamps provided raw materials for implements of this time such as the ground stone tools and finely flaked flintwork. This latter often imitated the first copper tools.

Chalk lamp

Copper axes

Dagger

Flint arrowhead

Polished stone axes

• Windmill Hill

Camp de Chassey •
• Cortaillod

• San Pedro de Estoril

• Los Millares

Eastern Mediterranean
Metal technology was highly developed in this area as evidenced by the rich finds from the Anatolian royal tombs and the treasures of Troy. Improvements in the plough and boat contributed to the growing prosperity on the island of Crete.

Bronze sistrum

Cretan ship

Gold jug

Cretan plough

Gold earring

• Troy
• Alaca Hüyük

• Beycesultan

Hal Saflieni • • Tarxien
CYCLADES

• Mochlos
• Ugarit
• Byblos

• Assur

• Mari

Megiddo •

Kish • • Uruk
• Jericho
Memphis • • Heliopolis   • Ur

Abydos • • Thebes

Egypt
Society prospered at home and abroad. Irrigation agriculture and foreign trade brought leisure and the materials necessary for advances in many areas such as metal working. Hieroglyphic writing was fully developed at this time.

Gold falcons head

Hieroglyphs

Shaduf

Sailing ship

Mesopotamia
Based on an efficient agriculture and active trade, Sumerian civilization reached its peak. This is indicated by highly developed techniques for working such metals as gold and copper as well as a full bronze metallurgy and the standardization of the cuneiform script.

Gold dagger

Cuneiform

Copper goddess

Plough

Iran-India
Writing, though undeciphered, appeared on the Indus Valley seals. Pottery utensils and toys and primitively worked copper tools are also representative of this short-lived civilization.

Seal impression

Feeding cup

Seal

Model cart

Metal weapon

• Harappa

• Mohenjo-Daro
• Lothal

Mesopotamia

Metal working in the form of bronze casting made great advances in spite of the fact that there were no local mineral supplies. Bronze melts at rather lower temperatures than copper and when melted flows more readily. The alloy could be cast in many specialized shapes – in closed moulds or by the lost wax method here illustrated. Bronze also yields harder, sharper, and so more efficient tools. Mesopotamia played an important part in developing and disseminating these skills to others. The necessity of trading for the needed minerals was itself a factor in the rise of Sumerian civilization.

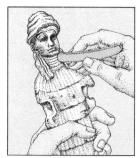
LOST WAX. *The object was modelled in wax.*

Leads were added for the metal to flow in.

The wax image was coated in plaster and baked.

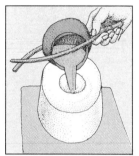
The metal was poured in to replace the wax.

The terracotta mould was then chipped away.

The casting was touched up for use.

Cast goddess, Ur

Egypt

Civilization and technology advanced together in Egypt, up to the flowering of the Old Kingdom. This was due to two factors: the unification of the country under stable rulers produced the conditions and patronage necessary for craftspeople to give of their best, and the improvement in metal tools made many technological innovations possible. Even the simple agricultural basis of the economy probably already benefited from such technical devices as the shaduf which employed a counter-weighted lever to lift water to the crops. Improved metal tools such as chisels, mallets, adzes and unhafted axes allowed the construction of more seaworthy boats for the Byblos run, to fetch the timber Egypt lacked but needed for such things as buildings and furniture. Hieroglyphs, which were first devised for communication and recording, were soon diverted to artistic and magical ends. This helps to explain why their functional improvement ceased at so early a stage.

Wall relief showing inscriptions of the names, titles and offering gifts to Wepemnofret

Boat building (after an Egyptian wall painting)

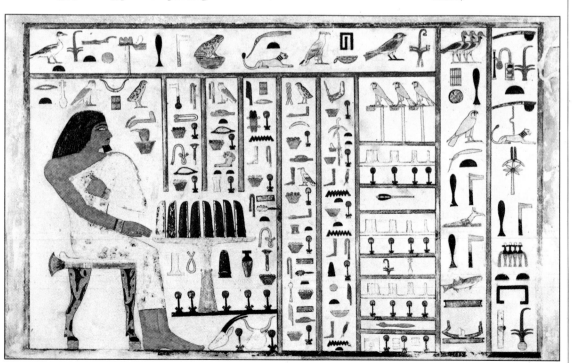

Shaduf

Eastern Mediterranean

Skilled metalsmiths in Anatolia worked in bronze and gold to produce the treasures of Alaca Hüyük and Troy. It was doubtless their ores from which Mesopotamia drew its metal supplies, and technical advances in metallurgy must have been exchanged between the two areas. Smelting, hammering, soldering, *epoussé* relief, sheathing and inlay were some of the known processes.

Gold jug, Alaca Hüyük, Turkey

Gold pendant from "Priam's Treasure", Troy

Western Mediterranean

Corn was still laboriously ground by hand but, for other tasks, simple physical aids like the wedge and lever must have been widely known. Spherical stone rollers found in Malta were used for manoeuvring building blocks. Final adjustments were effected with great levers, inserted in notches left in the blocks for that purpose.

Stone quern

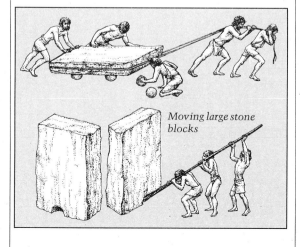

Moving large stone blocks

Continental Europe

High quality flint was mined from the chalk deposits at Grimes Graves in Norfolk. Radiating galleries led to the flint beds which were as much as 23 ft (7m) below the ground. Antler picks were used to remove the flint and to shape it into blocks or roughouts to be used for axes. The fashioning of the flint into working tools or weapons was left to the ultimate purchaser.

Antler pick

Chalk lamp

Flint dagger

Flint mine at Grimes Graves, Norfolk, England

Iran-India

The technology of the Indus civilization was not outstanding, its metal working, for example, was primitive. But the brilliantly carved stone seals argue for high craftsmanship and an advanced economic system. The model bullock cart provides evidence for wheeled vehicles.

Carved seal stones, Mohenjo-Daro, India

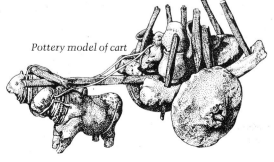

Pottery model of cart

Far East

Ground stone tools like the reaping knife were adequate for the needs of the food gatherers and early farmers of Japan and China.

Stone reaping knife

The Americas

The techniques of basketry and weaving, although certainly employed elsewhere, were widespread in this area. The dry conditions in Mexico and Peru have ensured the survival of such material.

Early basketry from Peru

Architecture *3000-2000 BC*

The civilizations which flourished at this time produced architecture of a scale and complexity that the simpler societies of the earlier millennia were incapable of achieving. In Mesopotamia, the temples of the predynastic period developed into grandiose monuments which dominated not only the cities they were meant to serve, but the whole of the valley floor. It has even been suggested that the ziggurats, the stepped mounds which supported the sacred shrines, were intended simply as artificial mountains. Though their design showed high skill, technically they were of the simplest: a mudbrick core encased in a weatherproof skin of burnt brick set in bitumen. The shrines on their summits have not survived, but at least the plans of the great temples associated with them have been recovered, as have those of the palaces which joined them later in the millennium. Both show the steady advances of building skills in more extensive plans, higher brick walls and longer spans of roof timbers. However, technical expertise is most clearly shown in much less ostentatious structures, the tombs. In the Royal Cemetery at Ur the true arch and dome were already employed, although it was over 2000 years before their advantages came to be fully recognized and exploited.

In Egypt, on the other hand, large-scale building was used for tombs rather than temples. The design, or more specifically the geometry, of the pyramids is astounding. Great organizational genius went into their construction. But the technical skills employed were crude compared with the arches of the Ur tombs. In the short period from the Step Pyramid of 2760 to the third Giza pyramid of 2300, pyramid building progressed as far as it usefully could in the direction of sheer size.

The Maltese temples, though of imposing size and sophistication, and the continuing megalithic tomb architecture of Iberia and western Europe also represent a kind of magnificent cul-de-sac.

The Indus civilization is more difficult to evaluate since the recovered evidence is scanty. Their civic buildings appear to have been less ambitious but still highly competent. The walls of Harappa, the granaries and Great Bath of Mohenjo-Daro and the brick-lined dock at Lothal are all functional structures. This element of usefulness rather than beauty or grandeur strikes us most forcibly on Indus sites, with their austere architecture, advanced grid town planning and even efficient public drainage system.

▨	Areas of major interest
●	Centres
▲	Sites

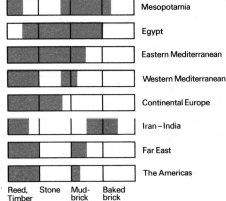

The Americas
This area lagged architecturally and such humble dwellings as the cave, tent and hut were still widespread.

Tholos tomb, Los Millares

Hypogeum, Malta

Tarxien Temple, Malta

Western Mediterranean
The Maltese temples and Iberian tholos tombs represent the most advanced architecture in this area at this time. The distinction between temple and tomb is often slight, and both could be either cut into the solid rock or built of stone above ground.

COMPARISON OF MATERIALS IN USE

	Reed, Timber	Stone	Mud-brick	Baked brick	
					Mesopotamia
					Egypt
					Eastern Mediterranean
					Western Mediterranean
					Continental Europe
					Iran – India
					Far East
					The Americas

Continental Europe
Domestic dwellings were simple; stake, hurdlework and thatch were the usual construction materials. The use of great blocks of stone in the megalithic tombs of western Europe shows that more ambitious architecture could be produced when necessary.

Long dolmen, Sonderholm

Chambered tomb, West Kennet   *Danubian dwelling*

▲ Sonderholm

▲ West Kennet

WURTTEMBURG

Los Millares ●

Hal Saflieni ● Tarxien

Eastern Mediterranean
Walled townships like Troy were maintained throughout the area. At Alaca Hüyük the tombs of the royal dead were storehouses of great wealth.

Tomb, Alaca Hüyük

● Troy
● Alaca Hüyük

Troy II

Far East
Architecture was restricted to house types of simple timber frame construction with thatched roofs, as in those of the Jōmon period in Japan and Yang Shao in China.

Jōmon dwellings

House, Pan Po Ts'un

▲ Pan Po Ts'un

Rectangular dwelling, Pan Po Ts'un

▲ Khafaje

● Ur

● Mohenjo-Daro

Great Bath, Mohenjo-Daro

House, Mohenjo-Daro

Iran-India
The civic buildings of Harappa and Mohenjo-Daro appear functional rather than aesthetic, competent rather than ambitious. House plumbing facilities and community bathing places are part of an innovative sanitation system.

Mastaba tomb, Giza   Sakkara ▲ Giza

Great Pyramids, Giza

Papyrus, date palm columns   *Step Pyramid, Sakkara*

House, Ur   *Brick arched vault*

Oval Temple, Khafaje

Ziggurat, Ur

Egypt
The leaf and bud columns show that elegance came as naturally to the Old Kingdom architects as did the planning of imposing masses of masonry, demonstrated most clearly by the development of the Great Pyramids of Giza from mastaba tombs and the Step Pyramid.

Mesopotamia
Monumental architecture is apparent in the region's ziggurats and temples. The brick arched vault was used in a tomb in the Royal Cemetery at Ur, and the town house suggests a high domestic standard of living.

Mesopotamia

The temples increased enormously in size and complexity, their principal feature now being the ziggurats – vast and solid mounds of mudbrick encased in a weatherproof skin of burnt brick set in bitumen. Holes were made in the casing to prevent it splitting in the rainy season. Though the shrines at their summits have not survived (a triple staircase led to the upper sanctuary at Ur), the mounds themselves, especially that at Ur, can be studied and shown to be well designed, both structurally and aesthetically. The much more modest tombs, however, are the more innovative in their use of the arch. A few large temple complexes contained in oval enclosures such as the one at Khafaje, were also constructed. A temple, altar, dwellings, workshops and stores were contained within three ascending terraces.

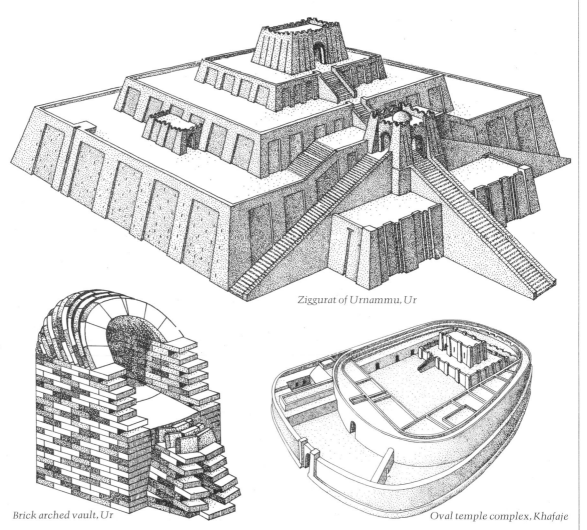

Ziggurat of Urnammu, Ur

Brick arched vault, Ur

Oval temple complex, Khafaje

Egypt

Perhaps the most famous architectural monuments in the world, the pyramids were built of stone with a rubble core as enlarged and elaborated versions of the humble mudbrick mastaba. The masses of masonry were partly symbolic, partly protective, and seemingly disproportionate for the sepulchral chambers they covered. They were worthy memorials but hardly inviolate. A remarkable ability in surveying, immediately obvious from their sheer bulk and proved by the accuracy of layout and orientation was necessary for their construction. The great pyramid of Cheops differed from the others in its greater bulk and internal layout. It had three separate chambers while the Chephren pyramid had one chamber with two approaches. Mycerinus' tomb had one chamber and one entrance.

Great pyramids at Giza: Mycerinus, Chephren, Cheops

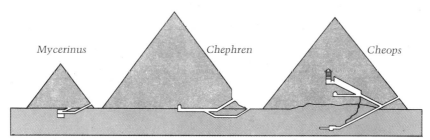

Mycerinus   *Chephren*   *Cheops*

Sections through Giza pyramids showing tombs

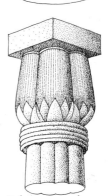

Capitals from temples imitate natural forms such as papyrus and date palm.

Eastern Mediterranean
Troy was a town long before the Argive Greeks appeared before its walls. Illustrated here is the second city of the nine which succeeded each other on this strategic site. This town of 2500 BC had extended city walls, several gateways and a large "megaron" (roof span 30 ft. [9.2 m] which may have been a council chamber.

Plan of Troy II

Western Mediterranean
Tarxien is the largest of the Maltese temple complexes which are among the earliest monumental architecture in the world. Certain of the limestone blocks used to construct the temples were decorated with relief designs such as the running spiral or all over pockmarking. Further west, in Iberia, the circular earth-covered tholos tombs of Los Millares consisted of an entrance passage separated into segments by port-holed septal slabs and a circular chamber lined with orthostats, topped by a corbelled roof. Some tombs had a low central pillar.

These tombs had well-constructed revetment walls and cult pillars which stood outside in the ritual enclosures. Sometimes coloured plaster was found on their inside walls.

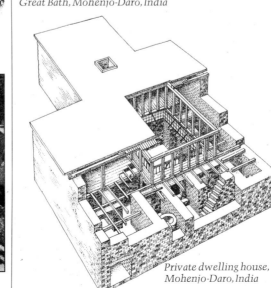

Tholos tomb, Los Millares, Spain

Tarxien Temple, Malta

Continental Europe
The immense megalithic chamber tombs required great community effort for manipulating blocks of stone weighing up to 100 tons into position. Some of these chambers contained kerbstones decorated with abstract designs. The West Kennet tomb was built of large boulders and had drystone walls. It was covered by a 350 ft (106 m) long mound.

West Kennet long barrow, Wiltshire, England

Iran-India
The Indus civilization made much greater use of baked brick which was utilized for private houses as well as for community structures such as a granary and the Great Bath; the latter was probably intended for ritual washing.

Great Bath, Mohenjo-Daro, India

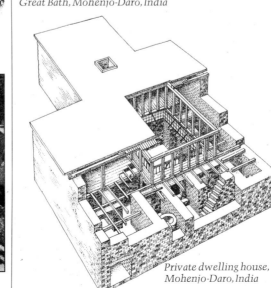

Private dwelling house, Mohenjo-Daro, India

Far East
Though villages and individual houses increased in size, both in the Huang-Ho Valley and along the Japanese coasts, architecture remained at an elementary level throughout the area. Building was largely restricted to timber and thatch, with some use of rammed earth for foundations.

Round Jōmon type dwelling, Japan

Rectangular Jōmon house, Japan

The Americas
For the New World, it is hardly yet possible to speak of architecture which was still of the very simplest at this period. The survival into more recent times of huts of lashed rods probably gives a fair idea of techniques available.

Partially constructed Chilca house, Peru

Art 3000 – 2000 BC

The Sumerians of the southern cities created the art forms of the civilization that was to outlast them. Royal stelae such as that of Naram-Sin (p. 90) are striking if always rather stiff. Treasures from the famous royal tombs of Ur dating from c.2600-2500 BC (and therefore contemporary with some of the finest Old Kingdom art of Egypt) give us an idea of the splendour of royal possessions – carved and inlaid harps and lyres, miniature masterpieces such as the gold and lapis goat and beautiful gold vessels and personal ornaments. Perhaps the finest art, however, was produced by the more Semitic people of the north, who absorbed Sumerian culture but made it freer and more vital. The best sculpture of this school comes from the temple of Ishtar at Mari. The bronze head, thought to portray Sargon of Akkad (p. 90) is another noble work. Votive figures placed in temples by worshippers sometimes show a cruder, more provincial style.

Most people would agree that in the visual arts the Egyptians, especially in this period, surpassed the Sumerians. The best portrait sculpture of the pyramid age has confident strength combined with a gift for showing individual character. The Egyptians were also masters of scenes carved in low relief and painted. From the Old Kingdom onwards these show everyday life in court and country estate with naturalism and sometimes a fine sensibility. Middle Kingdom art tended to be more austere; its royal portraits have lost the confidence of the Old Kingdom and show signs of inner conflict. It was in this period that it became the custom to supply the dead with carved wooden groups of soldiers, farmers and artisans of all kinds, shown with a lively charm. The Egyptian love of nature and realism appears also in their hieroglyphs, works of art in their own right.

The other region where art flowered was round the Aegean and outstandingly in the Cyclades and Crete. It was the art of cultivators and merchant sea-farers, all on a small scale, without royal grandeur. Nevertheless, many of the statuettes, mostly carved in white marble, show a sophisticated stylization that greatly appeals to modern eyes. The art that was associated with the unique Maltese temple architecture consists principally of stone-carved figures of the goddess, standing, sitting and reclining, nearly always immensely fat. The temple of Tarxien was decorated with well designed reliefs, mostly of spiral motifs.

Areas of major interest
● Centres
▲ Sites

▲ Puerto Hormiga

● Valdivia

Figurines, Puerto Hormiga

Figurine, Valdivia

Valdivian bowl

The Americas
The earliest known American potters of Ecuador now made curious little female figurines with huge headdresses. Potting began in Colombia with grotesque human and animal heads modelled on the rims of vessels and footed bowls.

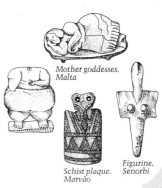

Mother goddesses, Malta

Schist plaque, Marvão

Figurine, Senorbi

Western Mediterranean
The outstanding work of this period is found in the small island of Malta. It consisted mainly of sculptures of the goddess, (one very large) and decorative reliefs in the temples. The passage graves of Spain and Portugal yielded many plaques engraved with religious symbols. Abstract human figures were carved in the island of Sardinia.

Continental Europe

Pottery was used for simple pots in Scandinavia and Britain while more elaborate forms were produced in the Balkans. Animal carvings and female figurines continued to be made of stone.

Beaker, Avebury

Elk head, Alunda

Idol, Vadastra

Chalk goddess, Grimes Graves

Danish pots, Skarpsalling

▲ Alunda

▲ Skarpsalling

Avebury ▲ ▲ Grimes Graves

▲ Gavrinis

▲ Marvão

▲ Vadastra

▲ Senorbi

MALTA

CYCLADES

CRETE

Sakkara ▲ Giza

Eastern Mediterranean

In Anatolia richly furnished tombs of chieftains at Alaca Hüyük contained bronze figurines of stags and bulls once set on standards. No doubt they represent many more works of art of a comparable kind. The artists of the Aegean, particularly of the Cyclades and Crete, now carved their finest statuettes (often in white marble) as well as producing elaborate pottery.

Bronze stag, Alaca Hüyük

Cycladic idols

Harp player, Cyclades

● Alaca Hüyük

Minoan jug

● Mari ▲ Tel Asmar

● Ur ▲ Susa

Far East

When farmers first spread into northeast China they developed the Lung Shan culture, distinguished by remarkable pottery shapes, usually in a fine black ware. In Japan the Jōmon pottery was by now highly ornate in its plastic decoration, and equally fantastic figurines were modelled.

Pottery jug, Shantung

Jōmon pot

Jōmon figurine

Huen steamer, Honan

Pot, Lan-chou

● Lung Shan
SHANTUNG

● Yang Shao
HONAN

INDUS VALLEY

● Harappa

● Mohenjo-Daro

Peacock vase, Harappa

Dancing girl, Mohenjo-Daro

Priest King, Mohenjo-Daro

Seal, Mohenjo-Daro

Terracotta toys, Indus valley

Scribe, Sakkara

Bas relief, Sakkara

Statue, Sakkara

Hetep-Heres' chair, Giza

Singer, Mari

Gaming board, Ur

Stele of Naramsin, Susa

Votive figure, Tel Asmar

Bull harp, Ur

Egypt

The sculptors of the Old Kingdom, mostly working from Memphis, made monumental royal statues, lifelike and very human portrait figures, delicate, detailed scenes in low relief. During the revolution art was debased but with the Middle Kingdom it revived. There were now new centres at Thebes and other places in Upper Egypt. Jewellery and personal effects were of exquisite design.

Mesopotamia

Grave goods from the royal cemetery of Ur reveal the sumptuous decorative art lavished on the possessions of the elite in gold and semi-precious stones. Royal stelae with figures in relief come from the southern cities, some of the best sculpture from the north (Mari).

Iran-India

A few statuettes of high quality and small heads in stone or bronze, elaborately uncouth figurines, some excellent clay models of bulls and very fine seal stones depicting animals and divinities represent the Indus fine arts. Painted pottery, usually in black on bright red, is inspired. It sometimes shows animal, bird and plant motifs.

Mesopotamia

The harps from the royal cemetery had sounding boxes inlaid with mosaic patterns and mythological subjects and bore bull and calf heads of wood, overlaid with gold and inlaid with lapis. Two styles of Early Dynastic art in the north are well represented by the vigorous, yet highly civilized singer, Uranshe, and the strangely staring votive figure from the Abu temple at Tell Asmar.

Statue of a female, Tell Asmar

Statuette of Uranshe the singer, Mari

Gold bull from harp, Ur

"Bull harp", lapis lazuli and gold, Ur

Egypt

The limestone statue (early Dynasty V) of a seated scribe well shows the individuality and naturalism of Old Kingdom sculpture in spite of his formal posture. King Pepi II, on his mother's knee, but shown as a miniature adult pharaoh, illustrates the slight decadence that set in towards the end of Old Kingdom times. The scene from Ti's tomb, in which a cowherd carries a calf across a ford, is full of sensitive detail.

Wall relief of cowherd and calf, Tomb of Ti, Sakkara

Seated scribe, painted limestone, Sakkara

Alabaster statue of King Pepy II and his mother, Sakkara (?)

Eastern Mediterranean

The typical Cycladic statuettes are beautiful but highly abstract. A few works of art come nearer to realism. A masterpiece among these is the seated figure of a harpist from Keros. It is in pure white marble. A companion piece from Keros portrays a double-flute player. Both have the curiously flattened back-tilted heads in vogue after about 2800 BC.

Marble figure of man with harp, Keros, Cyclades

Western Mediterranean
The clay model figure of the goddess reclining on a couch is the most unusual of all the Maltese female figurines. She is bare-topped, but a fringed skirt drapes her mountainous thighs. In Portugal engraved schist plaques were placed in later megalithic tombs. Though reduced to geometry, they represent female figures and are related to the eyed goddess idols of Los Millares.

Plaque, Marvão, Portugal

"The Sleeping Lady", Hal Saflieni, Malta

Beaker pot, England

Continental Europe
Pottery of the Beaker culture is characterized by fine impressed decoration often made with the rims of shells or with a cord wrapped spirally round the vase. Most pottery was made of a fine grit-tempered clay and coated with a burnished slip. The corpulent fertility goddess with its ample breasts and thighs was carved in a rough fashion out of chalk.

Chalk figure of a goddess, Grimes Graves, Norfolk, England

Iran-India
The two best, and most well-known miniature sculptures from the Indus civilization are the bronze dancing girl and the broken stone figure of a priest of divinity, both from Mohenjo-Daro. The sensuous and lithe movement of the girl contrast with the solid arrogance of the man. The trefoils on his robe may have religious meaning.

Bronze statuette of dancing girl, Mohenjo-Daro, India

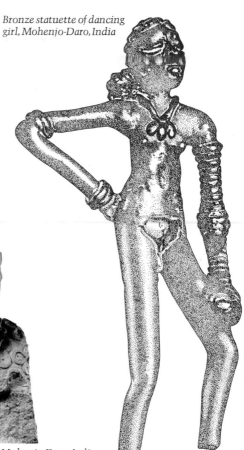

Steatite figure of priest-king (?), Mohenjo-Daro, India

Far East
The fine Lung Shan pottery of the late New Stone Age of China is represented by distinct tripod shaped vessels which imitate metalwork. Figurines of the middle phase of the Jōmon culture of Japan already show some fantasy.

Tripod jug, Wei-Fang, China

Earthenware figurine with a top knot, Middle Jōmon period, Japan

The Americas
The grotesque animal figure modelled on the rim of a large bowl dates from about 3000 BC. An example with a human face from the same shell mound has been called "one of the oldest anthropomorphic representations in aboriginal American art".

Clay figurine, Puerto Hormiga, Colombia

Region	Economy	Centres	Events and developments	People
Mesopotamia		Uruk, Kish, Ur and other Sumerian cities. Mari and Assur in the North.	Establishment of city-states and dynasties. Empire of Sargon of Akkad c.2350. Fall of Ur 2003.	Gilgamesh 2700? Sargon of Akkad Gudea of Lagash Ur-Nammu of Ur
Egypt		Memphis Heliopolis Abydos Thebes after 2040	Dynasty I-III followed by Old Kingdom 2700-2180. Social revolution and foreign infiltration. Middle Kingdom 2040.	Imhotep Cheops Pepi 1 and 11 Menthuhotep
Eastern Mediterranean		Jericho, Megiddo, Byblos, Ugarit, Alaca Hüyük, Beycesultan, Troy, Cyclades, Mochlos.	Growth of towns and small states in Palestine and Syria. Maritime trade, including the Aegean. Amorites invade Levant c.2200. Troy II falls c.2200. Indo-Europeans in Anatolia.	
Western Mediterranean		Hal Saflieni Tarxien Los Millares San Pedro de Estoril	Large and small villages, some fortified. Copper trade brings East Mediterranean influence to Iberia. Upset of settlements before 2000.	
Continental Europe		Chassey Cortaillod Windmill Hill New Grange	Further spread of farming throughout area. Further development of megalithic tombs and their spread to Scandinavia.	
Iran-India		Harappa Mohenjo-Daro Lothal	Fully developed Indus civilization with cities and ports, from c.2500.	Unknown (Script not deciphered)
Far East		Later Yang Shao Lung Shan Togaruishi	Farming spreads into E. and N.E. China. Hunting, fishing and food gathering. continues in S. China.	
The Americas		Tehuacán Valley Virú Valley Valdivia	Hunting and food gathering over most of continent. Settled farming beginning in Mexico and Peru. Earliest maize in Mexico.	

The economy bar graph indicates relative proportions of these factors: Irrigation ≋ Agriculture ☘ Hunting ⚔ Urban life ⌗ Trade ⚘

Religion	Technology and inventions	Architecture	Art and literature
Sumerian pantheon fully developed, numerous lavish temples and ziggurat mounds dedicated to each city's patron deity.	Copper and gold working followed c.2600 by full bronze metallurgy with lost wax casting. Cuneiform script. War chariots.	Ziggurats and temples, palm columns with cone and shell mosaics. Later palaces, walled cities. Royal cemetery of Ur c.2500.	Figure sculpture in stone and bronze. Bas reliefs, inlays in shell, lapis and other substances. Cylinder seals.
National pantheon fully developed. Divinity of pharaoh declines as sun-god Re's power grows. Nobility also began to claim immortality through burial rites.	Copper and gold working. Masonry building from c.2700. Sea-going ships. Hieroglyphic script. Calendar.	Mastaba tombs. Step Pyramid and temples c.2700. Pyramids from 2600. Sphinx. Fluted stone columns, carved stone palm columns, squat obelisks.	Portrait sculpture in stone and wood. Mural painting and painted reliefs. Calligraphy. Pyramid texts.
Range of local cults including fertility and mother goddess.	Copper, gold and silver working leads to Early Bronze Age. Sea-going ships. Occasional use of iron in Anatolia.	Walled towns. Shrines. Great halls or megara in Troy and Greece.	Human and animal figurines in metals, stone and terracotta, especially Cycladic idols. Fine stone vessels. Cretan carved seals.
Maltese temples: animal sacrifice, divination, libation. Mother Goddess with prominent fertility and chthonic aspects. Communal burial widespread.	Predominantly stone using but copper implements on increase especially in Iberia.	Maltese temples and hypogea. Walled bastioned forts. Megalithic and rock-cut tombs. Corbelling.	Figurines especially of mother goddess. Spiral and other large reliefs in Maltese temples. Engraved plaques.
Communal burial suggests at least respect for ancestors, but practice declined at end of period.	Stone using. Perfection of polishing stone and flint. Flint mining.	Megalithic dolmens, passage graves and gallery graves. Lake villages and substantial village houses in wood or stone.	Abstract and geometric engraving on megalithic tombs in Ireland, Brittany and Spain.
Many female figurines and probable cult scenes on seals, especially involving bulls. Ritual Great Bath at Mohenjo-Daro, fire altars at Kalibangan.	Copper and bronze metallurgy (poor) with continued use of stone; two-wheeled ox-carts.	Temple with lustral bath. City streets and houses on grid-iron plan. Ventilated granaries. Harbour works. Most building in plain, fired brick.	Small sculptures in stone and bronze. Figurines of animals and divinities in terracotta. Seal stones. Painted pottery.
Unknown	Chipped or polished flint and stone. Potters turntable in China c.2500.	Well-built hut villages.	Fine ceramics. Figurines.
Unknown	Pottery in Colombia and Ecuador. In Mexico first pottery c.2300. Cotton growing and weaving in Peru and Chile.	Settled village huts in Mexico after 2500. Beehive huts in coastal Peru.	Grotesque ceramic modelling in Colombia from 3000 BC. Figurines in Ecuador from 2300.

2000–1000BC

The Bronze Age world entered the second millennium greatly changed by the incursion of barbarians and Semitic nomads in the last centuries of the previous millennium. These incursions were still to continue and the further expansion of the Indo-European peoples during this period was of the utmost importance for the future. It remains obscure, however, since it so largely happened in lands beyond the reach of written records. This millennium also saw the rise and fall of the Hittites and the Hurrians and the Assyrians' first spasmodic successes.

One outstanding event was the first attainment of high civilization in Europe – that of the Minoans in Crete. Their palaces and administrative records kept on clay tablets show how much they owed to the orient, yet the whole style and spirit of Minoan life and arts was quite different from the pomp and circumstance of the great river valleys.

While in both Mesopotamia and Egypt the forms of civilization created during the previous three thousand years were maintained (in many ways even reaching the height of their power and international influence), this second millennium BC alerts us to the approaching birth of Western civilization. Side by side with the climax and decline of the Bronze Age came the first rise of Greeks and Hebrews.

Equally pregnant of the future was the sudden emergence of the bronze using culture of the Shang Dynasty out of the long-lived New Stone Age of northern China, and the earliest hints of ceremonial centres and monumental sculpture among the Olmecs of Mexico.

As might be expected for an age of great power rivalry, some of the most important technical advances of the second millennium were in instruments of war. The light battle chariot with its pair of spoked wheels provided a fast-moving mount from which the warriors could shoot arrows and hurl spears. Used for concerted charges, the chariotry revolutionized the conduct of pitched battles such as Megiddo and Lagash. With it went the smaller, more powerful composite bow, which intensified fire power. Another new weapon of even more lasting importance was the sword, probably invented in central Europe and widely adopted from the sixteenth century BC.

The most significant technical invention of this present period was undoubtedly the production of carbonized iron. This difficult technique was first perfected by the Hittites about the middle of the millennium, but they guarded it as a vital military secret, and it was only after their fall in the late thirteenth century that their smiths seem to have been dispersed and the new, more plentiful metal was generally adopted in the Near East and eastern Mediterranean. In Egypt it was hardly in use before 1000 BC and it took several more centuries for blacksmithing to reach western Europe.

If iron was the most lastingly important of material inventions, alphabetic writing was more than its equal as an intellectual advance. It was probably with the seventeenth century BC that the Hittites adapted cuneiform to their Indo-European language, while the Minoans of the Old Palaces from the first used a pictographic script, developing the more efficient Linear A in time for it to be used throughout the island in New Palace times. The early Greek of the Mycenaeans was written in Linear B both on the mainland and in Crete from the fifteenth century. At much the same time the Chinese Shang were employing a script ancestral to the historic form.

Like the Mesopotamian and Egyptian writing of the third millennium these scripts were no more than partially phonetic with sounds based on syllables and a vast range of qualifying signs. They were both immensely laborious and inefficient. To invent a system based on a sign for every sound required genius – and probably also courage against the vested interest of the scribes. For just as iron was to put good tools into the hands of the common man, so the alphabet put

Detail of a limestone relief showing attendants at a festive gathering, Tomb of Vizier Ramose, Dynasty XVIII, Thebes, Egypt.

The Phaistos Disc, Crete, has inscriptions stamped on its 6 in (15 cm) clay surface.

Faience "snake goddess" figurine from Crete dressed in the fashion of the Minoan court.

Phoenician ivory plaque showing a goddess flanked by two goats, Ugarit, Syria.

Late Minoan pitcher in the "Palace" style found at Knossos, Crete.

writing within the reach of non-professionals.

It seems that the invention was made by Semitic peoples in Palestine and Syria, that land where hieroglyphs and Mesopotamian cuneiform were both familiar. It may have been made in the eighteenth – seventeenth centuries BC, and a number of forms are known by 1500 BC. The earliest example of a complete ABC tablet comes from the Ugarit of about 1400 BC. By 1100 BC an early Hebrew alphabetic script had been established and also, of infinite importance, the Phoenician form was being used at historic Byblos. This was to be carried throughout the Mediterranean after 1000 BC by the Phoenicians and, through the Greeks, give rise to all Western alphabetic writings.

In the fine arts, learning, and science, this second millennium is so richly endowed that a summary can hardly be attempted and an appreciation must be left to pp 124-135. Only a few points can be brought out here. In Mesopotamia Sumerian is thought to have died out as a spoken language by about 2000 BC, but in the academies Sumerian works were both copied and composed even while the Akkadian literature of Old Babylonia was being created. Sumerian tales about Gilgamesh were certainly current much earlier, but the first actual texts belong to early in this present period, as also was the great Akkadian *Epic of Gilgamesh,* surely the earliest profound imaginative work. It became so widely popular that later versions are known from the Hittite capital of Hattusas, from Ugarit and Megiddo. Its composition was approximately contemporary with the Middle Kingdom which also saw Egyptian literature at its height with such works as the *Tale of the Eloquent Peasant* and what has been called the first novella, *The Story of Sinuhe.* The Hittites had distinctive royal annals and a few myths and legends, but in general their literature was dominated by Babylonia.

The Old Babylonian age also excelled in science and learning – mathematicians going far, though mainly in a practical spirit, with arithmetic, algebra and geometry. It is doubtful whether the Egyptians in the Houses of Life could rival them in any subject except medicine, where their preoccupation with embalming corpses gave them special knowledge.

In architecture and the arts, on the other hand, Egypt outclassed Babylonia. Nearly all the buildings, obelisks, monumental sculpture and exquisite tomb reliefs that tourists flock to see at Luxor and Karnak, Abydos and Abu Simbel were created by the pharaohs of the New Kingdom between the fifteenth and late thirteenth centuries, the Amarna art making an astonishing break in the traditional sequence.

In Crete the art of the Old Palaces consisted largely of splendid painted pottery and relatively naive figurines, but with the New Palaces after 1700 BC came the outburst of mural painting, faience, stone and ivory carving and more elegant ceramics that make the Minoan civilization the most purely delightful of the Bronze Age World.

The centuries immediately after 2000 BC saw several significant beginnings. There was the emergence of Assyria as a growing power under kings ruling from Assur-on-Tigris in northern Mesopotamia, soon to be temporarily suppressed by the rival power of Babylon. In this city near modern Baghdad a dynasty of invading Amorites established itself and in the eighteenth century produced Hammurabi, one of the truly great men of ancient history. While his Second Semitic Empire did not last long it had a tremendous impact; from that time old Sumer and Akkad became Babylonia.

The prosperity of the Assyrians in the seventeenth century BC is proved by their merchant colonies in northern Anatolia, and it is here that (through the merchants' records) the Hittites first enter history. They were an Indo-European people who had come from the north and inter-married so freely with the native Hatti that it was their heavy, Armenoid features that became dominant – as can be seen in Hittite art. In about 1750 (contemporary with the death of Hammurabi) the Hittites founded a strong kingdom to be ruled from the fortified capital of Hattusas and extending into Syria.

A few decades before 2000 BC Menthuhotep II re-united Egypt after the breakdown that had followed the death of Pepi II, and the Middle Kingdom that he established (Dynasties XI-XII) has been called Egypt's Second Golden Age. A Theban prince himself, Menthuhotep shifted the capital there for a time and so began the rise of Thebes and its god Amun towards future grandeur. In about 1786, however, when Hammurabi was only at the start of his imperial conquests, the rule of the Pharaohs collapsed once more, the kingdom split up, and Semitic nomads, the Hyksos, took possession of Lower Egypt and ruled it from Avaris.

Another collapse has to be chronicled for this time. It was with the eighteenth century BC that the Indus civilization went into decline, probably largely caused by serious flooding of its cities and a deterioration of the whole environment. The final blow may have been struck by invading Indo-European peoples.

By 2000 the Levant was recovering from the Amorite invasions which had partly

Wall painting of a bluebird among roses, lilies and other flowers from Knossos, Crete.

Carved limestone sarcophagus with painted religious scenes, Hagia Triada, Crete.

Hammurabi of Babylon, one of the truly great men of ancient history.

Hammurabi's laws are inscribed on an 89 in. (223 cm.) high basalt stele found in Susa. The upper portion shows him receiving the symbols of justice from the Babylonian sun god.

destroyed its urban life. While the Amorites remained in control of the hill country and eastwards of Jordan, in the lowlands their mingling with the native population gave rise to the Canaanite civilization with its city-states and prosperous trading centres such as Ugarit and Hazor. (This was approximately the pattern of settlement the Israelites were to find when, much later, they were to wrest the southern part of the country from the Canaanites.) It may have been in the seventeenth century that the Hurrians now under Indo-European leaders, moved into Syria and took control of its petty states.

I believe I cannot be accused of lack of objectivity if I say that the happiest, most promising of all the beginnings of the twentieth century BC took place in Crete. This was the Middle Minoan or Old Palace period of archaeology. Without any sharp break from the more rustic traditions of the last millennium, royal families took command of the island, built palaces at Knossos, Phaistos, Mallia, and a little later, at Zakro, and made them not only centres of government and religious life but also of arts, crafts, industries and both local and international trade. Administrative accounts were kept on clay tablets – the first formalized writing in Europe. Kings and queens ruled in the name of the goddess, who remained the supreme deity. The Minoans created the civilized form of a worship that we have seen at a barbarous stage at Çatal Hüyük (p. 41) and in a more advanced but still unsophisticated form in the Malta of our last period.

In about 1700 BC an earthquake destroyed the Old Palaces and their towns, but society was resilient and they were rebuilt, with their architecture and court life richer and more elegant than before. This was the time when the famous faience "snake goddess" figurines were made.

During these centuries mainland Greece remained relatively barbarous and isolated from the civilized world. This was probably largely due to the arrival from the north of Indo-European tribes. They reached the south, destroying Lerna, by about 1900 BC. Abruptly in the sixteenth century BC there was an immense increase in wealth, culture and government in the small principalities – of which Mycenae was, and remained, the greatest. This is made visible in the renowned shaft graves of Mycenae, where men and women of the royal house were buried with an amazing treasure of golden masks, breast plates, ornaments, vessels and ornate bronze weapons. The bearded face-mask once

attributed to Agamemnon, though it belonged to an anonymous prince living four hundred years before the Trojan War, nevertheless seems to express the idea of an Indo-European warrior hero. There were many objects of Minoan workmanship in these graves and during the following century the Mycenaeans, as all the mainland people can now be called (Homer's "Achaeans" is an alternative), adopted almost all their artistic and religious forms from the Cretans.

One question of special interest is how Minoan Crete came to be subjected by their pupils in civilization, the Mycenaeans. A stupendous volcanic eruption that largely blew up the island of Thera (Santorini), burying a Minoan town on Thera itself, seems to have played some part in the fall of Crete. Of all the much disputed interpretations I prefer the simplest, which says that the final explosion took place in about 1500 BC (a little before the reign of Queen Hatshepsut), and that while falling ash may have done some damage to Crete, the main blow was the destruction of its fleet (merchant and defensive). Seeing the Minoans thus weakened and impoverished, the Mycenaeans seized the island in about 1450 (the date of the death of Thutmose III), burnt the other palaces and installed one of their princes to rule from the Palace of Knossos. From soon after this time Mycenaean trade in the eastern Mediterranean boomed and there were colonies in Rhodes and later Cyprus and trading posts in Egypt and throughout the Levant, notably at Ugarit and Byblos. The Mycenaeans also sailed westward into the still prehistoric world of the western Mediterranean. They did much trade with Italy and Sicily, and it has been thought that their hunger for metals led them to contacts as far to the west as Britain at the period of the final reshaping of Stonehenge.

In the western Mediterranean and much of the rest of Europe, 2000 BC marks the beginning of the early phase of the Bronze Age when this alloy displaced copper for small tools and weapons, though stone and flint were still used for heavy tools and such things as the delicate flint arrowheads of the bowmen. Across much of Europe north of the Alps there were further movements of the warrior peoples (almost certainly Indo-Europeans) who had spread westward in the previous millennium. They played an important part in diffusing the use of bronze and of gold. They also left conspicuous monuments in the round mounds or barrows under which they were buried with their weapons and ornaments. They and their descendants played their part in the development of Stonehenge, but the history of this unique monument is discussed below.

Northern Europe, owing to remoteness and lack of local ores, remained in a neolithic stage of culture during this early Bronze Age of their neighbours, metallurgy coming to them with a burst in mid-millennium.

I have been forced by the crowding facts of its history to break our present period into two parts, so considerable is the distinction between the "beginnings" of Assyrians, Babylonians, Hittites, Minoan kingdoms and Europe's early Bronze Age and the developments that followed after about 1600 BC. The Near East and Mediterranean became increasingly a world of contending great powers led by more or less ambitious kings with well-equipped armies. With the other face of power politics, of empire building, campaigns and pitched battles went international diplomacy with the coming and going of embassies between royal seats of government, tribute and the exchange of gifts and royal brides.

One brilliant new invention gave a kind of unity to this militaristic world. The Indo-European peoples had always been associated with the horse and wheeled vehicles: now the clumsy solid-wheeled cart or wagon was replaced in warfare by the light chariot balanced on a pair of spoked wheels. Probably invented by the Hurrians in Syria, it spread with such speed among the powers that it is drawn across their history as a synchronistic line. In the sixteenth century chariotry was employed by the Indo-European aristocracy of Hurrians, Hittites, Mycenaean Greeks, and Kassites of Babylonia; it was adopted by the Egyptians from the Hyksos (among whom were Hurrians) and carried as far eastward as India by the migrating Aryans. It reached China, perhaps a little later, with the Shang dynasts. Always, as the cavalry of later times, chariotry was of great expense and limited to the noble.

In 1595 Mursilis I, one of the earlier kings of the Hittite Old Kingdom, made a sudden campaign down the Euphrates, capturing Babylon and ending the Amorite line of Hammurabi. The fall of this famous city shook the ancient world, and although the Hittites did not hold it, the throne was seized by Kassites, like the Hurrians a mountain people from the Iranian north, who had acquired Indo-European rulers. For four centuries Babylonia was ruled by a Kassite dynasty.

The stage was now set for the second half of our present period and the power struggle between Babylonians, Assyrians, Hurrians, Hittites and Egyptians, a struggle centred on possession of the northern Levant (particularly Syria) which controlled the all-important trade routes between east and west, north and south. It is a story so complex and so boring for most of us, that I have decided that I can best serve the purpose of this book by synchronizing some of its events with the history of Egypt.

When Babylon fell to the Hittites the Hyksos were still ruling Lower Egypt to well above Memphis and were in league with the princes of Kush (Egyptianized Nubians whose kingdom extended southward from the First Cataract at Aswan). Between the two, Theban princes were in humiliating subjection to the Hyksos. By 1600 BC the Thebans sought to "deliver Egypt and smite the Asiatics" and after bloody campaigning they succeeded, the Hyksos were driven back into Canaan and the victor, Ahmose, became the first pharaoh of the New Kingdom. For the whole of his mighty

King Thutmose III, sometimes called the Napoleon of Egypt. He is shown making a sacrificial offering in this white marble statue from Thebes.

Judgment of Anhai, from a papyrus Book of the Dead. Anhai is led by Horus while her soul is weighed by Anubis, Thoth recording the result.

Mural detail showing musicians and dancers from the tomb of Neb-Amun, Dynasty XVIII, Thebes.

The Colossi of Memnon, Luxor. These two monolithic royal statues are all that remains of the great funerary temple built by Amenhotep, son of Hapu.

Dynasty XVIII (1570-1304) the capital remained at Thebes, and its god Amun, linked with the sun god Re of Heliopolis, became king of the gods with his greatest temple at Karnak. Egypt emerged as an imperialist power, determined to control both the Levantine states from which the hated Hyksos had come and the presumptuous Kingdom of Kush. Thutmose I (c.1528-1510 BC), the first pharaoh to be buried in a rock-cut tomb in the Valley of the Kings, won victories in both directions. Indeed he was so successful in the north that he defeated the rising Hurrian power of the Mitanni in Syria and northern Mesopotamia and triumphantly crossed the Euphrates. These earlier pharaohs of Dynasty XVIII ruled at much the same time as the princes of Mycenae were buried in the shaft graves. Soon after the death of Thutmose I we can assume that the Shang had appeared in China and that Scandinavia entered its belated Bronze Age.

Queen Hatshepsut was a worthy daughter of Thutmose I. When her half-brother husband died, she took the double crown for herself – the first great, regnant queen in history. Girlish of face, she often had herself portrayed with the dress and attributes of a male pharaoh. Reliefs in her beautiful temple tomb in western Thebes (Deir el-Bahari) include lively scenes from the expedition she sent to Punt (Somalia?) for myrrh, gold, baboons and ivory. From a painting in her vizier's tomb comes visual evidence of contemporaneity: a line of unmistakable Minoan envoys bear vessels of forms well known from the land of Crete. Minoans appear again in paintings from the time of Hatshepsut's successor, and one carries a bull-head rhyton like the famous examples from Knossos and Zakro.

This successor was Thutmose III, sometimes called the Napoleon of Egypt. Control of the Asian territories had weakened since his grandfather's day, and he led many campaigns against rebellious states of the Levant and against the Mitanni, now a strong Hurrian kingdom. One of his most decisive victories was at the ancient city of Megiddo; later he defeated the Mitanni and emulated his ancestor by crossing the Euphrates. The tale of his exploits was inscribed on commemorative stelae and on the imposing buildings he added to the temple complex at Karnak. Megiddo was described in picturesque detail, the earliest known account of a battle.

Thutmose III's organization of the tributary states of Asia and of Nubia endured for nearly a century. Babylonian, Assyrian and Hittite kings sent placatory gifts. Wealth flowed into Thebes. It was during his long reign (1490-1436) that Knossos was occupied by the Mycenaean Greeks and it is probable that before the end of it Stonehenge had been completed.

The imperial luxury of Thebes reached its height with the reign of Amenhotep (Amenophis) III, a pleasure-loving, cultivated man quite unlike his Napoleonic grandfather. He further beautified Thebes with the temple that dominates modern Luxor. His gifted architect and namesake, Amenhotep son of Hapu, also built for him the great funerary temple on the west bank, of which nothing survives but the monolithic royal statues that came to be known as the Colossi of Memnon.

During this reign, in about 1380 BC, the ambitious Suppiluliamas became king of the Hittites and sought to crush the Mitanni, now allied with the Egyptians against him.

Amenhotep's son and successor is that most controversial of pharaohs, the "heretic" Akhenaten, a genius and mystic who strove to replace the myriad gods of Egypt by a monotheistic faith in the visible sun, or Aten. He revolutionized art as profoundly as he did religion, and probably wrote himself the lovely "Hymn to the Sun" which, through later Canaanite adaptations, inspired Psalm 104.

In about 1370 he and his queen, Nefertiti, left Thebes for the holy city they had built at el-Amarna – where they could worship the Aten among gardens and great temples open to the sun. Amarna art, with its love of nature, shows a Minoan quality, possibly introduced by Cretan refugees. The citizens of el-Amarna bought fine flasks of scented oils from the Mycenaeans, now the leading traders of the eastern Mediterranean.

The dream life at el-Amarna lasted only some fifteen years before the conservative forces recovered power and the double crown returned to Thebes on the head of the boy Tutankhamun. Amun-Re, Osiris, and all the ancient gods and their temples were restored.

One of the most significant finds made at el-Amarna was that of the palace archives of Akhenaten and his father. Written mainly in the then international diplomatic language of Akkadian, these tablets not only give a sudden insight into the cynical world of power politics, but also contain many synchronous cross-references. The great majority are letters to the two pharaohs from their "brother" monarchs of Babylonia, Assyria, Mitanni and the Hittite kingdom, and from their "servants," the regents of the factious vassal states – including Byblos, Tyre and Sidon.

Neither pharaoh had done much to maintain their power in Asia and the Hittites were challenging it. Near the end of

Water offering to the mummy, wall painting from the tomb of Neb-Amun, Thebes.

Mural from Tell el-Amarna, Egypt, shows the two daughters of Akhenaten and Nefertiti.

A painted casket showing Tutankhamun in battle was among the treasures found in the Pharaoh's tomb in the Valley of the Kings.

Hatshepsut, the first great regnant queen in history, often portrayed with the attributes of a male pharaoh.

Akhenaten and Nefertiti shown worshipping the Aten or visible sun.

Akhenaten's reign the Mitannian king was assassinated, and in about the year of Tutankhamun's premature death Suppiluliamas crushed the Mitanni and took all Syria.

The last pharaoh of Dynasty XVIII was in fact a former viceroy and general, Hahremhab, who followed a policy of law and order and of eliminating all memory of Akhenaten. It may possibly have been during his reign that the Hebrew Descent into Egypt took place, their settlement being in the eastern Delta.

The XIX Dynasty set about restoring Egyptian control of Palestine and Syria. Seti I (whose fine funerary temple stands at Abydos) and his son, the famous Ramesses II, led more or less successful campaigns into Syria against the Hittites and the petty princes allied to them. In 1286 the climax was reached with the Battle of Kadesh (on the Orontes river); Ramesses II himself fought with gallantry and averted an Egyptian defeat. He was to have accounts of the battle inscribed in several temples (including Abu Simbel) claiming a great victory; a Hittite account has also been found one thousand miles away in Hattusas. It will surprise no one in the twentieth century AD that the Hittite king also claimed Kadesh as a great victory. In fact it was indecisive and after some years the two great powers made an "eternal" treaty dividing their sphere of influence approximately at Byblos.

At home Ramesses II certainly re-established the idea of the wealth and grandeur of the pharaoh. He is famous most of all for his vast buildings with their colossal statues of himself. Of these his additions to the titanic hypostyle hall at Karnak, the Ramesseum in western Thebes and the Nubian temples of Abu Simbel are the most spectacular. He also built a new capital, Pi-Ramesse, in the eastern Delta. It is thought that Ramesses II was the oppressive pharaoh of the Exodus and that the labour forced upon the Hebrews was the building of this capital. It seems that Moses, having led them in the worship of Yahweh, then a god centred on Mount Sinai, brought them into the wilderness in about 1250 BC. At that date Hazor, north of Galilee, was still a flourishing Canaanite city; among other luxuries it imported oils from the Mycenaeans – as the citizens of el-Amarna had done a century before. The oil jars prove that round about 1230 BC Hazor was burnt and there is little doubt that this was the sack by Joshua recorded in the Bible (*Joshua II*) as the Israelites approached the northern limits of their conquest and settlement of Canaan. It should be noted that by now the Canaanites of the coastal strip can be called Phoenicians. Under

the leadership of Tyre they were founding their prosperity on the ancient timber trade, the purple dye of murex shells and metal working.

It was also at about this time that the Mycenaeans, still at the height of their maritime power and wealth, were exposed to some threat that caused them to strengthen their citadels – as best seen in the cyclopean walls, lion gate and underground cistern at Mycenae itself. This same threat may possibly have provoked them to launch the Trojan War at some date before the end of the century.

A fresh era of violence and folk migrations comparable to that at the end of the second millennium was in fact beginning. When Ramesses died in c. 1224 BC Egypt seemed secure, but already in his son's reign the kingdom was attacked from the west by a motley confederation of Libyans with refugee peoples from overseas. This incursion, driven on by famine, was part of a displacement of populations from the coasts and isles of the central Mediterranean probably caused by the pressure of migrants moving down from the north. Many folk took to their ships, whole families together, and for this reason were referred to as Peoples of the Sea.

The first onslaught was repulsed, but by the beginning of the twelfth century the whole eastern Mediterranean was in turmoil. Uprisings and invasions (particularly by Phrygians from Thrace) in Anatolia at last shattered the desperate Hittite resistance, and a disorganized horde of Sea Peoples and others rolled southward – through Syria. On land the families of the fighting men travelled in ox-carts, while a fleet of ships moved in concert with this horde. Egypt was now ruled by the last of her great, military pharaohs, Ramesses III, who had already beaten off a second attack from the Libyan deserts. In about 1170 this pharaoh defeated the land forces in Canaan. The ships of the Sea People were allowed to reach the Nile delta where they were routed in a naval battle portrayed for us in the huge, fortress-like temple (Medinet Habu) in western Thebes that still stands almost complete.

The destruction of the order that the Hittites had imposed on Syria led to the breakdown of the trade routes on which so much prosperity had depended. The Mycenaean civilization of the palaces disintegrated, art became plebeian and provincial, and many people left their homeland for settlement overseas, more barbaric folk filtering in.

The same collapse of trade and government also affected northern Mesopotamia where the Assyrians for a time went under in their long see-saw of power with Babylon. However, by

Ramesses II fought with gallantry and averted an Egyptian defeat in the Battle of Kadesh.

The Lion Gate, Mycenae, Greece, was placed outside the circle of shaft graves later excavated by Schliemann.

the time Tiglath-Pileser came to the throne in c.1115 BC the fortunes of this most military-minded of peoples had swung up once more and, in spite of further troubles, their future as the greatest power of our next period was already conceived. The situation both here and in Syria was complicated by an influx of yet another Semitic people in succession to the Akkadians and Amorites, the Aramaeans, from the Syrian deserts.

Meanwhile Egypt's defeat of the Peoples of the Sea brought her only temporary respite. After Ramesses III, Dynasty XX weakened, and its end in 1075 BC is held to mark the end also of the New Kingdom and of the true pharaonic age. Indeed, their repulse did not prevent a section of the People of the Sea from remaining in the Levant. The Philistines occupied the southern coastal plain of Palestine (giving their name to the country), wresting it from the Canaanites and the recently settled Israelites. Archaeology supports the tradition that a strong element of the Philistines came from the Aegean, deriving in some manner from the shattering of Mycenaean power. Within the last few decades of the second millennium their mounting pressure on the Israelites provoked Saul to lead the resistance, and, despite the disaster of Mount Gilboa, to open the way for David and Solomon and their united kingdom in our next period. So at one and the same time the "Grandeur that was Egypt" grew dim while the unique genius of the Jewish people rose in brilliance.

While chronicling the crowded history of the civilized world of the Near East and eastern Mediterranean after 1600 BC I have included brief references to a few of the chief events in the regions which remained in the relative obscurity of prehistory. I must now try to make the story more complete.

In spite of contacts with higher civilization there were no profound changes in the life of the peoples of the western Mediterranean but this was the time when local monumental creations (particularly on the islands) now familiar to all present-day sightseers were developed undisturbed. Rock-cut tombs were at their height at Anghelu Ruju but even more remarkable were the hundreds of tombs, some with symbol-carved entrances, at Castellucio near Syracuse. The massive *naveta* tombs of Minorca began to be built early in the period, but the well-known defensive towers, the *talayots* of this island and Majorca only towards its end. Other such towers, the Sardinian *nuraghi* and Corsican *torre*, probably the strongholds of small chieftains, seem to date back rather earlier.

The middle Bronze Age (from c.1450) in northern Italy was prosperous owing to its metal ores and close contact, probably involving immigration as well as trade, with the highly progressive bronze manufacturers of central Europe. For Spain and Portugal, on the other hand, this was a sluggish time, although in the southeast (Almeria) there were semi-urbanized communities trading with the eastern Mediterranean – as can be seen in the rich grave goods from the cemetery of the fortified hill-top settlement of El Argar.

In western Europe the barrow-building warrior aristocracy was still supreme, and especially prosperous in Brittany and Wessex. We have seen that these people played a part in developing the British henge monuments in the last millennium (p.97) and their descendants were now responsible for the architectural evolution of that unique temple – Stonehenge.

Soon after 2000 BC the Beaker people were concerned in the extraordinary enterprise of transporting the bluestones from south Wales. There seems no doubt that the next stage, the tremendous effort of bringing the colossal sarsen stones over a distance of some twenty miles, shaping and erecting them, was organized by the chieftains who were buried (as were their women folk) in the round barrows that cluster near Stonehenge. Although the foundation of their wealth was in cattle, this elite traded with Ireland and central Europe. It was formerly thought that their closest bond was with the Mycenaeans as eager customers for their metals. For a time radiocarbon dates appeared to show that the whole mighty enterprise on Salisbury Plain had been completed before the first Mycenaean princes were laid in the shaft graves. Now, however, there has been another turn of the kaleidoscope and it is admitted that the completed design of sarsens and bluestones as we see it today dates from 1500-1400 BC and is therefore contemporary with the early Mycenaean age. To sum up, I will set out approximate time-equations for the long history of Stonehenge: (1) The original New Stone Age sacred enclosure = the step pyramid of Zoser, or if this is a little too early, the Royal Cemetery of Ur and the pyramids of Giza; (2) The Beaker phase with bluestone circle = the Middle Kingdom of Egypt and the first rise of Babylon; (3) The final construction by Wessex chieftains = the shaft graves of Mycenae, or the height of the Egyptian New Kingdom under Queen Hatshepsut and Thutmose III.

By the end of the fifteenth century Britain and all western Europe were entering the middle phase of their Bronze Age (correspond-

Ceremonial spearhead of Shang period has a white jade blade and a turquoise mosaic inlaid bronze socket.

Shang bronze ritual wine vessel or tsun, Anhui, China. These elaborate vessel types either served as receptacles for meats and wine or were used for ritual ablution.

ing with the late Bronze Age of the eastern Mediterranean); the supply of copper and tin was better organized and casting techniques approached those of Sumeria, a thousand years earlier. Weaponry in particular was developed, now including long rapiers.

At about the same time the peoples of the north European plain and Scandinavia were entering their long-delayed early Bronze Age. The smiths, learning methods from central Europe, produced outstandingly fine weapons and personal ornaments, often enriched with intricate spiral designs. In the later centuries of the second millennium groups of huge round barrows were raised in Denmark and under some of these oak coffins were found within which woollen garments, bonnets and caps were preserved. Valuable bronzes were cast into bogs as votives for the gods – among them the famous Trundholm sun chariot.

Towards the end of our present period, when the Peoples of the Sea were active in the orient, folk migrations affected much of Europe, making a sharp break with the past in many regions. The outcome of these movements will be discussed in the next chapter.

The retarded but brilliant opening of the north European Bronze Age was almost exactly contemporary with the even more sudden and brilliant first Bronze Age of China. The whole purpose of this book will have been vindicated if it dispels the persistent popular belief that Chinese civilization is the most ancient in the world. Neolithic traditions had in fact persisted until about 1500 BC. The existence of a long line of Shang kings was recorded in the eighth century BC Book of Documents, but they were judged to be legendary until two of their capital cities were discovered. The earlier one was in central Honan, but in about 1400 BC the capital was shifted northward to Great Shang near Anyang. Here were the houses and temples of the all-powerful ruling dynasty where men and animals had been buried as foundation sacrifices. In one place a whole company of soldiers, with five charioteers and their vehicles and horses, had been slaughtered and buried together. Altogether 852 human victims were identified – compared with which the sacrifices at the Royal Tombs of Ur of a thousand years before appear restrained. In many of the tombs were fine jades and cast bronze vessels of the most amazing beauty and elegant stylization. Their shapes and motifs were to endure until the Han period.

A most curious custom of the Shang kings had been the taking of oracle by heating ox bones and tortoise shells. They sought guidance on matters from military tactics to the weather

and royal toothaches. Often questions and answers were inscribed on the bones, and these, together with a few signs on bronzes, are the earliest known Chinese characters. They are contemporary with the Linear B tablets of the Mycenaeans.

In 1027 BC the Shang dynasty was brought to an end by the invading armies of the Chou, apparently driving in from the west. The new dynasty was to endure for nearly eight centuries and to support many of China's greatest thinkers.

In Meso and South America the second millennium saw the beginning of the cultures that were later to attain high civilization, and for that reason it is called the Early Pre-Classic or Early Formative period. Some of the most significant developments were in South America. The art of potting seems to have spread southward into the highlands of Peru from its earliest centres in Columbia and Ecuador. It is found at Kotosh by about 1800 BC at a settlement that is far more remarkable for temples, including that of the Crossed Hands, built of stone with mud mortar and raised on a platform. In the coastal valley maize, peanuts and probably manioc were introduced to the great benefit of the food supply. Villages grew in size and the farmers and fisher folk advanced their religious life with temples and adjoining ceremonial buildings – as at Chuquitanta.

In Mexico and Guatemala potting was spreading by 2000 BC having probably begun rather earlier in the Tehuacán valley and on the Pacific coast of Panama, where it was made by simple communities dependent on the produce of the sea. With potting went the manufacture of a variety of figurines, probably for domestic cults. Although there was an increase in the size of villages (including now the Oaxaca valley) and in their houses and amenities, there is no certain evidence for ceremonial centres before 1000 BC. It may be, however, that a ceremonial organization of society had already been created on the hot Gulf coasts of the Tabasco-Vera Cruz region, where the Olmec culture with its famous "big heads", pyramids and plazas would be flourishing soon after 1000 BC.

In North America there are no great changes to record. Maize cultivation was spreading in the southwest and protein supplies were increased by the introduction of beans. In the southeast, especially Florida and Georgia, communities that had not yet adopted agriculture began to make simple pottery. The enormous abundance of salmon along the northwest coast enabled fishing groups to construct permanent villages by about 1500 BC.

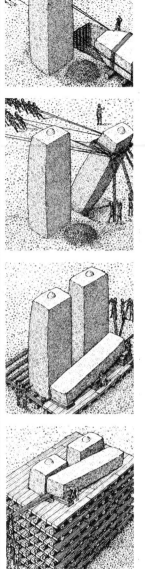

The raising of the sarsens and lintels at Stonehenge must have proved almost as difficult as their transportation. It seems that a foundation pit was dug with one side in the form of a sloping ramp and the facing side vertical. Stakes were driven in against the vertical side to prevent the chalk being crushed by the sarsen stone as it was raised. The sarsen was then moved towards the ramp on rollers, and the end levered up until the stone over-balanced into the pit. The sarsen was hoisted by means of levers, timber packing, struts and finally gangs of men hauling on ropes. The lintels were probably manoeuvred into position by means of levers and a platform built out of alternate stacked lengths of timber. The lintel was raised a foot or two at a time on temporary supports and the platform gradually built, and planked, beneath it until it was level with the tops of the sarsens.

The Trundholm sun chariot from Denmark, one of the valuable bronzes cast into bogs as votives for the gods.

Technology *2000-1000 BC*

This period saw the further development and elaboration of bronze working. New techniques such as riveting, soldering and particularly sheet metal work made the production of large-scale items possible. Moreover, advanced casting procedures using clay cores required much smaller amounts of metal. These skills spread to new areas and were widely imitated so that by the end of the period craftsmanship in central Europe was as competent as in the Near East. China apparently discovered the alloying of bronze for itself and developed it in unparalleled directions. Though they lagged in sheet metal work, Chinese casting of ritual vessels was far in advance of anything bronzesmiths were producing elsewhere.

Smiths in Anatolia now began to master the special methods of extracting useful metal from the unpromising iron ores. It was, however, only in the next millennium that knowledge of this new material spread to other areas making its impact on their cultures.

But with the full mastery of bronze working, other crafts received an enormous boost, notably carpentry. The appearance of the light horsedrawn chariot owed almost as much to the development of good wood working tools as it did to the introduction of the horse. Boat building benefited equally and the Egyptian tomb decorations of the New Kingdom show many innovations – both in their own ships and those of their opponents. Lavishly crafted furniture was a further result of these improved tools.

Writing was invented several times in the period and some changes were apparent. While early scripts had all incorporated a phonetic element, the Minoan Cretans went further with two syllabic scripts, Linear A and Linear B, in which phonetics predominated. They were written in abstract characters not pictographs. In the Levant the Hittites employed a form of hieroglyphs written in alternating directions, most of the symbols being pictographic. But they also used cuneiform, adapted to their own language, which they borrowed from Mesopotamia. The Chinese began using ideographs – characters representing whole ideas – which were directly ancestral to their present day language.

Advances in knowledge for its own sake are also characteristic of this millennium, notably Babylonian observations on mathematics and astronomy. It has been claimed, however, that these same interests are evident as well in such far-afield places as the stone circles of Britain.

Areas of major interest
• Centres

Ground stone projectiles

Metates

Bone awl

Axe

Loom

The Americas
Ground stone and bone continued to be used for weapons and tools as the New World progressed towards food producing. Intricate textiles of cotton and wool were woven on looms or twined by hand.

▲ Kotosh

Comb mould

Bone comb

Basket

Spear mould

Pottery brazier

Bronze razor

Bronze tanged knife

Bronze dagger

Western Mediterranean
Highly competent bronze work was produced particularly in the Po valley of northern Italy. Pottery and other natural materials were used for ornaments and moulds.

COMPARISON OF MATERIALS IN USE

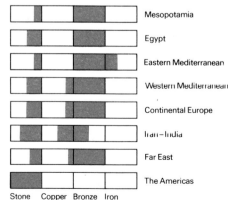

Mesopotamia

Egypt

Eastern Mediterranean

Western Mediterranean

Continental Europe

Iran – India

Far East

The Americas

Stone Copper Bronze Iron

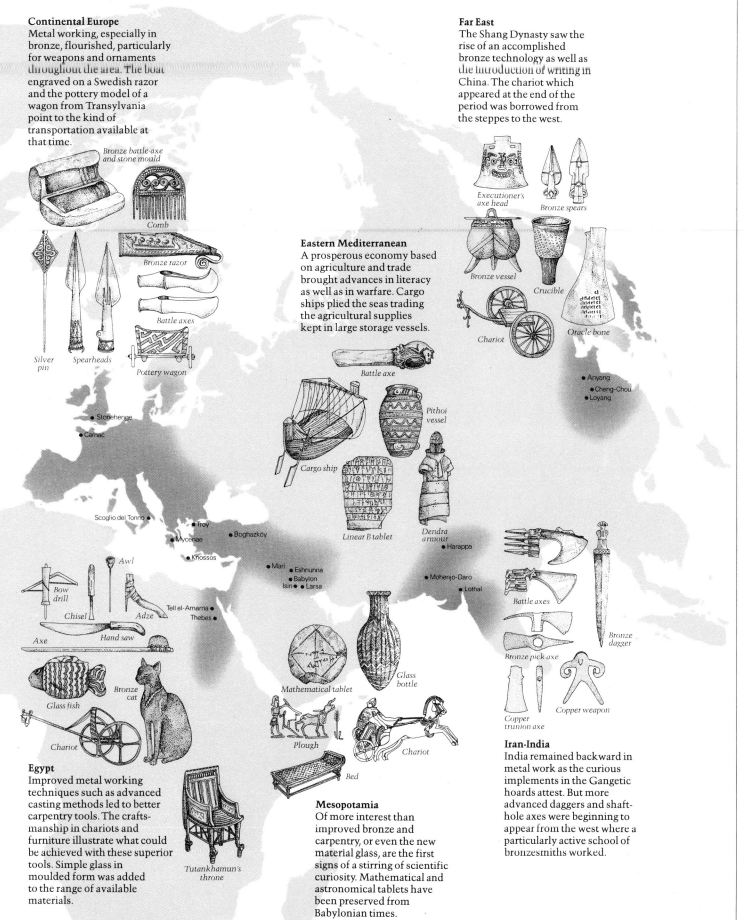

Continental Europe

Metal working, especially in bronze, flourished, particularly for weapons and ornaments throughout the area. The boat engraved on a Swedish razor and the pottery model of a wagon from Transylvania point to the kind of transportation available at that time.

Bronze battle-axe and stone mould

Comb

Bronze razor

Battle axes

Silver pin

Spearheads

Pottery wagon

● Stonehenge

● Carnac

Far East

The Shang Dynasty saw the rise of an accomplished bronze technology as well as the introduction of writing in China. The chariot which appeared at the end of the period was borrowed from the steppes to the west.

Executioner's axe head

Bronze spears

Bronze vessel

Crucible

Chariot

Oracle bone

● Anyang

● Cheng-Chou

● Loyang

Eastern Mediterranean

A prosperous economy based on agriculture and trade brought advances in literacy as well as in warfare. Cargo ships plied the seas trading the agricultural supplies kept in large storage vessels.

Battle axe

Cargo ship

Pithoi vessel

Linear B tablet

Dendra armour

Scoglio del Tonno ●

● Troy

● Boghazköy

● Mycenae

● Knossos

● Mari

● Eshnunna

● Babylon

Isin ● ● Larsa

● Harappa

● Mohenjo-Daro

● Lothal

Battle axes

Bronze pick axe

Bronze dagger

Copper trunion axe

Copper weapon

Awl

Bow drill

Chisel

Adze

Axe

Hand saw

Tell el-Amarna ●

Thebes ●

Glass fish

Bronze cat

Chariot

Egypt

Improved metal working techniques such as advanced casting methods led to better carpentry tools. The craftsmanship in chariots and furniture illustrate what could be achieved with these superior tools. Simple glass in moulded form was added to the range of available materials.

Tutankhamun's throne

Mathematical tablet

Glass bottle

Plough

Chariot

Bed

Mesopotamia

Of more interest than improved bronze and carpentry, or even the new material glass, are the first signs of a stirring of scientific curiosity. Mathematical and astronomical tablets have been preserved from Babylonian times.

Iran-India

India remained backward in metal work as the curious implements in the Gangetic hoards attest. But more advanced daggers and shaft-hole axes were beginning to appear from the west where a particularly active school of bronzesmiths worked.

Mesopotamia

The chariot was introduced from regions to the west (probably northern Syria) and revolutionized warfare. Its invention was dependent on the domestication of the horse in the steppes and improvements in bronze wood working tools. Clay tablets have preserved early astronomical and mathematical computations – a familiarity with numbers was necessary not only for calculating grain yield but also for recording the suspicious conjunctions of heavenly bodies.

Clay tablet with mathematical equation

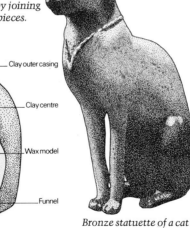

Assyrian horse-drawn chariot

Egypt

Carvers, carpenters and sculptors used these simple wood working tools not only for buildings, furniture and boats but for creating decorative masterpieces such as Tutankhamun's throne. This elaborate chair was made of gilded wood with inlays of silver, faience and coloured enamel. Further developments in the *cire perdue* or lost wax technique involving the use of clay cores resulted in a substantial saving in the amount of metal used.

CLAY CORES *The casting of expensive solid bronze items was no longer necessary and much larger objects could be manufactured by joining several smaller pieces.*

Clay outer casing
Clay centre
Wax model
Funnel

Bronze statuette of a cat

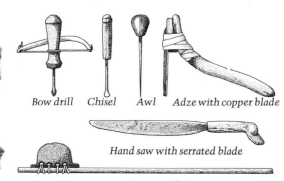

Bow drill   *Chisel*   *Awl*   *Adze with copper blade*

Hand saw with serrated blade

Tutankhamun's chair   *Axe with copper blade*

Eastern Mediterranean

The suit of armour from a tomb at Dendra was made of beaten plates of sheet bronze and hints strongly at the warfare in which the Mycenaeans indulged. Efficient trade with copper producing areas was often accomplished by boat as evidenced by the cargo of copper ingots found in a shipwreck off Turkey. This vessel had plied a trade between Cyprus and Greece. Minoan trade at an earlier date depended on Crete's agricultural wealth – wine, grain and olive oil. Huge jars or *pithoi* stored the produce received as taxes until it was needed to pay for imports or to support palace staff and craftspeople.

Armour, Dendra, Greece

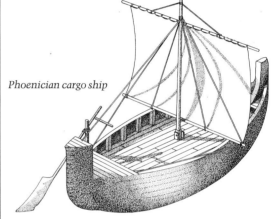

Phoenician cargo ship

Clay "pithos", Knossos, Crete

Western Mediterranean

The most advanced part of this area was northern Italy, where an active bronze industry flourished, supplied from the eastern Alps. At lakeside sites like Peschiera, at the foot of Lake Garda and close to the Adige and the Brenner Pass route, and again in the terremare south of the Po, industrial communities sprang up, advanced well beyond the subsistence farming stage. Pottery braziers or stoves for burning charcoal were among domestic equipment on sites through the Italian peninsula.

Double-edged razor, Italy

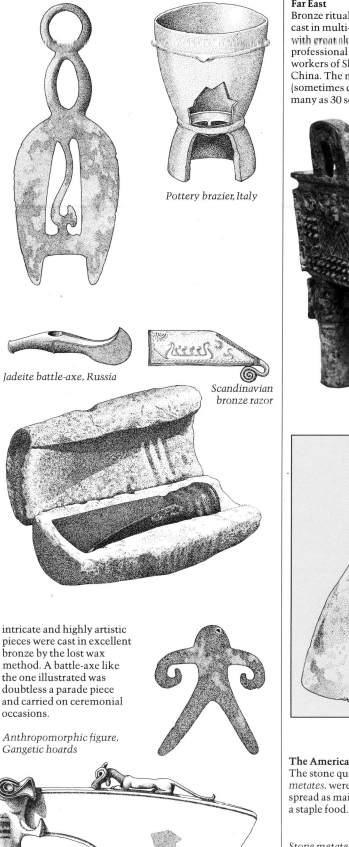

Pottery brazier, Italy

Continental Europe

Mining techniques were improved as ores from progressively deeper levels in the eastern Alps were worked. But there was still scope for the re-processing of scrap metal where natural sources were lacking as in Denmark. Bronze axes were traded widely across the continent in a time of growing hostilities. Decorated metalwork characterized ornaments and utensils.

Jadeite battle-axe, Russia

Scandinavian bronze razor

Bronze battle-axe in soap-stone mould, Denmark

Iran-India

The two ends of the region differed greatly in technological achievement. The bizarre objects from the Gangetic hoards in India are very primitive and usually still of copper cast in open moulds. But in Luristan, in the central Zagros, extraordinarily intricate and highly artistic pieces were cast in excellent bronze by the lost wax method. A battle-axe like the one illustrated was doubtless a parade piece and carried on ceremonial occasions.

Anthropomorphic figure, Gangetic hoards

Battle-axe, Luristan

Far East

Bronze ritual vessels were cast in multi-piece moulds with great skill by the professional bronze workers of Shang Dynasty China. The moulds (sometimes containing as many as 30 sections) were cast piece by piece in clay round a wax model. The relative position of each piece was ensured by dowels so that they could be reassembled in strict register. Channels and vents were added to let bronze in and air escape.

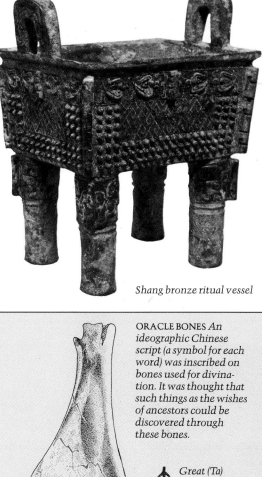

Shang bronze ritual vessel

ORACLE BONES *An ideographic Chinese script (a symbol for each word) was inscribed on bones used for divination. It was thought that such things as the wishes of ancestors could be discovered through these bones.*

Great (Ta)

Man (Jen)

Son (Tzu)

Flag (Yu)

The Americas

The stone querns, or *metates*, were now widespread as maize became a staple food.

The toughest local stone available was shaped to form a crusher, even more necessary with maize than with Old World cereals.

Stone metate, Mexico

Architecture 2000 – 1000 BC

The architecture of this period depends to a large extent on local developments rather than broad trends. In the first part of the millennium, palaces of remarkably modern appearance were designed in Crete. They not only served as administrative centres for powerful rulers but were constructed for comfortable living. The great central courtyards, bathrooms, interconnected living suites, sky-lights and gaily frescoed walls all reflected an interest in beauty as well as utility.

In Egypt a burst of temple building occurred during the New Kingdom of 1580-1070 BC. While no new techniques were employed, old ones were used in ever more impressive ways. The emphasis was on grandeur, imposing exteriors and dim and religious interiors. Most temple complexes consisted of a stone-walled courtyard, a hypostyle hall (roofed and supported by pillars) and a sanctuary. The santuary's central room housed the statue of the god and adjoining storerooms contained ritual objects. Tomb building for the most part gave way to more functional approaches, the imposing monuments having invited spoliation. But the tombs in the Valley of the Kings were monumental in the extreme and only one, that of Tutankhamun, preserved its contents.

The other centres of civilization made little advance architecturally. Quite apart from the use of perishable mudbrick, there was real decline in Mesopotamia, politically under the Kassites and economically as a result of the increasing salinity of the plains. Indus architecture, as we have seen, appeared unexciting, though incorporating advanced principles of town planning and drainage. Moreover, it disappeared with the collapse of civilization around 1750 BC in that area. Chinese architecture of the Shang dynasty is difficult to judge because of the sparse remains, and was probably far more elaborate than the surviving rammed earth foundations suggest. Any wealth of woodcarving or fabric hanging has vanished irrevocably. The royal tombs at least were very richly furnished.

But, as already noted, it is not only advanced civilizations which can aspire to a remarkable architecture. In Britain the megalithic tombs were followed by noteworthy stone and occasional timber circles. In the Western Mediterranean, elaborate rock-cut tombs and large-scale drystone fortifications were widely distributed. And while little architectural evidence remains, the first temples and monumental buildings arose at this time in Peru.

Areas of major interest
● Centres
▲ Sites

● Kotosh

▲ El Paraiso

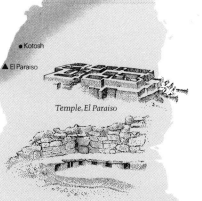

Temple, El Paraiso

Temple of Nitches, Kotosh

The Americas
The first ceremonial centres and imposing temple structures were erected in Peru at this time as at El Paraiso on the coast and at Kotosh in the highlands.

Western Mediterranean
Rock-cut tombs were found throughout the area but the fortified towers were more restricted. Variants did exist in the Balearics, Corsica and particularly Sardinia along with other more local monuments like the naveta megalithic tomb in Minorca.

Megalithic chamber, Minorca   *Nuraghe, Barumini*

Tombs, Cala Cave

COMPARISON OF MATERIALS IN USE

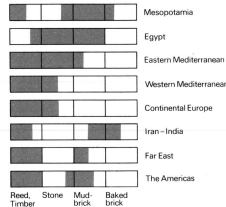

| | Mesopotamia |
| Egypt |
| Eastern Mediterranean |
| Western Mediterranean |
| Continental Europe |
| Iran – India |
| Far East |
| The Americas |

Reed, Timber   Stone   Mud-brick   Baked brick

Continental Europe

The architecture at this time varied in response to the peculiarities of each region. The farmstead of Wasserburg stood on a defended islet in a lake. The reconstructed mortuary house of Leubingen held a rich burial and was covered by a barrow. Stonehenge, focal point of a flourishing society in southern England, was the most extraordinary of the henge structures.

Farmstead, Wasserburg

Mortuary house, Leubingen

Stonehenge

Stonehenge

Leubingen

Wasserberg

MINORCA
Cala Coves

Barumini

Grave circle, Mycenae

Mycenae

Phaestos *Knossos*

Far East

The town houses of the Shang capital at Anyang were larger and more imposing than anything previous, but their rammed earth and timber construction leaves us little idea of their original appearance. The pit tombs of the royal cemetery are simple but much better preserved.

House, Anyang

Royal tomb, Anyang

Anyang

Eastern Mediterranean

The walls built by the Hittites to surround their city of Boghazköy and by the Mycenaeans to protect their town and royal cemetery were necessary defensive works. The palaces at Knossos and Phaestos represent the peak of Minoan architecture.

Town wall, Boghazköy

Palace, Knossos

Palace, Phaestos

Boghazköy

Ischali

Warka *Choga Zanbil*

Mohenjo-Daro

House, Mohenjo-Daro

Well, Mohenjo-Daro

Egypt

The great stone temples, which included many architectural masterpieces, sprang up thickly through the period of the New Kingdom. They were planned on firmly traditionalist principles, though some innovation like the brick arch from the Ramesseum was shown. Decorative obelisks had a religious significance.

Abu Simbel

Thebes
Deir-el-Bahari *Karnak*

Abu Simbel

Brick arch

Obelisk, Karnak

Temple, Deir-el-Bahari

Temple, Karnak

Mesopotamia

The temples and ziggurats of the Tigris-Euphrates were built of mudbrick, which necessitates a more stolid plan than stone. Surviving buildings do not show much advancement from the previous period.

Temple wall, Warka

Ishtar temple

Ziggurat

Temple, Ischali

Drainage system

Iran-India

Mohenjo-Daro and Harappa, with their town planning and drains, survived to about 1750 BC. They show an interesting rather than a great architecture –efficient but unexciting. Even this disappeared with the collapse of the Indus civilization.

Mesopotamia

The temple of Ishtar-Kitium at Ishchali, erected by the kings of Eshnunna, marks the end of the Sumerian phase of Mesopotamian architecture. Mudbrick was still used throughout but the plan was more complex, with a series of court-yards leading from the monumental gateways to the inner sanctuary of the goddess. Ziggurats continued to be built as at Choga Zanbil which was 174 ft (54 m) high.

Ziggurat, Choga Zanbil, Elam

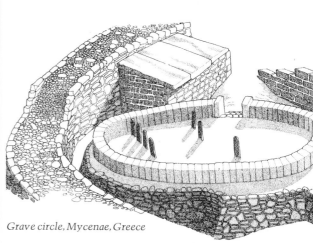

Temple complex, Ishchali

Grave circle, Mycenae, Greece

Egypt

Abu Simbel, one of Ramesses II's many temples, is no more than an artificial cave, but the scale of the project and the skill of the sculpture make it remarkable. The funerary temple of Queen Hatshepsut at Deir-el-Bahari was excitingly designed to take the fullest advantage of its setting. Constructional elements – ramps, stairs, colonnades, pillared halls – are simple but the results superb. Huge obelisks served religious purposes and the technical skill involved in their quarrying, transport and erection was of a very high order. They range up to 97 ft (30 m) in height.

Great Temple, Abu Simbel

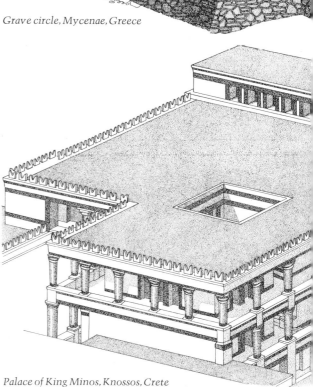

Palace of King Minos, Knossos, Crete

Temple of Hatshepsut, Deir el-Bahari, Thebes

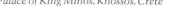
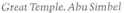

*Carved obelisk,
Temple of Amun, Luxor*

Eastern Mediterranean
The walls of Mycenae, Greece, were designed to protect the rich royal shaft graves of the noble dead as well as serving as defences for the living. The more ambitious Minoan architecture, however, was primarily dedicated to gracious living. Like the other Minoan palaces, Knossos had royal apartments, storage rooms and shrines built around a central court. Public rooms were on the second floor. Good stone was available and when used in conjunction with the timber framing gave the

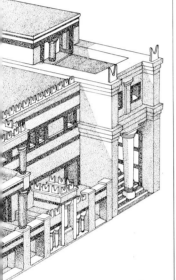

structure a measure of resilience very valuable in an earthquake zone.

Western Mediterranean
The cemetery of rock-cut tombs at Cala Coves in Minorca is carved into cliffs. Burial was by inhumation, earlier skeletons being swept to the back or thrown out to make way for their successors. Later tombs continued the tradition of communal burial. The Minorcan version was the naveta, which resembles an upturned boat. This was built of substantial but not enormous blocks of stone, set without mortar.

Naveta es Tudons, Minorca

Rock-cut tombs, Minorca

Continental Europe
Stonehenge is outstanding among the henge monuments in Britain – circular structures of stone or wooden uprights. Blocks of stone up to 54 tons were transported to this site from 24 miles (40 km) off, dressed to shape and erected. Others were raised to serve as lintels. The shaping included subtle architectural tricks like the swelling of uprights, the tapering of lintels, and the curvature of the circle of lintels over the outer ring, all intended to improve the visual, aesthetic appearance of the building. Within the main structure were subsidiary stones of

Stonehenge c. 1500 BC, Salisbury Plain, England

Stonehenge today

Mortuary house, Leubingen, Germany

around 4 tons weight. These were imported with immense labour from Prescelly, 132 miles (220 km) away in Wales. The site appears to represent the corporate achievement of a wealthy society, whose leading members lay in the barrows which cluster around. (The burial illustrated is of a similar but less architecturally inclined group in Germany.) Two major controversies have raged over this monument. The building's function has been strongly debated and questionable contact with Mycenaean Greece has been inferred from the architectural niceties.

Iran-India
An elaborate drainage system was one of the noteworthy achievements of the Indus civilization cities. The drains, like the streets, were clearly laid out and maintained by a civic

Drainage system, Mohenjo-Daro, India

Far East
The shaft tombs of the emperors at Anyang, China, are extremely simple architecturally. A pit in the bottom of the main shaft held the royal burial; offerings stood on the surrounding shelf and ramps gave access from ground level. All were cut from the compact but soft loess soil of the area. The buildings had rammed earth foundations but only these and the post-holes survive. The occasional bronze buried as a foundation offers hints at the richness of the structure.

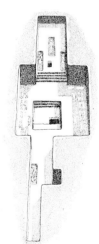

Royal tomb, Anyang, China

Shang period house, China

The Americas
El Paraiso in Peru was one of the first ceremonial centres. Terraces, steps and platforms were built of roughly dressed or natural

authority. Manholes at intervals allowed workers to clear them regularly of their accumulated rubbish. The house drains – an enclosed system of clay pipes – were connected to sewers by open brick gutters.

stone blocks set in mud mortar. Complexes of conjoined rooms were later filled with stone and earth and were used as a platform for the next storey.

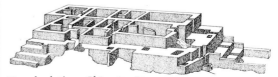

Temple platform, El Paraiso, Peru

Art 2000 – 1000 BC

In Mesopotamia the most interesting work was created by the Semitic peoples in the northern valley, especially in the enormous palace built at Mari early in the period. It had mural paintings and a collection of sculptures. The palace was destroyed by Hammurabi, whose own law stele is a good example of the maintenance of Sumerian tradition. The Kassites probably introduced sculpture in cut brick that was to be developed by the Assyrians.

The imperial spirit of the New Kingdom pharaohs is very evident at Thebes, much of it over-ripe, though some of the individual statues of pharaohs were of high quality. So, too, were the reliefs in the tombs of the nobles. By far the most remarkable event was, however, the revolution in the visual arts inspired by the "heretic" pharaoh Akhenaten. The old formal conventions were broken down, and a fresh life, movement and informality substituted. In the newly founded city of the Aten at el-Amarna, Akhenaten, Nefertiti and their daughters were shown eating, kissing and driving out together. The royal palaces contained charming murals of the bird, animal and plant life of the Nile. Even after the failure of this extraordinary enterprise and the return to Thebes, the Amarna style can be seen in many of the works from Tutankhamun's tomb.

In Anatolia the rise of the Hittite empire during the fifteenth century led to the development of monumental sculpture. Massive bas reliefs were carved on the foundation courses of palaces and temples and on natural rock surfaces. These kings and divinities were somewhat stiff and clumsy, yet conveyed a certain dignity.

The art of the Minoan Old Palaces is largely represented by magnificent painted pottery and some still very provincial figurines. It was the artists of New Palace times after 1700 BC who created an entirely new European art. It was not monumental like that of the oriental powers, but exquisite, lively, feminine, and intensely sensitive to nature.

The Mycenaean Greeks, from the sixteenth century onwards, imitate the Minoans in all their arts. Their more masculine values and lesser talent generally made their work more mechanical, while hunting and warfare became favoured subjects. The Lion Gate of Mycenae symbolizes this changed spirit.

Although the Shang emperors and their nobles are known to have elegant possessions, their art has to be judged by their ritual bronzes. These are superb, particularly the surface decoration of the more restrained pieces.

	Areas of major interest
●	Centres
▲	Sites

Head, Mexico

Head, Guatemala

▲ Tlatilco ▲ Mexico City

Relief carving, Cerro Sechin

Incised gourd, Huaca Prieta

GUATEMALA

The Americas
In the valley of Mexico and Guatemala, simple but well shaped pottery and figurines were made. The Peruvian temples of Kotosh and Cerro Sechin had a little simple relief carving and in Ecuador gourds were high decorated.

▲ Huaca Prieta
▲ Cerro Sechin

Hunting scene, Camonica Valley

Diadem, El Argar

Beaked jug, Minorca

Bone plaque, Altamura

Western Mediterranean
The early Bronze Age of the region did not produce much art, only simple craftsmanship in bone, pottery and bronze. While the rock-cut tombs in Sicily had relief carvings, in the Camonica Valley of north Italy thousands of rock engravings were made. In Spain the people of El Argar produced some ornamental bronze work.

Continental Europe
At the climax of their Bronze Age the Balkan peoples produced handsomely shaped pots, figurines and ornamental gold work. In Ireland and Britain fine gold ornaments and vessels were designed and after 1500 ornamental bronze work began in Scandinavia. In Norway and Sweden rock engravings now show ships, sunboats and human subjects.

Rock carving, Bohuslän

Rillaton cup, Cornwall

Bronze wagon, Trundholm

Gold hat Schifferstadt

Figurine, Kličevac

Far East
The territory of the Shang lay along the general line of the Yellow river in Shansi, Honan and Shantung. There superb bronze ritual vessels were cast, already assuming most of the specialized classic forms. There was also carving in jade. In Japan, Jōmon pottery and figurines became yet more ornate and decorative.

Ritual vessels

Jōmon amulet, Numazu

Jade amulet, Anyang

Figurine, Agatsuma

Eastern Mediterranean
From the beginning of the period Minoan artists of Crete painted and carved their masterpieces for palaces and country mansions. The Mycenaean Greeks of the mainland took over the Minoan styles and later spread them far overseas. The Hittites developed monumental bas relief carving on royal buildings and rock faces. Less sophisticated art forms continued in the Levant.

Goddess figurine, Knossos

Wall relief, Yazilikaya

Gold mask, Mycenae

Fresco, Knossos

Vase, Jericho

CORNWALL
Trundholm ▲ ▲ Bohuslan
Schifferstadt ▲
CAMONICA VALLEY
MINORCA
El Argar ▲
▲ Kličevac
▲ Altamura
▲ Mycenae
▲ Yazilikaya
Knossos ●   Atchana ▲
● Mari   ● Nuzi
▲ Susa
▲ Jericho
Tell-el-Amarna ●
Thebes ●
● Harappa
● Mohenjo-Daro
▲ Navdatoli
● Anyang

Iran-India
At the beginning of the period copper tablets (possibly amulets), engraved with pictographs and a variety of animals were added to the modest arts of the Indus civilization. Before 1700 the civilization was in decline.

Terracotta animals, Mohenjo-Daro

Urn, Harappa

Cup, Navdatoli

Copper tablet

Egypt
Thebes, with its temples and tombs of pharaohs and nobles, was now the great artistic centre. Tutankhamun's possessions reveal the richness of smaller works of art and fine craftsmanship. Akhenaten and Nefertiti developed their revolutionary art at el-Armarna, between Thebes and Memphis.

Tutankhamun's mask, Thebes

Mural, Thebes

Bust of Nefertiti, el-Amarna

Pectoral, Thebes

Bronze mirror

Mesopotamia
Although Semites took the lead in these Old Babylonian times, Sumerian art forms were maintained as can be seen in the stele on which Hammurabi's famous law code was inscribed, and the portrait head of this king found at Susa. The only considerable painting and the best sculpture comes from the palace of Mari. Kassite rulers introduced sculpture in moulded brick.

Vase, Susa

Goddess figurine, Mari

Hammurabi's head, Susa

Faience knob, Nuzi

Fresco, Mari

Mesopotamia
The magnificent palace built at Mari early in the period is the only place where important mural painting has survived in Mesopotamia. It is not known how many of its 300 rooms were decorated, but such scenes as we have show offerings and sacrifices being made to the god, all the participants wearing elaborate robes and head gear. These are stiff and uninteresting, but they are framed by some elegantly formalized trees and mythological beasts. The palace was once full of sculpture – including the handsome Lady of the Flowing Vase.

Wall painting from the palace at Mari

RIGHT: *Tudhaliyas IV carved in rock, Yazilikaya, Turkey. This sculpture of the king in his ceremonial robes is one of the finest reliefs at the Hittite sanctuary.*

FAR RIGHT: *Gold mask of Agamemnon (?), Mycenae, Greece*

"Bull leapers" fresco, Knossos, Crete

Egypt
The head of Queen Nefertiti from el-Amarna is probably the most famous work of art from the entire Bronze Age world. It was found in the workshop of the sculptor Thutmose and must date to about 1362 BC. It is of painted limestone, the eyes inlaid with rock crystal. This head is in fact not quite typical of the revolutionary art of el-Amarna, being too simply naturalistic. Nevertheless it is alive, personal – and tinged with tragedy. The pectoral jewel found in a casket in Tutankhamun's tomb is of gold inlaid with lapis, turquoise, chalcedony, carnelian and coloured glass. The winged scarab symbolizing the sun supports symbols of the moon. Like much of Tutankhamun's jewellery this is heavy and overcrowded. It cannot have been made more than ten years after the head of his mother-in-law, Nefertiti.

Tutankhamun's pectoral, gold cloisonné with glass and semi-precious stones, Valley of the Kings

Bust of Queen Nefertiti, polychromed limestone, Tell el-Amarna

Western Mediterranean
Thousands of engravings were cut on Italy's ice-smoothed rocks. They seem to have been made over a long period of time. Some depict hunting scenes, but many more are of houses, fields, domestic animals and ploughing.

Hunting scene engraved on rock, Camonica Valley, Italy

Iran-India
The Indus civilization begins to enter a period of decline soon after 2000 BC, but there is no reason to doubt that the artists continued their modest output, including their skilful modelling of sacred bulls.

Terra-cotta figure of a bull, Mohenjo-Daro, India

Eastern Mediterranean
Monumental Hittite sculpture flourished in the imperial age after c.1450 BC. The sanctuary of Yazilikaya near the capital of Hattusas, shaped from colossal rock fissures, is a late example, dating from the 13th century. The reliefs include scores of gods and goddesses and a few royal personages. Frescoes from Knossos range from life size to miniatures. The famous bull-leaping scene with its border simulating variegated stones is only 32 ins (80 cms) high. Two girls and a youth take part in the game. The Minoans followed the Egyptian convention of painting women with white skin, men with red. The finest of the gold masks from the shaft graves at Mycenae shows the strong, bearded face of a warrior prince.

Far East
The more ornate of the magnificent Shang bronzes is represented by the *yu* ritual wine vessel with its "tiger" motif. Other ritual vessels were far more restrained and elegant in style. Details were engraved on elaborate piece moulds before casting in many decorative motifs.

Shang Dynasty bronze ritual vessel, China

Continental Europe
The corrugated gold cup from a Cornish grave probably dates from about 1500 BC. Vessels much like it come from the shaft graves of Mycenae and it may reflect Mycenaean influence on Britain. In the northern Bronze Age the animal rock art was largely supplanted by other subjects, including ships. These might have religious meaning, being sun barges.

Engraving, Bohuslän, Sweden

The Rillaton gold cup, Wessex culture, Cornwall, England

The Americas
Without benefit of a potter's wheel the early farmers in the Valley of Mexico created their wares by coiling and hand modelling. Incision was the most frequent form of decoration, paint was used only in small quantities. Many female figurines, possibly used to promote crop fertility, were found in this area.
Head, Valley of Mexico

Region	Economy	Centres	Events and developments	People
Mesopotamia		Isin Larsa Babylon Eshnunna Mari	Isin-Larsa period 2025-1763. Empire of Hammurabi of Babylon 1792-1750. Kassites 1595, early Assyrians. Mitanni in N. Syria.	Hammurabi Tiglath-Pileser
Egypt		Thebes Tell el-Amarna	Hyksos domination leads to fall of Middle Kingdom 1640. New Kingdom 1570-1075 with conquests in Asia. Akhenaton's heresy. Attacks by Peoples of the Sea 1232, 1186.	Amenhotep 1, 111 Akhenaton Thutmose 111 Hatshepsut Ramesses II Moses Nefertiti
Eastern Mediterranean		Knossos Mycenae Troy Boghazköy (Hattusas)	Hittites move into Anatolia and found empire c.1750. Eruption of Thera. Minoan Empire collapses 1450. Trojan War c.1250. Sea Peoples sweep area c.1200. Phoenician cities established.	Minos
Western Mediterranean		Scoglio del Tonno (Taranto)	Local developments, e.g. nuraghi in Sardinia. Mycenaean trade to S. Italy, Sicily, Sardinia.	
Continental Europe		Stonehenge Carnac	Bronze working spreads throughout area, supported by trade network including amber. Warrior societies. Spread of Urnfield burial rites.	
Iran-India		Harappa Mohenjo-Daro Lothal	Collapse of Indus Civilization 1750. Survives at lower level in Ganges and Bombay areas. Aryan invasions into NW after 1500. Indo-Europeans into Iran even earlier.	
Far East		Loyang Cheng-Chou Anyang	Rise of Shang Dynasty in Honan 1500, overthrown by Western Chou 1027. Agriculture spreads throughout area.	
The Americas		Kotosh	Farming spreads slowly to all Mesoamerica. Maize introduced to S. America at end of period. Root cultivation in Amazon lowlands. Maize cultivation spreads to southwest N. America.	

The economy bar graph indicates relative proportions of these factors: Irrigation ≈ Agriculture ♀ Hunting ⚔ Urban life ⊞ Trade ⚇

Religion	Technology and inventions	Architecture	Art and literature
Sumerian pantheon continued by Semites. City gods.	Bronze plentiful. Glass, heavier plough in use. Babylonian astronomy and mathematics.	Period of comparative stagnation.	Decline of Sumerian art. Sumerian ceases at as living language. *Epic of Gilgamesh.*
Pantheon dominated by Amun of Thebes. Abortive challenge of Atonism. Osiris/Isis/Horus gaining ground.	Bronze becomes general, as also glass and faience. Fine carpentry. Horse chariot introduced.	Burst of temple building under New Kingdom, again under Ramesses especially at Thebes. Tombs in Valley of the Kings.	Vigorous art development under New Kingdom, especially under Akhenaton, particularly in fresco, stone reliefs, jewellery, furniture, sculpture. *Tale of the Eloquent Peasant. The Story of Sinuhe.*
Mother goddess, associated with doves and snakes. Tree cults, bull rites. Hittite pantheon.	Improved shipping. Chariot. Skilled pottery, metal working. Syllabic writing in Crete and Greece, alphabet in Levant. Iron technology mastered by Hittites.	Cretan palaces. Mycenaean, Trojan and Hittite citadels. Mycenaean shaft graves and tholos tombs.	Minoan and Mycenaean art in frescoes, jewellery, ceramics, sealstones, figurines, metal work.
Unknown. Possibly sun worship in North. Votive offerings in peat bogs and rivers.	Bronze working becomes generally adopted.	Nuraghi and giants' graves in Sardinia. Talayots in Balearics. Torri in Corsica. Rock-cut tombs especially in Sicily. Hut villages.	Craft competence in bronze and pottery, but later declining in north of area. Rock art in Camonica Valley, Monte Bego.
Sun and other heavenly bodies? Votive offerings in peat bogs and rivers.	Bronze working gains steadily in competence, especially for weapons. Evidence for skills in astronomical observation.	Stone and timber circles and alignments, Stonehenge (unique). Round barrows, timber built villages.	Skilled workmanship in bronze, but craft rather than art. Rock engravings in Scandinavia.
Forerunners of some Hindu gods recognized in Indus civilization. Vedic religion and literature introduced.	Rice farming. Bronze metallurgy replaces copper (Gangetic hordes).	Continuation of civic and domestic building in baked brick. City walls, drainage systems. Then return to simple mudbrick.	Continuation of seal engraving, small statues, painted pottery. Only the last survives the Indus collapse. *Rigveda.*
Range of divinities and ancestors demanding offerings and sacrifices. Oracle bone divination. Elaborate ritual vessels.	Brilliant bronze casting in multi-piece moulds. Writing on oracle bones, pictographic script. Chariots. Silk textiles.	Rammed earth foundations, timber superstructures. Elaborate royal shaft tombs.	Shang art, represented in bronzes, especially ritual vessels and jade carving.
Unknown.	Stone using cultures continue. Pottery spreads widely in Mexico, Peru and Guatemala.	First ceremonial centres in Peru. Kotosh before 1800.	Decorated pottery and figurines.

1000–500 BC

In our last period the beginnings of Western civilization and the modern world coincided with the climax and early decline of the ancient civilizations of Mesopotamia and Egypt. In the five hundred extraordinarily eventful years now to be considered the balance was clearly shifting towards the west. Although the Tigris-Euphrates valley housed the greatest power of the age, the Assyrian, although Babylon enjoyed a brief revival of wealth and fame, although the Indo-European might of the Persians loomed large towards the age's end, and although in the realm of religious and moral teaching the orient of India and China received a new light, the most potent centres of new growth, of new human outlooks, were now in the Mediterranean and were to remain there until AD 500.

In Palestine and Syria the Hebrews under Solomon had their moment of unity and worldly glory. Their religious growth flowered in the great prophets of the following centuries. The Phoenicians, seizing the opportunity offered by the collapse of the Mycenaeans and the Hebrew subjection of the Philistines, launched their immense sea trade and their colonization far to the west.

In western Asia Minor the Phrygians and then the Lydians created the wealth and luxury still conjured up for us by the names of Midas and Croesus.

In the early centuries the Greeks were in their Dark Age, reduced to illiteracy and with many refugees moving haphazardly overseas to settle the coast and isles of the east Aegean. Only with the eighth century came the thriving little cities, the Olympic games (776 BC), Homer, and the planned emigrations that established Greek colonies in the western Mediterranean and later in Cyrenaica and round the Black Sea. There they came into contact with the Scythic nomads of the Pontic steppes and helped to inspire their art.

Equally important, those Greeks who had fled to Ionia only a few centuries before now created the "natural philosophy" which took a rational view of the world as intelligible to man. It has sometimes been baldly stated that the modern world began at Ionian Miletus, the home of Thales and his disciples. Here was the intellectual counterpoint to the religious morality of the Hebrew prophets. In short, by 500 BC, the "Greek miracle" had been worked and all was ready for the classical age.

Nor was the western Mediterranean any longer outside the historical picture, as by now it was already set on the course that was to lead it to supremacy with the rise of Rome in our next period. The Phoenicians were already lining its shores with literate colonies; after the Assyrians weakened the home kingship of Tyre and Sidon, Carthage (traditionally founded in 814 BC) took the lead in trade and colonization. From the mid-eighth century the Greeks became their rivals, making many settlements in the south of Italy, Sicily, southern France and eastern Spain. These colonies and their contacts with the orient everywhere influenced the "barbarian" peoples of their hinterlands. In particular the Greeks profoundly affected the culture of the Etruscans in central Italy, later that of the Romans and other Italic tribes and the Celts. Elements of their civilization were introduced to the west long before being spread at second hand through the Roman Empire.

As everyone knows, Rome was traditionally founded in 753, but already before that time the Seven Hills had been settled by sturdy Latin shepherds and farmers. In the sixth century it became an Etruscan city ruled by the Tarquin kings and although it succeeded at last in establishing an independent Republic, at the end of our present period it was provincial and impoverished and appeared insignificant.

In France, Massalia and other Greek settlements traded with the Celts and Ligurians, introducing their rulers to some of the luxuries of civilization, particularly wine-drinking. The sumptuous burial of a

Although the woman on this sixth century Etruscan sarcophagus is dressed in the Greek style, the familiarity of the pose reflects the more equal position that women held in Etruscan society. Terracotta, Cerveteri, Italy.

Celtic princess at Vix and the quantities of amphorae and fine Greek pottery in the hill fort (oppidum) above exemplify the commerce that flowed up the Rhône valley and beyond. It is probable that this was also the main route by which tin from Cornwall and the Loire reached the Mediterranean world.

In Spain the presence of Greek settlements on the east coast and Phoenician in the southeast and on both sides of the Pillars of Hercules (Gibraltar) also had a powerful influence on the local peoples. In the east a distinctively Iberian culture was emerging, but the most remarkable happenings were in the southwest (Andalusia). The Phoenicians had founded Gades (Cadiz) as early as 800 BC. They came into contact with the mysterious kingdom of Tartessus and established a port there, probably on the Guadalquivir – a place that seemed to the Greeks on the edge of the accessible world. Thence came the "ships of Tarshish" of the Old Testament. The Tartessians developed their own shipping and traded with Ireland and Brittany; they may well have obtained Cornish tin through the Bretons. As trading partners with Phoenicians and Carthaginians the Tartessians became wealthy and developed a culture that had many oriental borrowings and yet remained their own.

There is no present evidence to support the old view that the Phoenicians themselves went to Cornwall. Yet in their marvellous ships they certainly explored Atlantic coasts, and we can suppose that the citizens of Tartessus and Gades welcomed with amazement the Phoenician fleet that in about 600 BC sailed down the Red Sea and circumnavigated Africa.

The late Bronze Age Europe which we have seen being stimulated by Greeks and Phoenicians in Italy, France and Spain was still being changed by the spread of those Urnfield cultures that had begun in our last period (p. 122). Originating in central Europe, by some admixture of actual migrations and trade contacts, they penetrated north Italy and Spain, eastern France, the Netherlands, and even just, Britain. Everywhere they vastly increased the quantity and quality of bronze and the skills of the bronzesmiths. Then, from about 700 BC, Europe's first iron using culture, the Hallstatt, grew out of the Urnfield tradition. Once again the earliest centres were in central Europe. With the many branches of the Hallstatt, historical flesh is suddenly on archaeological bones, for this was the earliest identifiable culture of the Celtic peoples.

Turning to the orient, we find India hardly emerging from the dark age following the collapse of the Indus civilization and the Indo-European incursions of 2000–1000 BC. Something of the Indus tradition survived in the southwest, yet renewed enterprise was greatest in a hitherto neglected region, the Ganges-Jumna basin, the land of holy waters that was later to be at the heart of Hindu life and culture.

Technology was backward. From the beginning of the period there were metal tools, but they were nearly all of copper and elementary in design. But by about 700 BC town life was returning, some cities, like Kaushambi on the Jumna, having fortifications faced with fired brick as in Indus times. Yet against this dusty archaeological background as it appears to us, the human mind and imagination were active. If the *Rigveda* was already composed in the previous age, the *Upanishads* ("secret teachings") and *Brahmanas* may date from the middle of our present period, although they were not to be written down for thousands of years. Then, in the last centuries of the sixth century, Buddha, the contemporary of Chinese Confucius, began his teaching.

In China we saw how the Shang dynasty was ended in 1027 when their Anyang capital was destroyed by the Chou, a warlike hierarchy apparently coming from the western highlands. They, even more than the Shang, were given to chariotry, their vehicles being light and more elegant and often drawn by four horses in place of two. They fought with the bronze halberd, composite bow and arrow and later the sword. Under the "Son of Heaven" or emperor there soon grew up a feudal society with hundreds of tiny city-states ruled from the palaces of tyrannical nobles, all bound to the monarch through social, military and religious ceremonies and obligations. They were an elite indeed, dressing in embroidered silks and furs, patronizing musicians and scholars and sending their sons to schools for the nobility.

Like many other feudal lords before and after them, these men fought, formed larger states and reduced the power of the emperor to a sham. Already he was hardly more than a puppet when in 722 BC a barbarian attack on the old capital in Shensi obliged the court to move east to Loyang. However, in this period southern and northern China were at last drawn into the area of civilization. Also the feudal states certainly supported some civilized ways and individuals. One of the smallest, that of Lu in Shantung, patronized Confucius, expounder of his notion of "goodness" who, like Plato, both founded an academy and tried in vain to lead rulers into the way of "right government." He was still travelling hopefully from state to state at the end of our period.

It is worth noting the extraordinary number of great thinkers living in this sixth century BC. Travelling westward with the sun, we find Confucius and Lao-Tse, founder of Taoism; the Buddha in India and Zoroaster in Persia; Thales, Anaximander and the other natural philosophers in Ionia and Pythagoras, the mystic mathematician, in Italy. Nearly all these were alive at the same time and were in their various ways striving to relate man to the universe not by the old means of myth and rite, but by new modes of intuition, morality and reason. How to account for it? The homes of the sages were strung out over many thousands of miles and most knew little of one another.

In the Americas the first half of the present millennium coincides with the Middle Formative or Middle Pre-Classic of archaeology. The Olmecs were now unquestionably in the van of progress. During the years when Solomon was building the Temple at Jerusalem, Olmec villagers were coming together and labouring to build monumental ceremonial centres such as those of San Lorenzo, La Venta and Tres Zapotes, and carving the famous "big-heads" that were a feature of all three centres. On an artificial platform courts, mounds and pyramids were laid out with formal precision. At La Venta, a small island in the midst of swamps, there was a ball court, prototype of the renowned courts of Mayan and Aztec times. The work that went into the big-heads was prodigious: they were carved from single blocks of basalt, the largest nine feet high. Basalt was also used for stelae with scenes cut in relief and for tombs, probably those of high priests. The Olmecs made small jade carvings and ceramic figurines. They often gave human subjects baby-like features. When these were combined with fangs and other feline attributes of a jaguar cult, the result is most sinister.

Olmec influence radiated to many parts of the country, particularly to the Valley of Mexico and to Oaxaca. The noble ceremonial centre of Monte Alban, just outside the modern town of Oaxaca, was founded c.700 BC and two hundred years later the first datable hieroglyphic in the Americas was set up.

In South America, although the old fishing economy persisted, there was an increased dependence on agriculture, including maize cultivation. Farming was also extending into Amazonian territory. From the beginning of the period, and therefore simultaneously with the Olmecs, the Chavín culture was spreading through the highlands and coasts of Peru. In the northern highlands, not very far from Kotosh was the ceremonial centre of Chavin de Huántar. It comprised sunken plazas and platform-like buildings with good masonry facings riddled with passages and chambers and embellished with sculptures. These show a strange assortment of animal features drawn from jaguars, condors and snakes. Among them are two divinities, a "smiling" god, largely feline, and a "staff" god with a rod in either hand. The Chavin people advanced weaving, often using the backstrap loom in place of twining, and in some coastal regions began the great tradition of plastic ceramics in the form of human heads and animals. As the Chavin culture is so distinctive, and occasionally seems to be associated with fortifications, it is possible that it was introduced by an invading people.

Meanwhile in North America, too, fresh enterprise coincided with the opening of the

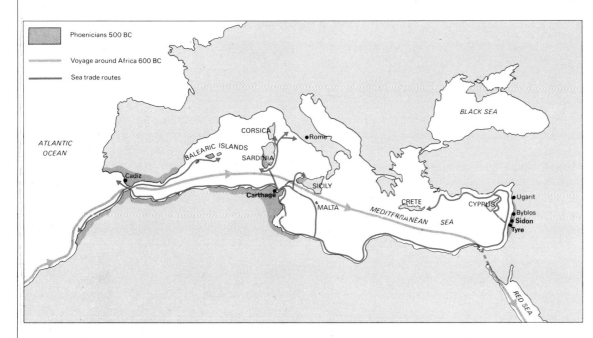

Phoenicians 500 BC

Voyage around Africa 600 BC

Sea trade routes

In vessels such as this early bireme found on an Assyrian wall relief the Phoenician sailors travelled throughout the Mediterranean world.

Among the technological advances of this period the further development and diffusion of iron working must be of prime significance. In particular its adoption on a large scale by the martial Assyrians greatly enhanced the might of their invincible armies. Its spread to the west took place mainly in this period, being stimulated in the Mediterranean by Greek and Phoenician colonies. In continental Europe it was associated, as we have seen, with the Hallstatt culture. It was just beginning to reach Britain and Scandinavia by 500 BC, though principally through imports. The Chinese reaction to the metal was characteristic. Iron working began under the Chou, probably towards the end of our present period, but from the first, perhaps thanks to their efficient furnaces, the Chinese learnt to cast it, a method requiring a very high temperature – and not mastered in Europe before mediaeval times. Their name for it meant "ugly metal" and it may have been for aesthetic reasons that it was not adopted by the aristocracy for their weapons until the following period.

The Assyrians were largely responsible for other new instruments of war. They developed the use of cavalry, consisting of mounted archers and lancers, as effective in this age as the chariotry had been before. It is possible that it was the Persians who invented the stirrup (they were playing polo by 525 BC). The most ingenious devices of the Assyrians were siege engines of various kinds, outstandingly the battering rams so often shown in their bas reliefs. Armoured, wheeled cars with either a great metal beak or a swinging ram, they were propelled by the soldiers inside against the gates or walls of fortified cities (p. 154).

The Phoenicians were probably in the lead in building longships with two banks of rowers below deck and with low beaked prows for ramming the enemy or shearing off his oars.

The peaceful arts of trade and communication also had their triumphs. We have seen how the brilliant idea of alphabetic writing was born in the Levant (p. 114). By the tenth century the Phoenicians had standardized their 22 letter (vowelless) alphabet and the Hebrews and Aramaeans theirs. Before 800 BC the Greeks had adopted and adapted the Phoenician alphabet, in comfortable time, it is thought, for Homer to be able to write down his epics half a century or so later. Its further transmission to Etruscans and Romans has been mentioned.

The other important advance was the invention for trading purposes of true coinage to take the place of barter or the many unstandardized forms of currency. The credit for this

In addition to well-designed works in bronze Hallstatt artists also produced decorative pottery such as this earthenware platter from Germany.

Bronze tiger's head inlaid with silver, Chou Dynasty, China.

first millennium. In the woodland region of the southeast, along the Ohio and Mississippi valleys, the former hunters and food gatherers began to cultivate various plants including sunflowers, gourds – and perhaps maize as well. They also made simple pottery. Most remarkable was a funerary cult which led them to bury their dead, sometimes dressed with red ochre, in house-like wooden constructions below large mounds. They had also taken another step forward in human enjoyment: they smoked tobacco. Most of their pipes were simple stone tubes but a chiefly grave contained one in the shape of a man with huge ear-plugs – an ornament of the elite.

A scene from an Attic vase shows the Greek hero, Theseus, slaying the Minotaur.

Homer. His epics have had undying influence on western civilization.

The Assyrian human-headed winged lions which served as guardians of palace gateways had five legs so they could be viewed realistically from all angles.

goes to the seventh century Lydians. At first the stamped coins were of electrum, but Croesus produced beautiful gold staters and silver shekels. The Greeks introduced coins stamped with a guaranteed weight and purity. The Greeks quickly embraced the idea and a hundred years later their cities were nearly all minting their own bronze and silver coinage. The practice quickly spread through the civilized world.

In literature and the visual arts the achievements of this great period are so many that I cannot do more than name a few of the most outstanding. Homer, of course, must come first, both for the wonder of his epics and their undying influence on Greek and all western civilization. If Homer had not been at work in the mid-eighth century (incorporating many memories of the Mycenaean age) Hesiod, one generation later, would have appeared a giant. With the seventh-sixth centuries came the Ionian natural philosophers with their speculative writings; further north up the coast of Asia Minor the Aeolian poets, greatest among them Sappho, were writing poetry more intense and more personal than anything attempted before. A popular literature of the sixth century is represented by the fables of Aesop.

The only other literature in this period of comparable significance for the future was that of the Hebrews, much of it incorporated in the Christian Bible. The Song of Solomon,

owing much to the Egyptians, was supposedly set down while the Greeks were in their illiterate Dark Age. The greatest age was the eighth century with Amos, Hosea and Isaiah who were all approximate contemporaries of Homer. Perhaps not many people think of Jeremiah as an almost precise contemporary of Sappho.

In Egypt, Babylon and Assyria literary activity was largely dependent on the past, more scholarly than creative. To one stupendous effort of this kind we ourselves owe so much that it must be chronicled. In the mid-seventh century the powerful Assyrian king, Assurbanipal, sent out his learned men and scribes to collect and then copy texts from all over Mesopotamia. The result of their labours, tablets stored in the royal library at Nineveh, is the source of much of our knowledge of Sumerian and Babylonian literature – including the famous discovery of the tablets of the Babylonian version of the "Flood" story from the *Epic of Gilgamesh*.

I have already mentioned the oral religious works in India – the Sanskrit *Upanishads* and *Brahmanas*. The older parts of the Persian *Axvesta* is of this period, including the *Gathos* of Zoroaster – like Jeremiah, a near contemporary of Sappho. In China there was the poetry anthology of the *Book of Songs* and at the very end of the sixth-early fifth century BC, the *Chronicles* and *Narratives of the States* of Tso-ch'iu Ming and the works of Confucius.

In the visual arts and architecture this present period is overwhelmingly rich. It is also highly eclectic. The increasing contacts between peoples through trade, travel, war, colonization and nomadism, led to influences and borrowings between them which were innumerable and sometimes hard to disentangle. The Neo-Babylonians, Assyrians, Urartians, Phoenicians, Greeks, Persians, Scythians and Etruscans were all within the web of influences. The Egyptians are not included only because while they gave much (particularly to the Phoenicians) they borrowed little. Indeed, in this late and troubled phase of Egyptian history artists did their best to reproduce the styles of earlier times.

1000–500 BC is the last period in which Mesopotamia remains a centre of interest. The three capitals of conquering Assyrian kings – Nineveh, Nimrud (Calah of the Old Testament) and Dur-Sargon (Khorsabad) with their citadels crowned by ziggurat, palaces and temples, were cities of great magnificence, rich in monumental sculpture. The old Babylonian and Sumerian inheritance was still with the Assyrian artists and builders but clearly modified. The most familiar and typical works were the colossal, monolithic, human-headed and winged bulls and lions that guarded gateways.

A new departure was to line palace rooms and passages with thin slabs of stone with bas reliefs that were originally painted. Some show processions, some narratives of battles, sieges or lion hunts. They are stiff, impersonal, yet at their best – outstandingly in their portrayal of animals – the reliefs are full of vigour and a kind of nobility. This school of sculpture was established by the reign of Assurnasirpal in the early ninth century and maintained through the imperial age. Setting it beside Greek dates, we see that it began during the Geometric Age when there was virtually no monumental sculpture or architecture in Greece, spanned the life of Homer and ended at about the time when the lions of Delos were being carved.

After the fall of Assyria and its cities, in the sixth century when the orders of classical architecture were being established in Greece, Babylon had its final and notorious burst of splendid extravagance. Nebuchadnezzar transformed ancient Babylon, constructing the great ceremonial way and Ishtar gate lined with friezes of lions, bulls and dragons in carved, glazed tiles (p. 158), and rebuilding the temple of Marduk which included a large hall lined entirely with gold. He also restored the ziggurat to eight or nine storeys and some 325 feet (100 m) in height. It was, almost beyond question, the original behind the Tower of Babel story in *Genesis*.

The flowering of Persian art also belongs late in this period. From the seventh century onwards there survive marvellous gold and silver drinking horns and rhyta ending in animals, real and fabulous, and vessels with pairs of animal handles. (The Greeks were later amazed by the rich furnishing of their enemies' banquets). These and other early Persian works of art and architecture show influence from Urartu, but later, as the Persians conquered most of the civilized world, they inevitably drew styles as well as actual craftsmen from their subject peoples. Cyrus the Great, who founded the Achaemenid empire in the mid-sixth century, built a capital at Pasargadae; he gave it Assyrian-style winged bulls at its huge gatehouse and set up a relief image of himself wearing a Syrian robe and an Egyptian head-dress – a combination that suggests Phoenician workmanship. Such was the eclecticism of the time! Cyrus' tomb at Pasargadae remains a well-known monument.

When Darius secured the throne in 521 BC he soon moved to create two even more famous works of monumental art: the rock sculpture of Behistun with its victory inscription in Old Persian, Elamite and Babylonian, and in 517, the ceremonial city of Persepolis, vast in scale and

Assurnasirpal, a great conquering Assyrian king.

Cyrus' tomb, Pasargadae, Iran.

King Darius shown at his royal palace at Persepolis receiving a high Median official.

with a most masterly blending of many styles. The relief carvings of delegations from all the satrapies of the empire are not only fine and full of human detail but make a true historico-anthropological exhibit of the peoples, costumes and equipment of the time. Persepolis, however, was not finished until about 460 BC although much had been done by the end of our present period, and while it is proper to accept it as yet another marvel of the marvellous sixth century, it is discussed in greater detail in our next chapter.

The art of the Scyths, whose mercurial history was so much involved with that of the Medes and Persians, demands attention for its individual force and beauty, as well as for its lasting influence on the Europeans of our last two periods.

The Scyths were true barbarians in their love of personal adornment and as nomads lavished their wealth on such display since their possessions had to be portable. Although they borrowed ideas from many of their contemporaries, notably from the Greeks of the seventh century and the Achaemenid Persians later, their art was distinctive. It is at its best in the splendid animal style of golden ornaments and vessels.

Of all the visual arts of 1000–500 BC that of the Greeks was, of course, to be the most significant. The period began for them in simple austerity. When the Phoenicians in

An Olmec jade carving with typical baby-like features.

One of the monumental basalt "big-heads" that were a feature of the Olmec ceremonial centres; Vera Cruz, Mexico.

Kouros figure known as the "Strangford Apollo", parian marble, Anaphe, Greece.

Tyre and Sidon and the Hebrews in Solomon's Jerusalem were living and building in the grand oriental tradition and when, for that matter, the Olmecs were sculpting their giant heads, Greek art is represented by the sober Geometric pottery of Athens, while its architecture was still rustic. Then in about 800 BC Greeks renewed the contacts with the Levant that their Mycenaean forebears had known so well and during the next two centuries potters and bronze workers in many parts of the Greek world were adapting oriental motifs and such fantasies as the griffon to their own ends. By the mid seventh century when Assurbanipal was filling his library amid all the wealth of Nineveh, the artists of Corinth were just beginning to find the magic of Greek vase-painting. By this time, too, the idea of stone colonnades, inspired from Egypt, was just beginning and by the end of the century the Doric and Ionic orders had been created. Progress accelerated and before Babylon fell, the Greeks were able to build noble Doric temples such as those we know at Corinth and Paestum and Ionic masterpieces such as the temple at Ephesus.

Just as the Greeks took the idea of monumental stone architecture from the Egyptians and transformed it, so, too with sculpture. Hitherto they had made only small figures, but by about 600 BC they were using their island marble to carve the naked youths *(kouroi)* who from the first had more sense of life and humanity than their Egyptian models. The story of how, during the sixth century, the youths assumed the "archaic" smile, were joined by the fully clad maidens *(kourai)* and gradually came to full life and naturalism is one of the most familiar in all art history. By this time, too, figure sculpture was animating the pediments and metopes of temple architecture.

At the beginning of the first millennium Italy was still part of the prehistoric world of Urnfield farmers. Although they were skilful bronze workers, art did not go much beyond handsomely embossed vessels and helmets. Then with the coming of Greek settlements and trading contacts with the eastern Mediterranean the Etruscan civilization was quickly kindled and by the seventh century Italy was part of the fully civilized world.

The Etruscans usually built their towns on hill tops; almost nothing survives of their early architecture, but probably already they were walled and gated in good, massive masonry – as they certainly were in our next period. They proved poor sculptors in stone, their talent being for working in bronze and terracotta and paint. They were also marvellous gold-

The Apollo of Veii, one of the figures which decorated the roof of the Etruscan Portonaccio Temple.

smiths and jewellers. Some would say that Etruscan art was hardly more than a branch of the Greek, yet their portrayal of human beings had an intense nervousness and nervous energy – the latter also apparent in their brilliantly-rendered animals. It was at its height in the sixth century in such works as the famous husband and wife sarcophagus from Cerveteri and the Apollo of Veii. The preservation of sixth century tomb paintings, full of lively scenes of everyday life, has provided a unique addition to our knowledge of Mediterranean art.

There is little to add to what has already been said about the more westerly part of the Mediterranean, except to single out Sardinia for the further elaboration of its *nuraghi* (p. 159) and the naive animation of its little bronze figurines. In France and Britain the building of *oppida* or hillforts had begun, but will be more fully treated with the flowering of the Celtic Iron Age, in our next chapters. In Denmark the perfect form of the *lur* horns (p. 156) makes them true works of art, while golden bowls, bronze helmets, shields and ornaments are full of vigour and good craftsmanship.

In China the bronze vessels of the Chou dynasty maintained the high standards and most of the regular ritual forms of the Shang, though in the seventh century the shapes might be over-elaborate as in the famous set of vessels from a tomb of Feng Hsiang.

For the Americas we have only to recall the ceremonial centres and marvellous sculpture of the Olmecs and the architecture and sculptural pottery of the Chavín.

I must end this account of our present period with a summary of the more political history of the lands of western Asia and the eastern Mediterranean. By this fully literate age there are inexhaustible sources of information from the records of the peoples concerned – the Hebrew history of the Old Testament is the most familiar in western civilization and the Assyrian annals perhaps the most reliable. One change that can best be mentioned here was the success of the Aramaeic language. By 1000 BC the incursions of the Aramaean Semites from the desert had largely subsided; they had established small kingdoms along the Euphrates and in Syria and had considerable influence in Babylonia. In general they absorbed the culture of the civilized peoples around them, but their language, written in alphabetic script, was adopted through much of Mesopotamia. It was spoken by the Jews from the time of the "Babylonian captivity" and was, of course, to be the language of Jesus. It was also adopted by the Persians of the

Achaemenid empire and so became the leading diplomatic language – as Akkadian had been in the last millennium.

At the centre of the political history of this period were the Assyrians with their appetite for conquest. The spearpoint of their ambition was, once again, to control the trade of western Asia and therefore to subject Syria and the Levant. The inevitable response of their neighbours was to form alliances (always unstable) against them. The configuration of peoples and powers around them had changed very greatly. Their most immediate opponents were regroupings of Hittites and Hurrians. Hittite city-states occupied territories from the Taurus Mountains down the Euphrates to a little beyond their chief city of Carchemish and southward even to the north Syrian coast. Adjoining the Hittite kingdoms, and Assyria's neighbours in the northeast, there was growing up the strong mountain kingdom of Urartu, centred on the Lake Van region of Turkish Armenia. The Urartians were of ancient Hurrian stock and may have been reinforced after the fall of Mitanni.

The Urartians were occasionally to be allied against the Assyrians with a people living to the west of them in Anatolia: the Phrygians. They are thought to have been Thracians who were forced eastward across the Bosphorus. They reoccupied several former Hittite cities, including Hattusas itself, and by the eighth century kings who seem to have held the legendary name of Midas had their capital at Gordion. To the south of them there emerged the Lydian kingdom, ruled from Sardis, on the Pactolus, and owing its "rich as Croesus" reputation largely to the gold found in this river. Both Phrygians and Lydians were in turn very much involved with the history of the Greek refugees who from the end of the second millennium had been settling the coast and islands of the peninsula: Dorians in the south, Ionians largely from Athens in the centre and Aeolians in the north. (By way of establishing links I will recall that Homer was an eighth century Aeolian, probably from Chios, that Sappho, in c.600 BC sang that she would not give her daughter for all the power of Lydia, and also took an interest in a fashionable headdress worn by the ladies of Sardis.)

Further north a new and very long lasting way of life was emerging on the vast open steppe lands stretching from the Hungarian Plain to the Gobi deserts. It seems that warlike tribes took to horse riding, and having the settled pastoralist farmers of the more fertile steppes at their mercy, led them into a true pastoral nomadism that produced a certain uniformity of culture right across the steppes, so that the nomads who attacked the Chou in China had a chain relationship with the Cimmerians and Scyths whom we shall find embroiled in our civilized Near Eastern world. Nearly all the warrior nomads at this time seem to have been of Indo-European stock, and wore snug tunics, trousers and felt boots. Even the raiders in China were said to have had red hair and green eyes! Other Indo-European peoples, mountainy men rather than nomads, were the Medes and Persians living south of Lake Urmia. Before their own imperial days, they became a threat to Assyria.

Beyond the obstacle to their expansion made by the Hittites, the Assyrians had to deal (after the splitting of Solomon's empire) with the tribal kingdoms of Israel and Judah, with Ammonites and Moabites, and the rich Phoenician cities. Egypt in her decline intervened, usually ineffectively, at last provoking her own conquest by Assyria.

Only towards their Babylonian neighbour was the policy of the Assyrian kings less aggressive. Recognizing their great cultural debt to the ancient south and their many historical ties, they were usually conciliatory of Babylonian pride, though in fact keeping the upper hand. From about the eighth century Babylonia was sometimes called Chaldea – best known from the biblical "Ur of the Chaldes". The Chaldeans were a branch of the Aramaean Semites who may originally have been settled in the extreme south of ancient Sumeria, but by the seventh century their kings had control of Babylon. Eastward of them the irrepressible kingdom of Elam was still thriving and was drawn into the Assyrian wars.

This, then, in roughest outline, is the setting in which for the three middle centuries of our present period the Assyrians dominated the political and military history of the Near East. It so happens that in the opening century they were in one of their periodic declines, while the Egyptians also were weak and taking little interest in Asian affairs. So there was no great power to prevent David from unifying his kingdom and founding Jerusalem on the hill from which he had driven the little Canaanite tribe of the Jebusites, none to intervene even when Solomon extended his rule to the Red Sea and the Euphrates and made his capital one of the most brilliant and civilized of the age. However, it did not need a great power to bring about the collapse of so much promise. Tribal envy of the power of Judah, armed by religious disapproval of the oriental extravagance and idolatry of the court, split the kingdom into Israel and Judah soon after

Solomon's death in 933 BC. It was only a little later that Egypt, led by a more vigorous, if usurping, Libyan pharaoh, Shoshenk (biblical Shishak) raided Jerusalem and carried off the rich temple treasure, including the golden shields of Solomon.

Thereafter the Hebrew kingdoms were caught up in the endless fighting and rivalry chronicled in the book of *Kings*. It can at least be said that Egypt, Assyria and Babylon fulfilled the worst monitions of the prophets.

With the ninth century the Assyrians were regaining their strength and building their army into the splendidly equipped, ruthlessly directed machine that made their name terrible to all within its reach. Assurnasirpal (883-859 BC) was the first king whose conquests surpassed those of Tiglath-Pileser in our last period. It has been said by a learned admirer of the Assyrians that "his track was marked by impalements, by pyramids of human heads and by other barbarities too horrible to be described." He won booty and tribute from Kurds and Urartians in the mountains, from the Hittite and Aramaean kingdoms of Syria and from Phoenicia he forced the Babylonians to sue for peace. With some of the treasure he built a great citadel and palace at Nimrud (Calah) and for the housewarming claimed to have feasted fifty thousand people, among them many foreign potentates, for ten days, providing some 18,000 cattle and sheep, 35,000 birds of many kinds and vast quantities of wine and beer. That was the Assyrian style. Just as Solomon had employed Phoenician craftsmen on his temple, so too did Assurnasirpal and his son Shalmaneser III. I have myself seen exquisite ivories, carved by them in the Egyptian manner, lifted from the dust of fallen Nimrud.

This son, Shalmaneser, who reigned for thirty-five years, was as tireless a campaigner as his father, particularly against the Urartians, who were now organizing resistance in the north, where he sacked the royal city, piled up the heads of its defenders, burnt many villages and then went to Lake Van where, as he said, "I washed my weapons in the sea and offered sacrifices to my gods". Shalmaneser also fought much in the west against a confederation of the kings of Syria and Palestine. Ahab, king of Israel, was among those whom he defeated at the battle of Karkar. Ahab, it will be remembered, had married a princess of Sidon, Jezebel, a marriage that brought him wealth but also the condemnation of Elijah. Although he himself remained with Yahweh, he built a temple of Phoenician Baal for his wife. Later, Jehu of Israel is among those recorded to have

brought Shalmaneser a great tribute of gold and silver vessels.

Assurnasirpal and his son had raised the first Assyrian empire to its height, but they fought for wealth and general domination, making no attempt to establish any permanent control over their victims. This was changed when in 745 BC, after civil strife and a revolt by the army, a military adventurer took the throne. His name was Pul (as it remains in the Old Testament) but this near contemporary of Homer assumed the name of Tiglath-Pileser and set about establishing an empire as wide as that of his namesake. What was new was his unification of the Second Empire under a

A relief of King Sargon II found at the royal palace, Khorsabad, Mesopotamia.

central government. Conquered lands were put under governors and forced to pay a fixed tribute. Rebellion was punished by ferocious means that included the deportation of peoples to distant parts of the realm.

Tiglath-Pileser fulfilled his ambitions, crushing resistance north, south and west. Of his exploits in the west, he is probably best remembered for his dealings with Ahaz, king of Judah, who offered treasure and his own submission in exchange for help against his enemy of Israel and those leagued with him. The greatest of the prophets, Isaiah, denounced this lack of trust in the Lord. Some years later, in the reign of Sargon (722-705 BC), Israel was finally destroyed and Judah left alone to maintain the worship of Yahweh.

Stability was never attained; fresh revolts and new alliances against the Assyrians meant almost perpetual warfare. Sargon (he had given himself this ancient Akkadian name) in addition to all the old enemies had to cope with Elam, with an ambitious Chaldean usurper in Babylon and with Egypt's ineffectual encouragement of Palestinian rebels. It was in his time, too, that nomad peoples began to impinge on western Asia. The Cimmerians, who had ruled north of the Caucasus, seem to have been pushed southward and having annexed northern Urartu, joined the Urartians against Sargon. The Scythians moved into their old territory and a few decades later were to drive the Cimmerians into their famous invasion of Asia Minor. Sargon also had dealings, sometimes friendly but more often hostile, with the Medes and Persians (Maddai and Parsua) now established southeast of the Caspian and thrusting into the Zagros.

The second Assyrian Empire approached its peak under Esarhaddon, who won the throne in 681 BC. He was a brilliant soldier but also a statesman prepared to follow conquest by conciliation. One of his first acts was to restore Babylon which (against traditional policy) had been wantonly destroyed by his father, Sennacherib. Again, after having to face an alliance of Medes and Cimmerians, he made a solemn pact with the Medes, exacting a promise that they would be loyal not only to himself, but to his son Assurbanipal after him. He also tried to seal a pact with the Scyths by marrying one of his daughters to their king.

Esarhaddon's most spectacular achievement was his conquest of Egypt. At this time the Nile was being ruled by a Nubian dynasty, the princes of Kush having grown stronger as the pharaohs weakened, until they themselves were able to take the double crown. The Assyrian's campaign against Egypt culminated in 671 when Memphis fell, the Nubian pharaoh fled and the new province was divided into satrapies. It was to be held for only fifteen years, but before its liberation by Psammetichus, a prince of Sais, Assurnasirpal had attacked Thebes and carried off much booty, including two obelisks – the first of many instances of these weighty monuments serving as trophies of war.

Under the Saite Dynasty XXVI Egypt had a brief interval of independence and prosperity, with Greek and Lydian mercenaries to control the Libyans and both Greeks and Phoenicians to develop Mediterranean trade. The second pharaoh, Necho, began to cut a canal from the Nile to the Red Sea and he commissioned the Phoenicians to circumnavigate Africa.

As for the Assyrians, Assurbanipal, having conquered Elam and brought its kings to drag his chariot through the streets of Nineveh, felt secure enough to leave the battlefield to his generals and make himself a patron of learning. Yet well before his death, and faster still under his two inadequate successors, the empire was disintegrating. Egypt's breakaway was followed by that of Babylon, when Nabopalassar won the kingdom with the support of the Chaldeans.

The most positive threat was from the Medes, now a powerful people led by ambitious kings. The Persians, too, were growing stronger under the Achaemenid family, but for the time were subject to the Medes. The Scythic horde meanwhile was active in western Iran and were in erratic support of Assyria. If it had not been for them the Medes might have struck sooner. As it was, once the Medes had allied themselves with Nabopalassar of Babylon, Assyria's position was hopeless. In 614 BC, the allies sacked Assur and Nimrud and two years later destroyed Nineveh, mightiest city in the world, and killed the Assyrian king. I cannot resist quoting from the biblical Vision of Nahum (the prophet may have lived near Nineveh) whose account of the fall of the city can speak for many other sackings in that bloody age.

> Woe to the bloody city!
> It is full of lies and robbery . . .
> The noise of a whip and the noise of rattling
>   wheels,
> And of the prancing horses, and of leaping
>   chariots.
> The horseman lifteth up the bright sword
>   and the glittering spear,
> And there is a multitude of slain . . .
> They stumble upon their corpses.

Breaking off to look further west, it was during the reigns of Esarhaddon and Assurbanipal that the Cimmerian nomads ravaged Anatolia. Having been originally

Ivory from Nimrud: Nubian with orynx, monkey and a leopard skin.

This marble statue known as the "Calf Bearer" is an early Kouros figure which came from the Acropolis in Athens, Greece.

dislodged by the Scyths many rode westward from Urartu and had descended on the prosperous kingdom of Phrygia by about 600 BC. It was after they had taken the capital of Gordion that, according to tradition, King Midas killed himself by drinking bull's blood. Phrygian power crumbled and never recovered.

The Cimmerians joined up with an invading Thracian people to assault the Lydians in the west – at that time ruled by Gyges and dominating the Ionian Greeks of the coast. When Gyges appealed to Assurbanipal for aid he can hardly have expected it to come since he had encouraged Psammetichus to expel the Assyrians from Egypt. The Cimmerians defeated and slew Gyges in battle and a little later Sardis was sacked. The Cimmerians went on to harry the Ionians, even destroying the sanctuary of Artemis in Ephesus. Ionian society with its refinement and intellect appeared to be in grave danger, but happily the Cimmerian horde began to break up and by about 640 BC the nomad threat had passed.

However, the Ionian cities were not left in peace (or rather to their own wars), for the Lydians recovered their force and the descendants of Gyges were as hostile to the Greeks as he had been. Alyattes, one of the most aggressive, regularly harassed Miletus until he was drawn eastward to repel the Medes. In 585 BC, after years of fighting, an eclipse of the sun coincided with a major battle. Lydians and Medes thought they must make peace and drew the boundary between them on the Halys River where their armies stood. This was the eclipse said to have been forecast by Thales of Miletus. Alyattes, whose parents had been a royal brother and sister had Croesus by one of his several wives, a native Carian woman.

There could hardly be two men more unlike than Alyattes the Lydian and his approximate contemporary in mainland Greece, Solon of Athens. The wise law-giver did much for the humbler citizens through land reforms and by admitting landless men to the Assembly as well as ending debt-slavery. Although he left power firmly in the hands of the upper class, he is judged to have taken a decisive step towards the Athenian democracy of our next period. After passing his laws in the later 590's, Solon set out for ten years of travelling through the Near East. The famous story that he visited Croesus at Sardis and warned him that no man should be counted happy until he is dead is, alas, impossible since Croesus became king of Lydia only in 560 BC. There is every reason to suppose, however, that Solon would have included Babylon in his

grand tour and witnessed the rebuilding of the city by Nebuchadnezzar, who had succeeded his father Nabopalassar in 605 BC.

After the fall of Nineveh the Babylonians had annexed most of Assyria, leaving the north in the hands of the Medes. The wealth of Babylon depended very largely on trade, and here she was handicapped by the Median presence. Nebuchadnezzar knew that he must hold Syria and Palestine against the Egyptian king Necho, who was campaigning there. He early defeated the Egyptians at Carchemish, but they continued to egg on the kings of Judah, and the Babylonians captured Jerusalem on three occasions (fulfilling the prophecies of Jeremiah) on the last destroying the city and transporting many of the rebellious Jews to Mesopotamia. Hence the "Babylonian Captivity" that was to bequeath to Christendom the image of the Whore of Babylon.

Nebuchadnezzar's death was followed by civil war and assassinations, but Babylonia was to enjoy one last burst of glory under Nabonidas. Yet, as is well known, the writing was on the wall. The Persians, hitherto subject to the Medes, now rose against them under Cyrus II and overwhelmed them at Pasargadae. Nabonidas naturally sided with the Persians.

Croesus, now at the height of his power and arrogance and ruling most of Anatolia, sought an oracle at Delphi and from it learned that if he marched against Cyrus "he would destroy a great empire." The empire, of course (with a typical Delphic twist) proved to be his own. Sardis was captured by the Persians (c.547) and tradition tells that the captive Croesus was already at the stake to be burnt alive when Cyrus reprieved him.

Whether or not he saved the Lydian, Cyrus was now free to turn against his ally, Nabonidas. Babylon had inherited the unpopularity as well as the riches of Assyria, and Isaiah's view that Cyrus was the "Chosen of the Lord" was not limited to the Jews, but was probably shared by many dissidents at home. Nabonidas's forces lost the battle of Opis and when Cyrus marched on to Babylon the gates were thrown open before him. This was in 539 BC. Almost at once the Jews (and other captive peoples) were freed to return to their own lands.

Babylonia, and soon after, Egypt, became satrapies of the Achaemenid empire. So with the end of our present period there also ended the long and often splendid history of the two founders of civilization as independent great powers. The acts of Darius in crushing the Ionian Greeks that led to further embroilment with Athens belong to our next chapter.

Technology *1000 – 500 BC*

The upheavals and displacement of peoples in the second millennium meant that iron working techniques were no longer limited to Anatolia but were transmitted to a far wider area. By 1000 BC, after a slow start, the techniques of working were producing a metal at least as good as bronze and within 500 years iron had largely displaced bronze for practical purposes from the Atlantic to the China Sea.

The superior hardness of iron was actually of much less significance than its commonness. While copper and tin were scarce, iron ore was plentifully distributed through most of the world. Bronze was a prerogative of the rich and powerful, primarily for weapons and display: iron was available to anyone cheaply enough for fashioning the simplest tools and agricultural implements. Moreover, in an age of conflict as this period was, iron weaponry was superior not only to bronze, but stone as well. The military might of Assyria owed as much to armoured wagons, grappling irons, wheeled siege towers and heavier chariots as it did to advanced military tactics.

While knowledge of the new metal was spreading, craftsmanship in the old was not standing still. The copper mines of Austria were delving ever deeper and more efficiently and the Late Bronze Age in Europe saw a massive increase in both quantity and quality of bronze goods. The quantity is shown by the appearance of large hoards of scrap metal, the reprocessing of which now became an industrial undertaking. In quality, swords, cauldrons and musical horns were added to the stock in trade of axes, knives and pins.

This period also saw the spread of writing. With an alphabetic system, writing could now be acquired by anyone in a few weeks instead of over many years. Related to this spread of writing and triggered by the same stimulus – trade – was the invention and rapid diffusion of minted money. When the seventh-century Lydians introduced true coinage, it was quickly and widely adopted as its advantages for international commerce were recognized.

The mastery of shipbuilding was largely responsible for the great increase in trade and the spread of cultural influences. While the Phoenicians were probably first in the production of long boats or galleys the Greeks constructed penteconters with a crew of 50. Moreover, seafaring was greatly enhanced by the work of two Greeks: Thales, who researched into navigation by the stars, and Anaximander, who produced what is alleged to be the first map of the world.

	Areas of major interest
•	Centres

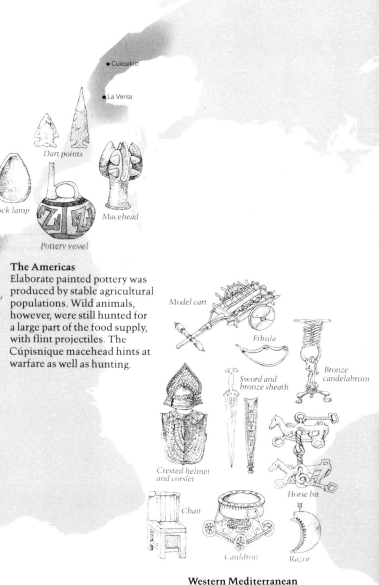

The Americas
Elaborate painted pottery was produced by stable agricultural populations. Wild animals, however, were still hunted for a large part of the food supply, with flint projectiles. The Cúpisnique macehead hints at warfare as well as hunting.

Dart points

Rock lamp

Macehead

Pottery vessel

Model cart

Fibula

Sword and bronze sheath

Bronze candelabrum

Crested helmet and corslet

Horse bit

Chair

Cauldron

Razor

Western Mediterranean
Italy became a great metal working area, both in bronze and iron under the Villanovans and their successors, the Etruscans. Domestic items such as the cauldron, chair, razor and candelabrum were produced in addition to such military hardware as the armour and sword. The horse bit and model cart show the increasing reliance on draught animals for transport.

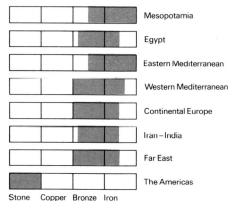

COMPARISON OF MATERIALS IN USE

				Mesopotamia
				Egypt
				Eastern Mediterranean
				Western Mediterranean
				Continental Europe
				Iran – India
				Far East
				The Americas

Stone   Copper   Bronze   Iron

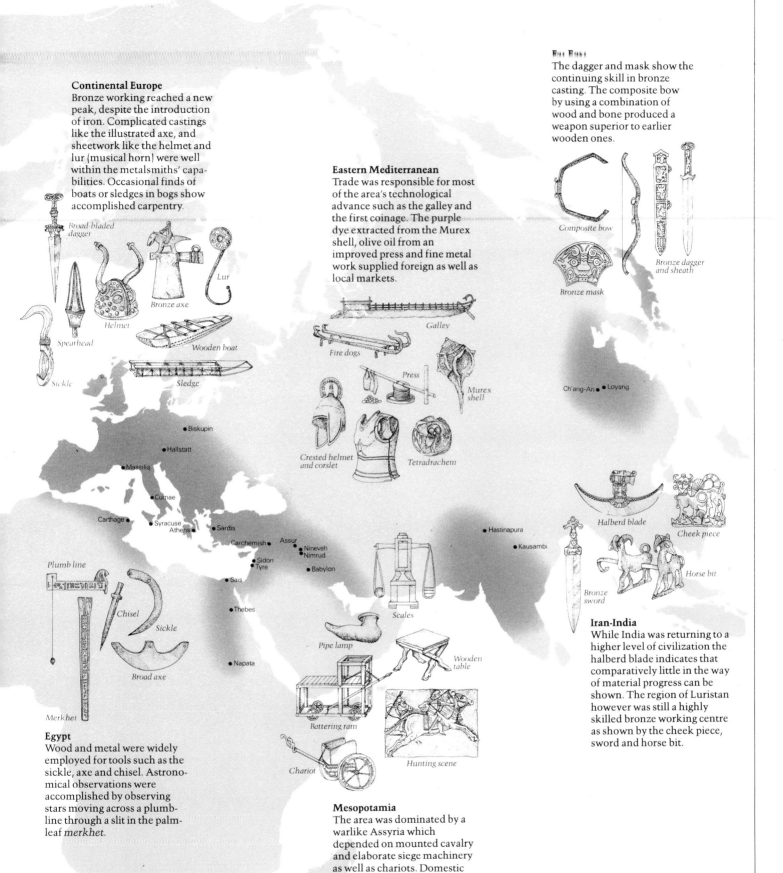

Continental Europe

Bronze working reached a new peak, despite the introduction of iron. Complicated castings like the illustrated axe, and sheetwork like the helmet and lur (musical horn) were well within the metalsmiths' capabilities. Occasional finds of boats or sledges in bogs show accomplished carpentry.

Broad-bladed dagger

Spearhead

Helmet

Lur

Bronze axe

Wooden boat

Sickle

Sledge

Eastern Mediterranean

Trade was responsible for most of the area's technological advance such as the galley and the first coinage. The purple dye extracted from the Murex shell, olive oil from an improved press and fine metal work supplied foreign as well as local markets.

Galley

Fire dogs

Press

Murex shell

Crested helmet and corslet

Tetradrachem

Far East

The dagger and mask show the continuing skill in bronze casting. The composite bow by using a combination of wood and bone produced a weapon superior to earlier wooden ones.

Composite bow

Bronze mask

Bronze dagger and sheath

- Biskupin
- Hallstatt
- Massilia
- Cumae
- Carthage
- Syracuse
- Athens
- Sardis
- Carchemish
- Assur
- Nineveh
- Nimrud
- Sidon
- Tyre
- Babylon
- Sais
- Thebes
- Napata
- Hastinapura
- Kausambi
- Ch'ang-An
- Loyang

Egypt

Wood and metal were widely employed for tools such as the sickle, axe and chisel. Astronomical observations were accomplished by observing stars moving across a plumbline through a slit in the palm-leaf *merkhet*.

Plumb line

Chisel

Sickle

Broad axe

Merkhet

Mesopotamia

The area was dominated by a warlike Assyria which depended on mounted cavalry and elaborate siege machinery as well as chariots. Domestic items such as the lamp, scales and table were also produced.

Scales

Pipe lamp

Wooden table

Battering ram

Chariot

Hunting scene

Iran-India

While India was returning to a higher level of civilization the halberd blade indicates that comparatively little in the way of material progress can be shown. The region of Luristan however was still a highly skilled bronze working centre as shown by the cheek piece, sword and horse bit.

Halberd blade

Cheek piece

Horse bit

Bronze sword

153

Mesopotamia

High quality iron weapons and the improvement of military tactics made the Assyrians almost invincible on the battlefield. The wheeled siege machine was a potent weapon against any enemy city. The sides would have been clad with hides to give protection to its "crew" – archers and javelin throwers on its tower, sappers to direct its ram against gate or wall, and large numbers of rank and file to push it into the attack. Cavalry was a new development, as horses were bred large enough and strong enough to carry an armed man. Though less heavily armed than chariots, they were much more rapid and more manoeuvrable. Bows and spears were carried.

Eastern Mediterranean

The Greek galley, reconstructed from a number of representations on painted vases, was between 35 and 40 feet (10½ – 12 m) long with a ram bow for offensive purposes. It had a crew of 26 rowers and steering was by means of an oar hung over the starboard (steer-board) quarter. While both oars and sails were used oars were preferred for naval vessels because of wind unreliability. On land, soldiers depended on weapons and tactics to carry the day. The crested helmet of bronze, with its protective cheek-pieces, would have been standard equipment. Its leather lining would have given the strength, sheet bronze itself offering little real resistance to an iron sword or spear. The minting of coins from the 7th century on greatly eased trading transactions. Each city struck its own series of fine coins in silver, gold, or later bronze.

Bronze crested helmet

Siege machine with battering ram

Assurbanipal hunting on horseback, alabaster plaque. Nineveh

Greek galley of 26 oarsmen

Egypt

Under foreign conquerors Egypt did not progress technologically. Even earlier it had relied on the deployment of vast reserves of forced labour during the annual inundation of the Nile and the backing of its wealth in gold. The Pharaoh Necho about 600 BC commissioned the cutting of a canal to join the Nile and the Red Sea, but this was not completed until after the Persian conquest of 525 BC.

TETRADRACHM OF ATHENS *Coins had a guaranteed weight and purity and were stamped with the issuing authority's mark.*

Western Mediterranean

Both the native Villanovans and immigrant Etruscans produced elaborate and accomplished metal goods. The four-wheeled cauldron cart with its pendant-decorated central bronze bowl of Etruscan manufacture reflects oriental influences in its design, the result of Phoenician trade. A wheeled laver is mentioned as one of the fittings in Solomon's temple. The candelabrum is more Greek in character, trade with that area being equally active. The sheet metal work of the Villanovans shown in the crested helmet and corslet may indicate a diffusion of techniques from beyond the Alps but they are clearly more local in their design. Helmets were frequently employed as lids for funerary urns.

Etruscan cauldron cart. Sesto Calende, Italy

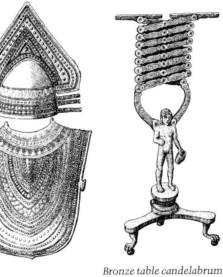

Villanovan crested helmet and corslet

Bronze table candelabrum

Continental Europe

The bronze axe with its mounted warrior from Hallstatt was used as a status symbol. It reflects the wealth pouring into this Austrian area in exchange for its salt and bronze. The horned and crested helmet from Vixo in Denmark was also probably used for ceremonial purposes. Its design was meant to be awe-inspiring but it was too unwieldy for battle.

Bronze axe, Hallstatt, Austria

Horned helmet, Vixo, Denmark

Iran-India

The bronze workers of Luristan continued to turn out their atttractive metal work in the lost wax technique. Horsebits were characteristic of the use of bronze after the introduction of iron although only the wealthy could afford to maintain horses.

Horse bits, Luristan, Iran

Far East

The composite bow combined slips of wood as well as bone. When a cast bronze grip and a lacquered finish were added a more effective weapon was produced. The way in which the bow bends back on itself when unstrung shows clearly the strength of the tension in it, even before the string was drawn.

Strung composite bow, China

Unstrung bow, China

The Americas

The knobbed macehead comes from Cúpisnique, a branch of coastal Chavin in northern Peru. Much skill was necessary to carve the stone into such a difficult shape, which was no doubt a useful one for warfare.

Knobbed macehead, Cúpisnique, Peru

Architecture 1000–500 BC

The Assyrians of the first millennium, supported by the wealth, prestige and drive of their military conquests, built walled cities of great magnificence along the middle Tigris. The main buildings included palaces, temples and ziggurats whose chief decoration was in the form of highly ornamental bas reliefs. Further south in Babylon, Nebuchadnezzar enlarged Hammurabi's city and used coloured glazed brickwork with figured designs to great effect. The highly decorated gateways, towering walls and hanging gardens combined to make Babylon one of the wonders of the ancient world.

The Persians, first at Parsagadae and later at Persepolis, also had carved stone motifs as their principal form of exterior decoration along with polychrome brickwork and relief slabs as in Mesopotamia.

In Egypt, Turkey and Syria, earlier styles of architecture persisted although the Phoenician style strongly influenced the Great Temple in Jerusalem.

Westward from the Aegean, however, this period saw the transformation of the king's megaron into the god's temple, the most notable advance being the addition of colonnades. In Greece, the introduction of stone in the sixth century to an essentially timber architecture encouraged the growth of "orders" – and the Doric was closely followed by the Ionic and in the next century by the more decorative Corinthian. Mural paintings, mouldings and statuary were effectively used to ornament one of the world's best known architectural forms – the Greek temple.

Further west the Etruscans were building their individual earth-covered tombs and the Sardinian nuraghe was further elaborated. Rome at this time was simply a provincial town.

In Europe, warring tribes and petty kingdoms depended on hillforts – earth and timber ramparts – for protection of their strongholds.

While little evidence remains of architectural developments in the Far East and India, monumental ceremonial centres containing platform mounds, pyramids and temples were built both in Mesoamerica by the Olmecs and in Peru by Chavín peoples. In addition to an early ball court at La Venta, relief-decorated stelae and ornate tombs were found in many of these centres. In North America, burial mounds containing wooden house-like constructions were also being built.

Areas of major interest
● Centres
▲ Sites

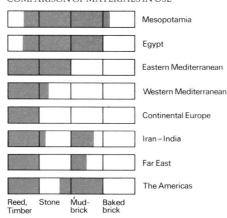

Ceremonial centre,
La Venta

Temple platform,
Cerro Sechin

Pyramid and shrine,
Cuicuilco

▲ Cerro Sechin
● Cuicuilco
● La Venta

The Americas
Temples in mudbrick or stone, frequently raised on massive platforms or pyramids were built in both Peru and Mexico. At La Venta a ceremonial centre served the religious and political needs of a far-flung population.

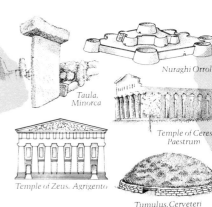

Nuraghi Orroli

Taula,
Minorca

Temple of Ceres,
Paestrum

Temple of Zeus, Agrigento

Tumulus, Cerveteri

COMPARISON OF MATERIALS IN USE

			Mesopotamia
			Egypt
			Eastern Mediterranean
			Western Mediterranean
			Continental Europe
			Iran–India
			Far East
			The Americas

Reed, Timber | Stone | Mud-brick | Baked brick

Western Mediterranean
Greek temples are well represented in the colonies around southern Italy and Sicily while the Etruscans produced local versions of oriental tomb architecture. More primitive structures such as the Sardinian nuraghi and the Minorcan taulas continued earlier traditions.

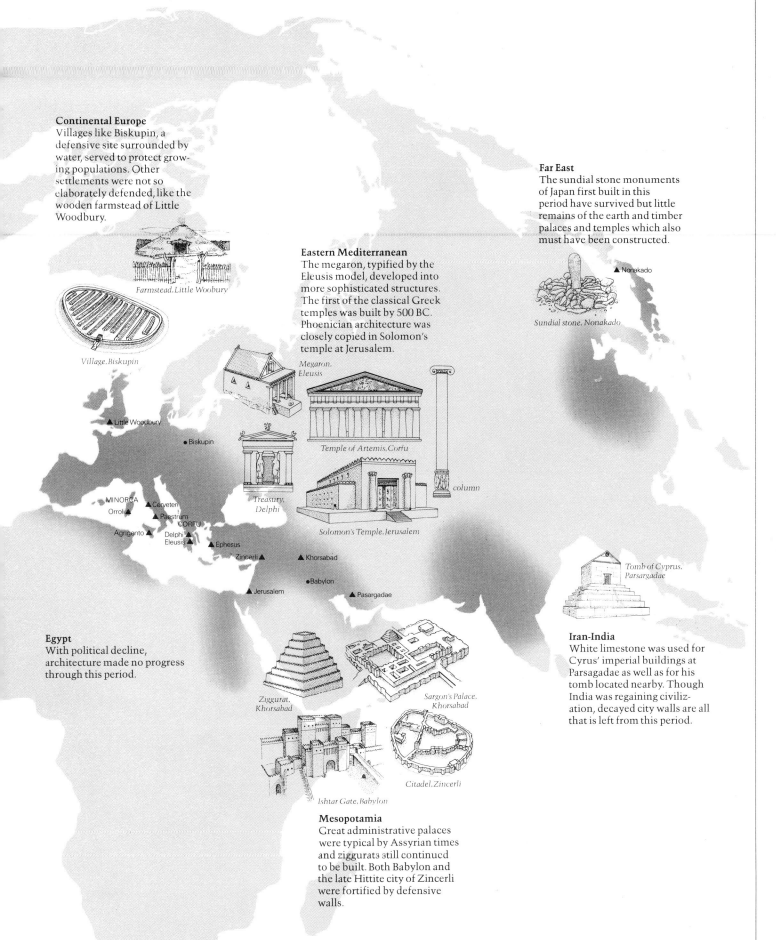

Continental Europe
Villages like Biskupin, a
defensive site surrounded by
water, served to protect growing populations. Other
settlements were not so
elaborately defended, like the
wooden farmstead of Little
Woodbury.

Farmstead, Little Woobury

Village, Biskupin

Far East
The sundial stone monuments
of Japan first built in this
period have survived but little
remains of the earth and timber
palaces and temples which also
must have been constructed.

▲ Nonakado

Sundial stone, Nonakado

Eastern Mediterranean
The megaron, typified by the
Eleusis model, developed into
more sophisticated structures.
The first of the classical Greek
temples was built by 500 BC.
Phoenician architecture was
closely copied in Solomon's
temple at Jerusalem.

*Megaron,
Eleusis*

Temple of Artemis, Corfu

*Treasury,
Delphi*

column

Solomon's Temple, Jerusalem

▲ Little Woodbury

● Biskupin

MINORCA ▲ Cerveteri
Orroli ▲
▲ Paestrum
Agrigento ▲ CORFU
Delphi ▲
Eleusis ▲ ▲ Ephesus
Zincerli ▲ ▲ Khorsabad
● Babylon
▲ Jerusalem ▲ Pasargadae

*Tomb of Cyprus,
Parsargadae*

Egypt
With political decline,
architecture made no progress
through this period.

*Ziggurat,
Khorsabad*

*Sargon's Palace,
Khorsabad*

Citadel, Zincerli

Ishtar Gate, Babylon

Iran-India
White limestone was used for
Cyrus' imperial buildings at
Parsagadae as well as for his
tomb located nearby. Though
India was regaining civiliz-
ation, decayed city walls are all
that is left from this period.

Mesopotamia
Great administrative palaces
were typical by Assyrian times
and ziggurats still continued
to be built. Both Babylon and
the late Hittite city of Zincerli
were fortified by defensive
walls.

Mesopotamia

Sargon II's capital at Khorsabad, built around 710 BC was contained within an area of one square mile and was surrounded by a double fortification wall. Besides the domestic quarters the palace included administrative halls, temples and a ziggurat. Wall reliefs and the human-headed winged bulls were carved in stone although the main structure was mudbrick. Babylon's construction required even less use of stone. The facing of brightly coloured glazed bricks applied to the great Ishtar Gate and Sacred Way completely masked the mudbrick construction.

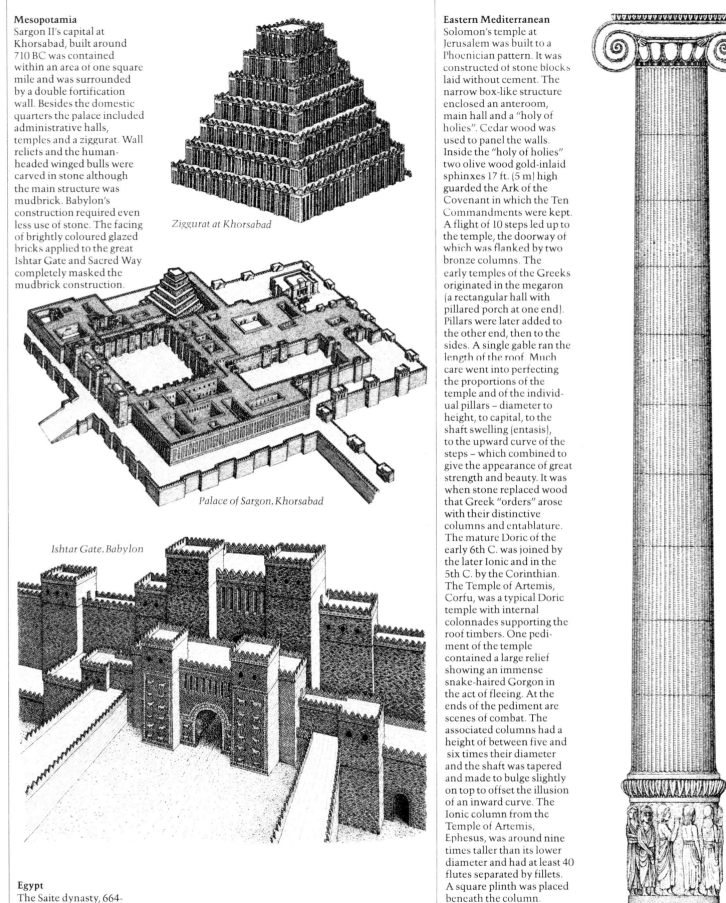

Ziggurat at Khorsabad

Palace of Sargon, Khorsabad

Ishtar Gate, Babylon

Egypt

The Saite dynasty, 664-525 BC, attempted to halt this region's decline by reviving past architectural glories, but with no success.

Eastern Mediterranean

Solomon's temple at Jerusalem was built to a Phoenician pattern. It was constructed of stone blocks laid without cement. The narrow box-like structure enclosed an anteroom, main hall and a "holy of holies". Cedar wood was used to panel the walls. Inside the "holy of holies" two olive wood gold-inlaid sphinxes 17 ft. (5 m) high guarded the Ark of the Covenant in which the Ten Commandments were kept. A flight of 10 steps led up to the temple, the doorway of which was flanked by two bronze columns. The early temples of the Greeks originated in the megaron (a rectangular hall with pillared porch at one end). Pillars were later added to the other end, then to the sides. A single gable ran the length of the roof. Much care went into perfecting the proportions of the temple and of the individual pillars – diameter to height, to capital, to the shaft swelling (entasis), to the upward curve of the steps – which combined to give the appearance of great strength and beauty. It was when stone replaced wood that Greek "orders" arose with their distinctive columns and entablature. The mature Doric of the early 6th C. was joined by the later Ionic and in the 5th C. by the Corinthian. The Temple of Artemis, Corfu, was a typical Doric temple with internal colonnades supporting the roof timbers. One pediment of the temple contained a large relief showing an immense snake-haired Gorgon in the act of fleeing. At the ends of the pediment are scenes of combat. The associated columns had a height of between five and six times their diameter and the shaft was tapered and made to bulge slightly on top to offset the illusion of an inward curve. The Ionic column from the Temple of Artemis, Ephesus, was around nine times taller than its lower diameter and had at least 40 flutes separated by fillets. A square plinth was placed beneath the column.

Ionic column from temple of Artemis, Ephesus

Temple of Artemis, Corfu

Solomon's temple, Jerusalem,

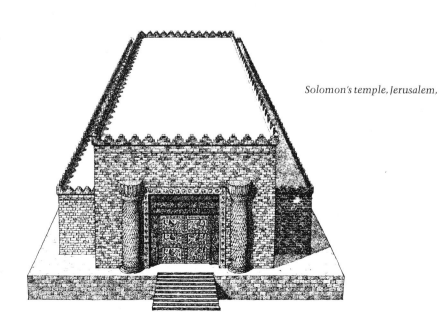

Western Mediterranean
Some early Sardinian nuraghi were later considerably enlarged and elaborated. The central tower at Orrubiu, containing a tall corbel-vaulted chamber raised in cyclopean masonry (large and uncoursed blocks without mortar) was surrounded by five interconnected towers. Other outer towers were built still later and linked with a curtain wall.

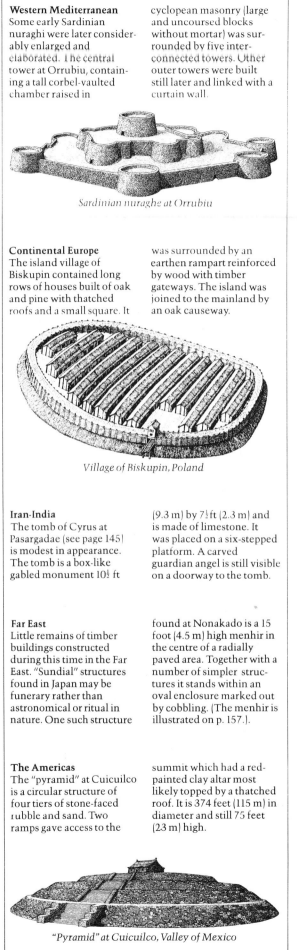

Sardinian nuraghe at Orrubiu

Continental Europe
The island village of Biskupin contained long rows of houses built of oak and pine with thatched roofs and a small square. It was surrounded by an earthen rampart reinforced by wood with timber gateways. The island was joined to the mainland by an oak causeway.

Village of Biskupin, Poland

Iran-India
The tomb of Cyrus at Pasargadae (see page 145) is modest in appearance. The tomb is a box-like gabled monument 10½ ft (9.3 m) by 7½ ft (2.3 m) and is made of limestone. It was placed on a six-stepped platform. A carved guardian angel is still visible on a doorway to the tomb.

Far East
Little remains of timber buildings constructed during this time in the Far East. "Sundial" structures found in Japan may be funerary rather than astronomical or ritual in nature. One such structure found at Nonakado is a 15 foot (4.5 m) high menhir in the centre of a radially paved area. Together with a number of simpler structures it stands within an oval enclosure marked out by cobbling. (The menhir is illustrated on p. 157.).

The Americas
The "pyramid" at Cuicuilco is a circular structure of four tiers of stone-faced rubble and sand. Two ramps gave access to the summit which had a red-painted clay altar most likely topped by a thatched roof. It is 374 feet (115 m) in diameter and still 75 feet (23 m) high.

"Pyramid" at Cuicuilco, Valley of Mexico

Art 1000 – 500 BC

The oldest centres of art in the Near East were now losing their force. Babylonian kings set up stelae deliberately imitating those of 3000 – 2000 BC, while in Egypt sculptors produced some quite good work in the manner of the Old and Middle Kingdoms.

The exception to the dying down of energy in these lands is provided by the conquering Assyrians. From the ninth century as part of the glorification of their capital cities they placed huge fabulous beasts at their gates and lined walls with carved and painted reliefs.

In the Levant the Phoenicians had gifted artist-craftspeople who usually worked in an eclectic style. Some of their finest ivory casting has been found at Nineveh; they supplied craftsmen to Solomon for his temple at Jerusalem – but hardly a trace survives.

By far the most significant centre of new life in the arts was, of course, in Greece, and above all in Athens. With the seventh century the miracle began. Renewed contact with the east brought in oriental motifs, and Corinth came to the fore with fine if still imperfect figure and decorative painting on ceramics. Then after 600 BC the sculptors evolved those famous figures of youths and maidens with their dawning archaic "smile", and in the ceramic art Athens created the exquisite art of the black figure vase painting. Much space has been given to the painted pottery of simple peoples, but there had never before been anything like this: the perfection of the formal motifs, the grace and humanity of the mythological scenes that come to us like illustrations from a book. By the end of the period figure sculpture as well as ornamental detail was allied with architecture.

Greek influence was widespread and helped to inspire further creativity most successfully among Etruscans, Scyths and ultimately Persians and Celts. While the Etruscans imitated Greek art, they adapted it to their own less moderate spirit. Their burial customs assured the survival of wall paintings. The Scyths were far less Greek dominated, their animal art in gold and silver owing much to their south Russian inheritance.

In the China of the Chou dynasty the output of ritual bronze vessels and jade carving was maintained but without much innovation. On the other hand in Mesoamerica higher civilization dawned at last among the Olmecs, creators of the famous "big heads" and other sculpture. In Peru the promise of things to come was already evident in the painted, sculptural Chavín ceramics.

Areas of major interest

● Centres

▲ Sites

Figurine. La Venta

Head. La Venta

▲ Tlatilco

▲ Vera Cruz
● La Venta

Jade figure. Vera Cruz

Figurine. Tlatilco

Chorrera vessel

▲ Chorrera

The Americas
As well as their famous "big heads" the Olmec sculptors made striking statuettes, sometimes in jade. In Peru the potters of the Chavín culture produced fine ceramics, now including human and animal shapes. In the ceremonial centre of Chavín de Huántar were relief sculptures portraying divinities.

Gold cup. Palestrina

Head of bull. Costig

Bronze warrior. Sardinia

Etruscan figurine

Askos. Benacci

Western Mediterranean
The Iron Age peoples of Italy, with moderate skills in potting and small bronze figure work, after Greek and oriental contacts evolved the civilized art of the Etruscans. Phoenicians, Carthaginians and Greeks spread minor civilized arts through their many colonies. Quaint bronze figurines distinguished Sardinia.

Far East
Under the Chou dynasty in the provinces surrounding the Yellow River, the Chinese continued to produce their ritual bronze vessels, establishing the classic forms. The latest Jōmon and the Angyo cultures of Japan included fantastic figurines.

Continental Europe
The Late Bronze Age-Iron Age "barbarians" of Britain and Europe developed their bronze work and produced some elaborate if primitive religious figure-work. In Denmark there was also good decorative work in bronze and gold, including the fine *lur* horns. The nomad Scyths of south Russia designed superb stylized animals, often in gold.

Eastern Mediterranean
Phoenician and Syrian artist-craftspeople, especially ivory carvers, often worked in the Egyptian manner. The Greeks emerged from their Dark Age to create their fine archaic statuary, their Corinthian pottery followed by the black figure vase painting of 6th century Athens and Sparta. Sculpture became an element of architecture.

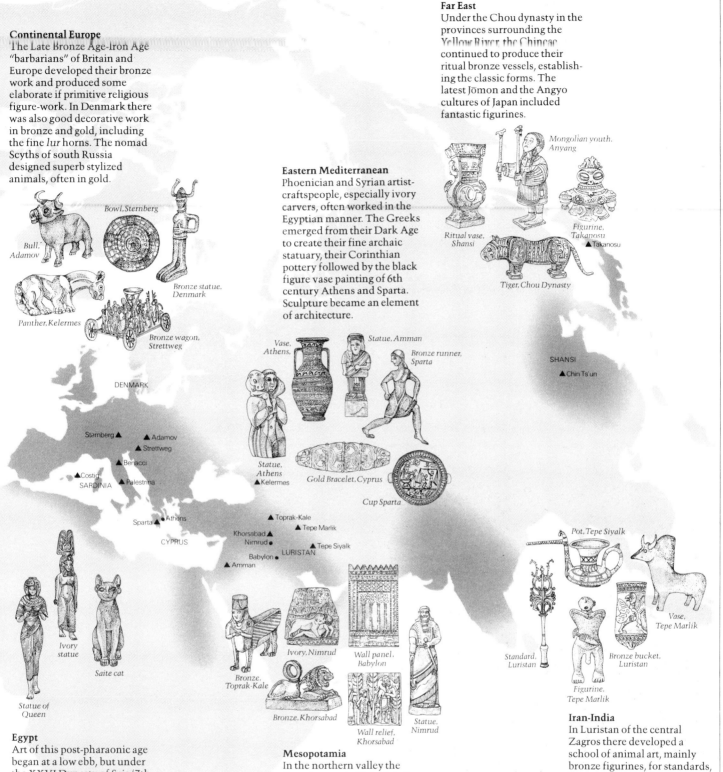

Bull, Adamov

Bowl, Sternberg

Panther, Kelermes

Bronze statue, Denmark

Bronze wagon, Strettweg

Mongolian youth, Anyang

Ritual vase, Shansi

Figurine, Takanosu

Tiger, Chou Dynasty

Vase, Athens

Statue, Amman

Bronze runner, Sparta

Statue, Athens

Gold Bracelet, Cyprus

Cup Sparta

DENMARK

Sternberg ▲   ▲ Adamov
▲ Strettweg
▲ Benacci
▲ Costig   ▲ Palestrina
SARDINIA

Sparta ▲ ● Athens
CYPRUS

▲ Toprak-Kale
Khorsabad ▲   ▲ Tepe Marlik
Nimrud ▲
Babylon ▲   ● Tepe Siyalk
LURISTAN
▲ Amman

SHANSI
▲ Chin Ts'un

Pot, Tepe Siyalk

Ivory statue

Saite cat

Statue of Queen

Bronze, Toprak-Kale

Ivory, Nimrud

Bronze, Khorsabad

Wall panel, Babylon

Wall relief, Khorsabad

Statue, Nimrud

Standard, Luristan

Figurine, Tepe Marlik

Bronze bucket, Luristan

Vase, Tepe Marlik

Egypt
Art of this post-pharaonic age began at a low ebb, but under the XXVI Dynasty of Sais (7th-6th C.) an effort was made to return to the styles of the Old and Middle Kingdoms. Good work was still produced in the minor arts.

Mesopotamia
In the northern valley the Assyrians embellished their capital cities of Nineveh, Nimrud and Dur-Sargon (Khorsabad) with monumental sculpture and fine furnishings. The Hurrians of Urartu specialized in ornamental metal. In Babylonia there was some imitation of early Sumerian art work.

Iran-India
In Luristan of the central Zagros there developed a school of animal art, mainly bronze figurines, for standards, horse-trappings and the like. In the west (Tepe Siyalk and Marlik) pottery and animal figurines had some distinction.

Mesopotamia

Friezes carved in low relief on large, thin stone slabs were a characteristic art form of the Assyrians from the 9th-7th centuries. They usually lined entrance ways or palace rooms, and frequently formed a narrative sequence of warfare, ritual or the chase. Like the Egyptians and Hittites (whose art influenced them) the Assyrians liked to show figures taking a short pace forward. The finest examples are at Nimrud, Nineveh and Khorsabad. In Nebuchadnezzar's Babylon, bricks moulded in relief and colour-glazed seem to have been favoured – as on the palace facade.

Hunting scene from Sargon II's palace, Khorsabad

Egypt

Animals played a great part in Egyptian art – as in their religion. They were not so much attributes of the gods as sacred creatures in their own right. An increase in animal cults seems to have gone with the general decline in Egyptian civilization and cemeteries with thousands of mummified cats are known. Many charming sculptures of them were made in a perfectly naturalistic style.

Saite period bronze cat

Eastern Mediterranean

The pottery known to classical scholars as proto-geometric and geometric was the principal art form during the 900-700 BC period. At first a few simple motifs were used sparingly, but with the full geometric, vessels might be covered with narrow zones of patterns and animal and human subjects such as chariotry and funerals. The colouring was usually dark brown on chestnut, and the shapes were both strong and formal.

Panel from Nebuchadnezzar's throne room, coloured glazed bricks, Babylon

Geometric period amphora, Athens, Greece

Western Mediterranean
The Sardinians who devised nuraghi also made delightful little bronzes, naïf but effective. One popular subject of many was the tribal chief in cloak and cap. The Etruscans could not approach the Greeks in stone sculpture, but their bronzes, free-standing or on vessels, were masterly.

Nuragic tribal chieftain, bronze, Sardinia

Horseman with bow, figure from Etruscan bronze bowl

Continental Europe
Much of the finest early Scythian animal art comes from rich burials in the Kuban. The gold panther (c. 1¼ ins: 3.5 cms) – may have been on a shield. The cloisonné inlay of the ear shows Persian influence. The Hallstatt art of central Europe corresponding to the Greek geometric is not generally distinguished. The unique ritual car shows the "goddess with the vase" (on her head) surrounded by naked warriors, attendants, a phallic man and a large stag.

Scythian gold panther plaque, Kelermes, Russia

The Strettweg Cart, bronze, Austria

Iran-India
The ancient settlement of Tepe Siyalk in western Iran, after being deserted for a time, was reoccupied by Indo-European people coming from the northeast. They made richly painted pottery in various forms.

Painted pot, Tepe Siyalk, Iran

Far East
By the time of the late Chou Dynasty, Chinese bronze smiths began to abandon their intricate vessel forms and to produce more naturalistic creations. Improved cutting and drilling methods also enabled jade to be treated in more elaborate forms. The statue of the Mongolian girl or Shamaness was cast in bronze and the birds held aloft were carved of jade.

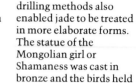

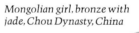

Mongolian girl, bronze with jade, Chou Dynasty, China

The Americas
As well as the gigantic heads for which they are famous, the Olmecs of the Gulf coast of Mexico made many small carvings for cult purposes, some of jade. They tended more or less towards the "baby face" style, sometimes with added jaguar features. The grimly down-turned mouth is part of this feline element.

Ceremonial jade figure, Vera Cruz, Mexico

Region	Economy	Centres	Events and developments	People
Mesopotamia		Assur Nineveh Nimrud Babylon	Ascendancy of Assyria until its destruction by rising power of Medes in 612 BC. Babylonian captivity c.600. Persia absorbs Medes and overthrows Babylon 539.	Assurbanipal Assurnasirpal Tiglath-Pileser III Nebuchadnezzar Semiramis Sargon II
Egypt		Thebes Napata Sais	Political decline, with Libyan and Kushite dynasties. Foreign invasions: Assyrian 670, Persian 525.	
Eastern Mediterranean		Athens Tyre Sidon Sardis Carchemish	Recovery in archaic Greece. Rise of city-states. Syro-Hittite states. Phoenicians ascendant in Levant, later subjected by Assyria. United kingdom of Judah and Israel under David with Jerusalem as capital 10th C. BC.	Homer David & Solomon Solon Croesus Thales Anaximander Sappho Isaiah
Western Mediterranean		Cumae Syracuse Massilia Carthage	Phoenician trade and colonies: Carthage 814. Villanovans, Etruscans. Greek colonies from 750. Conflict between these groups. Rome founded 753. Under Tarquin kings in 6th century.	Pythagoras Romulus
Continental Europe		Hallstatt Biskupin	Domination of continent by Urnfielders. Hallstatt culture in central Europe leads to Celts.	
Iran-India		Hastinapura Kausambi	Aryans move steadily eastwards into Ganges valley.	Gautama Buddha Cyrus I, II Darius Zoroaster
Far East		Sian Loyang	Western Chou 1027. Eastern Chou 700. Feudal societies with city-states in China.	Confucius Lao-Tse
The Americas		Cuicuilco La Venta Chavin de Huántar Monte Albán	Wide influence of Olmecs, but probably artistic and religious rather than political. Plant cultivation (gourds, sunflowers and possibly maize) in N. America.	

The economy bar graph indicates relative proportions of these factors: Irrigation ≈   Agriculture ✿   Hunting ✗   Urban life ⊞   Trade ⟑

Religion	Technology and inventions	Architecture	Art and literature
City gods, particularly Assur, Marduk.	Assyrian military technology: cavalry, siege engines, etc. Large-scale adoption of iron by Assyrians.	Assyrian temples, palaces, fortifications. Babylon's Ishtar Gate.	Assyrian wall reliefs. Babylonian glazed tiles. Syrian ivories.
Osirian worship. Amun and pantheon continue.	Stagnation in native crafts. Nile to Red Sea Canal. Iron introduced.	In decline, no new developments.	Decline. Archaistic revival under Saite dynasty especially in stone statuary.
Olympian pantheon. Temples and animal sacrifice. Delphic oracle. Phoenician pantheon. Temples, high places, obelisks. Animal and infant sacrifices.	Iron becoming general. Improved potter's wheel, kiln. Alphabetic writing. Coinage starting in Lydia. Improved shipping. Double bank of rowers in longships.	Development of classical architecture, particularly the great temple in Jerusalem after Phoenician models.	New start in geometric pottery painting, later sculpture. Rapid advances in both. Phoenician jewellery, metalwork, but largely imitative. Neo-Hittite statues and reliefs *Iliad, Odyssey* Hesiod's *Theogony* *The Song of Solomon.*
Greeks, Etruscans and Phoenicians all had their own gods.	Potter's wheel spreads. Greeks and Phoenicians carry writing, coinage, etc., throughout area. Iron technology.	Greek architecture carried to west. Etruscans build walls, temples and a wide variety of tombs.	Villanovan art on metalwork. Greek art imported in quantity by local peoples, much copied and adapted, especially by Etruscans. Sardinian bronze figurines.
Votive offerings.	Great increase of bronze in circulation; founders' hoards. Improved mining techniques in Central Europe. Iron spreading from South.	Poor timber and sod huts. Beginning of hill forts. Mines.	Bronzework shows high craftsmanship rather than artistry.
Vedic religion coalescing with native cults. Brahmanism. Upanishads. At very end of period Buddhism.	Little advance until late in period. Bronze.	Stone and brick city walls re-appear.	Unspectacular painted pottery. *Upanishads* *Brahmanas*
Range of Divinities and ancestor worship continuing. Confucius and Lao-Tse at very end of period.	Iron casting developed at end of period.	Timber architecture, not surviving. Roof tiles.	Chou art, continuing in bronze but also jade and lacquer. Jade carving. *Book of Songs*
Jaguar worship by Olmecs. Ceremonial centres developing. Funerary cult in N. America.	Stone and pottery-using cultures. Irrigation developed in Peruvian valleys.	Shrines on raised platforms in Valley of Mexico. Ceremonial centres on Mexican east coast. Mostly adobe in Peru and for all smaller buildings. First Mississippi burial mounds.	Olmec stone statues and statuettes. Chavin art on pottery and textiles.

500BC– AD1

This period saw the completion of the shift in the chief growing points in human advancement and power from the Near East towards the west. In the first two centuries the Persian empire can be seen as continuing the greatness of the ancient orient, including, as it did, all the original heartlands of Mesopotamia, Egypt, the Levant, Anatolia – and even the Indus. Indeed, it was larger, much better organized and for a time more successful in maintaining peace than any predecessor. Yet when in the opening decades of this period the Persians under Darius and Xerxes failed to defeat the brilliant, flexible Greeks, led by Athens, the future of the west was assured – rather as the future of England was assured when the Spanish Armada failed. The proof came with Alexander the Great's astounding conquest of the Persian empire from 334 to his death in 323 BC. In spite of the immediate splitting up of the empire into provinces, Alexander had succeeded in carrying Greek (Hellenistic) culture throughout its vast territories.

The shift to the west came near its culmination for the ancient world with the irresistible rise of Republican Rome. During the first two centuries of the period when the Greeks were enjoying the harvest of their classical age, the Etruscans were the highly civilized people of Italy and seemed by far the strongest. Yet after another two centuries Etruscans and Carthaginians had been cowed and the Greeks themselves made subject to Rome. By the end of the period the Egyptians and also the barbarian Celts had been conquered and Roman rule extended to the Channel coasts. With Octavian ruling as Augustus, the Roman republic had in reality become imperial.

Although no one could question that these tremendous events in the west were of supreme importance for the future of mankind, the orient also knew momentous changes. In India the Persian province of the Punjab was taken by Alexander, but soon liberated by the Mauryan princes. Of the second and greatest of them, Ashoka, it has been said that "his reign marks the first coherent expression of the Indian mind".

In China an age of philosophers and social thinkers followed Confucius, and the Ch'in dynasty (to which it owes its name) united the empire and sheltered it with a Great Wall. Cultural change and progress came with the Han rulers.

In Central America, Maya civilization was launched, glyphic writing and the calendrical cult begun. South American peoples advanced their prosperity by increasing food production through irrigation and terrace farming. Their craftspeople produced superb textiles and ceramics and curious works in gold.

The fulfilment of the Greek miracle in the high classical age of the fifth-fourth centuries was one of those wonderful outbursts of human creativity and greatness of spirit that light up the history of our species. Although Athens and its state of Attica, where the flame burned brightest, were politically powerful in the fifth century, turning a league formed against the Persians into a kind of Athenian empire dominating the rival Spartans, it is significant that one immediately thinks of this Hellenic age in terms of mind. In the arts – poetry, drama, sculpture and painting – in the intellectual fields of mathematics, philosophy and science, and perhaps above all in the new vision of people and society that inspired democracy, a small and largely barren country produced a shining treasure of genius on which we still draw. Behind it all was a way of looking at man never before experienced. It was related to the detachment of the Ionians, seeing man with his terrible limitations and yet with his innate worth. That worth, however, was still not divorced from transcendental ideas: man housed a spark that made him part of some divine reality and beauty. This produced a fully conscious philosophical belief in the rightness of democracy in contrast with the absolutism of oriental god-kings.

Bronze head of the Greek Delphic Charioteer, the surviving figure of a votive group which portrayed a chariot race and its victorious driver.

Pericles. He made election
by free males a reality in
Athens by 450 BC.

Darius III of Persia at the
Battle of Issus (333 BC) in
which he was defeated by
Alexander; mosaic,
Pompeii, Italy,

In the year 490 BC (when Buddha and
Confucius were still living) the Greeks
defeated the Persians under Darius at
Marathon, and Herodotus and Pericles were
born. These events well express the age to
come, for Herodotus as the first true historian
was to add much to the new view of mankind,
while by mid-century Pericles was to make
democratic election (if only by free males) a
reality in Athens, and by working with men of
genius (such as the sculptor Phidias) to make
it indeed "an education for Greece".

The yield of genius was extraordinary.
To take only a few samples, the first surviving
play of Aeschylus dates from 472, Sophocles'
first great tragedy from 468 and Euripides' from
455 – also the birth year of Thucydides. That
wonder of the world, the temple of Zeus at
Olympia, with Phidias' great gold and ivory
statue of the god, was begun in about 460.
The Parthenon was begun in 447 BC and the
Propylaea was built as a worthy entry to the
Acropolis. The Odeon concert hall was also
built at this time, and so were gymnasia and
baths for the citizens.

Yet for all their achievement and their
pursuit of the four virtues of courage,
temperance, justice and wisdom, they could
not hold back from man's terrible urge to
warfare. Pericles wanted Athens to be the
centre of power as well as of culture and so he
alarmed Sparta and her allies, most like herself conservative oligarchies, and then ensued
the tragedy of the Peloponnesian war and the
final defeat of Athens by 404. Fourth century
Athens was still intellectually great, though
mainly in a philosophy that theorized and
distrusted the springs of poetry. Plato was born
in the year (429) when Pericles died; two years
later Aristophanes began to teach the Greeks
to enjoy his mordant humour and to laugh
even at democracy. Thucydides, successor to
Herodotus, was there to write the disastrous
story of much of the Peloponnesian war, and
Aristotle was born just twenty years after its
end, in 384 BC.

One event deserves recall because it is so
well known and because it so well illustrates
the relentless steps of time. When Cyrus the
Younger's revolt against the Persian king had
failed, Xenophon, the future historian, was
among the leaders of the Greek contingent
stranded a thousand miles from any homeland.
The famous Retreat of the Ten Thousand took
them up the Tigris. At Nimrud the river had
shifted and they marched along the empty bed
looking far up at the mighty quays and
ziggurat. The huge and wealthy Assyrian city
of our previous period was almost deserted and

would soon be forgotten. This was in the year 401 BC.

The fourth century saw contests between Greeks and Carthaginians in the Mediterranean, particularly in Sicily, and,while Plato wrote his masterworks in Athens, endless internal struggles between Thebes, Sparta, Athens and their shifting allies. None realized that Philip, who in 359 had become king of the northern mountain land of Macedon, was to make their rivalries seem insignificant. He reorganized his kingdom, captured Thracian gold and silver mines, and won control of the pass to the south (the Thermopylae where Xerxes' Persian invasion had been repulsed in 480). The divisions and advantage-seeking of the southern city-states weakened all resistance, and in 338 Philip won his victory at Chaeronia and organized Greece under his own leadership.

The Macedonian now felt strong enough to fulfil the persistent Greek dream of war against the weakening Achaemenid empire of the Persians. Although he was murdered before he had won more than a foothold in Anatolia, his much greater son Alexander, between 334 and his death at Babylon in 323, conquered the whole vast territory even to northwest India. (His traditional cutting of the Gordion Knot at the old Phrygian capital would have been soon after his first crossing of the Hellespont in 334. He burnt Persepolis four years later.)

Like Napoleon in Egypt, Alexander campaigned with a following of scientists and historians, and he founded many cities across Asia. Greek architectural forms and Delphic inscriptions have been found in one of these foundations beside the distant Oxus. Something of the Greek ideal looks out from the faces of works of later Indian sculpture.

Of the descendants of Alexander's generals who divided his brief empire, the Seleucids were by far the most powerful – for a time ruling nearly all the Asiatic territories from Anatolia and Mesopotamia to the frontier of India. In the mid third century, however, they had to cede some of their eastern lands to the nomadic Parthians. The Seleucids remained great proselytizers for Greek civilization, founding Macedonian cities such as Seleucia and Antioch.

The other royal house sprung from an Alexandrine general was that of the Ptolemies in Egypt. There the strength of the ancient pharaonic tradition of culture was largely maintained in the Nile valley. Alexandria, however, rapidly became a brilliant cosmopolitan city, a centre of international scholarship and science that fulfilled its founder's

Alexander the Great, son of Philip of Macedon. During the course of 11 years he brought the entire Persian empire including northwest India under Greek control and in so doing inaugurated the Hellenistic Age.

Ptolemy II and his wife on a sardonyx cameo. Though Macedonian by birth and Greek in outlook, the Ptolemies ruled as pharaohs in Egypt.

Macedon. Yet memorable names and deeds are few. Across the Aegean the cities of Pergamum, Ephesus and Miletus flourished and were beautified; kings of Pergamum were strong enough to defeat the invading Celts and pen them into central Anatolia – where they gave their name to Galatia.

While the Seleucids and Ptolemies pursued their great affairs and the Greek cities their smaller ones, the new state was rising in Italy that would soon eclipse them all. Here was the next step in the westward shift of power to be completed in this period.

The Romans at the end of our last period were a poor but independent republic. During the next two centuries they were concerned to win control over Italy south of the Po by breaking the Etruscans and dominating the other peoples of the peninsula. First they made themselves the real masters of a modest federation of Latin neighbours, which succeeded in conquering the Sabines. The Etruscans held out through the fifth century, then, weakened by the usual internal quarrels and by invasion of Celts across the Alps, Veii fell to the Romans in 396. A few years later the Celts sacked Rome, but this brief setback only hardened the Romans: they annexed Latium, then the Campania from the Samnites. Learning by experience, they improved their weapons and tactics, and began their policy of control through engineered military roads. By the mid third century Rome, itself now a large city, ruled much of central and southern Italy and was so evidently a coming power that conflict with the Carthaginians still entrenched right along the African coast, in southern Corsica, Sardinia and western Sicily, and involvement with the Greek cities of south Italy and Sicily, were inevitable. Here one well-known name appears. In the 270s Pyrrhus, of Greek Epirus, used a large army and elephants to try to keep the Romans out of southern Italy and drive the Carthaginians out of Sicily. His unavailing victories made his name immortal.

The First Punic (Carthaginian) War, 264-241, brought Rome her earliest overseas province – Sicily – soon to be followed by Corsica and Sardinia. The Romans had shown their deadly will and energy when, landlubbers as they were, they built a large fleet and painfully mastered its use.

The Carthaginians determined to fight back by strengthening their forces in Spain, a policy boldly begun by their general, Hamilcar. When his son Hannibal took the command various provocations gave the Romans the excuse to declare war. Their plans were upset

highest purposes. There worked Archimedes (from Greek Syracuse) and Euclid; there was built the Museum with its splendid library and the famous lighthouse on the island of Pharos.

Unhappily the old struggle between Egypt and Mesopotamia for the Levant was revived in new form by the Ptolemies and Seleucids. One of the more bizarre episodes during the course of their alternating fortunes was when the Seleucid Antochus IV, soon after the recapture of Syria and Palestine from Egypt, determined to destroy Judaism in favour of the Greek gods. The temple at Jerusalem was dedicated to Olympian Zeus, and his altar, displacing that of Yahweh, became the "abomination of desolation". The rage aroused in the Jews led on to the revolt of the Maccabees.

In these Hellenistic centuries when Greek ideas and culture affected half the world, the affairs of the small land of their birth seemed relatively insignificant. Greece kept its prestige as the source of civilization, and there was still life and ambition in Athens, Sparta and

Hellenistic cameo of Alexander the Great and Roxane. Alexander was a great deal less successful at governing his vast, formerly Persian empire, than he was at conquering it. His adoption of Persian manners and dress and his marriage to a Bactrian princess Roxane alienated his fellow Macedonians. This situation was further aggravated by Alexander's assumption of divinity and its accompanying ritual. Whether he would have been able to maintain his empire is doubtful. In any event, on his premature death at the age of 32, his empire was split between his generals who had Roxane and her son murdered.

by Hannibal's bold decision to invade Italy. Largely thanks to the writing of the Greek historian, Polybius, Hannibal's crossing of the Alps with his elephants in 220 remains one of the epic stories of the western world. It coincided almost exactly with the Ch'in conquest of China and its unification behind a Great Wall of Emperor Ch'in-Shih-huang.

Celts in the north rallied to Hannibal and this still youthful military genius won his great victories; it seemed that Rome itself must fall. Yet the Carthaginians failed to invade the city, and after all the years and campaigns of the Second Punic War, by 201 BC Hannibal had to surrender to Scipio Africanus and Carthage became a tributary of Rome with territory no greater than modern Tunisia. So the western upstart ended the ancient Phoenician sea power of the orient. Rome took Spain with its silver and gold mines. Well before this Rome had seized Illyrian land across the southern Adriatic, a movement that brought her close to the Greeks in Macedon.

It seems amazing that the Greeks had not recognized what was happening in their world before 217, when there was a warning that there was "a cloud rising in the west". Even then an alliance that included Greece was foolish enough to appeal to Rome for aid against Macedon's ambitious king. Like the Assyrians for Babylon, the Romans still felt a certain veneration for Greece to whom they owed so much of their culture, and when the first of their armies landed in Greece it was in the name of "liberation". However, after some decades of Greek feebleness and disputes, "their patience was exhausted": first Macedon and then most of Greece were subjected – in

146 BC (just 200 years after the death of Plato). In that same year, after long clamour in the ruling Senate, the Romans destroyed the city of Carthage and sowed it with salt. They now had an African province with abundant corn. Another rich province fell to them peacefully when the last king of Pergamum gave them western Anatolia. By 100 BC Rome controlled nearly all the lands north of the Mediterranean – which was already virtually a "Roman lake".

The events of the last century of this period as the Romans extended their conquest both east and west are a familiar part of history and literature. The names of Pompey and Caesar, of Antony and Cleopatra, seem to belong to a different, more poetic, world. Yet their intrigues, coups d'état and conquests were mundane enough.

Pompey it was who ended the Hellenistic Seleucids' kingdom. From the second century they had lost their eastern territories to the formerly nomadic Parthians, a little known empire which at times stretched from Bactria to Babylonia. By 64 BC Pompey took the Seleucid heartland of Syria. He also captured Jerusalem and outraged the Jews by entering the Holy of Holies – but Judea was not to be completely annexed until the first years of our next period.

Soon after Pompey's oriental triumphs, Caesar won his in the west. From 58 BC he waged his often brutal campaigns against the fierce if divided resistance of the Gallic (Celtic) tribes of France and the Low Countries. They ended when Vercingetorix, after leading a successful rebellion, was captured at Alesia in 52 BC. (He was held for six years before being paraded in Caesar's

"Dying Warrior," marble, 490 BC, Greece.

Roman Triumph and then strangled.) The Roman frontier was now on the Rhine. In the years 55-54 Caesar had found time to make his two Pyrrhic invasions of Britain – dates which must be said here are too often confused with those of the later Claudian conquest.

It was just at this time that the Romans suffered their most terrible reverse at the opposite limits of their realm. The aging Crassus (who had put down the slave uprising of Spartacus) unwisely led an army against the Parthians in Mesopotamia, hoping to win glory as great as Caesar's – or even Alexander's. The army was caught at Carrhae (Harran) and thousands killed: the worst havoc was wrought by the arrows of the light cavalry, a proportion, no doubt, by those Parthian shots loosed as the horsemen wheeled away. One story is worth telling as, true or false, it reveals something of the part-Greek, part-barbarian oriental courts of the region. It tells that the Parthian king sent the head of Crassus to his tributary monarch of Armenia. The gift arrived during some royal nuptials at which an actor was reciting from Euripides' *Bacchae.* This Jason seized the trophy and declaimed the frenzied words which, in the tragedy, Agave addresses to the head of Pentheus.

So the Roman effort to push beyond the Euphrates failed, and before the end of this period a large army under Mark Antony was also routed by the Parthians.

It was in 49 BC in the midst of civil war that Caesar crossed the Rubicon and took possession of Italy. Soon after, having eradicated Pompey, Caesar made a winter campaign in Egypt, enjoying the company of Cleopatra then a little over twenty years old and as brilliant and dynastically ambitious as she was seductive. He confirmed her on the throne of Egypt – the seventh Cleopatra of the house of Ptolemy – and left her pregnant of a son.

In the various crises of civil war and the failure of the Senate to maintain government, Julius Caesar had several times been given office as temporary dictator, but when he returned to Rome, having crushed the last of Pompey's party, he claimed it for life: to be in effect an emperor. That may have been the main reason for his murder at a meeting of the Senate on the Ides of March 44 BC.

Octavian, still in his teens, had been adopted as Caesar's son and heir. The renewed civil fighting that broke out after the Ides of March, the appointment of the Triumvirate of Mark Antony, Octavian and the wretched Lepidus, their punishment of the party of Caesar's murderers (Cicero was among those executed) and the victory over them at Philippi

The Parthians were able to defeat the Roman army of Crassus at Carrhae in 53 BC by utilizing such tactics as the Parthian shot – an arrow loosed as the horseman wheeled away at high speed.

Supposed head of Cleopatra, Queen of Egypt. Octavian's disapproval of her marriage to Antony led him to declare war on Egypt. After the battle of Actium in 31 BC Egypt became a Roman province.

Julius Caesar (shown above) had several times been given office as temporary dictator but upon eradicating Pompey he claimed office for life. He adopted Octavian as his son and heir (shown right) who later took the title of Augustus and established the Roman Empire.

The Roman mosaic below shows Vergil writing the Aeneid *accompanied by two muses. When he died with his work unfinished, Augustus took some part in having the epic published.*

make a familiar narrative. For a time Octavian undertook the reorganization of Italy while Antony was to look after the eastern provinces.

The year 41 BC saw Mark Antony's first encounter with Cleopatra when she sailed up the Cydnus in splendour to meet him at Tarsus. He spent the winter with her in Egypt – outdoing Caesar in leaving her with twins. During the years that followed Antony's costly failure against the Parthians, his growing subservience to Cleopatra, his marriage to her and abandonment of his wife, Octavian's sister, most of all the suspicions he aroused in Rome by heaping Cleopatra and her offspring with titles and honours, made it easy for the cool, ruthless, immensely capable Octavian to break with him and declare war.

The battle of Actium, when Cleopatra's ships withdrew, was in 31. It is historically true that Antony stabbed himself, thinking Cleopatra dead, and died in her arms; true also that she killed herself by snake bite – though it was after an interval during which she seems to have hoped to captivate the cold Octavian and save her throne. So by 30 Egypt became a province of Rome, one that could supply the city with enough grain for four months of the year. A little later Octavian took the title of Augustus, and although the legal forms of the Republic were duly observed, in fact established the Roman empire. He was worshipped by many of his subjects during his lifetime and after his death his cult as a god was part of the imperial religious observances.

Augustus was a typical Roman of his time in that while he felt a sentimental admiration for Greek culture, he combined it with a dedication to Rome and Roman values. His was in fact a golden age of Latin writing. Vergil (70-19 BC) published his *Georgics* in 29, and when he died with the *Aeneid* not perfectly finished Augustus himself took some part in having the epic published. Catullus, the intense poet of love between the sexes, was some seventeen years Vergil's senior and Horace five years his junior. Ovid was writing as well at this time.

For the rest of the century he was ceaselessly occupied with reconstructing the administration and the army, extending the European frontier to the Danube, enhancing Rome and creating a true *Pax Romana*. So, when Jesus of Nazareth was born – in fact in about 4 BC at the end of the reign of Herod the Great – the Roman Empire, in which his ministry was to be lived, was reaching one of its summits of prosperity and power.

The furthest limit of the shift of innovation and achievement towards the west can be recognized in the exuberant rise and expansion of the Celtic peoples. Their first advance stimulated by contacts with the Greeks of Massilia was mentioned in the last chapter, and they have already appeared more than once in the present section as barbarian intruders upon the civilized world. Barbarians still only just emerging from the mists of prehistory they remained until the last century or two BC. Yet when brought under Roman rule this gifted and vigorous people was to add rich sources of talent, wealth – and trouble – to the empire.

The cradle lands of the Celts, their language and culture were in central Europe north of the Alps and extending into western France where they can be seen as descendants of the creators of the first iron-using culture of Europe, the Hallstatt. They came in time to dominate France and Belgium to the Rhine, north Italy, much of Spain and the British Isles, while Galatia was an outpost left from their migrating thrusts eastward. (From all this area varieties of their Indo-European speech now survive only on its western fringes in Scotland, Wales, Ireland and Brittany.)

Their culture, including their marvellous decorative La Tène art, was developing its character during the two great classical centuries of Greece. Their art in fact grew out of the Hallstatt tradition through the stimulus of imported Greek and Roman decorative design – particularly on wine vessels. This art also absorbed something from the animal designs of the Scyths.

From as early as 500 BC Greek writers bring the Celts into history as a distinctive people united by more than language. They were said to be tall, fair and excitable, with a love of personal display, wine-drinking and fighting. They were in fact much given to warfare between the tribes into which they were divided, and increasingly during the period they built hilltop strongholds which tended to develop into regular settlements. They are usually called *oppida* in France and hillforts in Britain.

In most regions the Celts were ruled by a warrior aristocracy much given to horses. They were probably the last to adopt (fifth century) and the last to employ, the two-wheeled battle chariot that had originated in the second millennium. Much of their finest art was lavished on their shields, helmets, weapons, horse harness and chariot fittings.

The religion of the Celts had much in common with the more primitive stages of other Indo-European peoples. They recognized a variety of divinities, widespread or with local habitations, and propitiated them through

The Turoe stone from Ireland is carved in the Celtic La Tène style.

The silver "Gunderstrup Cauldron" is decorated with the heads of Celtic divinities.

175

sacrifices of cattle and human beings. Their famous druids, mostly members of the aristocracy, had considerable power. They were part priest, part seer, part shaman – and there is more reason to believe in their human sacrifices than in their possession of philosophy. A few, like Divitacus, the druid friend of Cicero and Caesar, may have understood something of classical thought. The extraordinary Greek-influenced religious sculpture of Provence (a shrine in the Entremont oppidum near Aix and Roquepertuse) dating from the third-second century well represents the Celtic mingling of civilization with barbarity. As well as strangely dignified sacred figures, this sculpture clearly represents the Celtic cult of trophy heads.

It was in the early fourth century, just before the birth of Aristotle, that several Celtic tribes invaded northern Italy by the Alpine passes, settling in Lombardy, Emilia and down the Adriatic coasts. They were known to the Romans as Galli. From here fast-moving

warrior bands made forays as far to the south as Sicily. Rome itself was sacked in 390 and remained under threat until the Romans succeeded in trapping and destroying a huge Gallic army at the battle of Telamon in 225.

Further east, it is assumed that there had been an earlier Celtic migration into the Balkans to account for mercenaries serving in the Peloponnese in c. 369. It must have been some disaster in the early third century that caused a horde of Celts to invade Macedonia in wintertime. Whole families were moving in their wagons – a migration recalling that of the Sea Peoples in the eastern Mediterranean almost a thousand years earlier. Before the Greeks could wear them down they had done much pillage and even attacked Delphi. The Greeks subsequently hung a set of the long Celtic shields as trophies in the temple of Apollo, where they could be compared with the old Persian shields already in the shrine.

It was tribes from this migration that swung eastward across the Dardanelles and

Found in the Celtic shrine of Roquepertuse, France, was this limestone "Janus head" so called after the double-facing Roman god.

enjoyed a life of successful banditry in Anatolia before being settled in Galatia.

The history of the Celtic penetration of Spain remains shadowy. Early Celtic-speaking groups had probably been arriving late in our previous period, others certainly came by land or sea during the fifth century and perhaps later. While the Tartessians and Iberians continued to prosper and to develop their culture (including stone sculpture) in the south and east, the Celts were concentrated in the north and west, spreading also into the wild and primitive interior. After mingling with local folk they tended to develop in ways distinct from their kinsmen north of the Pyrenees. Their many *castros* can, however, be compared with Gaulish and British *oppida* and forts.

In spite of the long survival and brilliance of their language, literature and art, particularly in Ireland, the history of the Celts' invasions of Britain is again far from clear. As in Spain, they had probably begun during the late Bronze Age of our last period (1000 – 500 BC) and continued through the present period. One of the most easily distinguished groups was that of the Parisii who settled in Yorkshire, their chiefs being buried with their chariots as was the custom in their homelands of the Marne. The only historically recorded invasions were those of the Belgae from the lower Rhine mentioned by Julius Caesar as having taken place not long before his own raids. These Belgae, ruling in the southeast and south of England, came to have political as well as trading contacts with Gaul and the Romans in the last century BC, importing wine, fine pottery and other goods of civilization and adopting coinage. During this century and up to the conquest by Claudius, La Tène art had a late flowering in Britain, producing some of its leading masterpieces.

In Scandinavia this period covers the pre-Roman Iron Age of archaeology. It was not a very prosperous time in the north perhaps because the Germanic tribes were cut off by the Celts – who were more interested in their Mediterranean contacts. Iron came into use only very slowly. This is the time of some of the famous "bog people," the amazingly well-preserved bodies of men and women (including Tollund Man) who had been sacrificed to the gods or executed for crimes and then consigned to the bogs.

In India, which through its Indo-European inheritance of language and religion was not in fact so utterly remote from the Celtic world as distance would suggest, Achaemenid Darius had conquered the northern Punjab in 516 BC, making it the twentieth satrapy of the Persian Empire. Achaemenid cities such as Charsada

and Taxila grew up on caravan routes that assured their prosperity. Persian influence now encouraged the adoption of a coinage and the use of iron – also the Aramaeic alphabet soon to be modified to suit Indian languages. Sanskrit remained the language of learning and literature.

We have already seen how, with the spread of the Indo-Europeans eastward into the Ganges-Jumna basin, this became the centre of the steadily evolving Hinduism. The doctrine of transmigration was accepted by the Hindus and their more fanatical sect of the Jains, and they had been taught by Buddha and by Mahavira, founder of the Jains, that release from the sad cycle of rebirth could be obtained only by right belief, right conduct and right action on the part of each individual.

The caste system was now becoming firmly established, part of it based as it originally was on colour. The fair westerners ruled the natives whom they called *Dasyus* (slaves). There were three groups of the higher castes, the brahmans or priests (who have

The amazingly well-preserved head of Tollund Man from Denmark belonged to one of the "bog people" either sacrificed to the Iron Age Scandinavian gods or executed for crimes.

Scythian gold plaque from southern Russia shows two men sharing a drinking horn – perhaps as a gesture of friendship.

sometimes been likened to druids), the warriors and the merchants. The aboriginals below them were to become untouchable *sudras* or outcasts.

The two great epics of the time, the *Mahabharata* and *Ramayana*, are always irresistibly compared with the *Iliad* and *Odyssey*. Though one is concerned with a family feud, the other with the adventures of Prince Rama of Oudh, together they give a picture of a maturing civilization with powerful kingdoms, walled towns and spacious, if simple, palaces. In eastern India small states, both tribal republics and principalities, were being welded into larger units, the greatest of them becoming Maghada with its capital at Pataliputra (Patna). Here were self-contained villages in forest clearings; craft guilds under guild masters were an important part of social life.

In 326 BC a clear shaft of historical light breaks into this rather dim picture. Alexander the Great crossed the Indus and soon entered Taxila – where the Greeks were at once amazed by the naked Jain ascetics, widow-burning and marriage markets. They had very little difficulty in taking the Persian satrapy: in the crucial battle the elephants of the Indian army proved more dangerous to their own side than to the invaders, and the chariots useless.

Alexander would have liked to conquer the Ganges lands, but his troops at last rebelled and he had to withdraw along the Indus. Soon after his death the Greeks as a ruling power were driven out of the Punjab by a national rising led by a young warrior, Chandragupta Maurya – who then made himself king of Maghada. He came to rule most of northern India as a typical good oriental despot, maintaining a large army, many spies and a pleasant lacquered palace at Pataliputra. He built a royal road to the northwest frontier and his foreign trade extended as far afield as Egypt and China.

The greatest ruler of the Mauryan empire was to be Chandragupta's grandson, Ashoka, who succeeded in 273. He launched a successful war against Kalinga (Orissa) but was so much horrified by the slaughter and suffering he had caused that he became a total convert to Buddhism, renounced warfare and began to rule his kingdom under the "law of piety."

This conversion was almost as important for Buddhism as that of Constantine was to be for Christianity. It was raised from a still obscure sect to be the official religion of a very considerable empire. Ashoka with his family visited the Buddhist holy places, and at each one of them, and other spots besides, set up his famous sandstone columns in the Persian style, highly polished and crowned with lions and other symbols. On some, gentle admonitions to his subjects were carved. The ashes of Buddha were divided up and great numbers of *stupas* or *dagobas* built to enshrine them. Rock-cut temples and cells, the interiors highly polished, were copied from Persia, and it is very probable that many craftsmen employed in Persia and left unemployed by the destruction of Persepolis and other effects of Alexander's seizure of the Achaemenid empire, moved into the service of the Mauryans and began to beautify their cities – hitherto without stone architecture or style.

Ashoka sent Buddhist missionaries far afield even to Antiochus of Syria and Ptolemy of Egypt. More important for the future was his family mission to Lanka (Sri Lanka) which converted the king and all his court. Buddhism has continued there ever since.

After Ashoka died in 232, the Mauryan empire began to break down and by the second century, when it ended, India was being violently affected by movements of nomadic hordes on the steppes to the north. The Grecian element in the population of the Punjab was reinforced when Greeks settled in Bactria were driven across the Hindu Kush by Saka nomads from beyond the Oxus. The Saka themselves invaded India and set up petty kingdoms there. In about 140 the Parthians, a part of this great nomad upheaval, seized Taxila.

The history of the nomadic hordes along the whole sweep of the Eurasiatic steppes during this period is too complicated and fast changing to be chronicled. At its beginning the Scyths of the Pontic regions were still strong and making the great royal burials so vividly and accurately described by Herodotus. The richness of these royal tombs is even better shown at Pazyryk in the Altai where in the fifth-third centuries BC eastern kinsmen of the Scyths left burial mounds so constructed that they served as a deep-freeze preserving marvellous textiles, pictorial felt hangings and fantastic horse headdresses. Some of these grave furnishings show strong Chinese influence. The bodies buried at Pazyryk prove that mongols were now mingling with the Indo-European stock; the men had been tattooed with impeccable displays of nomadic animal art.

Towards the end of the period Scyths were largely destroyed by a steady westward thrust of the Sarmatians. As for the movements into India, they had been set off by the expanding power of the Hsiung Nu nomads of the Gobi who pushed out their eastern neighbours, the Yueh Chi. These people were among those whom the Chinese wished to hold in check by the construction of their Great Wall.

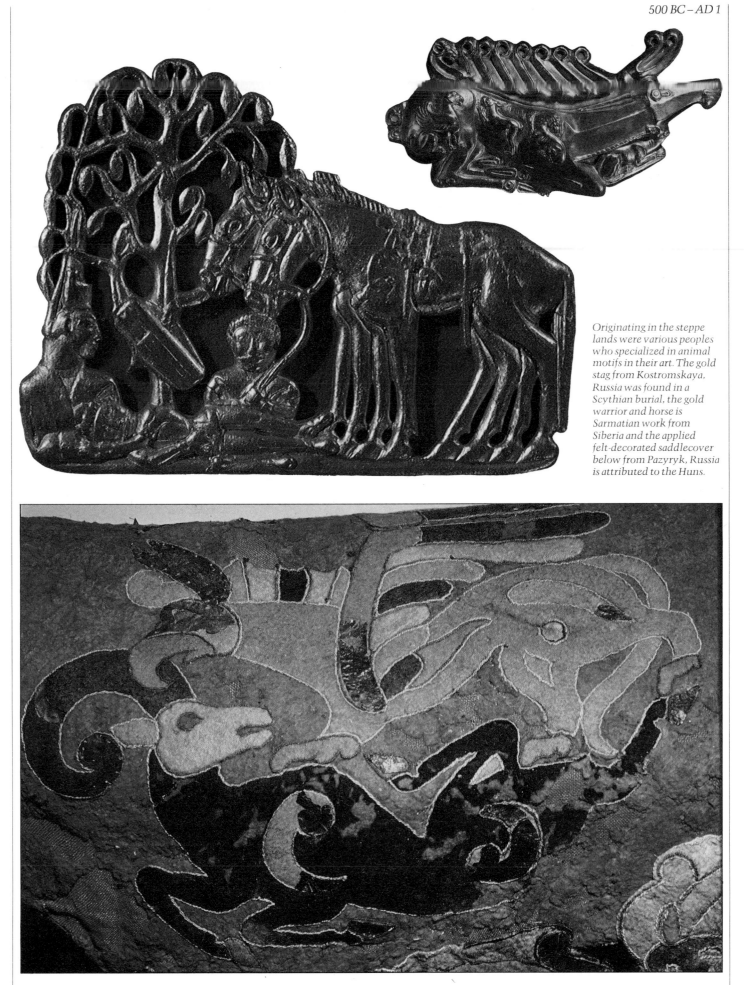

Originating in the steppe lands were various peoples who specialized in animal motifs in their art. The gold stag from Kostromskaya, Russia was found in a Scythian burial, the gold warrior and horse is Sarmatian work from Siberia and the applied felt-decorated saddlecover below from Pazyryk, Russia is attributed to the Huns.

In China itself the Chou regime was weakening before and during the period known as the age of the Warring States (402-221 BC) when there was not only internal fighting between states but attacks from the nomads. Yet it was an age of growing trade and of prosperous country towns, also an age of philosphers such as Motzu who believed in universal love and pacifism and Mencius who developed Confucian teaching. Iron was coming more freely into use for weapons as well as tools.

The rising state was in fact that of the Ch'in who had remained relatively obscure during the height of the Chou but now fought southward from their northern homeland. They may have owed some of their success to their adoption of good iron swords. In 256, when the Romans were in the middle of the First Punic War, the Ch'in killed the last, vestigial, Chou emperor and soon took control of all rival states. As a more civilized commentator observed "Ch'in has the same customs as the barbarians. It has the heart of a tiger of wolf.... It knows nothing about etiquette and virtuous conduct and if there be any opportunity for material gain, it will disregard its relatives as if they were animals."

Nevertheless by 221 their ruler established himself as Ch'in-Shih-huang "First Emperor" of a unified Chinese empire. Various northern states had been building sections of earthen wall against nomad attack; these the emperor now faced with stone and linked together to form a continuous rampart. Its effectiveness was greatly increased by the invention of the crossbow which enabled defenders to pick off the mounted nomads at a range far beyond that of their own composite bows.

Ch'in-Shih-huang's government was efficient in administration, in unifying the script and the currency, but he tyrannically suppressed free intellectual debate, ordered a burning of the books – and so was execrated in later times.

The rule of his house was not to last. By 206 BC it had been displaced by the Han dynasty, coming from the same northern region as the Chou and Ch'in. (Although the west has adopted the name of the Ch'in for the country, the Chinese like to call themselves "men of Han.") The first two centuries of the Han empire, when the "Son of Heaven" ruled from the "City of Eternal Peace," coincided with the expansion of the Roman republic. While it was equally rich and powerful, despite the name of the capital, it was no more peaceloving – at least in earthly terms.

Deservedly the most renowned emperor of the early Han, Wu-ti (140-86 BC), was known as the Martial Emperor and waged most extravagant campaigns. By one of them he lost tens of thousands of men and horses in order to capture a breeding stock of the Ferghana steeds, so much larger and more beautiful than the sturdy steppe horses which the Chinese, like their nomad enemies the Scyths and Sarmatians, had hitherto employed.

Wu-ti, however, was also an admirable ruler. He caused the construction of great canal systems, organized the iron and salt industries and developed the famous Silk Road to the west on which so much of the imperial wealth depended. The Romans had by now come to appreciate this loveliest and most comfortable of all textiles. They knew China as the Land of Silk. Caravans of silk-laden camels set out from the Han capital, through Kansu to Samarkhand and on to Antioch and the Mediterranean coast. Guard posts were set up along the route and Wu-ti waged war against the Hsiung-nu, always a danger to his northern provinces and the Silk Road.

There are good written sources for the history of the Han – indeed there was a court historian Ssu-ma, castrated by Wu-ti for his criticisms but permitted to remain in office. Yet owing to the funerary customs of the wealthy, it is archaeology that can provide the most amazingly full, dazzling and intimate

The Chinese silk necessary to make this cloth found in a chieftain's burial at Pazyryk, Russia, no doubt arrived via the Silk Road from the Han capital through Samarkhand on the way to the Mediterranean coast.

pictures of the life of all classes in that age.

In a number of ways it seems that the Han empire can better be compared with those of the Near Eastern Bronze Age rather than with contemporary Rome. In spite of its religious philosophies it had not experienced the mental revolution of Greek intellectual detachment and rationalism. In the matter of burial of the elite with full provision for the enjoyment of the good things and services of this world for use in the next, it is obvious to compare Han China with the Egypt of the Old and New Kingdoms. Confucius had been relieved by the substitution of tomb figurines for the sacrificial holocausts of Shang times.

Already some very fine models were put in Ch'in tombs, but now they contained group models of all manner of men and women and animals set in houses and farms. In one, with over two dozen painted clay figures, dancers and acrobats perform with a band of zither, pipes, gongs and drums.

The dead were also provided with sumptuous personal treasures. The Marquess of Tai, for example, who died in c.160 BC, had been buried in a score of silk robes and cloaks, accompanied by fifty rolls of silk, exquisite lacquer work, wooden models of 162 servants of her household, as well as countless female accessories, cosmetics and false hair. The painted silk banner draping her coffin showed

Green jade Han Dynasty horse's head from China.

Bronze vessel of Han Dynasty China.

One of the tomb figurines of Han Dynasty times which replaced the sacrificial holocausts of the Shang era.

the Marquess herself framed by dragons of a species still being portrayed under the rule of Chairman Mao.

The burials that have won world fame are those of Liu Sheng, brother of Wu-ti, and his wife and cousin Tou Wan, who died some half century after the Marquess. They were found in close-fitting suits of thousands of pieces of jade linked with gold and had been provided with horses and carriages and many treasures. Among these none was more lovely than the gilt bronze lamp held by a kneeling lady. It had been given to Tou Wan by her grandmother, a powerful royal dowager, who had it designed for her own palace of Eternal Trust.

In Japan people of the long-lived Jōmon culture, in many areas still largely dependent on fishing, maintained their simple way of life through much of the Warring States era in China. Then, early in the third century BC, strong continental influences that included both Chinese and Korean elements began to enter Kyushu and to spread gradually eastward among the Jōmon communities. The greatest change was in the adoption of rice-growing in regular paddy fields, but before long the potter's wheel was introduced, probably from Korea, and bronze weapons and bells were imported and soon also made locally.

The resulting bronze-iron culture is known as the Yayoi. Its arrival may from the first have involved a considerable immigration, and certainly was in time to be associated with the mongolization of Japan – the mongolian element having been slight among the Jōmon folk. The immigrants seem to have tended to form a ruling class, humble when compared with their Celtic contemporaries in Britain, but clearly marking the start of social stratification.

This modest Yayoi aristocracy sometimes buried their dead in stone cist-graves of Korean type, but a more common custom was burial in large lidded jars, or opposed pairs of jars. Before the end of the period they might be furnished with imported Chinese bronze mirrors, glass beads, coins and weapons.

The cultivators lived in villages near their rice fields in sturdy round or oval houses with heavy thatch supported on ridge poles, sometimes with a upper roof over the ridge. For the storage of their rice they built substantial granaries raised on piles. After the long retardation due to their isolation, by the end of our era the Japanese were evidently on their way to the literate civilization that would dawn in our next period.

In Meso and South America, 500 BC – AD 1 falls mainly within the Late Formative or Pre-Classic period in archaeological terms. Olmec civilization still persisted and its influence was widespread in Mesoamerica, but it was to decline and disappear with the abandonment or destruction of its ceremonial centres. Meanwhile, as the Olmec as a distinct tradition was coming to an end, that of the Maya was emerging more strongly. In the Guatemalan lowlands what was to become the grand Mayan ceremonial centre of Tikal had been founded by the beginning of the period and temples of plastered masonry were already being built there by 300 BC.

At Monte Albán in the Oaxaca Valley of southern Mexico, we saw that the first stelae inscribed with hieroglyphs were probably set up in c.500 BC. Among the ceremonial buildings of this early capital of the Zapotec people was the pyramid platform called the Mound of the Dancers, after a well known series of contorted, naked figures incised on stone slabs. Instead of dancers, they may well represent mutilated sacrificial victims. They are associated with hieroglyphic inscriptions that already include the bar and dot numerals later to be used by the Maya as well as evidence for calendrical reckoning (p. 187).

Meanwhile very significant advances were taking place in the Valley of Mexico. Its people had long lagged behind their southern neighbours, but were now taking the first tentative steps towards their future dominance.

Superb textiles figured with grotesque humans, birds, animals and monsters were found in the Paracas Necropolis in Peru.

Considerable temple building was undertaken – for example at Cuicuilco to the southwest of the great lake that filled the Basin. In a side valley there was already some settlement at Teotihuacán, destined to become the magnificent ceremonial capital of a powerful state.

In South America the Chavín culture that had given a certain unity to Peru was breaking up, though it continued to flourish for a time in its own heartlands round Chavín de Huantár and also along the south coast. Here, as is shown by the cemetery of the Paracas Necropolis with its mummified burials, the the most superb textiles were being woven for cloaks, shirts and other garments. They are figured with grotesque humans, birds, animals and monsters, all in the richest colours. There was some increase in the working of copper and gold ornaments – and goldsmiths were active also in Colombia.

Towards the very end of the period there were signs of the creative change that was to flower in our last period. In Colombia the ceremonial centre of San Agustín had probably been founded, in Peru the Mochica and Nazca cultures were emerging on the coasts, and in the Bolivian Andes near Lake Titicaca the famous Tiahuanaco had already been settled, though still far from days its greatest.

In North America there was considerable advance in the southwest, although it was not achieved until near the end of the period. Then out of the old Cochise tradition, as better cultivation of maize and other plants allowed an increase in population, there grew flourishing farming societies with quite substantial villages. These belonged in the mountainous regions to the Mogollon peoples, and in the hot deserts of Arizona to the Hohokam. In these desert lowlands irrigation was necessary from the first, and it is clear that there was at this time a very strong influence, if not an actual immigration, from Mexico. A well known settlement of the early Hohokam people is Snaketown on the Gila river near Tucson. Here Mexican borrowings can be seen in cotton textiles, figurines, ornaments such as nose and ear plugs, and in time in the construction of a ballcourt and ceremonial mounds. Both Mogollon and Hohokam people were to develop excellent painted pottery.

In the east the life of the Woodland moundbuilders did not show any very significant change, although a branch of it known as the Hopewell culture had evolved by about 200 BC and evidently prospered, since its creators were able to import such materials as obsidian, mica and shells over quite long distances. The Woodland people of the whole Ohio-Mississippi region continued to devote themselves to the piling of huge burial mounds and other earthworks that were probably ceremonial in purpose.

Figure of a baby in typical Olmec style. The influence of their distinctive art style persisted throughout Mesoamerica.

Technology *500 BC – AD 1*

Technological progress in our last two chapters depends almost entirely on engineering as no new raw material was exploited during this time. Advances in iron working, however, were responsible for one of the few new means of production – that of blowing glass. Previous materials had been unsuitable for the necessary tubes.

Social factors were largely responsible for the lack of technical innovation among the Greeks, for instance, but mechanical devices, such as the water organ, fire engine and steam turbine were produced in great numbers, even if they were treated like toys. More practical developments were the Archimedean screw, cogwheels, pulleys, pumps, levers, lathe and valve bellows which were adapted for various purposes.

In Athens, Alexandria and other centres, scientists and scholars such as Hero, Ctesibius and Philo studied and designed equipment for both military and civilian purposes. They also wrote engineering manuals and interested themselves in logic, astronomy and navigational problems.

China under the Han dynasty produced another technological explosion. Their most important single contribution was the invention of the horse collar, which along with shafts and traces resulted in the first efficient harnessing of the horse's strength. Iron workers using improved bellows achieved temperatures high enough for the casting of their metal many centuries before this could be done in Europe. The crossbow, with its cocking and trigger device, and the wheelbarrow well demonstrated Chinese ingenuity at this period.

Great progress, too, was made in the New World. In Mexico the Olmecs devised a remarkable and highly effective calendar and glyphic script. Their Calendar Round was a numerical way of dividing the year: two interlocking cycles of 20 numbers and 18 months gave, with the addition of five extra days a 365 day year. In Colombia metallurgy was being perfected in gold, silver, copper and alloys. In Peru the major developments were in the form of major works of irrigation and terracing.

Another advance which, though increasing the efficiency of investment of effort, can only marginally be considered technological, was in the matter of imperial administration. Where the Assyrians had failed, the Persians succeeded, and the Macedonians and Romans, and not forgetting the Han, improved even on their efforts.

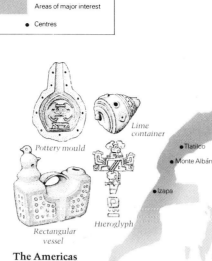

	Areas of major interest
●	Centres

Pottery mould

Lime container

● Tlatilco
● Monte Albán
● Izapa

Rectangular vessel

Hieroglyph

The Americas
Pottery was often made in moulds in this area, as the specimens from Peru and Ecuador show. Carved shells were also used as containers. Writing in the form of hieroglyphs made its appearance in the Mayan areas.

● Paracas

Egypt, Eastern, Western Mediterranean
The spread of Hellenism and then of the Roman armies produced a similar technology in the three Mediterranean regions. The steam turbine and hydraulic organ demonstrate the Greek mind at its most inventive while more practically useful for time telling and field irrigation were the water clock and Archimedes screw. Older skills, often in improved forms, are represented by the shield and body armour, the furniture (in stone and bronze as well as wood) and the trireme (developed from the bireme by the addition of a third bank of oars). More widely applied were the improved grape press, lathe and military catapult, all exploiting new principles or new applications of old ones.

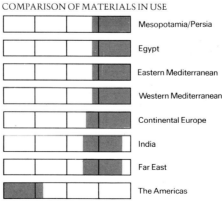

COMPARISON OF MATERIALS IN USE

Mesopotamia/Persia

Egypt

Eastern Mediterranean

Western Mediterranean

Continental Europe

India

Far East

The Americas

Stone Copper Bronze Iron

Continental Europe

The Dejbjerg wagon shows the level of technological expertise achieved by "barbarian" Europe. Iron was general for swords and spears, and even ploughshares and delicate surgical instruments were now being produced in that metal. Bronze was still used, however.

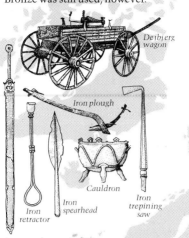

Dejbjerg wagon

Iron plough

Cauldron

Iron spearhead

Iron retractor

Iron trepining saw

Iron sword in scabbord

Far East

The cast iron implements and complicated crossbow are only some of the wide range of products encountered under the inventive Han dynasty. The chariot was continued, the model cooking stove being a contemporary appliance.

Cast iron adze

Cast iron axe

Trigger mechanism for cross bow

Clay model stove

Chinese cross bow

Chinese chariot

Bactrian leading camel

Coins

Sword scabbard

Mesopotamia/Persia

The camel, in both the one and two humped forms, was the most important means of transport. Coinage also emphasizes trade movements through the area. The distinctive sword scabbard, however, continues an older tradition of decorated metalwork.

• Ch'ang-An

La Tène •   • Heuneberg

• Bologna

Tarquinia • • Rome

Carthage •   • Syracuse
     • Athens

• Taxila

• Alexandria

Babylon • • Seleucia
     • Susa
        • Persepolis

Sarnath • • Rajgir

• Sanchi

Pottery vessel

Pot

Soakpits

Black polished ware

India

While evidence of metallurgy or other technical expertise is lacking, an extremely varied range of pottery has been preserved. This includes highly competent Northern Black Polished Ware as well as coarse jars subsequently used for lining soakaways.

Steam turbine

Grape press

Hydraulic organ

Couch leg

Lathe

Armour

• Meroe

Catapult

Archimedes screw

Stone chair

Water clock

Greek trireme

Mesopotamia/Persia

Persia's major contribution was in the field of imperial organization. Its coinage, such as the Darics of the Achaemenid royal house, were accepted from the Aegean to India, and symbolized the peaceful movement of trade over vast distances. Minted money did not, of course, disappear with the Persian Empire; Alexander and his successors maintained it, striking their own pieces, and with Persian independence under the Parthians, local issues resumed again. Trade was also enhanced in this difficult terrain by more widespread use of both the one and two-humped camel which greatly facilitated transport.

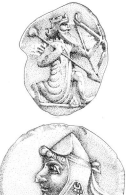

TOP: Achaemenian gold coin
BELOW: Parthian drachma

RIGHT: Bactrian leading camel

Egypt, Eastern, Western Mediterranean

The trireme was merely a bigger and better bireme with a third bank of rowers and composite keel. The number of oarsmen varied between 120 and 200, and those in the third bank sat furthest inboard. Presses for grapes and olives were much improved by incorporating the principles of lever, pulley and winch. The catapult represents a whole range of military weaponry powered by rope torsion, but with few applications elsewhere. Though not very efficient, the water clock was the best attempt until very much later to measure the passage of time. Archimedes, the greatest engineer of his age, developed the screw pump to lift water from mines. Hero of Alexandria developed a device for opening temple doors using hot air but his "steam engine" was considered by many to be no more than a scientific toy.

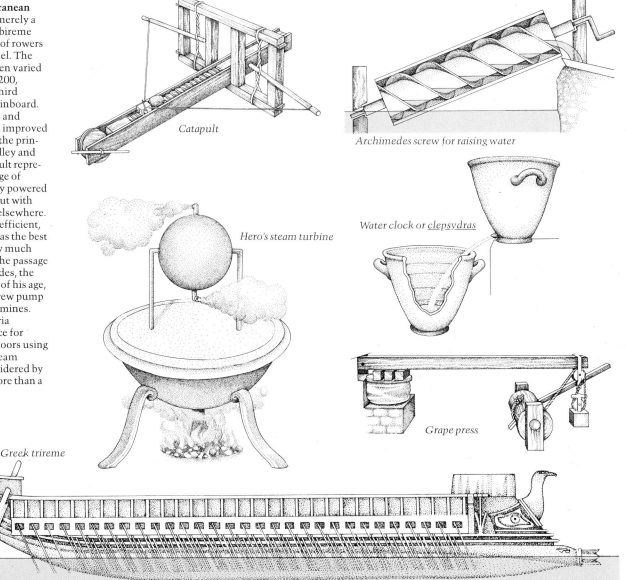

Catapult

Archimedes screw for raising water

Hero's steam turbine

Water clock or clepsydras

Greek trireme

Grape press

Continental Europe

The Dejbjerg wagon from Denmark incorporates a number of improvements on previous vehicles such as 14-spoked wheels with multipiece felloes and lavish bronze plate decoration. The Celtic craftsmen introduced a roller bearing of wooden pins in a bronze race, to facilitate the turning of the wheel on its axle. A simpler and more obvious development can be seen in the plough – where iron was probably used to preserve the wood of the plough from excessive wear rather than to ease its passage through the soil. Before long an even more significant improvement was made – the addition of a coulter (a heavy knife blade, which cut the sod for turning the furrow).

Dejbjerg wagon

Roller bearing on Dejbjerg wagon

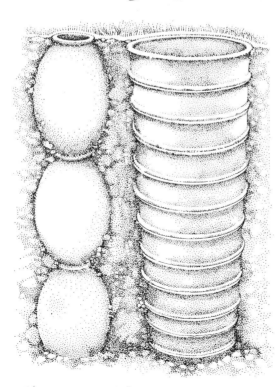

Iron plough

India

The pottery-lined soakaway pits, and even the highly competent northern black polished ware show that material technological equipment made little progress. Advances in theoretical knowledge however, were of enormous importance, particularly in the field of mathematics. It was here that the efficient use of the zero sign in conjunction with positional notation was first perfected, making figures a tool for calculation, not just a method of recording.

Northern black polished ware

Soak pits, Hastinapura, India

Far East

In China progress in the casting of iron led to socketed forms of axes which differ greatly in comparison with the wrought iron forms of the west. Greater skills were required in producing these tools but they suffered from a certain brittleness of the material. The iron, in effect, merely strengthened and protected the edge of what were really wooden tools – a very economical use of the metal. Inventiveness is even more apparent in the development of the crossbow, with which the defenders of the Great Wall kept the desert nomads at bay. This is most apparent in the trigger mechanism which gave an efficient arrow release. It was cast in bronze in three ingeniously interlocking parts. This weapon was far superior to the composite bow due to its easier loading and greater range.

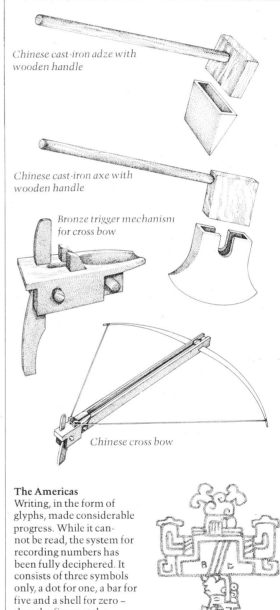

Chinese cast-iron adze with wooden handle

Chinese cast-iron axe with wooden handle

Bronze trigger mechanism for cross bow

Chinese cross bow

The Americas

Writing, in the form of glyphs, made considerable progress. While it cannot be read, the system for recording numbers has been fully deciphered. It consists of three symbols only, a dot for one, a bar for five and a shell for zero – thus the figure at the bottom of the accompanying illustration is 8. The main purpose of this system was to record dates in the Calendar Round. Two interlocking cycles of 20 numbers and 18 "months" gave (plus 5 extra days), a 365 day year.

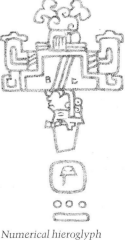

Numerical hieroglyph

Architecture 500 BC – AD 1

Once the major structural and aesthetic problems of the Greek temple had been solved, the formula could be repeated indefinitely on any site and at any scale, with variation limited to stylistic decoration. In particular, the leafy Corinthian capital achieved immediate popularity. With the spread of Hellenistic civilization around the Mediterranean, east to the Punjab and west to the Atlantic, this most typical of Greek buildings was carried with it. Much more interesting for its later significance was the development of the Greek theatre, which posed a new set of problems that called for new answers. There was no difficulty where a suitable hillside could be carved into shape. Where only a level site was available, the structure had to be built up, and the properties of the arch had to be explored for this purpose. In Italy there was not always good limestone, so that brick and concrete had to be investigated as substitutes.

Improvements in old techniques were being perfected in Europe also. Earthen ramparts were made more stable and more formidable by means of various systems of timber lacing and facing. At the same time, they developed from refuges into towns or *oppida*, with a corresponding elaboration of the timber architecture within them.

In the Middle East, the city of Persepolis marks the peak of local architectural development, with its monumental stairways and pillared halls. Persepolis is famous for its architectural sculptures which lined the stairways showing processions of nobles, courtiers and tribute-bearers.

In India the new religion of Buddhism provided the impetus for temples and monuments to house the sacred relics. The rock-cut chaitya halls and stupas were the result. Hellenistic influences came through Bactria and Gandara at an opportune moment to affect the Indian religious, architectural and artistic development.

In China, most building continued in timber, doubtless in grander and more lavish versions as the Han Dynasty centralized the country's wealth. There are interesting tomb models but little more, until one reaches the frontier of the empire. There the Great Wall was completed to keep out nomadic raiders.

In Mesoamerica the ceremonial centre of Tikal was begun and temples of plastered masonry were being built. Pyramid platforms were constructed by the Zapotec people while in the Valley of Mexico considerable temple building was undertaken.

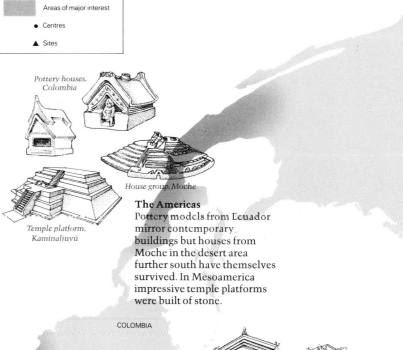

Areas of major interest

● Centres

▲ Sites

Pottery houses, Colombia

House group, Moche

Temple platform, Kaminaljuyú

The Americas
Pottery models from Ecuador mirror contemporary buildings but houses from Moche in the desert area further south have themselves survived. In Mesoamerica impressive temple platforms were built of stone.

COLOMBIA

▲ Moche

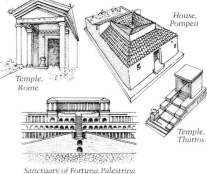

House, Pompeii

Temple, Rome

Temple, Tharros

Sanctuary of Fortuna, Palestrina

Western Mediterranean
Greek temple architecture was carried to the west, though often adapted to local taste, as at Rome and Praeneste. Houses were more typically Roman. The Temple at Tharros reflects the contribution of another culture to that area – that of the Phoenicians.

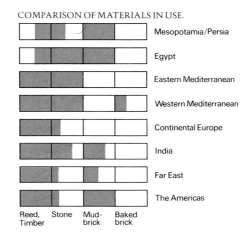

COMPARISON OF MATERIALS IN USE.

Mesopotamia/Persia

Egypt

Eastern Mediterranean

Western Mediterranean

Continental Europe

India

Far East

The Americas

Reed, Timber · Stone · Mud-brick · Baked brick

Continental Europe
Protective settlements were widespread over this area. The crannog at Milton Loch was an artificial timber-based island, the broch of Mousa a drystone tower, the Heuneberg a hill fort of earth and mudbrick.

Lakeside settlement, Milton Crannog

Broch, Mousa

Hillfort, Heuneberg

Eastern Mediterranean
The principles of Greek temple architecture are most widely recognized in the Parthenon. The Propylea, monumental entrance to the Athens Acropolis, belongs to the same tradition. In the Xanthos monument these principles have been modified while the theatre at Epidaurus represents another line of Greek architectural development.

Parthenon, Athens

Propulea, Athens

Theatre, Epidauros

Monument, Xanthos

Far East
The Great Wall of China and some contemporary tombs have survived due to massive masonry or subterranean location. Pottery models and tiles provide evidence of less permanent structures.

Tomb, Shantung

Model house

Han Dynasty tile, Szechwan

Great Wall, China

SHANTUNG

SZECHWAN

SWAT VALLEY

MAGADHA

Capital, Pataliputra

Kushinagara, Magadha

Stupa, Swat Valley

Great Stupa, Sanchi

India
The Mauryan Empire, with its capital at Pataliputra and its origins at Magadha was responsible for the revival of monumental architecture in India. Its greatest monument is probably the stupa at Sanchi, the finest of many. Also shown is a humbler example from the Swat Valley.

Pharos, Alexandria

Temple of Isis, Philae

Temple, Kom Ombo

Temple, Edfou

Egypt
The Hellenistic tradition is clearly seen in the Pharos at Alexandria. Up the Nile, however, native temple architecture prevailed at such sites as Philae, Kom Ombo and Edfou.

Lycian tomb

Tomb, Naksh-i-Rustam

Column, Persepolis

Persepolis

Mesopotamia/Persia
The city of Persepolis and Darius' palace form the most famous sites of the area and period. One innovation was the animal forms on sculptured column capitals. At nearby Naksh-i-Rustam, Darius' tomb was cut into the cliffs but a different style is apparent in the Lycian tomb.

Mesopotamia/Persia

Darius built Persepolis as a capital for his vast empire. The city was built on a natural rock terrace and although the mudbrick buildings and enclosing wall no longer survive, some of the supporting columns, sculptures and relief-decorated stairways still remain. Other stone carvings are evident on the monumental facade of Darius' tomb at Naksh-i-Rustam.

Tomb, Naksh-i-Rustam

Ornamental stairway and columns, Persepolis

Egypt

The Pharos of Alexandria was one of the Ancient World's Seven Wonders, built to serve as a lighthouse. Though its design was Hellenistic, its colossal size was more clearly Egyptian. The great gateway and relief-decorated towers at the Temple of Horus, Edfu, continued a more traditional local style.

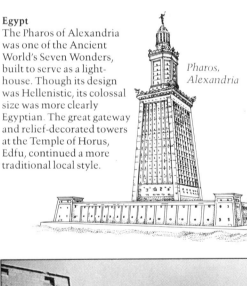

Pharos, Alexandria

First pylon, Temple of Horus, Edfu

Eastern Mediterranean

The Parthenon was the temple of Pallas Athene, the patron goddess of Athens. It was built in 447-432 BC by Pericles and once housed Athene's giant ivory and gold statue. The temple consists of a central cella, in which the old megaron plan can still be recognized, surrounded by colonnades. The outer row contained 46 pillars. The Elgin Marbles adorned the triangular gables and friezes along the sides. The Greek theatre was also a religious building of a more simple architectural design. The orchestra was a complete circle with an altar. The theatre was carved into the rock of a suitable hillside, only the screen behind the stage and a "proscenium" requiring building up.

The Parthenon, Athens, Greece

Greek theatre plan

Theatre, Epidaurus, Greece

Western Mediterranean

Pompei's single-storey houses were based on a standard plan: largely blank walls fronted the streets; an entrance led into a central courtyard; a hole in the roof lit the atrium. The main reception and living rooms were grouped around and the kitchen quarters were tucked in at the back. Concrete was invented to supply strength to the Italian tufo used in constructing the Temple of Fortuna Primigenia.

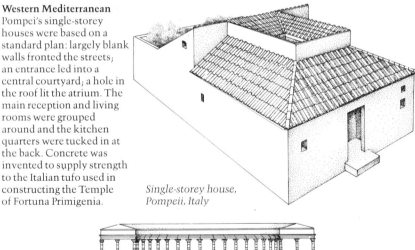

Single-storey house, Pompeii, Italy

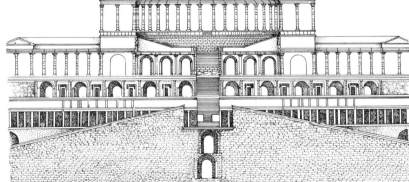

Temple of Fortuna Primigenia, Palestrina, Italy

Continental Europe

The broch at Mousa, Shetland, Scotland, like other structures developed in similar circumstances (the nuraghi of Sardinia), was a defensive stronghold, a refuge for a small community in a region of plentiful stone. The broch is a circular tower of two skins of unmortared stone, allowing a stair to wind up between the two to a parapet walk, at Mousa over 39 ft (12 m) above the ground. A single small doorway opens to the outside. The interior court was surrounded by timber lean-to structures against the stone wall. The hillfort and wooden houses at the Heuneberg had more complicated defences. After a double bank and ditch with earthen causeway the western wall was constructed in the "timber-box" technique combining timber frame and stone rubble filling. The other surrounding settlement walls were of sun-dried mudbrick on limestone.

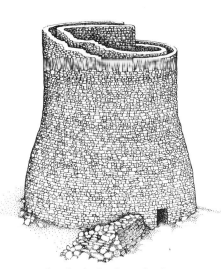

Mousa broch, Shetland, Scotland

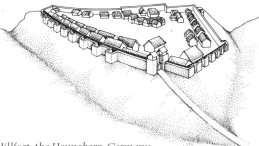

Hillfort, the Heuneberg, Germany

India

The Great Stupa at Sanchi, Bhopal, was built about 240 BC by the Mauryan emperor Ashoka. Its function was to house a relic of the Buddha and as such it is distantly related to the barrows of central Asia and Europe, being equally a funerary deposit beneath a hemispheric mound. It was much enlarged to its present form under the Andhra dynasty, 72-25 BC, who also added the railings and gateways. Like the Egyptian pyramid, the Mesopotamian ziggurat or the Mexican temple mound, a complicated symbolism is embodied, determining strictly the orientation and proportions of the monument. However elaborate the design, the technical means of construction in all these cases were very simple. The gateways for example, are straight translations into stone of timber originals. The mound and railings are quite plain here, but the four gateways at the cardinal points were lavishly decorated in relief.

Great Stupa and gateway, Sanchi, Bhopal

Far East

Pottery house models from c. 202 BC have been preserved in tombs although the light-walled, timber-framed originals no longer exist. However, the Great Wall has been restored in recent centuries. This monument is attributed to Ch'in-Shih-huang, Ch'in emperor of 232 BC. While fortified boundaries between Chinese states had been built well before, he had the idea of joining up existing stretches into a continuous boundary for 1920 miles (3200 Km).

Model of Han house

The Great Wall of China

The Americas

A temple platform at Uaxactún shows the complexity of Mayan architecture by the Chicanel phase of about 300 BC. It has the characteristic apron mouldings and on each face the stairway is flanked by monster masks. The structure is 26 ft (8 m) high, and is of adobe coated with white plaster (stone being scarce in the area). The temple which had crowned the summit was a simple structure of poles and thatch.

Temple platform, Uaxactún, Guatemala

Art 500 BC–AD 1

Greek art as it emerged into its full classic age must be given first place both for its own unique perfection and for its widespread and lasting influence. Having left behind archaic stiffness, Greek sculptors produced their works of a calm and idealized naturalism, often as an integral part of temples and other buildings. The red figure mode of vase painting had recently been devised by the Athenians, and now gave artists the flexibility to create the most exquisite figured and formally decorated ceramics the world has ever known. In the Hellenistic Age sculpture became more elaborate, dramatic and individual.

Greek art continued to influence many neighbouring peoples, including the Etruscans, whose art perhaps reached its peak c.500 with the fine terracottas of the sculptor Vulca at Veii, and after that tended to decline.

The Romans, as their Greek inspired art developed in later Republican times, may also have learnt something from the Etruscans. By the end of the period their sense of personality was evident in fine portrait sculpture and they were beginning to paint attractive landscapes. The Roman art of mosaic began in the fifth century BC. Greek, and to a less extent Etruscan influence, was important in the first inspiration of the La Tène art of the Celts that flourished all through this period.

In Egypt, even under the Ptolemies, Greek influence had little effect on the art; outside Alexandria reliefs and other sculpture in the great temples of the age still show the ancient styles. In Achaemenid Persia, too, these influences were weak, the sculptors of Susa and Persepolis being far more indebted to Assyrian tradition. In the whole region from central Asia to eastern Europe affected by the Scyths and other nomads, there was a bewildering blend of Chinese, Persian and Greek elements mingled with the old animal style of the steppes.

Indian sculpture revived in architectural reliefs and the famous Ashoka columns – where Persian influence was strong. Hellenistic Greeks greatly affected sculpture in the north-west. In China, while some fine tomb figures in bronze and clay were already being made in Ch'in times, it was with the Han that they became numerous and of great beauty. Lacquer work and painting on silk were also exquisite.

In the Americas the late Olmec style was dying out, while Monte Albán and early Mayan sculpture was beginning. In Peru the minor arts of pottery and textiles almost attain to greatness.

Areas of major interest
● Centres
▲ Sites

MEXICO

▲ Oaxaca

Figurine. Oaxaca.

Carved boulder. San Agustin

Textile. Paracas

Olmec figurine. Mexico

▲ San Agustin

Zoomorphic vessel

● Paracas

The Americas

While the influence of the Olmec "baby face" style lingered on, growing points were now in upland Mexico, at Monte Albán and other places in Oaxaca and in the Petén where Mayan art was stirring. Fifth century Peru produced superb textiles. The Chavín pottery tradition persisted in some regions, and the coastal Mohica and Nazca cultures began late in the period.

Head. Etruscan

Capitoline wolf. Rome

Head. Elche

Etruscan earring

Wall painting. Tarquinia

Western Mediterranean

During the earlier centuries the Etruscans produced their sculpture and murals in which archaic Greek tradition tended to prevail over classic naturalism. The Capitoline Wolf is an Etruscan work (the suckling twins a Renaissance addition). In Iberia and in the south of France contact with Greek colonists stimulated stone sculpture.

Continental Europe
In the 5th century the Celtic peoples began the evolution of their La Tène decorative art style. Many of the finest works in this style were on weapons and ornaments of the last two centuries BC. As well as adapting some classical motifs, the Celts used animal forms that were still being brilliantly executed by the Scyths and other steppe nomads.

Eastern Mediterranean
Greek sculptors – Phidias, Praxitiles, Lysippus – carved their masterpieces both in free-standing figures and temple pediments and metopes – best known from the Parthenon and Olympia. Red figure vase painters produced exquisite and lively scenes from mythology and everyday life. Greek influence predominated throughout the area.

Far East.
In the China of the Ch'in and early Han dynasty, pottery tomb figures developed charm and often beauty. There were also exquisite small works in bronze and jade. The influence of Chinese styles on the more easterly of the nomads is seen in the marvellous Pazyryk finds.

*Janus head.
Roquepertuse*

*Gold stag.
Kostromskaya*

*Cauldron.
Gundestrup*

*Ewer.
Basse-Yutz*

*Battersea
shield*

Rhyton, Bucharest

*Venus de Milo,
Melos*

Greek vase

*Nike of
Samothrace*

*Jockey,
Artemisium*

*Hermes and
infant*

*Delphi
charioteer*

*Bronze bell.
Hitaka*

Horseman, Pazyryk

*Lacquered
cup*

Man-Ch'eng

Leopard, Man-Ch'eng

Figurine, Shensi

SHENSI

▲ Gunderstrup
▲ Battersea
▲ Basse-Yutz
▲ Roquepertuse
● Elche
● Tarquinia
● Rome
▲ Bucharest
▲ Samothrace
▲ Delphi
Olympia ▲ ▲ Athens
Artemisium ▲ ▲ Melos
▲ Kostromskaya
▲ Oxus
▲ Hamadan
● Susa
● Persepolis
● Alexandria
▲ Memphis

GANDHARA

Sarnath ● * BIHAR

Priest's head

*Statue of
Tauret*

*Apis bull.
Memphis*

*Cameo.
Alexandria*

Funerary mask

*Wall relief.
Persepolis*

*Gold Armlet.
Oxus*

*Archer,
Susa*

Rhyton, Hamadan

*Ibex
amphora
handle*

*Figurine.
Bulnadibagh*

*Lion capital.
Sarnath*

*Yakshi, Didargani,
Bihar.*

*Head,
Gandhara*

Egypt
Temples of the period were unrestrainably covered with relief sculpture in the traditional manner, sometimes rather more sensual in feeling. An intensifying of animal cults encouraged small animal sculpture. Greco-Roman influence shows in realistic portrait heads.

Mesopotamia/Persia
The sculptured friezes of early Achaemenid Susa and Persepolis plainly owe much to the Assyrian tradition – possibly coming also from Uratu. Persian artist-craftspeople excelled in designing splendid ornaments and vessels for the banqueting table. Something of the animal art of the steppes still makes itself felt.

India
Under the Mauryan empire architectural sculpture now appeared on Buddhist buildings and on the famous Ashoka column, some of which supported elephants, lions and bulls. Here Persian influence was strong. Free-standing figures of *Yakshis* (nature spirits) were carved.

Mesopotamia/Persia

Persian Achaemenid princes used splendid vessels for their banqueting tables and dishes. Beakers with pairs of animal handles were among them, but most popular of all were drinking and libation horns with animal terminals – winged lions, bulls, rams.

The low reliefs on the walls and stairways of Persepolis owe much to Assyrian art.

Gold rhyton, Ecbatana

Wall relief of Mede and Persian, Persepolis

Egypt

In this later end of their history, Egyptian sculptors continued to carve reliefs and sculptures in traditional forms. There was an increase in animal cults and hence in small animal figurines. These representations show a keen observation of nature. Faience as well as stone and bronze were used for these figures, and attempts were made to capture the characteristics of the sacred animals in the various mediums. The female hippopotamus, Tauret (Thoueris) stood for fecundity and aid in childbirth.

Faience figure of Tauret

Eastern Mediterranean

Artists had an honourable status in Greek society so that we know the names not only of sculptors such as Phidias and Praxitiles but also of many vase painters. Greek sculptors of the classical age increased the naturalism and anatomical correctness of their figures. Most, even of their free-standing sculptures, were made for temples. Praxitiles' famous Hermes (340 BC) comes from the temple of Hera at Olympia. The 5th century saw the exquisite art of red-figure vase painters at its best.

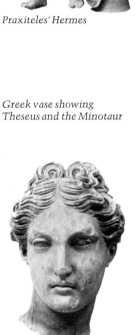

Praxiteles' Hermes

Greek vase showing Theseus and the Minotaur

Western Mediterranean

After 500 BC Etruscan art began to decline, although mural paintings such as those from Tarquinian tombs perhaps now showed their greatest life and vigour. The colourful wall paintings reflected the everyday life and customs of the Etruscans. Banqueting scenes perhaps expressed the hope that a good life would continue after death. Greek elements remained dominant not only in tomb paintings but in gems, pottery and bronze work, but the Etruscans tended to prolong the old archaic style, and they continued to produce excellent work in bronze and terracotta. Big sculptures in terracotta were produced for religious buildings in Etruria similar to the earlier Apollo of Veii (p. 147).

Etruscan head

Fresco, Tomb of the Leopards, Tarquinia, Italy

Continental Europe

The La Tène decorative art style which the Celts developed in central and western Europe from the 5th century BC initially owed something to Greek motifs, but these were soon turned into graceful curvilinear forms, balanced but assymetrical, such as those on the Battersea Shield (c. 100 BC). The early La Tène bronze flagon with coral and enamel inlay shows that the Celts borrowed also from Scythic animal art. The decoration on this wine vessel may reflect a Celtic sense of humour in that a tiny duck on the spout appears to be pursued by larger creatures on the lid and handle.

Basse-Yutz flagon, France

"Battersea Shield," Thames at Battersea, England

India

Under the Mauryan dynasty sculpture in the form of stone carving on capitals and colossal female figures or *Yakshis* predominated. A *Yakshi* is a native spirit of Dravidian origin and these carvings represent a purely Indian folk art, the Ashoka capitals being mainly Greek in conception. Techniques learned from earlier wood and ivory carvings were used in these early stone representations which were prototypes for later images of the Buddha.

Yakshi, moulded terracotta plaque, Kausambi.

Far East

While the Scyths and neighbouring nomads are mostly renowned for the brilliantly stylized animal art of their goldsmiths, the frozen royal tombs of Pazyryk (Altai) preserved some surprising art in perishable materials, including a felt appliqué wall hanging with a mounted warrior. The parcel gilt-bronze leopard inlaid with silver and garnets was found in the tomb of Princess Tou Wan and was probably used as a weight.

Crouching leopard, Mancheng, China

Felt applique hanging, Pazyryk, Siberia

The Americas

Among all the emergent art forms of this Pre-Classic (Formative) period of American art, none is more remarkable than the 5th century textiles from southern Peru – mostly from the Paracas Necropolis mummy bundles. They are woven with pattern and grotesque animal and human figures in brilliant colours.

Textile, Paracas Necropolis, Peru

Region	Economy	Centres	Events and developments	People
Mesopotamia/Persia		Susa Persepolis Babylon Seleucia	Persian empire of the Achaemenids from 639 BC. Alexander's conquests 334-323. Seleucid dynasty to 63. Rise of Parthians.	Xerxes
Egypt		Alexandria Meroe	Alexander's conquest 332. Persian re-conquest 341. Ptolemaic dynasty until Roman annexation 31. Flowering of trade and scholarship at Alexandria.	Ctesibius Hero Ptolemy Cleopatra Euclid
Eastern Mediterranean		Athens	Greece repulses Persia 480 but succumbs to internecine wars. Rise of Macedon. Struggle between successor states ended by Roman conquest.	Philip of Macedon Alexander Pericles Socrates Plato Aristotle Aeschylus Phidias
Western Mediterranean		Tarquinia Bologna Syracuse Carthage Rome	Celtic invasions and Roman advance destroy independence of Etruscans. Republican Rome then absorbs Greek colonies, overthrows Carthage and advances east, west and north to English Channel.	Archimedes Pythagoras Julius Caesar Augustus Cicero, Vergil
Continental Europe		La Tène Heuneberg	Introduction of iron. Greek and Etruscan trade in west and centre followed by Roman conquest to Rhine and Danube towards end of period.	Cassivellaunus Vercingetorix
India		Taxila Rajgir Sanchi Sarnath	Persian conquest of Punjab. Alexander's campaign. Mauryan Empire. Saka invasion. Establishment of caste system.	Mahavira Ashoka Chandragupta Maurya
Far East		Ch'ang-An	Warring states 405-221. Ch'in dynasty 221-206. Han empire unites China 206. Yayoi period in Japan c.300.	Wu-ti
The Americas		Monte Albán Tlatilco Izapa Paracas	Conquests by Monte Albán in C. Mexico. Maya emerges to south. Local developments in Peru.	

The economy bar graph indicates relative proportions of these factors: Irrigation ≈ Agriculture ✤ Hunting ⚹ Urban life ⊞ Trade ⚘

Religion	Technology and inventions	Architecture	Art and literature
Zoroastrianism Mithraism Manichaeism	Efficient imperial administration and road system. Wider use of camel.	Persian road building. Pillared halls, monumental stairway at Persepolis.	Achaemenid art as manifested in wall reliefs, gold and silver vessels, gold jewellery. Scythian art impinges from Asiatic steppes. *Axvesta*
Pantheon continues especially Isis, Horus and Osiris.	Hellenistic civilization unites these areas. Technology based on full use of wrought iron, mechanics on rope torsion, pulley, lever, primitive screw and gears. Lathe, valve bellows, first waterwheels, glass blowing, Archimedean screw, map-making. But on the whole the brilliant inventiveness of Greeks especially of Alexandria e.g. motive force of steam remained completely unexploited.	Earlier traditions continue to decline. Greek styles introduced to Alexandria.	Native art gradually supplanted by Hellenistic.
Olympian pantheon. Mystery religions e.g. Orphic and Eleusinain take greater hold. Philosophy develops as an alternative.		Greek temple architecture develops to peak, then turns to stylistic variations – Doric, Ionic, Corinthian. Theatres.	Peak of sculpture and vase painting reached early followed especially with latter by rapid decline. Greek drama of Aeschylus, Sophocles, Euripides, Aristophanes. Works of Herodotus, Thucydides, Plato, Aristotle.
Greek, Phoenician and Etruscan gods. Roman state gods, the Capitoline triad, imposed by Roman rule. Druidism, sacred groves, human sacrifices, offerings.		Greek temples widely copied. Brick and concrete architecture developed in Italy. Earth and timber continue in use elsewhere.	Etruscans adapt Greek art to local taste in tomb and vase painting and statuary. Romans continue the process. Greek art itself declines steadily. Phoenician restricted largely to metalwork and jewellery. Works of Catullus, Horace, Livy, Cicero, Vergil, Ovid, Seneca.
Local gods, votive offerings. Bog bodies in Denmark and N. Germany.	Spread of iron technology, salt boiling, enamel.	British hill forts, becoming oppida-towns. Oppida through central Europe.	La Tène art develops in C. Europe, spreads widely. Thracian art develops in and around Bulgaria. Scythian art in steppes.
Brahmanism continues to develop into Hinduism. Jainism. Buddhism rises and spreads slowly throughout region.	Iron technology. Northern polished black pottery. Writing re-introduced. Knowledge and use of monsoon winds for navigation.	Rock-cut temples (chaityas), stupas, Ashoka pillars. City walls reappear.	Magnificent stone carving associated particularly with Buddhist stupas and temples. Greek influence through Alexandria. *Mahabharata* *Ramayana*
Philosophical religion, especially Confucianism, Taoism.	Widespread use of cast iron. Crossbow invented.	Great Wall of China, road building. Buildings in timber and tile with virtually no archaeological evidence surviving.	End of Chou art style. Han more naturalistic. Lacquer work, ceramics especially tomb figures, calligraphy.
Calendrical religion of the Maya. Local gods elsewhere.	Cyclical calendar devised by Olmecs. Glyphs, forerunners of writing. Goldwork in Colombia. Irrigation and terracing expand in S. America.	Stone temples in Mexico, early Maya temple platforms. Roofing by corbel only. Burial mounds and other earth-works in Mississippi basin.	Olmec traditions surviving. Elaborate textiles in Peru.

AD1–500

In these first five centuries of our era the "shift to the west" given so much emphasis in the last two periods reached a climax in power with the earlier Roman empire, but during the last hundred years had already been put into sharp, if temporary, reverse. Even within the empire this reversal is well expressed by Constantine's creation of Constantinople at the ancient Greek colony of Byzantium. He had hoped it would be possible to rule the east from the city without losing grip on the west, but this proved impossible. The Romans had checked then conquered the Celtic barbarians, but could not hold out against the untamed Germanic peoples from beyond the northern frontiers. In the end it was to be the tenacity of Byzantium that was to make the revival of the Christian west possible.

In a very different sense the triumph of Christianity, for the future the most important event of this period, was itself a manifestation of the swing back towards the east. For here was a religion founded in the Semitic Levant and spread by a Greek from Anatolian Tarsus.

Beyond the eastern frontiers of the empire, the Persian Sassanids crushed Rome's long-standing enemies the Parthians (in AD226) claiming to be the true descendants of the Achaemenids.

India was first invaded by the Kushans, a branch of the Hueh-chi nomads who, however, soon settled down, their kings becoming Buddhist and also patrons of Sanskrit scholarship. Buddhism had by now become a saviour religion and Buddha a divinity. The Kushans were eclipsed by the Gupta Empire, founded by a second Chandragupta at just about the time that Constantine adopted Christianity. It was an ideal regime under which Hinduism was at its greatest and the visual arts, literature and science flourished in conditions of pious prosperity.

It was probably during the lifetime of Jesus that Buddhism began to reach China from India. Although the great Han Empire did not break up until 220 and its artists were still capable of producing such masterpieces as the famous "flying" horses from a general's tomb at Wu-wei, it was weakening and with it (temporarily) the Confucian ideal. Buddhist teaching therefore found ready listeners. After the collapse of the Han Dynasty, followed by internal strife and the occupation of the north by nomads, it encouraged a withdrawal from public duties for a life of contemplation of nature and a cultivation of the fine arts of poetry, painting and calligraphy. These were to flourish particularly under the southern dynasty of East Ch'in, almost contemporary with the Gupta of India. Partly through their colony in Korea and partly by direct contact the Han built up a luxury trade with Japan. At first Japan consisted of a number of rival kingdoms, but in time that of Yamato won the hegemony. In about AD400 its rulers adopted the Chinese language and script for official purposes, starting Japan on the road to literacy.

This period is the first in which the Americas demand a leading place. It witnessed the first attainment of high civilization in Mesoamerica and of its dawn also in South America. It is, indeed, one of the most striking features of a study of contemporaneity that by the later centuries of this period the first civilizations in Mesoamerica were reaching their peak just when the Roman empire was falling to ruin.

The coincidence is given piquancy by the fact that the New World reached this high civilization while technologically very backward. No form of wheel was ever to be in practical use there and all impressive material achievements were the work of human muscle. The Maya had no metals throughout their Classic Age, learning their use only later when metallurgy spread up from the south. In Peru and Colombia gold, silver, copper and tin had been worked since the previous period. Even there mining methods, furnaces and other equipment remained primitive.

Ceiling of the Capella of the Baptistry of the Orthodox at Ravenna, Italy.

The artists of the Han empire were capable of producing such masterpieces as the flying horses found in Wu-wei even while the dynasty was on the verge of collapse.

In parts of Mexico the Zapotecs were enlarging Monte Albán, while the people of Teotihuacán built their huge pyramids of the Sun and Moon early in the period. Both places were true cities as well as ceremonial centres: Teotihuacán probably reached a population of well over 100,000, including many specialist craftspeople. The people of Cholula (Pueblo) perhaps a colony of Teotihuacán, raised the largest pyramid of all – 180 feet (55·4m) high and covering 25 acres. Meanwhile, down on the Gulf coast to the north of the former Olmec territory, a large administrative and religious centre with temples, pyramids and palaces grew at El Tajin.

It was the Maya who were to surpass them all as intellectuals, builders and artists. Their Classic Age opened in about AD 300 – once again in chronological line with the East Ch'in, the Gupta and the adoption of Christianity by Constantine.

Most of the mighty works of Maya architecture visible today date from after 500, but owing to the strange practice of adding skin after stone skin to their buildings, many contain original versions of earlier date. The cradle of the advanced Mayan civilization was in the Petén lowlands of Guatemala and part of Mexican Chiapas. There it was that the

The Roman empire was at its greatest extent during the reign of Trajan (98-117). By this time Britain had been occupied and Rome's eastern boundary stretched from the Caspian to the Red Sea after his conquest of the Dacians. The Romans' *mastery of the Western world is held to begin at 201 BC when Sicily, Corsica, Sardinia and southern Spain were added to the empire after two wars with the Carthaginians. In 44 BC, the time of Julius Caesar's death, Gaul, most* *of the Iberian peninsula, Greece, a good part of Asia Minor and some coastlands along the Black Sea had been annexed. During the reign of Augustus, Judea and Egypt became provinces and Europe was penetrated as far as the Danube.*

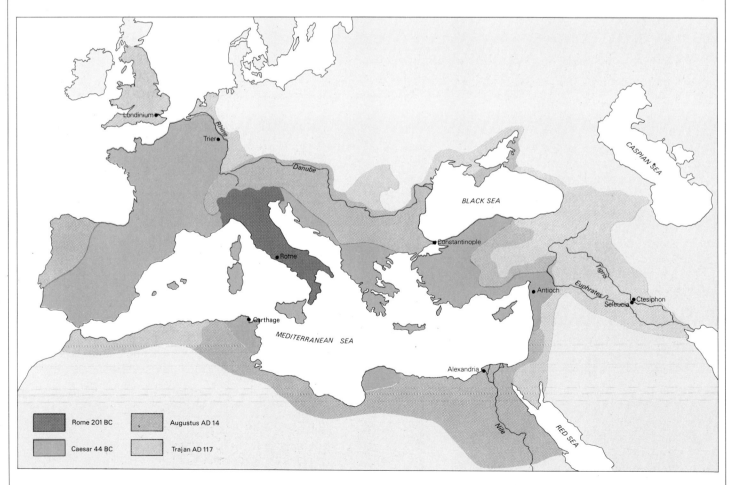

■ Rome 201 BC		⠂ Augustus AD 14	
■ Caesar 44 BC		Trajan AD 117	

glyphic writing and calendar cults were first developed and where, therefore, the intellectual life of priestly astronomer-mathematicians was most subtle and advanced. The earliest known Mayan calendar stone is at Tikal in the Petén and dates from the year AD 292; at nearby Uaxactún the oldest is 328, and away to the east at Copán, 460. By this last date Mayan sculptors had developed their fine and distinctive style.

In South America the local cultures of the end of our last period now emerged as organized states. As in Mesoamerica, though usually on a smaller scale and lacking architectural style, there were ceremonial centres serving scattered farming populations. A northerly example at San Agustín, Colombia, has mounds and sculptures that still show the fearsome jaguar features of Chavín times. The Mochica in the coastal valleys of northern Peru built large adobe pyramid-mounds. Although like all the South Americans they had no writing, they speak to us now through their superb modelled pottery, with its portrayals of everyday life, pleasant and unpleasant. In southern Peru the Nazca preferred to paint their vessels with animals, monsters and divinities. Gold, silver and copper were freely used for ornaments, and the Mochica used bronze for some of their tools.

The one centre, however, that comes close to rivalling those of Mesoamerica, is the famous Tiahuanaco on Lake Titicaca, 13,000 feet (4000m) up in the Bolivian Andes. Here was a great temple complex entered through the massive, monolithic "Gateway of the Sun." Architectural development had certainly begun in this present period and it is not impossible that the gate was hewn before its end. The figure at the centre is the "staff god" of ancient tradition.

So by the year 500, when Rome and its western empire had collapsed and still barbarian peoples seized control over most of Europe and North Africa, the Maya and other peoples of Mesoamerica and Peru and adjacent lands were still advancing towards the heights of their various civilizations. If these seem to us strange and remote when compared with those of the Old World, that is largely due to our inability to read much of the Maya script and to the lack of writing elsewhere.

Was there also something more brutal and sinister about them? I used to think that there was, particularly those of Middle America, with their terrible divinities distinguished by skulls and flayed skins and an appetite for eating human hearts. There is something threatening and perverse in their art, even the

This model of a Mochica warrior is dressed for battle in tunic and helmet and wields a heavy mace (possibly bronze) and shield.

The Pyramid of the Sun was part of the huge ceremonial centre at Teotihuacán whose population was probably at least 100,000 individuals.

Roman glass jug with snake thread decoration.

best Maya works, some of which are very beautiful. And it is a fact that religious sadism increased, reaching its height, of course, after the Aztec conquests of fourteenth-fifteenth centuries. The great square of Montezuma's capital of Tenochtitlán had its rack of sacrificial skulls when the Spaniards entered it. At least one can say the Sumerians and Egyptians of 3000-2000 BC and the Chinese of 500 BC–AD 1 grew more humane and gave up their religious immolations. Yet anyone who has followed these eight steps of time must be appalled by the ceaseless slaughter and cruelties of Old World warfare. Was anything the Aztecs were to do much worse than the brutalities of the Roman arena in this present period? Perhaps the answer is that while in their art, through which alone they can address us, the Americans were uninhibited in displaying their sadism, they manifested so little of the counterbalancing virtues of humanity. Little or none of the intimacy, gaiety and love of nature of the Egyptians, the lively enjoyment of the Minoans, the lofty idealism of the Greeks, or the humanity and dignity of the Romans is apparent.

The main historical interest of AD 1–500 must be the counterpoint of the Roman Empire and Christianity: the still expanding Roman Empire, so great and seemingly secure when Augustus died in AD 14 during Jesus' youth; Christianity growing and spreading within it like a creeping plant, yet still seeming no more than a minor nuisance when first-second century emperors tried their persecutions; intellectual stiffening of Christian theology with Greek philosophy and an increase of converts of high social rank after AD 200; the coming together of the two themes when Christianity was accepted as the official religion of the empire; the fall of Rome to the Goths seen by Augustine in North Africa as an act of God, and the part played by the churches' institutions in conserving something of classical culture for Christendom.

Looking back upon the five centuries, this dramatic contrapuntal form is conspicuous, but it would have been a great seer indeed

The decoration on the engraved bronze Desborough Mirror continued earlier La Tène and Celtic styles. It may have belonged to a woman of high position, of whom there were many in Celtic society. Similar mirrors and ornaments have been found in burials.

who could have recognized it much before the mid-point of the period.

The first century of the empire is crowded with famous names and events – even if many of them have become so through excessive popular interest in the wickedness of certain emperors. In the last years of his reign, Augustus tried to advance his northern frontier from the Rhine to the Elbe with the intention of shortening it. The Germanic tribes annihilated Varus and three Roman legions in AD 9 and in spite of the quite successful counter-attack by Germanicus begun in the year of Augustus' death, the Rhine frontier had to be accepted. At the eastern extremity of his realm, Augustus was still having trouble with the Parthians, and, although of a very different kind, with the Jews. The Romans were prepared to do what seemed to them reasonable to accommodate the strange exclusiveness and fanaticism of Jewish religion and to give its people degrees of self-government. However, complaints against the rule of a son of Herod the Great were so troublesome that in AD 6 Augustus removed him and Judea was united with Syria under Roman governors. Herod Antipas became tetrarch of Galilee.

When Tiberius succeeded his great kinsman as the second emperor, he was already 56, taciturn and without Augustus' political tact, purpose and prestige. He was soon in trouble with the senate and still more with other members of his imperial (Julio-Claudian) family. The first great events of the Christian story fall within his reign. He had just (AD 27) made the mistake of quitting Rome for Capri (where his supposed debaucheries were to be made the most of by Tacitus) when John the Baptist began preaching by the Jordan.

The crucifixion of Jesus is thought to have been in 29, 30 or 33 at a time when Herod Antipas had gone down to Jerusalem for the Passover. Paul's conversion was in c.35. Over the next dozen years he was preaching and shaping his own ideas mainly in Damascus, Antioch and Tarsus.

Meanwhile, Tiberius had died at Capri in 37 and been succeeded by Caligula, son of Germanicus. Already the next year this unbalanced young man enraged Jews throughout his empire by his edict that all must pay him divine honours. He sought and succeeded in pleasing the Roman mob with brutal shows in the arena. If only a few of the tales of perverse atrocities he staged are true, he was an unrivalled sadist, while his megalomania was such that the story of his senatorial horse does not seem impossible. In 40, after putting down a Gaulish revolt,

Caligula made preparation for an invasion of Britain, but his troops mutinied and he was assassinated in the following year. His uncle Claudius, who thus unexpectedly was raised to the purple, revived the plan, and being a shrewd and capable as well as somewhat grotesque human being, he promptly executed it. Much of southeastern Britain had been united and ruled from Colchester (Camulodunum) by the Belgic king best known as Cymbeline – but more correctly as Cunobelin who had become king in about AD 10. He was probably grandson of Cassivellaunus, a powerful tribal leader, who had opposed Julius Caesar nearly a century before. There had been many political contacts between British kings and Rome, while Roman merchants made good profits in exchanging wine, ceramics, glass and trinkets for the British corn, cattle, gold, silver, iron, hides, slaves, hounds and pearls.

Cunobelin died in about 41, and his son Caratacus, with a brother, began to extend their kingdom at the expense of neighbouring tribes and even to threaten trouble in Gaul. When one of the defeated kinglets (Verica) fled to Rome, he provided an obvious excuse for invasion that chimed in well with Claudius' wish for glory, the need to keep certain Rhineland legions out of mischief, and hopes for exploiting Britain's mineral wealth. One other small motive there may have been; the Romans did not extend their normal religious toleration to the savage rites of the Druids, and had been trying to stamp them out in Gaul. Britain, and particularly Mona (Anglesey), was the recognized home of Druidism.

So in AD 43 the Roman army crossed from Boulogne to Richborough, meeting no serious opposition until the British confronted them on a river line, probably at Rochester on the Medway. The Romans won a two-day struggle, the Britons still using chariots directly descended from the originals of 2000-1000 BC. Soon Claudius was summoned to enter Camulodunum as a conqueror. He arrived with some of the Praetorian Guard and a show of elephants – the first of the genus *elephas* to set their large feet on British soil since the Ice Age. Camulodunum remained the temporary capital and a temple for the divine Claudius was built there.

Caratacus withdrew to Wales to rouse the tribespeople to resist, and they in turn enlisted the Brigantes of Yorkshire, with the result that the conquest of upland Britain was to take several decades – and was never of course to reach Ireland or the Scottish highlands. Caratacus was finally betrayed by the

Nero started his reign with good intentions but his personal instability and the evil atmosphere around him exposed him to all the corruptions of power.

The political, military and administrative skills of Augustus were largely responsible for the continuing expansion of the Roman Empire. When he died in AD 14 there was no apparent reason why the Empire should not last indefinitely, so powerful and secure did it seem.

Brigantine queen Cartamandua and paraded in Rome. There he asked the famous question "Why do you, with all these great possessions, still covet our poor huts?"

Meanwhile the southern lowlands were quickly subdued, the hillforts proving unable to withstand the Roman military. Legate of Legion II was the future emperor Vespasian, who captured a score of such strongholds, including mighty Maiden Castle in Dorset. There and at many other places the native capitals were moved down to lower ground where Roman-style towns could be built. Soon the old Celtic warrior aristocracy had exchanged their "poor huts" for villas.

During the years after 43, when the Romans were finding the conquest of Britain not altogether easy, Saint Paul was making his great journeys as missionary to the "gentiles" in Syria, Anatolia and Greece. It was during the third, starting in about 51, that he stayed in Ephesus and got into dire trouble with the imagemakers of Artemis, that Goddess who had been so powerful in Anatolia since her days in the Çatal Hūyūk of our second period. In spite of Roman disapproval, the hatred of orthodox Jews and their own dissensions, Christian communities were multiplying all round the eastern Mediterranean – and in Rome itself.

Claudius had no luck with his wives. The third, the beautiful young nymphomaniac Messallina, bore him a son (named Britannicus in honour of the new conquest) before she was executed for intrigue and depravity. The fourth, his niece, persuaded him to set aside Britannicus as his successor in favour of her own son by a previous marriage. To clinch the matter she had Claudius poisoned. In this auspicious fashion, Nero became Emperor.

Through the influence of his tutor, Seneca, Nero started his reign with the intention of restoring the good government of Augustus. But, as with his uncle Caligula, his personal instability and the evil atmosphere in which he had always lived exposed him to all the corruptions of power. The murder of his mother and execution of Seneca and his wife (after he had become infatuated with Poppaea) were only the most personal of his cruelties. He was popular with the mob for indulging them with even more "bread and circuses" and by his public displays of himself as musician, poet and charioteer. He had at least one imperial success, a compromise settlement with the Parthians in the struggle over Armenia.

The Parthian campaign partly coincided with disaster in the extreme west. Oppression by officials administering the subject parts of Britain provoked Boudicca (Boadicea), queen of the East Anglian tribe of the Iceni, to revolt. This occurred in AD 60, or 61, at the very moment when the Roman governor had crossed to Anglesey and amid wild scenes destroyed the Druids and their sacred groves. Before they were ruthlessly put down, the rebels had slaughtered some 70,000 people at Camulodunum, Londinium and Verulamium (St Albans). In defeat, Boudicca took poison. (While it is correct that the queen would have ridden to war in a chariot, it would not have been as massive as the vehicle of her memorial on Westminster Bridge, nor would it have

AD 69, the Year of the Four Emperors or Tetrarchs, brought the unhappy revelations that the imperial throne could be bestowed by the army or seized by powerful generals.

fire in Rome. The story that Nero fiddled while the city burned probably comes from his public performances as a musician; it certainly appears to be quite untrue. His many enemies did, however, spread the rumour that he had instigated the fire and then, according to Tacitus, "Nero fabricated scapegoats – and punished with every refinement the notoriously depraved Christians, as they were popularly called. Their deaths were made farcical. Dressed in wild animals' skins they were torn to pieces by dogs, or crucified, or made into torches…". Traditionally both St Peter and St Paul lost their lives at this time – but Paul's execution may in fact have been earlier. It was in this Rome of corruption and persecution that St Mark wrote his gospel.

Soon after the end of this first Roman persecution of Christians and five years after Boudicca's uprising, the empire was shaken by another revolt. After many years of guerilla warfare and unrest, in the year 66 the Zealots led the First Jewish Revolt which, like that of the Iceni, had temporary success but was inevitably crushed. It was during this bitter struggle that the monastic establishment at Quamran (quite probably known to both John the Baptist and Jesus) was destroyed and some of its religious texts left in caves to be discovered as the Dead Sea Scrolls. In 70 the future emperor Titus besieged and captured Jerusalem and largely destroyed the city, including the great new temple begun by Herod the Great. Very large numbers of Jews scattered as refugees. Those who remained under Roman rule were wisely led by rabbinical scholars who in time were recognized by the Romans as supreme patriarchs.

Before the wretched end of the Jewish Revolt, Rome had seen a change not only of emperors but of dynasty. An aristocratic conspiracy, further provincial revolts and finally his desertion by both army and Senate led to Nero's suicide in 68. The chaos of AD 69, the Year of the Four Emperors or Tetrarchs, brought the unhappy revelations that the imperial throne could be occupied by men who were not of Julian or Claudian blood, that it could be conferred in places other than Rome, and, above all, that it could be either bestowed by the army or seized by generals.

Luckily the throne ended in the possession of a general of bourgeois good sense and long experience: Vespasian, first of the three Flavian emperors. During the decade of his rule he secured peace and used it to reform the army, administration and treasury, to build roads and consolidate frontiers. It seems appropriate that

scythes on its wheels).

Events leading up to another tragic death of a contrasting kind coincided with that of Boudicca. On Saint Paul's return from his third great mission, his Jewish enemies in Jerusalem obliged the Roman authorities to arrest him and hold him in "protective custody." There followed his appeal to Caesar (Nero), the long voyage and shipwreck on Malta, then two years of "free custody" in Rome before his trial and execution.

Nero's persecution of the Christians was during the year 64-65, following the terrible

Pliny the Elder wrote the famous *Natural History* in his reign. His noted humour was maintained into his last words: "Alas, I think I am about to become a god."

Vespasian was also one of the architects of Rome, restoring fire damage, and above all building the Colosseum as a gift to the Roman people on the land of Nero's Golden House.

This gigantic amphitheatre, though its dedication was one of Vespasian's last acts, was not to be used until the brief reign of his soldier son, Titus (AD 79-81). These years were marked by two famous events, the tremendous eruption of Vesuvius that overwhelmed Pompeii and Herculaneum, and killed Pliny the Elder as he observed it from a naval ship, and in the following year (80) the opening of the Colosseum by a hundred days of unsurpassed spectacle and bloodshed. The number of wild beasts and men killed was enormous: Suetonius mentions that 5000 animals, including elephants, were slaughtered in one day. It must be remembered that the emperors did not create the Colosseum just for grandeur and to please the populace. It was also a means of political and psychological control of the citizen mob.

So well did Titus succeed in handling his subjects that when he was carried off by fever he was "the darling of the world." His brother, Domitian, third and last of the Flavians, was a far less amiable character. He went far with self-deification, angering the Senate by this oriental style of kingship. He, however, continued to manipulate the citizens with games and hand-outs – even forming a new school of super gladiators as much beloved by the crowds as present-day football stars. He was having difficulty with Dacians, Germans and Sarmatians along his northern frontiers and this was one of the reasons that prevented his best known general, Agricola, from advancing from his defeat of the Welsh and North British tribes to complete his conquest of Scotland. Agricola's campaigns are well known to us since the great historian, Tacitus, was his son-in-law and wrote a flattering biography. Its composition must have roughly coincided with that of the gospels of Matthew and Luke.

Domitian was assassinated (to the delight of the Senate) in AD 96 near the end of the much troubled first century of the Roman empire. Of the following century Gibbon wrote: "If any man were called to fix the period in the history of the world during which the condition of the human race was most happy and prosperous, he would, without hesitation, name that which elapsed from the death of Domitian to the accession of Commodus".

Looking both backward and forward from AD 100 it can be seen how, in spite of turmoil in Rome itself and occasional local revolts, the empire itself could indeed provide a happier life. For many of its peoples and most of the time the blessing of the *Pax Romana* prevailed on both land and sea. Travel and trade were vastly easier, desirable goods flowed freely within the frontiers, silk, spices, gems and other high luxuries came from China and India (large hoards of Roman coins have been found in southern India). Ever since the time of Vergil the more educated classes had cultivated a taste for country beauties and rural life. Gardens great and small were another pleasure, and one that spread quickly through the provinces. The great villa at Fishbourne, built for a romanized Celtic prince as early as AD 75, stood in a formal garden. All these delights were expressed not only in poetry but also in paint – as can best be seen in the murals preserved for us at Pompeii. Medical care must have improved with the leadership of Galen, "prince of physicians," born at Pergamum in 130. The *dolce vita* was certainly available to most free men, and even slaves could sometimes attain to it.

Trade and prosperity encouraged architectural magnificence in provincial cities old and new. Among the best known in the Levant are Petra, with its rock-cut temples, the chief city of Nabataean Arabs, and from the second century capital of Roman Arabia, and Baalbek (Heliopolis), city of the Sun God, with its sumptuous Great Sanctuary buildings. In the western provinces and North Africa, cities were being developed on the Roman plan, with temples, fora, public baths and theatres or amphitheatres. In Rome itself grandiose building projects were adopted by emperor after emperor, outstanding being Trajan's new forum and the architecturally brilliant Pantheon, the dome that has stood for nearly two thousand years.

If urbanization and the extravagant consumption of imported luxuries by the aristocracy contributed to the debasement of the coinage (inflation) that so often troubled the empire, at least no one suffered from the advice of professional economists.

The earlier part of Gibbon's "most happy and prosperous" age was presided over by two excellent emperors, both of Spanish birth though descendants of Roman settlers. Trajan (98-117), a great soldier, conquered wealthy Dacia beyond the Danube, and also defeated the old Parthian enemy, capturing the capital, Ctesiphon on Tigris (known to all tourists for its one huge surviving vault) and sailed down

RIGHT: Roman fresco found at Pompeii shows the well-travelled hero Ulysses resisting the lure of the Sirens.

the river to the Gulf. During the brief period that these conquests beyond the Euphrates were held, the empire was at its greatest size.

Trajan's best memorial has been his famous column, still standing near his forum. This hundred foot column of parian marble was spiralled with scenes from the Dacian campaigns which unrolled would measure 650 feet (200m). They tell much about the Roman army and navy, the dress and habits of the barbarians and the hideous savagery of warfare at the time.

Trajan was widely loved as a good ruler and was recognized as "best of the princes" even by the Christians. The number of Christians was growing especially, thanks to St Paul, in Anatolia and Syria. Pliny the Younger, whom Trajan had sent to northern Anatolia, was worried by the size of the communities – the reason being as always, their refusal to honour the imperial cult. The Emperor advised him that he must pardon those who repented and ignore anonymous denunciations, to do otherwise, he wrote, would be "the worst of precedents and out of keeping with the spirit of the age."

It must be remembered that in this second century the Christians were only one sect among many. The mystery cult of Mithras at this time seemed a strong rival, its spread through the empire encouraged by the army.

Hadrian (117-138) was an exceptional man, strong, capable and talented in the arts. His central policy was to bring greater unity to the provinces behind stable frontiers. For this purpose he made many reforms in administration and financial management and also travelled to almost every part of his empire. On his first tour, which took him through Gaul to the Rhine and (in 122) across to Britain, he initiated the building of the stone wall from Tyne to Solway that bears his name. This most northerly of Roman frontiers with its forts, fortlets and turrets is as much his popular memorial as the column is Trajan's. His later journey up the Nile is remembered chiefly for the drowning of his favourite, the beautiful young man, Antinous, and for the record of the musical sounds coming from the Colossi of Memnon at Thebes (p.119).

Hadrian, too, was a great builder and it was his decision to rebuild devastated Jerusalem as a Roman city that, unintentionally, provoked the worst trouble of his reign. The Second Jewish Revolt (132-135) of the hero Bar-Kokhba led to the capture of Jerusalem and a brief nationalist government before its inevitable defeat and further scattering of the Jewish people. The Roman city was built. A famous

Tiberius Caesar, in whose reign the first great events of the Christian story fall.

Julia, wife of Tiberius Caesar.

Marcus Aurelius was the greatest of the Antonines, and was famous as a Stoic philosopher and as author of the Meditations. *But*

Caligula sought and succeeded in pleasing the Roman mob with brutal shows in the arena.

when the Pax Romana *was threatened he did his noble best to save it. He led successful campaigns against the Parthians and Germans.*

Head of Arcadius, Byzantine emperor (AD 395-400), found near the Forum.

discovery was that of Bar-Kokhba letters, and pathetic remains of some of his followers, in a cave on the west shore of the Dead Sea, not very far from Quamran.

Hadrian's greatest buildings (apart from his Wall) are the Pantheon at Rome and his enormous and marvellous "villa" at Tivoli, outside the capital. He could not spare much time to enjoy it. His personal quality is revealed in the exquisite little poem he addressed to his soul during his last illness: "*Animula, vagula, blandula…*".

Shortly before his death, Hadrian had adopted Antoninus Pius as his heir. This founder of the Antonine house, with none of Hadrian's brilliance or restlessness, proved a pacific, stay-at-home ruler. In the west, however, his name is associated with a temporary advance of the British frontier beyond the Scottish lowlands to the shorter Forth-Clyde line. It might also be said that it was at this time educated men were given a clearer view of the earth. Ptolemy of Alexandria, the great geographer, realized that it was a sphere with mingled land and water masses, established latitudes and longitudes, and using a conical projection mapped the known inhabited world – from Britain to a shapeless China (p.230).

Marcus Aurelius (161-180), as a man so much the greatest of the three Antonines, and famous as a Stoic philosopher and author of the *Meditations*, was denied the peace he could so well have employed. Suddenly the *Pax Romana* was threatened – and he did his noble best to save it. German tribes were thrusting across the Danube and into Italy, the Parthians again aggressive in Mesopotamia and Armenia, and there was an internal rebellion. His campaigns were on the whole successful, Parthian Ctesiphon and Seleucia fell. Yet when the Stoic died the old stability had gone and his son, Commodus, too carefully educated by Aurelius, was no more stable. When this unhappy young man, who thought of himself as Hercules, was strangled in his bath, Rome and the court entered a spell of civil strife and murder recalling the worst days after Nero.

Septimus Severus (193-211) from Leptis Magna in North Africa and the first emperor who had to learn Latin as a second language, was a brave and tireless soldier who contrived to hold the empire together. More and more, however, he and his successors had to placate the army with high pay and privileges. The army itself became more professional and far less Roman. Not only soldiers but officers too were often barbarian recruits from inside or outside the frontiers. The cost of maintenance increased enormously and also the taxes to

Septimus Severus (193-211) from Leptis Magna in North Africa and the first emperor who had to learn Latin as a second language was a brave and tireless soldier who contrived to hold the Empire together.
This family portrait was amended at a later date to remove the figure of one of Severus' sons after the child's death.

Constantine in the Edict of Milan (313) gave religious toleration to the Christians and restored their property. As Constantine also announced his own acceptance of the faith it became virtually the imperial religion.

Diocletian reorganized the whole imperial structure, dividing it into two parts, so recognizing the ever-present distinction between the oriental east and the young western provinces.

support it; so prosperity declined and bureaucracy tended to increase. It is to us a familiar picture.

Among the disruptive forces that Severus and many of his third century successors feared, was the mounting power of the Church. Writing in his reign, Tertullian said "We are but of yesterday and we have filled every place belonging to you: cities, islands, fortresses, towns, assemblies…the palace, the Senate, the law-courts; the only thing we have left to you for yourselves is your temples". It was by now this fear that prompted the Christian persecutions. One of those to suffer under Severus was the wise and tolerant convert to the faith, St Clement of Alexandria, who saw Greek thought as preparing the way for Christianity. Origen was his pupil.

Severus died in York where he had been campaigning against the Scots; his son, Caracalla followed his policy of unifying the empire by granting Roman citizenship to all its freeborn men – a gift no longer worth what it once had been. It was also in his reign that there was the first hint of future terror: the Goths, a Germanic people who had moved eastward from Scandinavian Gotland, attacked the frontier north of the Danube. It did not seem serious: Caracalla could afford to build his gigantic baths in Rome. The more immediate threat appeared to be from the Persian Sassanids when, claiming to be the true inheritors of the Achaemenids, they overthrew the Parthian empire in AD 226 – a few years after the collapse of the Han empire in China.

The Germanic onslaught began in earnest from about 249 when the Goths went into the Balkans and shortly afterwards killed the emperor Decius in battle. Together with the Heruli they continued to harry from the Black Sea to the Aegean and in Greece itself. Meanwhile, from 253, the western empire was also attacked, the Alamanni and Marcomanni invading north Italy and Gaul, the Franks and Burgundians plundering across the Rhine. Resistance was weakened by frequent struggles for the imperial throne by nominees of the armies, but during the 270's the Romans had considerable successes against the barbarians – until the empire could be restored by Diocletian who took the throne in 284.

This son of an Illyrian freedman, acting with extraordinary clarity and determination, reorganized the whole imperial structure, dividing it into two parts, so recognizing the always-existing distinction between the Greek and oriental east and Italy with the young western provinces. Territorial divisions were also completely reframed at a lower level of

RIGHT: View across the Forum towards the round "Temple of Romulus". The Basilica Nova of Maxentius and Constantine is in the background.

Constatine founded Constantinople on the site of the old Greek town of Byzantium. It was perfectly situated for trade and self-defence and for controlling frontiers both east and west.

administration, an effort made to prevent military control of the throne, and the currency reformed. All this was to be effective for a time, but it meant the imposition of a totalitarian state, with emperors remote from the people in courts of oriental grandeur. Diocletian showed his extraordinary strength of purpose by not waiting to die or be murdered in royal harness, but retiring to his fine villa at Split and cultivating his garden.

In his efforts to cement the empire together, Diocletian was bound to oppose the Church, which he recognized as forming a state within a state. In 303 (five years after the earliest calendar stele at Tikal) he issued a harsh edict depriving Christians of Roman citizenship and therefore of holding any office, and ordering the destruction of churches and sacred books; a little later it was decreed that the clergy were to be imprisoned and forced by torture to sacrifice to the gods.

It was in truth far too late for such measures to succeed; in fact they encouraged resistance. When, in spite of Diocletian's reforms, his retirement was followed by disputes over the succession, there was a sudden reversal of policy–culminating in the Edict of Milan (313) under which Constantine gave religious toleration to the Christians and restored their property. As Constantine also announced his own acceptance of the faith it became virtually the imperial religion. Tolerance was, however, the legal condition and there was nothing to deter Julian the Apostate (361-363), a nephew of Constantine, from declaring himself a pagan and trying to re-instate the ancient gods. It was not until 378 that Theodosius ended official neutrality and outlawed paganism, many temples being nationalized and made into museums.

Constantine the Great's second manifestation of greatness (apart from military brilliance) was his foundation of Constantinople (324-330) on the site of the old Greek town of Byzantium. It was perfectly situated for trade and self-defence, and for controlling the frontiers both east and west. The transfer of the main imperial capital from Rome also recognized the great relative importance of the eastern empire. As it turned out the west never fully recovered from the events of the third century. Rome declined while Constantinople and its Byzantine empire prospered and were to remain a bastion of Christian civilization until they fell to the Turks over a thousand year later.

There is a parallel here between the Old World and the New. The Byzantine Empire can be dated from AD 324-1453, the (admittedly less coherent) Mesoamerican high civilization from AD 300 to the Spanish conquest of 1520.

In 325, when the building of Constantinople had just begun, Constantine summoned the first of the Ecumenical Councils of the Church to meet at Nicaea. It found against the Arian heresy that denied the full divinity of Christ and recognized Rome, Antioch and Alexandria as the Patriarchal sees. At about this time, too, Constantine's mother, St Helen, made excavations at Jerusalem and brought back the True Cross and many other acceptable relics.

It is totally impossible here adequately to chronicle the events of the spasmodically disintegrating western empire during the later fourth and fifth centuries. The confusion of rival emperors, of assassinations, of uprisings and Christian schisms, of barbarian invasions and campaigns against them, is too great. I cannot do more than pick out a few names and events that are most familiar.

Some of the more positive and happier events sprang from the Christian church, now able to proselytize. It was, for example, most fortunate that the Ostrogoths and Visigoths now living north and west of the Black Sea were converted to the faith (in its Arian form) in c.340, their bishop Wulfila translating the Bible into Gothic. It so happens that St Jerome, whose great work was to be the revision of Latin translations of the Bible that issued in the Vulgate, was born in this same year of 340. A few words about his curious life will give a revealing picture of the age. Studying in Rome, he made researches into the early Christian relics in the Catacombs; in about 366 he travelled in Gaul and settled in the fine city of Trier; after a dream in which he was divinely rebuked for being "not a Christian but a Ciceronian" he went to the deserts of Chalcis and lived as a hermit–four years made familiar by innumerable mediaeval paintings of his "temptations". He moved to Constantinople and then Rome, where he came near to being elected pope. In 385 he abandoned Rome for the orient, was joined by Paula and other Roman women determined to live in celibacy in the Holy Land. Together they visited the sacred sites of Palestine, convents in the Egyptian desert, and finally came to rest in Bethlehem, where Jerome and Paula presided over monastic houses. Jerome did not die until 420, ten years after the Goths had sacked Rome.

Although every kind of internal trouble within the empire weakened its resistance, it was, of course, the attacks, invasions and settlements of the Germanic, and a few nomadic steppe, peoples who brought about the final collapse of the west. These huge folk movements were in large part started by the Huns, a Turco-Mongol people who can be identified with none other than the Hsuing-Nu who had troubled the Chinese in our last period and set up a temporary state in north China in the fourth century AD. A Roman historian described them as small, squat and beardless, with "horrible faces", riveted to their horses where they ate, drank and slept; they could neither plough nor cook. The sudden drive of the Huns to the west, launched in 363, caused a chain reaction and precipitated the invasions of the Roman empire. First the Indo-European Alans were caught up, then the Hunnish horde crossed the Don, displacing the Ostrogoths who in turn displaced the Visigoths (who appealed for protection to the Emperor Valens). In 376, 70,000 Visigoths crossed the Danube. Roman mismanagement of their refugee problem led them to revolt against their protectors: Valens was heavily defeated and himself killed at the battle of Adrianople in the Balkans. Although Theodosius made a treaty with the Visigoths and used many as soldiers, they were now inside the empire as a nation under its own kings. Meanwhile the Huns occupied eastern Europe with a nomadic empire stretching to the Urals. Their further pressure caused north German Vandals and Alans to break into Gaul in 406. They later advanced southward, through Spain and into north Africa (429).

After Theodosius' death in 395 the Visigoths, under their king Alaric, roused from their short quiescence, threatened Constantinople itself, pillaged Athens, Corinth and Sparta, then went by way of Illyria into northern Italy. It was now that Theodosius' Vandal general, Stilicho, recalled the legions from the west – including Britain. He was virtually ruling the west in the name of the feeble emperor Honorius. Temporarily he drove the Goths from Italy. Then in 408 Stilicho was assassinated, and within two years Alaric was in Rome. It was also in 410 that the British, stripped of the regions and being raided by Saxons, made a vain appeal for Honorius' help.

King Alaric behaved with moderation, appointing a puppet ruler and withdrawing from Rome. Yet the shock to the Roman world was enormous. Many said that Rome's disaster was due to the betrayal of her gods. This was one of the great contrapuntal moments in the Roman-Christian story, for St Augustine, roused both by the disaster and the outcry against Christianity, began his great work on the *City of God*, in which he interpreted the fall of Rome "made with hands" in the light of the city of God, "eternal in Heaven".

The period of regular settlement of the barbarian peoples within the empire now began, particularly the Visigoths, Burgundians and Alans (round Orleans) in Gaul, the Franks to the north of them and the Saxons along the north coasts. This was the time of those comically famous Saxons, Hengist and Horsa. However fanciful their names, the British king Vortigern, doing what he could to protect the land from still wilder tribes, such as the Picts and Scots, invited Saxon mercenaries to his aid. This was probably in c.430 – earlier than Bede's familiar date of 449. It would have been about a dozen years later that they began to plunder and take the land for themselves.

Now the Huns were on the move again. Under their king Attila they crossed the Rhine in 451. They devastated northern Gaul until they were defeated by the Romans in alliance with the Visigoths at the battle of Troyes. Attila veered off into Italy, where luckily for the Roman government, now at Ravenna, he died in 453. His followers broke up and were driven far to the east, where various Hun states were to become a thorn in the side of the Byzantines.

Almost before the Italians could appreciate the death of Attila, Rome was sacked by the Vandals. Still the broken western empire struggled on, a sham with emperors controlled by barbarian puppet-masters. This pretence was ended when in 476 the last little emperor, most ironically named Romulus Augustus, was deposed by the barbarian general, Odoacer, who set up no puppet but declared himself ruler in the name of the Byzantine emperor.

The period was to end in good fortune for the west. Theodoric the Ostrogoth had been educated in Constantinople and when his people ravaged Greece, the eastern emperor Leo was able to relieve the pressure by commissioning Theodoric to lead them against Odoacer. This he did after 488, when 100,000 Ostrogoths crossed into Italy. Theodoric the Great in fact made himself king of Italy and was accepted by the Senate – though nominally a Roman general under the eastern Emperor. The Ostrogoths were settled in the country, most of them in the north. Contriving to keep on moderately good terms with Clovis, ambitious and still barbarous king of the Franks, Theodoric was able to bring peace and prosperity to Italy. He graced his court with scholars such as Cassiodorus and Boethius, while the populace were still granted their bread and circuses. The city of Rome was in part restored and Ravenna made more splendid; some provinces were recovered.

The mosaic at the top comes from S. Pudenziana in Rome and is of Christ teaching the Apostles. The others, from Ravenna, show the Baptism of Christ (above), from the Arian Baptistry, and the Good Shepherd and his flock from the ceiling of the Galla Placida (right).

Theodoric's reign and the absorption of his Ostrogoths in Italy is already pointing towards the future, when the vigorous Germanic peoples were to blend Roman and Byzantine cultural traditions with their own and create the Christian civilization of the Middle Ages.

I am going to end these steps through time with a contemporary of Clovis and Theodoric whose name seems utterly remote from theirs: with "King Arthur" of Britain. Once thought to be entirely a figure of myth and legend, he is now recognized as a very real hero of the resistance of the Romanized Britons to the Saxons, Angles and Jutes now crossing the North Sea, settling the country. Arthur was not so much a king as a military leader in the late Roman tradition, gathering together Britons mainly from the west and north. He can be imagined at the head of a force of cavalrymen in chain mail, formidable to the unorganized barbarians. After various lesser battles, Arthur won the great victory of Mons Badonicus that was to check the advance of the invaders for some half century. Neither the date nor the place of this true Arthurian victory is exactly known. It is quite probable, however, that it was won in AD 499.

Technology *AD 1–500*

The Roman engineers, in spite of the prevalence of slave labour and their insufficient iron-working skills for full exploitation of the new ideas of the screw thread and gears, were able to apply several new principles. Three fields only need be mentioned to illustrate the point here. The watermill was the first new (and a very effective) harnessing of a natural power source since the invention of the sail. Much use was made of the storage of power in twisted rope, notably in military artillery, and chemical research resulted in Greek fire as an offensive weapon. The Romans invented the extremely elaborate hypocaust heating system and from their surgical instruments seem to have been capable of a number of complex operations even though their ideas on anatomy and physiology were extremely unscientific.

China's burst of inventive activity, already noted for the preceding period, continued unabated – so much so that it is frequently difficult to apportion discoveries correctly between the Christian and pre-Christian eras. Here, too, cogwheels and the watermill were invented independently of the west. Of much greater significance for the future was the discovery of a technique for making paper, an enormous improvement on papyrus or calf skin (vellum). A mash of plant fibres was shaken to an even layer on the mesh of a sieve and later stuck to the wall to dry. Lesser inventions like the seismograph, the folding umbrella and the reintroduction of stoneware were also made in this period.

In India considerable progress was made in medicine and more importantly in mathematics. At last a system of representing integers and the zero sign were developed together, so that calculations could be worked with the symbols themselves. Previous systems could be used only for recording the result of a problem worked out by some other method.

Developments in the New World included the perfection of the Maya glyphic script and the further elaboration of the calendar with the Long Court system. Improved techniques for casting and alloying various metals resulted in highly decorative ornaments. In Ecuador, finely separated particles of gold and platinum were alloyed together. Other techniques included the use of hard solder, hammer welding and lost wax casting.

	Areas of major interest
●	Centres

The Americas

Metal came into more general use, particularly in the Andean region. It was used especially for jewellery and figurines, but simple functional objects like fish hooks were also made. Mayan glyphs were further elaborated and the ribbed pounder was for beating out bark for use as paper.

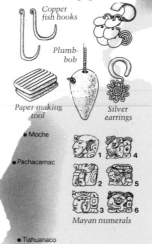

Copper fish hooks

Plumb-bob

Paper-making tool

Silver earrings

Mayan numerals

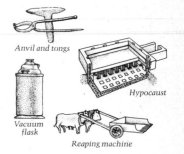

Anvil and tongs

Hypocaust

Vacuum flask

Reaping machine

Eastern, Western Mediterranean, Continental Europe

Roman ingenuity and practicality in engineering in the widest sense continued well into this period. Waterwheels or mills (mainly used for grinding corn or extracting olive oil) were used throughout the Roman empire. Other mechanical machines included a simple reaping device and the crane. Hypocausts which provided underfloor heating and vacuum flasks for food warming were among the domestic inventions of the time. Manufactured tools included surgical instruments. Roads were constructed for both administrative and military purposes. The developments in armour and war engines contributed greatly to the army's successes.

COMPARISON OF MATERIALS IN USE

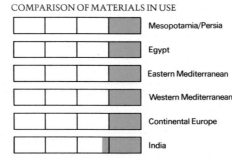

	Stone	Copper	Bronze	Iron	
					Mesopotamia/Persia
					Egypt
					Eastern Mediterranean
					Western Mediterranean
					Continental Europe
					India
					Far East
					The Americas

Far East
The use of the forge in Japan simplified the production of iron helmets. In China measuring devices such as the seismograph and gauge and coins were produced in metal while pottery was still more appropriate for decorative objects and models.

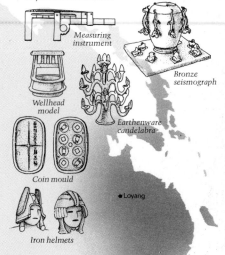

Measuring instrument

Bronze seismograph

Wellhead model

Earthenware candelabra

Coin mould

• Loyang

Iron helmets

Armoured soldier

"Tortoise" shields

Crane

Roman road

Waterwheel

• Londinium

Mobile assault tower

Surgical instruments

• Trier

• Rome

• Constantinople

• Antioch

Seleucia • Ctesiphon

• Alexandria

• Pataliputra

• Ajanta

Egypt
The city of Alexandria and the Egyptian army and government shared fully in Roman imperial development, but the inventiveness of the Egyptian Greeks had declined and there was no noteworthy technological progress.

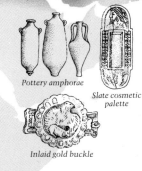

Pottery amphorae

Slate cosmetic palette

Inlaid gold buckle

Mesopotamia/Persia
This region had little to add to world progress in technology. Earlier traditions were followed in producing items in clay, metal and stone.

India
India's contribution at this time was to abstract thought rather than to material progress. For example, the discovery of the cycle of the monsoon winds enormously improved India's sea connections with the west.

Mesopotamia/Persia
This region no longer figured in the forefront of technological advance. Its great amphorae certainly demonstrate skills both in pottery making and in trade, but both were long practised. New developments would arise after its conquest by Islam in 641.

Pottery amphorae, Babylon

Egypt
Roman civilization determined technological advance in this area and whatever native tradition remained was to be shortly swept away by the Muslim conquest in 634.

Eastern, Western Mediterranean, Continental Europe
Roman roads were practical and enduring engineering works on an extraordinary scale. They incorporated a number of innovations in their metalling, camber and surveying. Their effect on the history and economics of their time, and for long afterwards, was enormous. They were found throughout the Empire stretching from one boundary to another. The armour such as that worn by the Triarius usually consisted of a bronze helmet and breast plate with a rectangular leather-coated wooden shield trimmed with iron. Spears and thrusting swords protected the individual soldier while siege engines were used in assault manoeuvres. The

Triarius' armour c. AD 200

Mobile assault tower

hypocaust which supplied underfloor heating was an important part of the Roman bath complex. Vitruvius' water mill harnessed a new source of power with an ingenious and effective use of simple gears to alter the direction and ratio of the drive. It worked on the principle that the water flowing beneath the vertically set wheel struck the blades, thus causing rotation. The connected millstone rotated five times to one turn of the water-wheel. It was more versatile than earlier wheels and could handle a greater volume of work. The crane, needed for lifting in large-scale building construction, was worked by a system of pulleys and winches. The power source was a tread wheel.

Roman road, Blackstone Edge, Lancashire, England

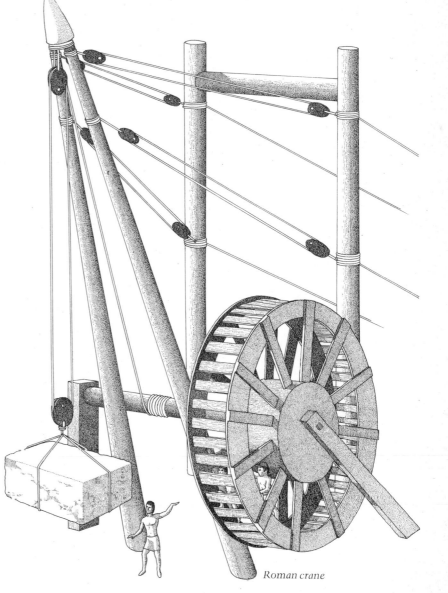

Roman crane

Hypocaust, Roman villa, Chedworth, England.

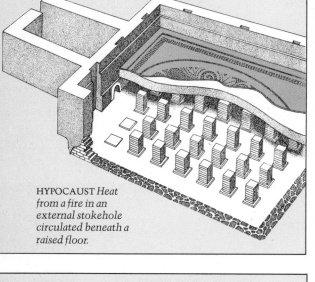

HYPOCAUST *Heat from a fire in an external stokehole circulated beneath a raised floor.*

WATER MILL, VITRUVIAN TYPE *This was a vertical undershot wheel driving a horizontal millstone by the use of gears.*

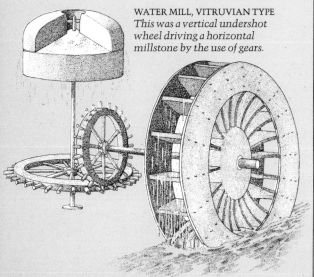

India

Further progress in medicine and astronomy was made in this period. Some contact with Hellenistic and Roman thought via the Arabian Sea trade routes on both these subjects is evident. The period also saw the mastery of the full system of positional notation with the use of a zero sign in mathematics. The first documentary record of this is in the *Puranas* of the 5th century, though as we have seen (p. 87) it was being worked out from a much earlier date.

Far East

The Han Dynasty seismograph was able not only to detect earthquake shocks but also to indicate the direction from which they came. A bronze jar moved forward with the shock waves. Slight movement was sufficient for a bar on the pendulum to move a trigger attached to the jaw of one of the eight bronze dragons on the outside of the jar. As the jaw opened, it released a ball into the mouth of a bronze frog on the stand, waiting to receive it. The apparatus was artistic as well as ingenious and effective. The bronze measuring instrument is similar to modern examples and it needs no further description. The coin mould however, is of interest because even until very recent times, coins in China were cast, not struck as was usual further west. The details on the back of the mould were concerned with the strict control of coinage.

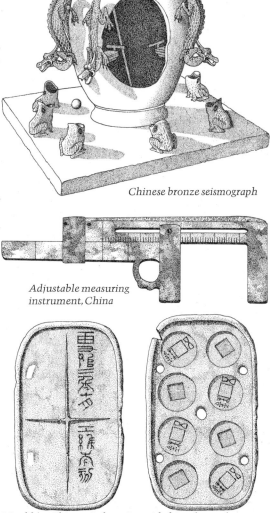

Chinese bronze seismograph

Adjustable measuring instrument, China

Mould for Chinese 5-shu coins with date of manufacture

The Americas

The Maya employed intricate glyphs in the form of grotesque faces. The main purpose of these was in recording dates by the Long Count. Since the Calendar Round (see p. 187) repeated after 52 years, a similar but longer cycle covering recordable history was devised.

1

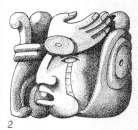

2

3

4

5

6

Architecture *AD 1–500*

The complex civilization of the Romans called for utilitarian as well as majestic structures. Although "Greek" temples continued to be built (with suitably changed dedications) from Colchester to Baalbek, the future lay firmly not with the repeatable formula but with the new problem, not with the temple but with the theatre, the public baths, other civic buildings, and also, if not buildings in the usual sense of the term, the bridge and the aqueduct. All these led to experiment and advance in the use of the arch and of brick-faced concrete, with the object of roofing over larger areas safely, durably and impressively. The Pantheon at Rome had the entrance facade of a classical temple but the dome behind it was entirely novel and not surpassed in size until a thousand years later.

Later in the period and more obviously in the Byzantine east than in the Roman west, the greatest building effort went into the churches, not only because they needed to house the largest number of people at one time, but because to be worthy of God they had to be the finest that their builders could achieve. From the fourth century onwards, architecture meant above all ecclesiastical architecture.

So too elsewhere in the world. In India, the architecture of the Gupta dynasty was directed primarily to temples, rock-cut or free standing, and to the related stupas. And for very similar reasons. In the Far East, however, timber structures were felt to be as adequate for the gods as they were for men. The most impressive surviving monuments are tombs, both in China and Japan, less because they were the grandest structures being erected at the time than because their burial has ensured their preservation. The plans for these ceremonial buildings incorporated a great deal of cosmic symbolism.

Temples come into their own again in the Americas. The motive force which raised the great pyramids and temples of Teotihuacán was a religious one, so too with the temples of the Maya. Their corbel vaulting may have been primitive by comparison with contemporary work in the Old World, but it was far in advance of anything earlier in the American continent. Similar development of the ceremonial centre can be demonstrated in South America, where the great site of Tiahuanaco was rising in this period.

Areas of major interest
• Centres
▲ Sites

Temple, Yaxchilán

Temple, Uaxactún

Kaminalijuyú ▲ Yaxchilán ▲ • Uaxactún

The Americas
This period saw the rise of the Early Classic Period in the lowlands of the Petén in Guatemala. At such sites as Yaxchilán and Uaxactún, ceremonial centres containing platforms, pyramids and temples were built and re-designed over a period of several hundred years.

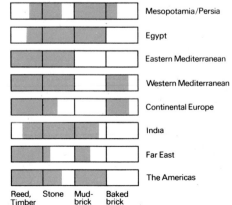

Temples, Baalbek, Lebanon

Basilica Nova of Maxentius, Rome

Hadrian's Wall, England

Arch of Titus, Rome

Eastern, Western Mediterranean, Continental Europe
The number and variety of the illustrations give some idea of the wealth of building under the Roman Empire. From the early imperial age, shown in the Maison Carrée and the huge temple complex at Baalbek, Hellenistic influence was gradually phased out as new systems and principles were explored. The Pantheon, rebuilt by Hadrian, couples a traditional facade with an outstandingly novel building. By the time of the Basilica of Maxentius and the Christian cathedrals of Syria and Old St Peter's, the arch and the vault (first seen in the Royal Cemetery of Ur in 2500 BC), had completely displaced the column and the architrave. A similar progression can be seen in theatres, as at Aspendus and El Djem, and in tombs at Petra and Santa Costanza. Roman inventiveness created new forms such as Hadrian's Wall and the aqueduct of the Pont du Gard where there were no Greek models.

COMPARISON OF MATERIALS IN USE

	Reed, Timber	Stone	Mud-brick	Baked brick
Mesopotamia/Persia				
Egypt				
Eastern Mediterranean				
Western Mediterranean				
Continental Europe				
India				
Far East				
The Americas				

Pont du Gard, Nimes, France

Amphitheatre, El Djem, Tunisia

Pantheon, Rome

Maison Carree, Nimes, France

Old St. Peters, Rome

Syrian cathedral

Temple of Ed Deir, Petra, Jordan

St. Constanza, Rome

Aspendos theatre, Turkey

Far East
Still the only building to survive are the tombs, as at Loyang, but increasing archaeological remains, contemporary representations and deciphered literary descriptions of Loyang and Chang-An allow much more detailed reconstructions.

Ceremonial building, Chang-An

Brick tomb, Loyang

Fortified house, Wu-Wei

● Ch'ang-Sha ▲ ● Loyang

▲ Wu-Wei

▲ Nimes

● Rome

El Djem ▲

▲ Aspendos
SYRIA ● Hatra
▲ Baalbek
● Ctesiphon
▲ Uruk

▲ Petra

▲ Kalabsha
▲ Esna

● Ajanta

▲ Aihole

Temple of Khnum, Esna

Temple of Mandulis, Kalâbsha

Tomb, Hatra

Palace at Ctesiphon

Temple of Gareus, Uruk

Durga Temple, Aihole

Temple facade, Ajanta

India
The Durga temple at Aihole is representative of the architecture of the Gupta period, 320-600 AD whose temples were small, flat-roofed and mortarless. The 27 rock-cut caves of Ajanta are lavishly decorated with paintings and sculpture. A temple was carved into the stone hillside in front of the cave hollow.

Egypt
The temples of Khnum at Esna and Mandulis at Kalâbsha are among the last traditional Egyptian buildings constructed during the Roman occupation.

Mesopotamia/Persia
The Parthian Temple of Gareus at Uruk and the Sassanian palace at Ctesiphon show that the superiority of the arch had at last come to be fully realized (over 2000 years after it was first used here). These buildings are closer to contemporary Roman construction than to their Mesopotamian predecessors. The tomb at Hatra is an altogether simpler structure.

Mesopotamia/Persia

Ctesiphon passed about 225 AD from the Parthians to the Sassanians. The key feature of their palaces was an audience chamber in the form of a huge but shallow brick vaulted hall, 100 ft. (31 m) high, set in an elaborately recessed facade. The hall or *iwan* became a feature of later Muslim architecture. The vault's kiln-baked brickwork spanned a distance of 83 ft. (24 m). The *iwan* was composed of obliquely set arch rings which provided support during construction as well. There are hints of late Hellenistic architecture in details of the brick facade such as the blind arcading (the constant hostility between Parthians and Romans, and later between Sassanians and Byzantines, in no way prevented regular cultural contacts). The palace shown is a reconstruction of an early Sassanian one. The substantial remains surviving on the site were built by King Chosroes, in the mid-6th century.

Palace of Ctesiphon, near Baghdad

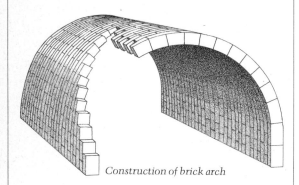

Construction of brick arch

Egypt

The Temple of Khnum at Esna was one of the very last manifestations of pharaonic architecture, which just survived into the Christian era. As has been apparent in these pages, it lingered surprisingly long, perhaps because of the strength of its traditions, built up over 3000 years. Indeed, the religion it was created to serve continued to a much later date. But the spread of this worship was in an acceptably Hellenistic, now Romanized, setting. The heavy masonry, pilasters and concave cornice were more firmly wedded to the Nile valley, and even there these gradually gave way to influences from the Mediterranean.

Temple of Khnum, Esna

Eastern, Western Mediterranean, Continental Europe

The Romans applied Hellenistic architecture with a pragmatic common-sense. At the Maison Carrée at Nîmes, for instance, the exterior consisted of Romanized Corinthian columns supporting a richly carved entablature. When no Hellenistic models for an aqueduct were available, the Romans produced a structure 882 ft. (271 m) long with three tiers of arches 155 ft. (47 m) above the River Gard. The masonry was laid dry except for the top tier. The second century tomb facade known as Ed Deir at Petra is also colossal (151 ft: 46 m high). The tombs were cut into rock and closely resemble temples. The Pantheon in Rome, while not the first round temple, was one of enormous scale. Seven recesses housed statues of the gods and one served as an entrance. The huge dome was illuminated by a 30 ft. (9 m) round opening. Gilt bronze decorated the exterior of the dome. In theatre building, the new developed alongside the old. The theatre at Aspendos (only the stage building survives complete), is closely in the Greek tradition. But the amphitheatre, as at El Djem, was a completely new and purely Roman development, as its ostentatious use of the arch shows. Hadrian's Wall was a permanent military installation built across the north of England, Vaults were built which, when concrete-filled, became extensions of the arch.

Pont du Gard aqueduct, Nîmes, France

Temple of Ed Deir, Petra, Jordan

Hadrian's Wall, England

Roman amphitheatre, El Djem, Tunisia

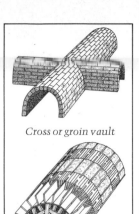

Cross or groin vault

Tunnel or barrel vault

Maison Carrée, Nîmes, France

Theatre, Aspendos, Turkey

Interior of dome, Pantheon, Rome

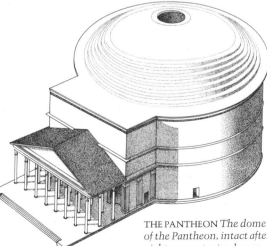

THE PANTHEON *The dome of the Pantheon, intact after eighteen centuries, has an internal diameter of 142 ft. (43 m). Its construction was made possible by a highly skilled use of concrete.*

India

The Durga Temple at Aihole, one of seventy-odd temples at that site, is of the chaitya form and late Gupta in date, probably 5th century AD. It consists of a rectangular nave, here flat-roofed (barrel vaults were less usual) terminating in an apse which contains the principal shrine. The entrance is in the form of a porch at the other end, and the whole cella is surrounded by an ambulatory. The masonry was mortar-less and rather large and thick. Like the rock-cut chaitya halls or "cave temples" of Ajanta, it goes back to prototypes of timber buildings well before the Maurya period, which have not survived. The carved stone copies, allow easy reconstruction of the timber originals.

Durga temple, Aihole, India

Far East

Ceremonial buildings which were of great size and complexity have to be reconstructed largely from written descriptions. One palace at Loyang was described as "A two-storeyed fane with double eaves, having eight apertures and nine chambers; compass drawn like the Heavens and squared off like the Earth; telling the seasons and conforming to the cardinal directions". A massive timber framework supported these structures which were crowned by tiled roofs.

Ceremonial building, Ch'ang-An, Shensi, China

The Americas.

Careful excavation at Uaxactún has shown a long succession of building phases as the temple was progressively enlarged and beautified. A broad flight of steps led up to an open square on a platform over-looked by three imposing buildings. The height of these was necessitated by the use of the corbel vault, the arch being unknown.

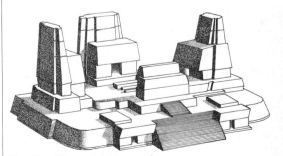

Temple at Uaxactún, Guatemala

Art AD 1–500

To emphasize the significance of the beginning of the high civilizations of Mesoamerica from c. AD 300, it is justifiable to set aside the claims of the Old World and open with the New.

In the valley of Mexico the city of Teotihuacán was flourishing and widely influential; in addition to rather limited architectural sculpture, mural painting was already practised. In Oaxaca, where advances toward civilization had begun early at Monte Albán, Zapotec culture was now fully established. It was, however, the Mayan high civilization that developed in the Guatemalan lowlands round Tikal and Uaxactún, but soon spread more widely, that was to have by far the highest achievement in the arts. The Maya had already adopted the principal of vitalizing the heavy masses of their buildings with decorative sculpture; one of the early stele from Tikal shows the priest-king dwarfed by a colossal headdress that was to become such a familiar figure a little later.

In the Old World, of course, the Roman empire dominates the age. Its art derived directly from the Hellenistic tradition. Indeed, in the earlier centuries much of it was executed by Greeks, while wealthy Romans robbed Greece of many of her finest sculptures and also had them copied on a commercial scale. The Roman character and the grandiose demands of imperial monuments brought about obvious changes of feeling. Moreover, in the western provinces such as Gaul and Britain much provincial work was produced.

In Near Eastern art, including Parthia, where a mingling of Hellenistic with Persian and other local elements persisted on a generally low level, there was one curious revolution. The lines of figures seen in profile, which had prevailed for so long, were, during the 1st century, turned round and shown full face: this new principal of "frontality" spread to the eastern empire and greatly affected Byzantine art. In India both Buddhist and Hindu religious art evolved their iconography – the Gupta age marking one of the high peaks of Indian culture.

In China the courtly art of the Han was maintained with its grace and artificiality – best known throught tomb figures. The infiltration of Buddhism encouraged the contemplative life and the perfection of the arts of subject painting and calligraphy. Rock-cut shrines with Buddhist painting and sculpture spread across the north, even among the nomad intruders. The export of Chinese tomb figures to Japan gave rise to the local *Haniwa* style.

Areas of major interest
● Centres
▲ Sites

MEXICO

● Monte Albán

PERU

The Americas

By about AD 300 true Mayan art had emerged in architectural sculpture and relief figures on calendar stelae. The Maya also sculpted fine vessels and made painted and modelled pottery. The people of Tenochtitlán used sculpture less freely, but had already developed mural painting. Zapotec art developed in Oaxaca (Monte Albán). Figure sculpture was plentiful at San Agustín, Colombia, while in the coastal valleys of Peru fine painted and modelled pottery characterized the Mochica and Nazca cultures.

God figurine Monte Albán

Jade mask, Mexico

Mayan incense burner

Warrior vase, Peru

Mochica pot

Eastern, Western Mediterranean

Greco-Roman art generally prevailed round the Roman Sea, although local schools are often recognizable. Imperial Roman art was at its best in realistic portraiture and historical narrative. After Constantine, portrayals tended to be more stylized and Christian subjects are developed, particularly in funerary sculpture. The Romans also practised landscape and architectural painting and the mosaic art.

Far East

Artists of the late Han dynasty continued to produce excellent small sculptures such as the famous "flying horses" from Wu-wei. After the fall of the Han dynasty calligraphic and other painting was perfected under the southern dynasty of East Ch'in. With the growth of Buddhism its art forms spread; they are well represented in the thousand Buddha caves.

Continental Europe

During the brief period before the Claudian conquest of AD 43 La Tène art enjoyed an Indian summer in Britain. Masterpieces such as the bronze Desborough mirror were produced. After the Conquest something of the Celtic spirit occasionally showed itself – in unclassical sculpture. Generally, however, Roman provincialism prevailed. Before 500 the Germanic peoples began to produce fine jewellery.

Brooch, Denmark

Cup, Hoby

Head, Gloucester

Desborough Mirror

Sassanian horse

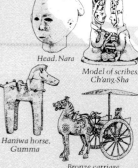

Silver plate

Mesopotamia/Persia

Some examples of the best early Parthian art come from the edge of the empire – from Palmyra. Fresco painting, including scenes from a Mathraeum, are known from Dura Europos. In a new age of prosperity after the Sassanid conquest of 220, an effort was made to restore something of the Achaemenid past.

Head, Nara

Model of scribes, Ch'ang-Sha

Haniwa horse, Gumma

Bronze carriage, Wu-Wei

Handscroll detail

GUMMA

▲ Nara

GLOUCESTER ▲   ▲ Desborough   ▲ Hoby

DENMARK

Seine-et-Oise ▲

▲ Wu-Wei   ▲ Ch'ang-Sha

● Rome

● Constantinople

▲ Begram
▲ Hadda

▲ Sarnath

SYRIA

▲ Sanchi

● Alexandria
▲ Hawara

● Ajanta

Fresco, Ajanta

Monks' statue, Hadda

Roman bust

Statue of Augustus, Rome

Tetrarchs, Constantinople

Figurine, Begram

Greco-Roman statue

Gravestone

Augustus cameo

Roman painting

Sarcophagus detail

Spanish fibula

Flask, Syria

Mummy case, Hawara

Lamp

Glass bowl, Alexandria

Funerary painting

Buddha, Sarnath

Torso, Sanchi

Egypt

The Egyptians were greatly influenced by the Romans even in those traditions uniquely theirs, i.e. the decoration of mummies. Glass and bronze were widely used.

India

Indian art was now divided between a Greco-Roman influenced province in the northwest (under the Kushans) that gave rise to the Gandhara schools of sculpture, and a native development out of the earlier Mauryan tradition. This art of the Guptas (including Ashoka) is wholly Indian and religious – serving both Hindu gods and the Buddha. The finest painting can be seen in cave temples of Ajanta.

225

Mesopotamia/Persia
The Parthians were of probable Scythian origin and warlike in nature. Their art was formed from an unstable blend of Hellenistic and Achaemenid traditions and is recognized by the 1st century AD. Among a small amount of surviving Parthian art is a silver bowl showing the god Silenus accompanied by his followers, which is dated around AD 200.

Parthian silver plate

Egypt
The Greco-Roman presence in Egypt and the blending of ideas is well illustrated by a funerary portrait of a classical gentleman being handled by Anubis. It was he who escorted the dead to the underworld. This was the period when realistically painted portraits were attached to mummies. These portraits replaced the earlier Hellenistic plaster masks. The painting was done on wooden tablets and were made during the lifetime of the sitter.

Wall painting of Anubis accompanying soul to afterworld

Eastern, Western Mediterranean
From the first the Romans showed a genius for realistic portrait sculpture, and developed a taste for narrative historical scenes, such as those on Trajan's column. Also from the beginning, landscape and architectural painting with perspective of an imperfect kind was already highly accomplished. Mosaics, sometimes works of art, more often journeyman stuff, spread thoughout the empire. The best Roman metropolitan sculpture could have great natural charm. Much surviving relief carving is funerary – from tombstones and sarcophagi. Among minor arts the Romans cut cameos and painted miniature portraits on glass. Some of the early Christian art which flourished in this area is well known from the decorations at Ravenna (p. 215)

Bas relief figure from a tombstone

Sardonynx cameo of Emperor Augustus

Greco-Roman figure of a young girl

Portrait of a girl, Pompeii

Detail of a Christian sarcophagus, Rome

Continental Europe

While most western provincial art was fully Romanized, though often pedestrian, an occasional spark of a very un-Roman spirit appears – particularly, perhaps, in Britain where Celtic art was to have a post-Roman revival. This limestone head from a life-sized statue is only Roman in its hairstyle.

"Gloucester head", limestone with red colouring

India

Indian painting of the period survives principally in cave temples. The earliest are in the famous Ajanta caves of Hydrabad, where they range from the 1st to 5th centuries. These murals give colourful insights into the court life of Gupta kings. Within the Gupta empire Indian Buddhist art reached its peak. At Mathura and Sarnath Buddha statues have a serene beauty. While early statues portrayed Buddha as equal to his audience, later representations made him of enormous scale.

Cave painting, Ajanta

Buddha in the pose of preaching, Sarnath, India

Far East

Some of the finest late Han tomb figures are the bronzes from the tombs of a 2nd century general at Wu-Wei. As well as the well known "flying horses" a number of carts and human figures were buried with him. The horses were originally brightly painted. The handscroll titled "Admonitions of the Imperial Preceptress" by Ku K'ai Chih is the oldest surviving example.

Painted handscroll, Ku K'ai Chih, China.

Bronze model of a horse carriage and driver, Wu-Wei, China

The Americas

The Mochica potters of the southern coastal valleys of Peru produced an amazing range of figure pottery, including animals, birds and a rich variety of human studies, including portrait heads. The jaguar maintained its ancient religious significance. The Mayas favoured grotesque monsters as decoration.

Mayan pottery incense burner

Jar showing jaguar attacking a man, Mochica, Peru

Region	Economy	Centres	Events and developments	People
Mesopotamia/Persia		Seleucia Ctesiphon	Parthians. Sassanians from 226. Great increase of trade to Mediterranean via Petra and Palmyra.	
Egypt		Alexandria	Roman province. Pre-eminence of Alexandria rivalled by Antioch. Byzantine province. Iron spreads from Meroe into sub-Saharan Africa.	
Eastern Mediterranean		Antioch Constantinople	Gradual rift between eastern and western halves of Roman Empire. New capital at Constantinople/Byzantium.	Jesus of Nazareth Constantine
Western Mediterranean		Rome	Imperial Rome as ruler of known world, under increasing threat from civil war and external Barbarian attack. Split between E. and W. West succumbs c.400.	Trajan Hadrian Pliny Nero Diocletian Marcus Aurelius Galen Augustine
Continental Europe		Trier Londinium	Roman Empire extends to Rhine/Danube, Trajan adds Dacia. Trade beyond. Westward pressure of peoples builds up and breaches frontier. Migration period.	Boudicca King Arthur Caratacus Cunobelin Alaric Attila
India		Pataliputra Ajanta	Andhra Empire 32 BC. Kushan invasion from NW 50 AD. Gupta dynasty 320. Ephthalite invasion 5th century.	Chandragupta
Far East		Loyang	Han dynasty to 220. Spread of civilization to Yangtze valley. Unification of Japan 4th century.	
The Americas		Teotihuacán Monte Albán Tikal Uaxactún Mochica Tiahuanaco Pachacamac	Rise of Teotihuacán and Tiahuanaco. Mochica, Zapotec, Nazca and Mayan civilizations. Basketmaker villages in southwest N. America.	

The economy bar graph indicates relative proportions of these factors: Irrigation ≈ Agriculture ✿ Hunting ⚔ Urban life ⌗ Trade 𝕊

Religion	Technology and inventions	Architecture	Art and literature
Zoroastrianism. Some infiltration of Judaism and Christianity. Nestorianism.	Comparative stagnation.	Ambitious use of brick vaults.	Parthian and Sassanian art style in rich metalwork and textiles.
Isis. Judaism. Christianity leads to Coptic Church. Origins of monasticism.	Roman application of some Greek inventions, e.g. widespread use of waterwheel, but advance decidedly sluggish. Torsion-powered artillery. Underfloor heating.	Hellenistic/Roman	Hellenistic, Coptic and Byzantine art styles. Especially in textiles, funerary portraiture.
Christiany becomes widespread. Edict of Milan 312. Doctrinal disagreements frequent.		Beginning of divergence of Byzantine architecture from main Roman stream.	Imperial Roman art developing Greek cast to become more formal Byzantine art. *New Testament* Works of Plutarch, Josephus, Eusebius
Roman pantheon. Deified emperors (political rather than religious). Mithras and Isis. Christianity prevails.		Full development of brick and concrete construction. Aqueducts, roads, temples, theatres. Amphitheatres, villas, public baths, military forts, town walls.	Imperial Roman art: fresco mosaic, realistic portrait sculpture, statuary, bronze figurines. Works of Juvenal, Tacitus, Pliny.
Within empire, Roman gods challenged by Isis, Mithras, Christianity. Bog bodies in Denmark.	Advances in horse-riding, cavalry.		Provincial Roman. La Tène continued in Ireland. Germanic art style developed in north.
Brahmanism changing into Hinduism. Vishnu and Shiva. Hinduism spreads through coastal SE Asia, Buddhism into C. Asia.	Advances in medicine. Decimal system of mathematics with full use of positional notation perfected.	Gupta architecture, rock-cut and free-standing temples, stupas.	Gandara, Mathura art styles. Peak of Hindu art and architecture under Guptas. Ajanta frescoes. *Puranas* Works of Kalidasa.
Buddhism spreads through China and Japan.	Very fruitful period: paper, horse collar, watermill, wheelbarrow, seismograph, folding umbrella, cog wheels.	Timber architecture magnificent but surviving only in records. Japanese tombs.	Haniwa tomb figures. Later Han. Growth of Buddhist art. Tomb figures, bronze horses. Eastern Ch'in painting and calligraphy.
Mexican gods of sun, moon, rain, maize, feathered serpent, etc. Similar range in Peru.	Gold, silver and copper in Peru. Obsidian continues in Mexico. Maya elaboration of calendar and script.	Pyramids of Teotihuacán. Corbel vaulting in Mayan temples and palaces, elaborate stairways. Temple platforms. Monolithic gateway at Tiahuanaco.	Maya art developing, stone reliefs on calendrical stelae. Mochica art, especially figured pottery.

Atlas of
Archaeological
site maps

Ptolemy of Alexandria, the great geographer, realized the earth was a sphere with mingled land and water masses, and established latitudes and longitudes. He used a conical projection and mapped the then known inhabited world from Britain to China.

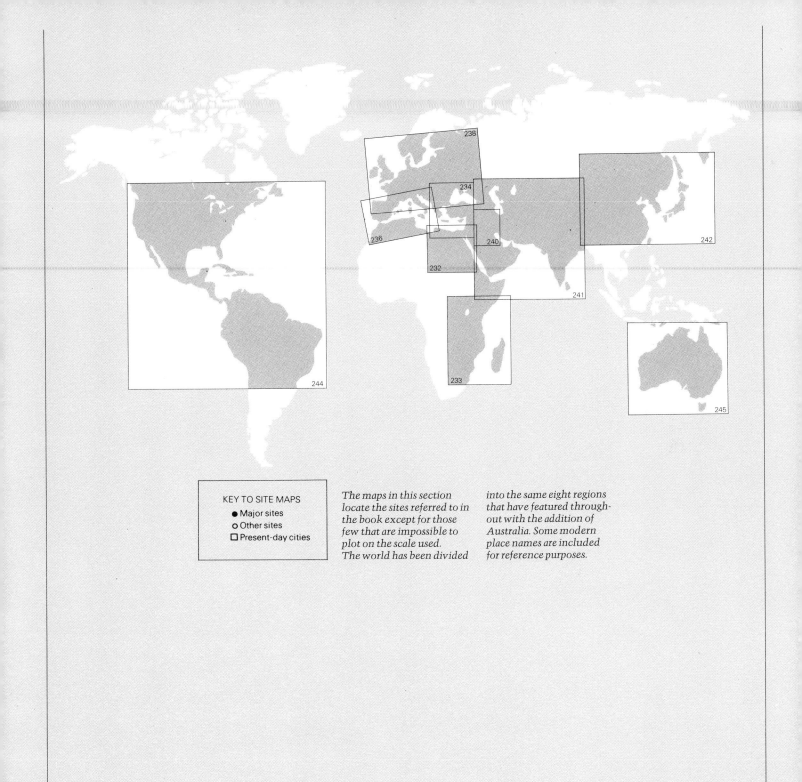

KEY TO SITE MAPS
● Major sites
○ Other sites
□ Present-day cities

The maps in this section locate the sites referred to in the book except for those few that are impossible to plot on the scale used. The world has been divided into the same eight regions that have featured throughout with the addition of Australia. Some modern place names are included for reference purposes.

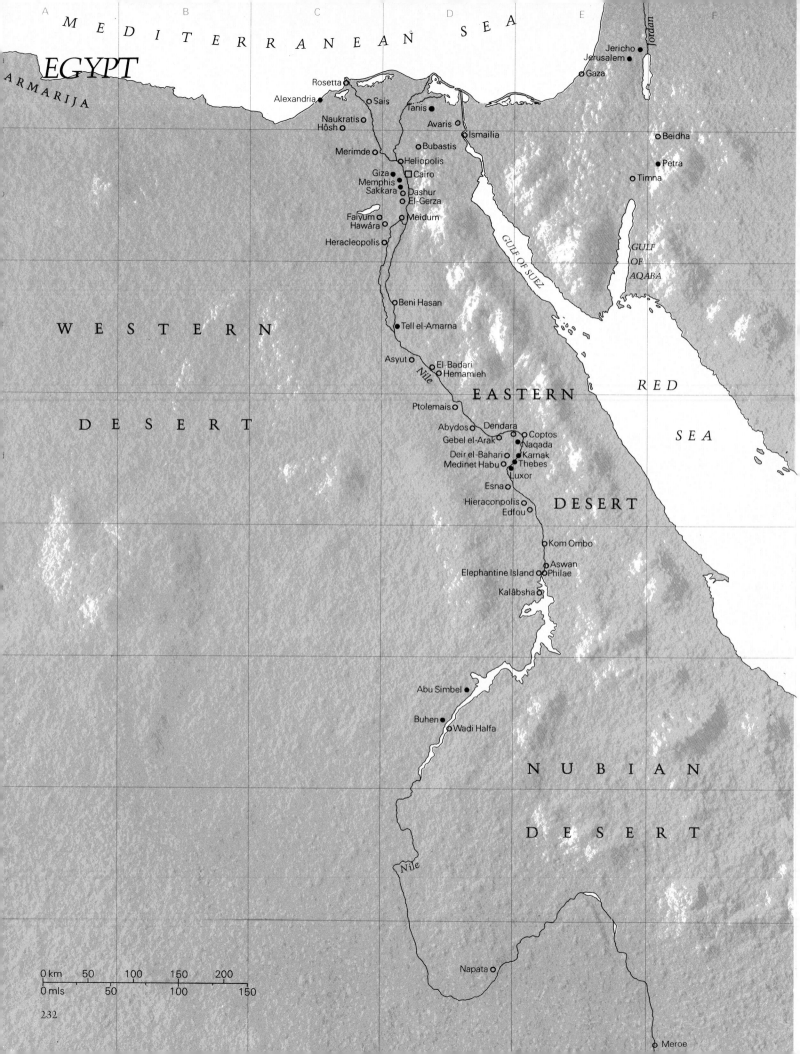

MEDITERRANEAN SEA

A   B   C   D   E   F

EGYPT

ARMARIJA

Jordan

Jericho

Jerusalem

Gaza

Rosetta

Alexandria

Sais

Tanis

Avaris

Ismailia

Beidha

Naukratis

Hôsh

Petra

Bubastis

Timna

Merimde

Heliopolis

Giza   Cairo

Memphis

Sakkara   Dashur

El-Gerza

Faiyum   Meidum

Hawára

Heracleopolis

GULF OF SUEZ

GULF OF AQABA

WESTERN

Beni Hasan

Tell el-Amarna

Asyut   El-Badari

Hemamieh

EASTERN

RED

DESERT

Ptolemais

SEA

Abydos   Dendara

Gebel el-Arak   Coptos

Naqada

Deir el-Bahari   Karnak

Medinet Habu   Thebes

Luxor

Esna

Hieraconpolis   DESERT

Edfou

Kom Ombo

Aswan

Elephantine Island   Philae

Kalâbsha

Nile

Abu Simbel

Buhen   Wadi Halfa

NUBIAN

DESERT

Nile

0 km   50   100   150   200

0 mls   50   100   150

232

Napata

Meroe

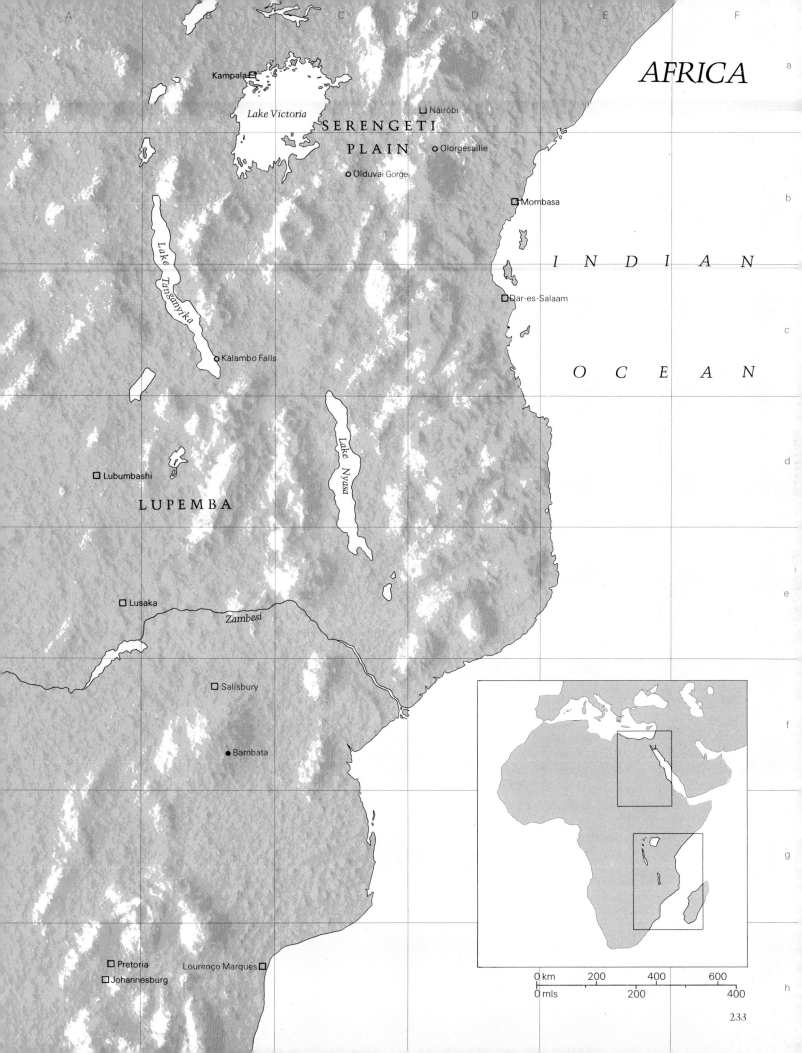

AFRICA

a

Kampala□

Lake Victoria

SERENGETI
PLAIN

□Nairobi

○Olorgesailie

○Olduvai Gorge

□Mombasa

b

I N D I A N

Lake Tanganyika

○Kalambo Falls

□Dar-es-Salaam

c

O C E A N

Lake Nyasa

□Lubumbashi

d

L U P E M B A

□Lusaka

Zambesi

e

□Salisbury

f

●Bambata

g

□Pretoria   Lourenço Marques□
□Johannesburg

0 km   200   400   600

0 mls   200   400

h

233

EASTERN MEDITERRANEAN

ADRIATIC

SEA

MACEDONIA

THRACE

o Philippi

BOSPHOR

o Samothrace

PHRYGI

• Troy.

o Nea Nikomedia

△ Olympus (Mt.)

THESSALY

AEGEAN

LESBOS

CORFU

EPIRUS

Otzaki o

Larisa o

• Dimini

• Sesklo

CHIOS

Pergamum o

LYDIA

Gediz   • Sardis

o Smyrna

• Actium

Chaeronia o

SEA

ITHACA

• Delphi

• Ephesus

PELOPONNESE

Corinth o

Mycenae •

Dendra •

Olympia o

Lerna •

Tiryns •

Eleusis •

Epidauros o

Franchthi Cave

o Athens

o Miletus

IONIAN

CYCLADES

SEA

Artemision o

• Sparta

o Melos

RHO

CRETE

Mallia

Mochlos o • Palaikastro

M

Knossos •

Gournia o   o Zakros

Kamarea Cave o

Vasiliki

E

Agia Triadha

Phaestos

o Apesokari

D

I

T

E

R

R

A

N

• Haua Fteah

BLACK SEA

A · B · C · D · E · F

Constantinople
Fikirtepe
US

Alaca Hüyük
Yazilikaya ●○ Boghazköy

Sakarya
Ankara
Gordion

Halys

Kultepe

Euphrates

KONYA
PLAIN

Beycesultan

Sakagozi
Tell Hala
Zincirli
Carchemish
Carrhae

Hacilar

Catal Hüyük

TAURUS MOUNTAINS

Tarsus
Mersin

Issus

Aspendos

Can Hasan

Tell Atchana
Antioch
Aleppo

Mureybet

Belbusi

Minet el-Beidha

Xanthos

Ugarit
Hama

Rhodes
ES

CYPRUS

Khirokitia

Byblos ○ Baalbek

Beirut

Sidon

Tyre

A

Eynam
Hazor

E
A
N
Nahal Oren
Mt. Carmel
Megiddo
Caesarea
El Wad
Kebara

Tiberius
Nazareth

S
E
A
Wadi en Natuf
Jericho
Amman
Ghassul

Bethlehem
Jerusalem
Lachish

Alexandria

Beidha

Petra

235

WESTERN MEDITERRANEAN

BAY OF

BISCAY

P Y R E N E E S

Châteauneuf-les-Martigues

○ Aurignac

○ Lespugue   ○ Mas d'Azil

Altamira ● ○ El Castello   ○ Lortet

Ebro

○ Cogul

Douro

□ Madrid   Castellón ●

MINORCA

Costig
Es Tudons ○○
Cala Coves ○

Tagus   ○ Marvão

MAJORCA

San Pedro de Estoril ○   Parpalló ●

IBIZA

Guadiana

○ Anto do Silval   ○ Elche

Guadalquivir

G U A D A L Q U I V I R

A N D A L U S I A

T

El Argar ○ ○ El Garcel

● Los Millares

● Almeria   □ Algiers

○ Cadiz

M   E   D

○ Gibraltar

□ Tangiers   M   *Oued Chéliff*

A T L A S   M O U

236

A   B   C   D   E   F

Rhône

A L P S
VAL
CAMONICA
○ Sesto Calende   ● Peschiera
Adige
Tartaro
● Benacci ●Bologna
● Savignano

A D R I A T I C
Savu
S E A

a

b

● Grimaldi

○ Arretium

● Massilia

CORSICA

○ Telamon
● Tarquinia
Cerveteri ● ● Veii
○ Rome

Tiber

● Coppa Nevigata
● Tavoliere   ● Molfetta
○ Altamura
Matera ● ● Scoglio del Tonno
● Romanelli

c

● Filitosa

LATIUM
CAMPANIA
● Cumae
● Pompeii
● Paestum

○ Palestrina

● Praia-a-Mare

d

T Y R R H E N I A N

SEA

● Anghelu Ruju

SARDINIA

● Tharros   ○ Orrubiu
● Barumini
○ Senorbi

○ Lipari

e

● Addaura

S I C I L Y

M E D I T E R R A N E A N

Agrigento ●   Pantalica ○   Stentinello
Castelluccio ●   ● Syracuse

E

A

N

● Carthage □ Tunis

Ggantija
Hal Saflieni ○○ Tarxien
Hagar Qim ○ Borg in Nadur
Hagrat

f

N T A I N S

○ El Djem

S

E

A

g

0 km   100   200   300
0 mls   50   100   150   200

h

● Leptis Magna

237

CONTINENTAL EUROPE

NORTH

SEA

BAY OF

BISCAY

ADRIATIC

SEA

Mousa

Skara Brae Maeshowe

Klosterfoss Oslo Alunda

Stockholm

Perth

Milton Loch

Gundestrop

Graubolle Sonderholm

Dejbjerg Tollund

Trundholm Copenhagen

Skarpsalling Bohuslan

Mullerup Egemarke Kivik

Hoby

Turoe New Grange

MEATH

PRESCELLY MTS.

Scarborough

Star Carr

Gloucester Desborough

Birdlip Grimes Graves

Windmill Hill

Avebury Londinium Colchester

West Kennet Swanscombe

Stonehenge Thames

Maiden Castle Little Woodbury Woodhenge

Amsterdam

Rhein

Berlin Biskupin

Woldenberg

Vettersfelde

Sittard

Brussels Köln-Lindenthal Leubingen

Elbe

Oder SIL

Trier

Steinheim

Seine-et-Oise Fère-en-Tardenois Basse Yutz Prague

Paris Schifferstadt Unĕtice

Carnac Essé

Gavrinis

Seine

Střelice Adamov

Vix

Gneiding Dolni Vĕstonice MORAV

Alesia Sternberg Heuneberg Vogelherd WACHAU

Grand Pressigny Solutré Willendorf

Robenhausen Mondsee Vienna

Camp de Chassey Wasserburg

La Tène Cortaillod

La Madeleine Lascaux Bern Aichbühl Hallstatt Strettweg Budapest

WURTTEMBURG

ALPS

Loire

Font de Gaume Laussel

La Gravette Peche Merle Vačé Lengyel

Brassempouy Vezère

Dordogne

TARN

Lortet Aurignac Vučedol

Lespugue

Mas d'Azil Roquepertuse

PYRENEES

Ebro

Rhône

Tiber

238

0 km   100   200   300

0 mls   100   200

□ Moscow

Kapova Cave o

o Pushkari

● Kostienki

□ Warsaw

Vistula

ESIA

PONTIC STEPPES

Don

Dnepr

o Mezhirich

Dneister

o Moldova

A

o Kostromskay

o Trusesti

o Kelermes

o Cucuteni

o Borodino

o Maikop

o Tartaria

CAUCASUS MTS

Stakčevo

Vinča
□ ● o Kličevac
Belgrade Lepenski Vir

o Vadastra

o Bucharest

o Cernavoda

BLACK   SEA

o Gumelnita

o Glasinac

Danube

□ Sofia

o Karanovo

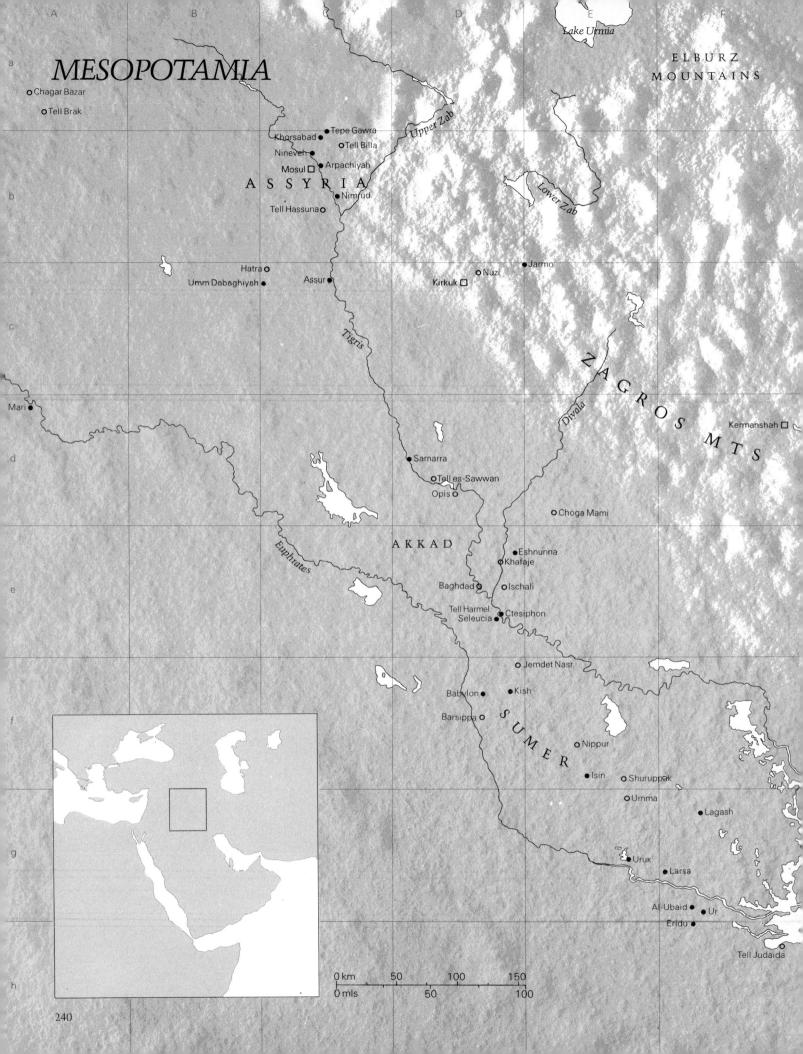

MESOPOTAMIA

○ Chagar Bazar

○ Tell Brak

● Tepe Gawra

Khorsabad ● ○ Tell Billa
Nineveh ●
Mosul ☐ ● Arpachiyah

A S S Y R I A

● Nimrud
Tell Hassuna ○

Hatra ○
Umm Dabaghiyah ● Assur ●

○ Nuzi
Kirkuk ☐

● Jarmo

Upper Zab

Lower Zab

Tigris

**Z
A
G
R
O
S**

Divala

Kermanshah ☐

**M
T
S**

● Samarra
○ Tell es-Sawwan
Opis ○

○ Choga Mami

A K K A D

● Eshnunna
○ Khafaje

Baghdad ○ ○ Ischali

Tell Harmel ○
Seleucia ○ ● Ctesiphon

Euphrates

○ Jemdet Nasr

Babylon ● ○ Kish

Barsippa ○

S U M E R

○ Nippur

● Isin ○ Shuruppak

○ Umma

● Lagash

● Uruk
● Larsa

Al-Ubaid ● ● Ur
Eridu ●

Tell Judaida ●

Lake Urmia

**ELBURZ
MOUNTAINS**

0 km   50   100   150
0 mls   50   100

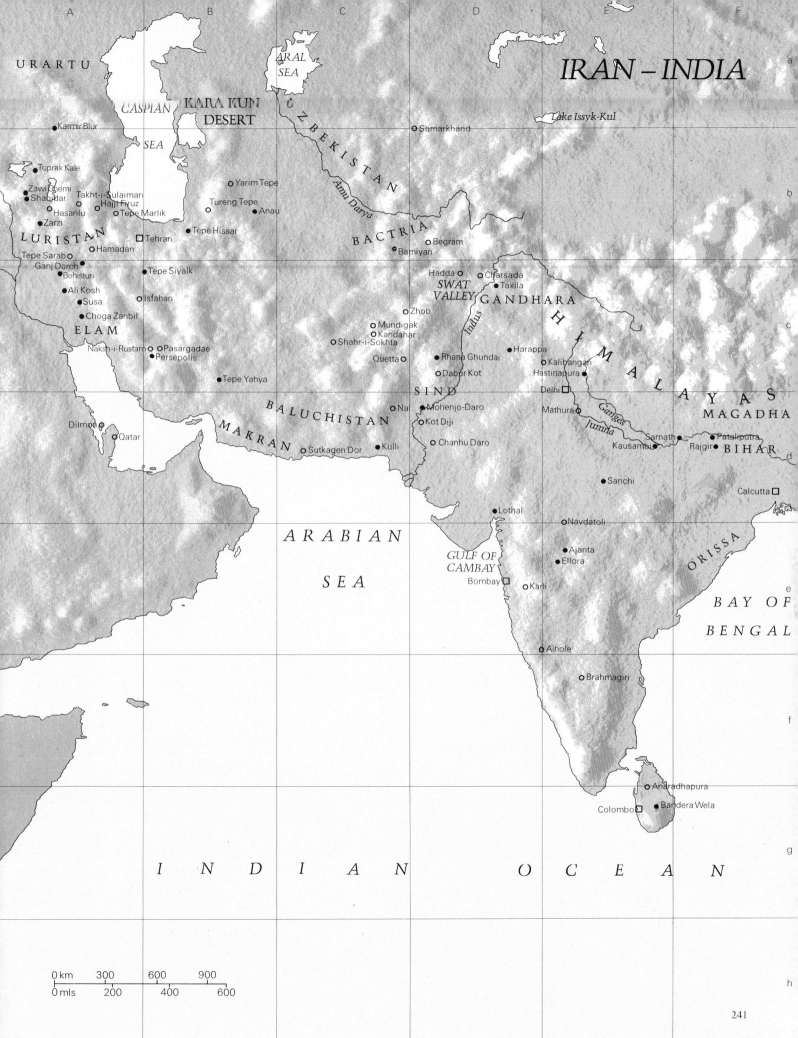

URARTU

CASPIAN
SEA

KARA KUM
DESERT

ARAL
SEA

Lake Issyk-Kul

Karmir Blur

Toprak Kale

Zawi Ogemi
Shanidar
Hasanlu
Zarzi

Takht-i-Sulaiman
Hajji Firuz
Tepe Marlik

LURISTAN

Tehran

Tepe Hissar

Tepe Sarab
Ganj Dareh
Behistun
Ali Kosh
Susa
Choga Zanbil

Hamadan

Tepe Siyalk

Isfahan

ELAM

Naksh-i-Rustam
Persepolis

Pasargadae

Yarim Tepe

Tureng Tepe
Anau

UZBEKISTAN

Amu Darya

BACTRIA

Samarkhand

Bamiyan

Begram

Hadda
SWAT
VALLEY

Charsada
Taxila

GANDHARA

Zhob

Mundigak
Kandahar
Shahr-i-Sokhta

Quetta

Rhana Ghundai
Dabur Kot

Indus

Harappa

Kalibangan
Hastinapura

HIMALAYAS

Delhi

Ganges

MAGADHA

Tepe Yahya

Dilmun

Qatar

BALUCHISTAN

MAKRAN

Sutkagen Dor

Kulli

Nal

SIND

Mohenjo-Daro
Kot Diji

Chanhu Daro

Mathura

Jumna

Kausambi

Sarnath
Rajgir

Pataliputra

BIHAR

Sanchi

Calcutta

Lothal

Navdatoli

ARABIAN

SEA

GULF OF
CAMBAY

Bombay

Ajanta
Ellora

Karli

ORISSA

Aihole

Brahmagiri

BAY OF

BENGAL

Anaradhapura

Colombo

Bandera Wela

INDIAN   OCEAN

0 km   300   600   900

0 mls   200   400   600

241

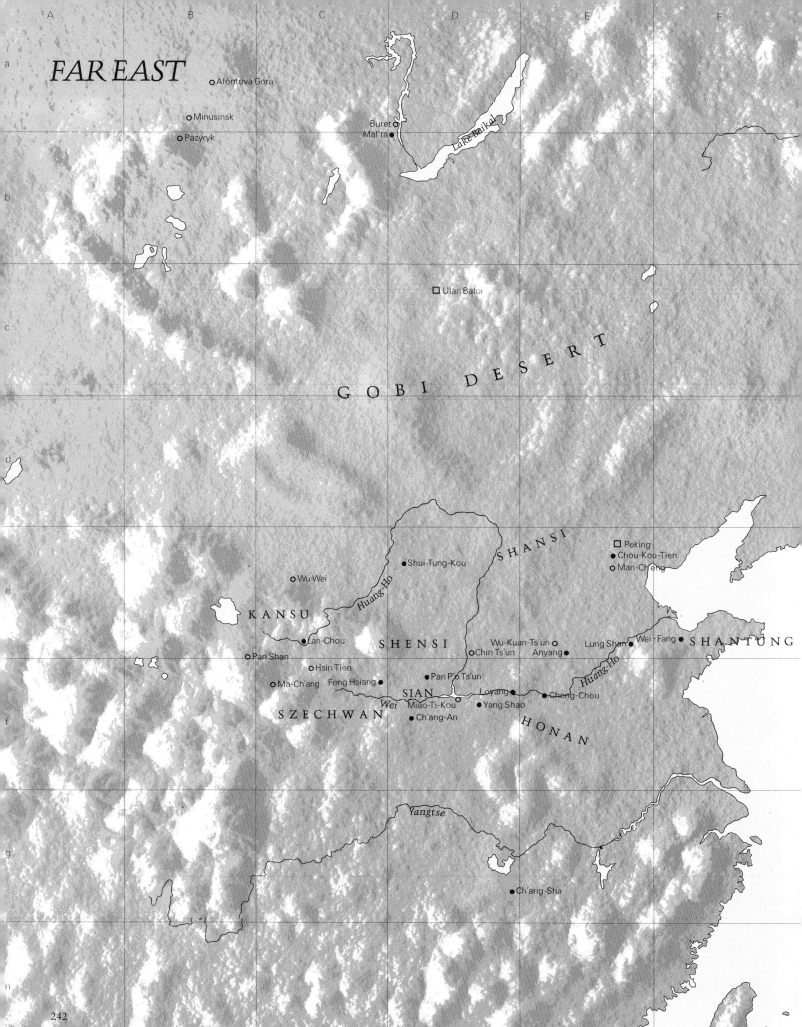

FAR EAST

○ Afontova Gora

○ Minusinsk

○ Pazyryk

Lake Baikal

Buret ○
Mal'ta ●

□ Ulan Bator

G O B I   D E S E R T

□ Peking

● Chou-Kou-Tien

○ Man-Ch'eng

S H A N S I

● Shui-Tung-Kou

○ Wu-Wei

Huang-Ho

K A N S U

● Lan-Chou

S H E N S I

Wu-Kuan-Ts'un ○

Lung Shan ● Wei-Fang ● S H A N T U N G

○ Pan Shan

Chin Ts'un ○

Anyang ●

Huang-Ho

● Hsin Tien

● Pan P'o Ts'un

○ Ma-Ch'ang   Feng Hsiang ●

SIAN   Loyang ●

Cheng-Chou ●

Wei   Miao-Ti-Kou

● Yang Shao

S Z E C H W A N

● Ch'ang-An

H O N A N

Yangtse

● Ch'ang-Sha

242

● Fu-Nan

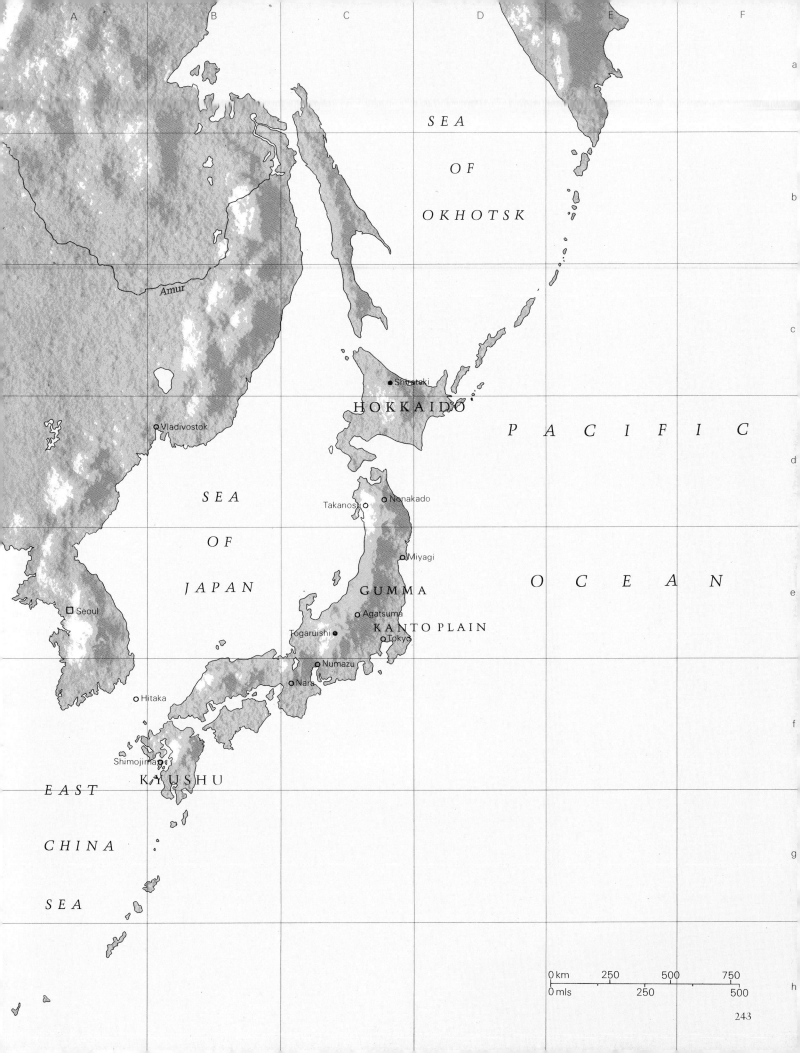

SEA

OF

OKHOTSK

SEA

OF

JAPAN

PACIFIC

OCEAN

EAST

CHINA

SEA

Amur

Vladivostok

● Shiratoki

HOKKAIDO

Takanosu ○   ○ Nonakado

○ Miyagi

GUMMA

○ Agatsuma

Togaruishi ●

KANTO PLAIN

○ Tokyo

○ Numazu

○ Nara

○ Hitaka

Shimojima ○

KYUSHU

□ Seoul

| 0 km | 250 | 500 | 750 |
| 0 mls | | 250 | 500 |

THE AMERICAS

A   B   C   D   E   F

ROCKY MOUNTAINS

□ San Francisco
Danger Cave ○
● Scottsbluff
Colorado
● Sandia
La Jolla ○
Bat Cave ●
● Folsom
Snaketown ○
COCHISE
● Clovis
Missouri
● Adena
□ New York
□ Washington
● Cahokia
Rio Grande
Mississippi
○ Moundville
○ Marksville

A T L A N T I C

P
A
C
I
F
I
C

O
C
E
A
N

○ El Tajin
OCAMPO
Teotihuacán
Tlatilco ● ○ El Riego
Cuicuilco ● ○ Vera Cruz
Coxcatlan ● Tehuacán Valley
Monte Albán ● Tres Zapotes
Oaxaca ● La ○ ● Palenque
Mitla ○ ● Venta ● Uaxactún
Izapa ○ Yaxchilán ○ ● Tikal
TEHUACAN VALLEY ○ Copán
Kaminaljuyú □ Guatemala

● Chichén Itzá
□ Havana

C A R I B B E A N   S E A

Las Huacas ○ □ San José
Puerto Hormiga
Chiriquí ○ ● El Jobo □ Caracas
Coclé ○ □ Panama ● Manzanillo
Cerro Mangote ○ ● Momil
A
N
D
E
S
Orinoco

● San Agustín
Quito ○
Jama ○ ○ El Inga
Guangala ○
A
N
D
E
S
Valdivia ●

Negro

CHICAMA VALLEY
Chiclayo ○ ○ Cúpisnique
Huaca Prieta ● ● Moche
CASMA VALLEY
● Chavín de Huántar
Cerro Sechín ● ○ Lauricocha ● Kotosh
Rio Seco ○ ○ El Paraíso
Lima □ ● Pachacamac
Paracas ○
A
N
D
E
S
NASCA VALLEY
○ Pucára
Lake Titicaca
● Tiahuanaco

0 km   250   500   750

0 mls   300   600   900   1200

AUSTRALIA

Weipa

Darwin Oenpelli

Millstream

Kenniff Cave
The Tombs

Wilgie Mia

Koonalda Cave

Perth
Mammoth Cave

Tartanga
Fromm's Landing Devon Downs
Kow Swamp
Keilor
Wilson's Promontory

Sydney

Canberra

OCEAN

Amazon
Tapajos
Tocantis

245

Gazetteer

Page numbers are followed by map grid reference.

Abu Simbel 232Df
Abydos 232Dd
Actium 234Cd
Adamov 238Ff
Addaura 237De
Adena 244Eb
Adige River 237Bb
Afontova Goru 242Ba
Agatsuma 243Ce
Agia Triadha 234Ef
Agrigento 237Df
Aichbühl 238Eg
Aihole 241De
Ajanta 241Fe
AKKAD 240De
Alaca Hüyük 235Db
Aleppo 235Ed
Alesia 238Cf
Alexandria 232Ca, 235Bh
Ali Kosh 241Ac
Almeria 236Df
Altamira 236Cc
Altamura 237Ed
Al Ubaid 240Fg
Alunda 238Fb
Amman 235Eg
Amu Darya River (see Oxus)
Amur River 243Bc
Anaradhapura 241Ef
Anau 241Bb
ANDALUSIA 236Cf
Anghelu Ruju 237Bd
Antioch 235Ec
Anto do Silval 236Bf
ANYANG 242Ee
Apesokari 234Ef
Arpachiyah 240Cb
Arretium 237Cc
Artemision 234Ce
Aspendos 235Bd
Assur 240Cc
ASSYRIA 240Cb
Aswan 232Ee
Asyut 232Dc
Athens 234De
Aurignac 236Ec, 238Bg
Avaris 232Da
Avebury 238Be

Baalbek 235Ef
Babylon 240Df
BACTRIA 241Cb
Baghdad 240Db
Bahrein (see Dilmun)
BALUCHISTAN 241Cd
Bambata 233Bf
Bamiyan 241Cb
Bandera Wela 241Eg
Barsippa 240Df
Barumini 237Be
Basse Yutz 238Df
Bat Cave 244Cb
Begram 240Db
Behistun 241Ac
Beidha 232Fb, 235Eh
Belbusi 235Be
Benacci 237Cb
Beni Hasan 232Dc
Bethlehem 235Eg
Beycesultan 235Ad
BIHAR 241Fd

Birdlip 238Be
Biskupin 238Fe
Boghazköy 235Cb
Bohuslan 238Ff
Bologna 237Cb
Borg in Nadur 237Ef
Borodino 239Cg
BOSPHORUS 234Fb
Bouray (see Seine-et-Oise)
Brahmagiri 241Ef
Brassempouy 238Bg
Bubastis 232Db
Bucharest 239Bg
Buhen 232Df
Buret' 242Dg
Byblos 235Ef
Byzantium (see Constantinople)

Cadiz 236Bg
Caesarea 235Dg
Cahokia 244Db
Cala Coves 236Fe
CAMPANIA 232Dd
Camp de Chassey 238Df
Camulodunum (see Colchester)
Can Hasan 235Cd
Carchemish 235Ed
Carnac 238Bf
Carrhae 235Fd
Carthage 231Cf
CASMA VALLEY 244Eg
Castellón 236Ee
Castelluccio 237Ef
Çatal Hüyük 235Cd
CAUCASUS MTS 239Fg
Cernavoda 239Bg
Cerro Mangote 244Ee
Cerro Sechin 244Eg
Cerveteri 237Cc
Chaeronia 234Dd
Chagar Bazar 240Aa
Ch'ang-An 242Df
Chanhu-Daro 241Dd
Ch'ang-Sha 242Dg
Châteauneuf-les-Martigues
    236Fc
Chavín de Huántar 244Eg
Cheng-Chou 242Ef
CHICAMA VALLEY 244Ef
Chiclayo 244Eg
Chin Ts'un 242De
Chichén Itzá 244Dd
Chios 234Ed
Chiriqui 244De
Choga Mami 240Ed
Choga Zanbil 241Ac
Chou-Kou-Tien 242Ee
Chuquitanta (see El Paraiso)
Clovis 244Cb
COCHISE 244Bb
Coclé 244Ee
Cogul 236Ed
Colchester 238Ce
Constantinople 235Ab
Copán 244Dd
Coppa Nevigata 237Ea
Coptos 232Ed
CORFU 234Bc
Corinth 234Dd
CORSICA 237Bd
Cortaillod 238Df
Costig 236Fe

Coxcatlán 244Cd
CRETE 234Ef
Ctesiphon 240De
Cucuteni 239Bg
Cuicuilco 244Cd
Cumae 237Dd
Cúpisnique 244Eg
CYCLADES 234Ee
CYPRUS 235Ce

Dabur Kot 241Dc
Danger Cave 244Bb
Danube River 239Ah
Dashur 232Db
Deir el-Bahari 232Dd
Dejbjerg 238Ed
Delphi 234Dd
Dendara 232Ed
Dendra 234Dd
Desborough 238Cd
Devon Downs 245Ec
Didarganj (see BIHAR)
Dilmun 241Ad
Dimini 234Dc
Diyala River 240Ed
Dneister River 239Bf
Dolni Věstonic 238Ff
Don River 239Ee
Dordogne River 238Bg
Dur-Sargon (see Khorsabad)

Ecbatana (see Hamadan)
Edfou 232Ed
Egemarke 238Ed
ELAM 241Ac
El Argar 236Df
El-Badari 232Dc
ELBURZ MTS 240Fg
El Castello 236Cc
Elche 236Ef
El Djem 237Cg
Elephantine Island 232Ee
Eleusis 234De
El Garcel 236Df
El-Gerza 232Db
El Inga 244Ef
El Jobo 244Fe
Ellora 241Ee
El Paraiso 244Eg
El Riego 244Cd
El Tajin 244Cc
El Wad 235Dg
Ephesus 234Fd
Epidaurus 234Dd
EPIRUS 234Bc
Erech (see Uruk)
Eridu 240Fh
Eshnunna 240De
Esna 232Dd
Essé 238Bf
Es Tudons 236Fe
Euphrates River 235Fc, 240Ce
Eynam 235Ef

Faiyum 232Cb
Feng Hsiang 242Cf
Fère-en-Tardenois 238Cf
Fikirtepe 235Ab
Filitosa 237Bd
Folsom 244Cb
Font de Gaume 238Cg
Franchthi Cave 234Dd
Fromm's Landing 245Ec
Fu-Nan 242Bh

Gades (see Cadiz)
GANDHARA 241Dc
Ganges River 241Ed
Ganj Dareh 241Ac
Gavr'inis 238Bf
Gaza 232Ea
Gebel el-Arak 232Dd
Ggantija 237Ef
Ghassul 235Eg
Gibraltar 236Cg
Giza 232Db
Glasinac 239Ah
Gloucester 238Bd
Gneiding 238Ef
Gordion 235Bc
Gournia 234Ef
Graubolle 238Ed
Grand Pressigny 238Cf
Great Lakes 244Da
GREAT PLAINS 244Ec
Grimaldi 237Ac
Grimes Graves 238Ce
Guadalquivir 236Bf
Guangala 244Ef
Gulf of Aqaba 232Eb
Gulf of Cambay 241De
Gulf of Suez 232Db
Gumelnita 239Bh
GUMMA 243Ce
Gundestrop 238Ec

Hacilar 235Ad
Hadda 241Dc
Hagar Qim 237Ef
Hagia Triada (Agia Triadha)
Hagrat 237Ef
Hajji Firuz 241Ab
Hallstatt 238Fg
Hal Saflieni 237Ef
Halys River 235Cc
Hama 235Ee
Hamadan 241Ab
Harappa 241Dc
Hasanlu 241Ab
Hastinapura 241Ec
Hatra 240Cc
Haua Fteah 234Dg
Hawára 232Db
Hazor 235Eg
Heliopolis 232Db
Hemamieh 232Dc
Heracleopolis 232Db
Heuneberg 238Ef
Hieraconpolis 232Ed
Hitaka 243Af
Hoby 238Ed
HOHOKAM 244
HOKKAIDO 243Dd
HONAN 242Ef
Hopewell 244Eb
Hôsh 232Ca
Hsiao-T'un (see Anyang)
Hsin Tien 242Cf
Huaca Prieta 244Eg
Huang-Ho River 242Ef

IBIZA 236De
Indus River 241Dc
Ingaladdi 245Ea
Ionia 234Fc
Ischali 240De
Isfahan 241Ac
Isin 240Ef
Ismailia 232Db
Issus 235Ed
ITHACA 234Cd

Izapa 244Cd

Jama 244Ef
Jarmo 240Ec
Jemdet Nasr 240Df
Jericho 232Ea, 235Eg
Jerusalem 232Ea, 235Eg
Jordan River 232Fa
Jumna River 241Ed

Kalâbsha 232Ee
Kalambo Falls 233Bc
Kalibangan 241Ec
Kamares Cave 234Ef
Kaminaljuyú 244Dd
Kandahar 241Cc
KANSU 242Ce
KANTO PLAIN 243Ce
Kapova Cave 239Fd
Kara Kun Desert 241Ba
Karanovo 239Bh
Karli 241De
Karmir Blur 241Aa
Karnak 232Ed
Kausambi 241Ed
Kebara 235Dg
Keilor 245Ec
Kelermes 239Ff
Kenniff Cave 245Fb
Khafaje 240De
Khirokitia 235Cf
Khorsabad 240Cb
Kirkuk 240Dc
Kish 240Df
Kivik 238Fd
Klicevac 239Ag
Klosterfoss 238Eb
Knossos 234Ef
Köln-Lindenthal 238De
Kom Ombo 232Ee
KONYA PLAIN 235Bd
Koonalda Cave 245Dc
Kostienki 239Ee
Kostromskaya 239Ff
Kot Diji 241Dd
Kotosh 244Eg
Kow Swamp 245Ec
Kulli 241Cd
Kultepe 235Dc
Kushinagara (see MAGADHA)
KYUSHU 243Bf

Lachish 235Eg
Lagash 240Fg
La Gravette 238Cg
La Jolla 244Bb
Lake Baikal 242Db
Lake Garda 237Cb
Lake Issyk-Kul 241Da
Lake Nyasa 233Cd
Lake Tanganyika 233Bc
Lake Titicaca 244Fg
Lake Urmia 240Ea
Lake Victoria 233Ba
La Madeleine 238Cg
Lan-Chou 242Ce
Larisa 234Dc
Larsa 240Fg
Lascaux 238Cg
Las Huacas 244De
La Tène 238Dg
Laussel 238Cg
Lauricocha 244Eg
La Venta 244Cd

246

Lengyel 238Fg
Lepenski Vir 239Ag
Leptis Magna 237Eh
Lerna 234Dd
LESBOS 234Ec
Lespugue 236Ec, 238Bg
Leubingen 238Ee
Lipari 237Ee
Little Woodbury 238Be
Loire River 236Fa, 238Bf
Londinium 238Ce
Lortet 236Ec, 238Eg
Los Millares 236Df
Lothal 241Dd
Loyang 242Df
Lu (see SHANTUNG)
Lung Shan 242Ee
LUPEMBA 233Bd
LURISTAN 241Ab
Luxor 232Dd
LYDIA 234Fc

MACEDONIA 234Ca
Ma-Ch'ang 242Cf
Maeshowe 238Cb
MAGADHA 241Fd
Maiden Castle 238Be
Maikop 239Eg
MAJORCA 236Ce
MAKRAN 241Bd
Mallia 234Ef
Mal'ta 242Db
Mammoth Cave 245Cc
Man-Ch'eng 242Ee
Manzanillo 244Ee
Mari 240Ad
Marksville 244Dc
MARMARIJA 232Aa
Marvão 236Be
Mas d'Azil 236Ec, 238Cg
Massilia 237Ac
Matera 237Ed
Mathura 241Ed
MEATH 238Bd
Medinet Habu 232Dd
Megiddo 235Eg
Meidum 232Db
Melos 234Ee
Memphis 232Db
Merimde 232Cb
Meroe 232Fh
Mersin 235Dd
Mezhirich 239Cf
Miao-Ti-Kou 242Df
Miletus 234Fd
Millstream 245Cb
Milton Loch 238Bc
Minet el-Beidha 235Ee
MINORCA 236Dd
Minusinsk 242Ba
Mississippi River 244Dc
Mitla 244Cd
Miyagi 243Ce
Moche 244Eg
Mochlos 234Ff
Mohenjo-Daro 241Dd
Moldova 239Bf
Molfetta 237Ec
Momil 244Ee
Mondsee 238Ef
Monte Albán 244Cd
MORAVIA 238Ff
Mosul 240Cb
Moundville 244Dc
Mount Carmel 235Dg
Mount Olympus 234Cc
Mousa 238Cb

Mullerup 238Ed
Mundigak 241Cc
Mureybet 235Fd
Mycenae 234Dd

Nahel Oren 235Dg
Naksh-i-Rustam 241Bc
Nal 241Cd
Napata 232Dh
Naqada 232Ed
Nara 243Cf
NASCA VALLEY 244Eg
Naukratis 232Ca
Navdatoli 241Ed
Nazareth 235Eg
Nea Nikomedia 234Cb
New Grange 238Bd
Nile River 232Dc
Nimrud 240Cb
Nineveh 240Cb
Nippur 240Ef
Nonakado 243Cd
Numazu 243Cf
Nuzi 240Dc

Oaxaca 244Cd
Oder River 238Fe
Oenpelli 245Da
Olduvai Gorge 233Cb
Olorgesailie 233Db
Olympia 234Cd
Opis 240Dd
ORISSA 241Fe
Orrubiu 237Be
Otzaki 234Cc
Oxus River (see Amu Darya)

Pachacamac 244Eg
Pactolus River 234Fd
Paestum 237Dd
Palaikastro 234Ff
Palenque 244Dd
Palermo (see Addaura)
Palestrina 237Dc
Panama 244Ee
Pan P'o Ts'un 242Df
Pan Shan 242Be
Pantalica 237Ef
Paracas 244Eg
Parpalló 236Ee
Pasargadae 241Bc
Pataliputra 241Fd
Pazyryk 242Bb
Peche Merle 238Cg
PELOPONNESE 234Cd
Pergamun 234FC
Persepolis 241Bc
Perth 238Cc
Peschiera 237Bb
Petra 232Fb, 235Eh
Phaestos 234Ef
Philae 232Ee
Philippi 234Db
PHRYGIA 234Fc
Pi-Ramesse (see Tanis)
Pompeii 237Dd
PONTIC STEPPES 239Bf
Praeneste (see Palestrina)
Praia-a-Mare 237Ed
PRESCELLY MTS 238Bd
Ptolemais 232Dd
Pucára 244Fg
Puerto Hormiga 244Ee
Pushkari 239De

Qatar 241Ad
Quetta 241Cc

Rajgir 241Fd
Ras Shamra (see Ugarit)
Rhana Ghundai 241Dc
Rhein River 238Dc
Rhodes 235Ae
Rhône River 237 Ag, 238Cg
Rio Grande River 244Cc
Rio Seco 244Eg
Robenhausen 238Df
Romanelli 237Fd
Rome 237Cc
Roquepertuse 238Ch
Rosetta 232Ca

Sais 232Ca
Sakagozi 235Ed
Sakkara 232Db
Samarkand 241Da
Samarra 240Dd
Samothrace 234Eb
San Agustín 244Ef
Sanchi 241Ed
Sandia 244Cb
San Pedro de Estoril 236Ae
SARDINIA 237Bd
Sardis 234Fd
Sarnath 241Ed
Savignano 237Cb
Scarborough 238Cd
Schifferstadt 238Df
Scoglio del Tonno 237Ed
Scottsbluff 244Cb
Seine-et-Oise 238Cf
Seleucia 240De
Senorbi 237Be
SERENGETI PLAIN 233Ca
Sesklo 234Dc
Sesto Calende 237Bb
Shahr-i-Sokhta 241Cc
Shanidar 241Ab
SHANSI 242De
SHANTUNG 242Fe
SHENSI 242De
Shimojima 243Bf
Shirataki 243Cc
Shui-Tung-Kou 242De
Shuruppak 240Ef
SIAN 242Df
SICILY 237Ce
Sidon 235Ef
SILESIA 238Fe
SIND 241Dc
Sittard 238De
Skara Brae 238Cb
Skarpsalling 238Ed
Smyrna 234Fd
Snaketown 244Bb
Solutré 238Cf
Sonderholm 238Ec
Sparta 234De
Star Carr 238Cd
Starčevo 239Ag
Steinheim 238Df
Stentinello 237Ef
Sternberg 238Df
Stonehenge 238Be
Střelice 238Ff
Strettweg 238Fg
SUMER 240Df
Susa 241Ac
Sutkagen Dor 241Cd
Swanscombe 238Ce

SWAT VALLEY 241Dc
Syracuse 237Ef
SZECHWAN 242Cf

TABASCO 244Cd
Takanosu 243Cd
Takht-i-Sulaiman 241Ab
Tanis 232Da
TARN 238Cg
Tarquinia 237Cc
Tarsus 235Dd
Tartanga 245Ec
Tartaria 239Ag
Tartaro River 237Bb
Tartessus 236Cf
Tarxien 237Ef
TAURUS MTS 235Ad
Tavoliere 237Ec
Taxila 241Dc
TEHUACAN VALLEY 244Cd
Telamon 232Cc
Tell Atchana 235Ed
Tell Billa 240Cb
Tell Brak 240Aa
Tell el-Amarna 232Dc
Tell es-Sawwan 240Dd
Tell Halaf 235Fd
Tell Harmel 240De
Tell Hassuna 240Cb
Tell Judaida 240Fh
Telloh (see Lagash)
Tell Yahya 241Bc
Tepe Gawra 240Cb
Tepe Hissar 241Bb
Tepe Marlik 241Ab
Tepe Sarab 241Ab
Tepe Siyalk 241Bc
Tepe Yahya 241Bc
Thames River 238Ce
Tharros 237Be
Thebes 232Ed
THERA 234Fe
THESSALY 234Cc
The Tombs 245Fb
THRACE 234Fa 231Fa
Tiahuanaco 244Fg
Tiber River 237Cc
Tiberius 235Eg
Tigris River 240Cc
Tikal 244Dd
Timna 232Eb
Tiryns 234Dd
Tlatilco 244Cd
Togaruishi 243Ce
Tokyo 243Ce
Tollund 238Ed
Toprak-Kale 241Ab
Tres Zapotes 244Cd
Trier 238Df
Troy 234Ec
Trundholm 238Ed
Trușești 239Bf
Tureng Tepe 241Bb
Turoe 238Ad
Tyre 235Ef

Uaxactún 244Dd
Ugarit 235Ee
Umma 240Eg
Umm Dabaghiyah 240Cc
Unětice 238Ff
Ur 240Fg
URARTU 241Aa
Uruk 240Eg
UZBEKISTAN 241Ca

Vače 238Fg
Vadastra 239Ag
VAL CAMONICA 237Ba
Valdivia 244Ff
Vasiliki 234Ff
Veii 237Cc
Vera Cruz 244Cd
Vettersfelde 238Fe
Vézère River 238Cg
Vinča 239Ag
VIRÚ VALLEY 244Eg
Vistula River 239Ae
Vix 238Cg
Vladivostok 243Bd
Vogelherd 238Ef
Vućedol 238Fg

WACHAU 238Ff
Wadi en Natuf 235Eg
Wadi Halfa 232Df
Wasserburg 238Ef
Wei-Fang 242Fe
Wei River 242Cf
Weipa 245Ea
West Kennet 238Be
Wilgie Mia 245Cb
Willendorf 238Ff
Wilson's Promontory 245Ec
Windmill Hill 238Be
Woldenberg 238Ee
Woodhenge 238Be
Wu-Kuan-Ts'un 242Ee
WURTTEMBURG 238Eg
Wu-Wei 242Ce

Xanthos 235Ae

Yamuna River (see Jumna)
Yang Shao 242Df
Yangtse River 242Dg
Yarim Tepe 241Bb
Yaxchilán 244Dd
Yazilikaya 235Cb

Zab River (Lower) 240Eb
Zab River (Upper) 240Db
ZAGROS MTS 240Ec
Zakro 234Ff
Zambesi 233Be
Zarzi 241Ab
Zawi Chemi 241Ab
Zhob 241Cc
Zincirli 235Ed

Index

Figures in italics indicate illustrations.

A

Abu Simbel 114, 120, *130*
Abydos 114
Achaemenid Empire 145, 148, 151, 169, 177, 178, 186, *186*, 210
"Achaeans" 116
Acropolis 168
Actium, battle of 174
Advanced Hunters 21, 23, 24, 28, 39
    art 22
    care of dead 21-2
Advanced Hunting cultures 19, 20
Adze 75, *187*
Aegean 42, 96, 106, 121, 170
Aeolians 148
Aeneid 174
Aeschylus 168
Aesop 144
Afanasyevskaya 94-6
Afganistan 44, 93
Africa
    architecture 25, *25*, 26, *26*, 29, *29*, 30, 51, *51*, 52, *52*
    art 33, 55, *55*, 66
    technology 25, 26, *47*, 47, 48, *48*
Agamemnon *135*
Agricola 206
Ahab 149
Ahmose 117-18
Ajanta 227, *227*
Akhenaten 119, *120*, 132
Akkad 93
Akkadians 92, 121
    language 119, 148
    literature 114
Alaca Hüyük 96
Alamanni 210
Alans 213
Alaric 213
Alaska 23
Alexander the Great 167, 169, *169*, 178
Alexandria 169
    Museum of 170
Alloying 87
Alphabet 113-14
Altamira 22, *34*
Alyattes 151
Amenhotep 111, 119
Amenhotep son of Hapu 119
Amenophis (Amenhotep)
Americas (the) 45, 71, 97, 122, 141-2, 182-3, 199
    architecture 20, *20*, 30, 50, *50*, 53, *53*, 76, *76*, 79, 102, 105, *105*, 128, *128*, 131, *131*, 156, *156*, 159, *159*, 191, *191*, 220, *220*, 223, *223*
    art 80, *80*, 83, 106, *106*, 109, *109*, 132, *132*, 135, *135*, 160, *160*, 163, *163*, 192, *192*, 195, *195*, 202, 224, *224*, 227, *227*

Chavin 141, 147, 156, 160, 183, 201
    funerary cult 142
    Maya 182, 191, 199, 200-2, 216, 220, 223, 227
    Mochica 201, *201*, 227
    Nazca 201
    Olmecs 141, 182
    peopling 22-3
    technology 24, *24*, 26, *26*, 46, *46*, 48, 72, *72*, 75, 98, *98*, 101, *101*, 124, *124*, 127, 152, *152*, 155, *155*, 184, *184*, 187, *187*, 216, *216*, 219, *219*
    Zapotecs 180, 200
Ammonites 148
Amorites 92, 93, 96, 114, 116, 121
Amos 144
Amun 118
Amun-Re 119
Anatolia 39, 40, 42, 43, 44, 68, 96
Anaximander 141, 153
Anghelu Ruju 121
Angles 214
Antinous 208
Antler 27
Antochus IV, 170, 178
Antoninus Pius 209
Antony 172, 173, 174
Aphrodite *2*, 171
Apollo 176
Arabian Gulf 92, 93
Aramaeans 121
Aramaeic language 147-8, 177
Arcadius 208
Archaeological terminology 11
Archaic period (Egypt) 88
Architecture 28-31, 40, 50-3, 76-9, 87, 102-5, 114, 128-31, 156-9, 188-91, 220-3
Ardrey, Robert 17
Arian heresy 212
Aristophanes 168
Aristotle 168, 176
Arpachiyah 56, 78, *78*
Art 22, 32-5, 54-7, 80-3, 88, 106-9, 132-5, 144, 160-3, 192-5, 224-7
    Amarna 119
    Assyrian 160, 162
    Celtic 175, 177
    Chou *142*, 147
    Etruscan 147
    Megalithic 71, *71*, 80, 83, *83*
    Minoan 114, *114*, *115*
    Old Kingdom 88, 89
    Olmec *146*, *183*
    Shang *122*, *123*
Artemis 204
Ashoka 167, 178, 194
Assurbanipal 144, 147, 150, *154*
Assurnasirpal 145, *145*, 149, 150
Assyria 43, 114, 168
Assyrians 120-1, 142, 148-9, 150
    architecture 156, 158, *158*
    art 160, 162, *162*
    technology 152, 154, *154*
Aten 119, 132
Athens 167, 168
Attila 213
Augustine 202, 213

Augustus 174, *174*, 202, 203, 204, *204*, *226*
Aurelius, Marcus *208*, 209
Aurignacians 21, 22, 23
Australia 22
    men in 22
    technology 25, *25*, 27
Australopithecines 17
Avebury 97
Axvesta 144
Aztecs 202

B

Baal 149
Baalbek (Heliopolis) 206
Babylon 114, 117, 145, 156, 158, *158*
Babylonia 114, 117, 148, 151
"Babylonian captivity" 151
Bacchae 173
Bactria 178
Balkans 69-70, 97, 176
Baluchistan 65
"Barbarians" 139, 140, 210
Bar-Kokhba 208-9
Barley 40, 70, 93, 97
    six-row 42
Barrows 122
Basketry *101*
Batons *21*
Battle-Axe people 97
Battle of Kadesh 120
Beads 41, 42, 43, 44
Beans 71, 97, 122
Beaker folk 97, 109, *109*, 121
Bede 213
Bedouins 89
Beersheba 67
Belgae 177
Beycesultan 68
Bible 120, 142
Big-game hunting 23, 45
"Big-heads" 141, *146*
Bireme *141*
Black figure vases *10*, 160
Blade and burin 20, 21
Boats 24, 44, 46, 62, 98
Boethius 213
"Bog people" 177, *177*
Bone 27
Book of Documents 122
Book of Songs 144
Boudicca (Boadicea) 204-5
Bow and arrow 21, 24, 44
Brahmanas 140, 144
Brahmans 177
Brigantes 203
Britain, 44, 70, 97, 116, 121, 213
    invasion of 177, 203
Britannicus 204
Broch *191*
Bronze 87, 96, 97, 98
    casting 100, 124, 126, *126*, 127, *127*, 152
Bronze age civilizations 42, 113, 114, 116, 121-2
Bucrania 41
Buddha 141, 177, *227*
Buddhism 178, 188
Burins 20, *26*

Burial customs
    barrows 116
    Çatal Hüyük 42
    Egyptian 67
    Hunters 21-2
    Jericho 40, 41
    Megaliths 71
    round mounds 97
Byblos 67, 68, 114, 120
Byzantine art *214-15*
Byzantine Empire 212
Byzantium 212

C

Caesar, Julius 172-3, *174*, 176, 177, 203
Calendar 87
Calendar Round 184, 187, *187*
Calendar stones 201
Caligula 203, 204, *208*
Camels 186, *186*
Camonica Valley *134*
Canaan 117, 120
Canaanites 96, 116, 119, 120, 121
Canals 43, 150
Capitals *104*
Caracalla 210
Caratacus 203
Carbon-14 9
Cartamandua 204
Carthage 139, 172
Carthaginians 167, 169, 170, 172
Cassiodorus 213
Cassivellaunus 203
Caste system 177
Castros 177
Catacombs 212
Çatal Hüyük 40, 41, *41*, 42, *43*, 50, 53, *53*, 54, 55, *55*, 56, 56-7
Cattle 42, 44, 65, 66, 70, 93, 94, 97
Catullus 174
Caves 21, 30, *30*, *31*, 43, 50, 70
Cave painting 21, 22, *34-5*, 44
Celts 140, 147, 170, 172, 175-7, *175*, *176*, 195, 202
Ceramics 66
Cereals 42, 44, 45
Ceremonial centres 141
Chaityas 188
Chalcolithic Age 61, 71, 96
Chaldea 148
Chaldeans 150
Chandragupta 199
Chandragupta Maurya 178
Chariots 113, 117, 124, *126*, 203
Chavin culture 141, 147, 156, 160, 183, 201
Chavin de Huántar 141
Cheops (Khufu)
Chephren (Khafra)
Chiapas 200
Chicama Valley 97
Ch'in Dynasty 180, 181
China 109, *109*, 122, 140, 142, 144, 180-2, 199,

219, *219*
Chinese silk *180*
Ch'in-Shih-huang 172, 180, 181
Cholula 200
Chou Dynasty 122, 140, 142, 147, 148, 160, 163, *163*, 180
Chou-Kou-Tien caves 17
Christianity 199, 202, 203, 210
Christians 208, 212
   persecution of 205, 210
Chuquitanta 122
Church 210, 212
Cicero 173, 176
Cimmerians 150, 151
City of God 213
City-states
   Canaanite 116
   Mesopotamian 90
Claudius 177, 203, 204
Cleopatra 172, 173, *173*, 174
Clovis 213
Coinage 142, 154, *154*, 177, 186, *186*, 219, *219*
Colchester (Camulodunum) 203
Colombia 97
Colosseum 206
Colossi of Memnon *118*, 119, 208
Commodus 206, 209
Communications 98, 142
Composite bow 113, 155, *155*
Cone mosaics 64, 78, *78*
Confucius 140, 141, 144, 180, 181
Constantine 178, *209*, 212, *212*
Constantinople 212, 213
Contemporaneity 7
Continental Europe 44, 45, 69, 70, 97, 116-7, 121-2, 147
   architecture 29, *29*, 30, *30*, 51, *51*, 53, *53*, 77, *77*, 79, *79*, 103, *103*, 105, *105*, 129, *129*, 131, *131*, 157, *157*, 159, *159*, 191, *191*, 220, *220-1*, 222, 222-3
   art 22, 33, *33*, 35, *35*, 55, *55*, 57, *57*, 64, 65, 68, 69, 81, *81*, 83, *83*, 107, *107*, 109, *109*, 133, *133*, 135, *135*, 161, *161*, 163, *163*, 193, *193*, 195, *195*, 225, *225*, 227, *227*
   technology 25, 26, 47, *47*, 48, 73, *73*, 75, 99, 99, 101, *101*, 125, *125*, 127, *127*, 153, *153*, 155, *155*, 185, *185*, 187, *187*, 216, *216-17*, 218, *218-19*
Copán 201
Copper 44, 46, 62, 68, 71, 72, 152
Copper Age 61
Copper working 69, 75, *75*, 97
Corn 97
Cotton 93-4, 97
Crassus 173
Cretacious period 13
Cretan palaces 128, 130, *130-1*
Crete 42, 96, 113, 114, 115, 116, 128, 134

Croesus 144, 151
Cromagnons *19*, 20, 21
Crossbow 184, 187, *187*
Crucifixion 203
Ctesibius 184
Ctesiphon 206, 209, 222, *222*
Cuicuilco 159, *159*, 183
Cult of skulls 40, 41
Culture 11
Cuneiform 62, 114, 124
Cunobelin 203
Cúpisnique 155, *155*
Cyclades 69, 88, *96*, 108, *108*
Cylinder seals 63
Cymbeline (Cunobelin)
Cyprus 43
Cyrene *10*
Cyrus the Great 145, *145*, 150
Cyrus the Younger 168

D

Dacians 206, 208
Dagobas 178
Danubians 69-70, 79, *79*
Darius 145, *145*, 167, 177
Darius II *168*
Dasyus 177
Dating 9-10
David 121, 148
Dead Sea Scrolls 205
Decius 210
Defences 40
Deir el-Bahari 118
Dejbjerg wagon 187, *187*
Delphi 176
Delphic Charioteer *166*
Denmark 45, 57, *57*, 155
Desborough mirror *202*
Desert culture 45
Diffusion 11, 18, 23, 44, 66, 69
Dimini 69, 79, *79*
Diocletian 210-12, *210*
Diviticus 176
Dolmen 70
Domestication of animals 39, 40, 42, 43, 45, 46, 49, *49*, 65, 71
   plants 39, 40, 42, 43, 45, 46, 49, *49*, 65, 71, 72, 97, 122, 142
Domitian 206
Dorians 148
Dress 21, *21*
Drills 74
Druids 176, 178, 203, 204
Durgas 223, *223*

E

Early dynastic
   Egypt 88
   Mesopotamia 90
Earthworks 70, 89
Easter Island 61

Eastern Mediterranean 42, 67-8, 96, 116, 176
   architecture 29, *29*, 30, *30*, 51, *51*, 52, *52*, 53, *53*, 77, *77*, 79, *79*, 103, *103*, 105, *105*, 129, *129*, 130-1, *130-1*, 157, *157*, 158, *158-9*, 190, *190*, 220, *220-1*, 222, *222*
   art 33, *33*, 35, *35*, 55, *55*, 56, *57*, 81, *81*, 83, *83*, 107, 108, *108*, 133, *133*, 134-5, 135, 161, *161*, 162, *162*, 193, *193*, 194, *194*, 225, *225*, 226, *226*
   technology 25, *25*, 26, *26*, 47, *47*, 48, 73, *73*, 75, 99, *99*, 125, *125*, 126, *126*, 153, *153*, 154, *154*, 184, *185*, 186, *186*, 216, *216-7*, 218, *218-9*
Ecuador 71, 97
Ecumenical Council 212
Edict of Milan 212
Egypt 43, 62-3, 66-7, *67*, 88-9, *92*, 95, 113, 114, 117-21, *118*, 148, 150, 174, 181
   architecture 29, *29*, 30, 51, *51*, 52, *52*, 77, *77*, 78, *78*, 103, *103*, 104, *104*, 129, *129*, 130, *130*, 157, 158, 190, *190*, 221, *221*, 222, *222*
   art 33, 55, *55*, 56, *56*, 81, *81*, 82, *82*, 107, *107*, 108, *108*, 118, 119, 133, *133*, 134, *134*, 161, *161*, 162, *162*, 193, *193*, 194, *194*, 225, *225*, 226, *226*
   literature 114
   technology 25, *25*, 26, *26*, 47, 48, 73, *73*, 74, 89, 98, 99, *99*, 100, *100*, 125, *125*, 126, *126*, 153, *153*, 154, *184*, 185, 186, *186*, 217, 218
Elam 92, 93, 148, 150
Elamites 63, 65, 93
El-Amarna 119, 120
El Argar 121
Elburz 44
Elijah 149
El Tajin 200
Enki 63
Enki 63
Enlil 90
Ensi 65
Epic of Gilgamesh 114, 144
Epidaurus *190*
Eridu 44, 63, 71
Esarhaddon 150, 151
Etruscans *138*, 147, 167, 170
   architecture 156, *156*
   art 163, *163*, 194, *194*
   technology 155, *155*
Euclid 170
Euripides 168, 173
Europe 140, 175
Evolution 17
Exodus 120

F

Faience 62, *62*
Far East 45, 65-66, 178-82
   architecture 29, *29*, 30, *30*, 51, 53, 77, *77*, 79, *79*, 103, *103*, 105, *105*, 129, *129*, 131, *131*, 157, *157*, 159, 221, *221*
   art 33, *33*, 35, *35*, 55, *55*, 57, 81, *81*, 83, *83*, 107, *107*, 109, *109*, 133, *133*, 135, *135*, 161, *161*, 163, *163*, 193, *193*, 195, *195*, 225, *225*, 227, *227*
   technology 25, *25*, 26, *26*, 47, *47*, 48, 73, *73*, 75, 99, *99*, 101, *101*, 125, *125*, 127, *127*, 153, *153*, 155, *155*, 185, *185*, 187, *187*, 217, *217*, 219, *219*
Farming 39, 43, 44, 65, 70, 72
Female figurines 22, 42, 54, *67*, 69
Ferghana steeds 180
Fertility cults 41, 43
Figurines 44
Fire 24
Fire altars 93
Fired brick 93
First Cataract (Nile) 66
Fishbourne 206
Flavians 205-6
Flax 44
Flint 21, 27, 43, 70
Folk movements 96, 97, 120, 122
Food production 41, 45, 46, 71, 72, 94, 97, 122, 142
Food supplies 41, 94
Forum *210*
Funerary cult 142
Funerary offering *92*

G

Gades 140
Galatia 170, 175, 176
Galen 206
Galley 152, 153, *153*
Gallic tribes 172, 176
Gateway of the Sun 201
Gathos 144
Gauls 213
Gavr'inis 70
Genesis 145
Georgics 174
Germanic tribes 203, 209
Germanicus 203
Ghassulians 68
Gibbon 206
Gilgamesh 89, *89*, 114
   Epic of 114
Glaciations 16
Glass 125, *202*
Goats 40, 42, 44, 66
Gordion Knot 169
Goths 210
Gourds 97, 142

Gravettians 21, 22, 23, 28
Great Shang 122
Great Wall of China 172, 178, 180, 188, 191, *191*
Greece 96, 116
Greeks 114, *143*, 148, 167-70, 172, 176
  architecture 188
  art 147, 160, 161, 192, 193 *193*, 194, *194*
  coinage 145
  Dark Age 139
  in India 178
  orders 145, 147, 156, 158, *158-9*
  philosophy 167, 168
  technology 184, 186
Grimes Graves 70, 101, *101*, 109
Grinding 24
Gudea 92, 96
Gunderstrup cauldron *175*
Gupta Dynasty 199, 224
  architecture 220, 221, *223*
Gutians 92
Gyges 151

H

Hacilar 50, 52, *52*, 68
Hadrian 208-9
Hadrian's Wall 208, 222, *222*
Hahremhab 120
Halafians 44, 61
Hallstatt culture 140, 142, *142*
Hamilcar 170
Hammurabi 114, *116*
  laws of *116*
Han Dynasty 180-1, 191, *191*
  architecture 188, 191, *191*
  art *181*, 194, *200*, 224
  technology 184
  tomb figurines 181, *181*, 227, *227*
Handaxe 17-18, *17*
Haniwa 224
Hannibal 170-2
Harappa 93
Harpoons 21
Hassuna 43
Hatshepsut 116, 118, *120*
Hatti 114
Hattusas 114, 120, 148
Hazor 116, 120
Hebrew Descent 120
Hebrews 144, 147, 149
  alphabetic script 114
  literature of 144
Heidelberg Man 17
Heliopolis 118
Hellenic Age 167
Henges 97, 121
Hengist 213
Herculaneum 206
Hermes *194*
Hero 184, *186*
Herod Antipas 203
Herod the Great 174
Herodotus 168, 178
Heruli 210
Hesiod 144
Hieroglyphs 62, *74*, 182, 187

187, 219, *219*
Hillforts 156, 175, 177, 188, 191, *191*
Hinduism 177
Hindus 140
Hittites 113, 114, 117, 119, 124, 148
  architecture 129, *129*
  art 132, *134*, 135
Hohokam 183
Holocene 16
Homer 142, 144, *144*, 145, 148
Hominids 17
Homo 17
Homo 16, 17
  erectus 17
  habilis 17
  sapiens 19, 20, *20*
Honorius 213
Hopewell culture 183
Horn of Africa 43
Horsa 213
Horses 94
Horus *94*
  Temple of 190, *190*
Hosea 144
Hougue Bie 70
Houses
  Arpachiyah *78*
  Chilca *105*
  Danubian 79, *79*
  Hassuna *78*
  Jarmo *52*
  Jōmon *105*
  Mohenjo-Daro *105*
  mudbrick and straw *53*
  Pan P'o Ts'un 79, *79*
  skin and bone *30*
  Tholos *78*
Houses of Life 114
Housing 43, 69
Hsiung Nu nomads 178, 213
Hungary 42
Huns *179*, 213
Hunting 71
Hunting magic 28, 41
Hurrians 93, 116, 117, 148
Huts 21, 28, *30*, *43*, *52*
Hyksos 117, 118
Hymn to the Sun 119
Hypocaust 216, 218, *219*
Hypogea 97

I

Ice Age 16, 23
  land bridges 16
Iceni 204
Ideograms 62, 124
Ides of March 173
Idols 41
Iliad 178
Imhotep 88, 97
Inanna 64
India 93, 140, 177-9, 199
  architecture 191, *191*, 221, 223, *223*
  art 140, 193, *193*, 195, *195*, 225, *225*, 227, *227*
  technology 140, 185, *185*, 187, *187*, 217, 219

Indo-Europeans 96, 113, 114, 116, 148, 175, 177, 178
Indus Civilization 93-4, 102, 105, *105*, 114, 135, *135*
Indus Valley 93
Ionians 148
Iran-India 44
  architecture 29, *29*, 30, *30*, 51, *51*, 53, *53*, 77, *77*, 79, 103, *103*, 105, *105*, 129, *129*, 131, *131*, 157, *157*, 159
  art 55, *55*, 57, *57*, 65, 81, *81*, 83, *83*, 106, *106*, 109, *109*, 133, *133*, 135, *135*, 161, *161*, 163, *163*
  technology 25, *25*, 26, *26*, 47, *47*, 48, 73, *73*, 75, 99, *99*, 101, *101*, 125, *125*, 127, *127*, 153, *153*, 155, *155*
Iron 180
  carbonized 113
Iron Age 177
Iron working 142, 152
  Chinese 142, 184
Irrigation 46, 93, 184
Isaiah 144, 149
Ishtar gate 145, 158, *158*
Israel 148
Israelites 116, 121
Italy 96, 97
Ivory 27, 68

J

Jains 177, 178
Janus head 176, *176*
Japan 65, 94, 182, 199
Java Man 17
Jebusites 148
Jeremiah 144, 151
Jericho 40, 52, *52*, 55, *55*
Jerusalem 147, 148, *159*, 170, 172, 203, 205, 208, 212
Jesus of Nazareth 147, 179, 199, 202, 203, 205, 212, 214-15
Jewish Revolts 205, 208
Jews 203, 204
Jezebel 149
John the Baptist 205
Jōmon culture 94, 109, *109*, 182
Joshua 120
Judah 148-9, 151
Judea 172
Julia *208*
Julian the Apostate 212
Jurassic Period 13
Jutes 214

K

Kalibangan 93
Kara Kun Desert 44
Karanovo 69
Karnak 114, 118, 120
Kassites 128, 132
Khafra (Chephren) 88, 94
Khirokitia 43, 50, 53, *53*
Khnum, temple of 222, *222*
Khufu (Cheops) 88
Kilns 72, 74, *74*
King Arthur 214
King List 65, 90
Kings 149
Kish 90
Knapping 40
Knossos 42, 116, 118, 119
  Palace of 116, 130-1, *130*
Korea 182
Kotosh 122, 141
Kourai 147
Kouroi 147, *147*, 151
Kush 117, 118, 150
Kushans 199

L

Lagash 90, 92, 113
Land bridges 16, 22, 23
Lakeside pile dwellings 70
Lake Titicaca 183
Lanka 178
Lao-Tse 141
Lapis lazuli 93
Lascaux *14-15*, 22, *35*
Late Hunters 11, 23, 39, 43, 44, 54
La Tène 175, *175*, 177, 194, 195, *195*, *202*
La Venta 141
Leakey, Mary 17
Legumes 40
Leo 213
Lepenski Vir *53*
Lerna 96, *116*
Levant 39, 40, 43, 68, 96, 114, 116, 117, 118
Libyans 89, 120
Linear A & B 113, 124
Lion gate, Mycenae *121*, 132
Literature 87, 144
Liu Sheng 182
Llamas 45, 71
Loess 16
Long count 216, 219, *219*
Looms 40
Los Millares 71, 96, 97, *105*
Lost wax casting *100*, 126, *126*, 127, *127*, 216
Lothal 93
Lugalzagesi 92
Lur horns 147, *153*
Luxor 114, 119
Lydians 148, 150, 151

M

Maccabees 170
Macedon 169, 172
Macedonia 42, 176
Maes Howe 70
Magdalenians 21, 22, 23
Mahabharata 178
Mahavira 177
Maiden Castle 204
Maize 45, 71, 97, 122, 142
  hybridization of 97
Makran 93
Mallia 116
Malta 97, 108, *108*
Maltese temples 76, 97, 102,
  105, *105*, 106
Mammoths 23
Manioc 122
Marathon 168
Marcomanni 210
Marduk 145
Mari *108*, 132, 134, *134*
Marquess of Tai 181
Mastaba tombs 67, 76, 78, *78*
Mathematics
  Babylonian 124, 126, *126*
  Indian 216
Matthew 206
Mauryan Dynasty 167, 178,
  194
Mayas 199, 200-2
  architecture 182, 191, *191*,
    200, 220, 223, *223*
  art 201, 227, *227*
  technology 216
Medes 150, 151
Meditations 209
Megalithic
  architecture 70-1, 96-97,
    102
  art 70-1, 80, 81, *81*, 83, *83*
Megaliths 61, 70, 97
Megaron 69, 79
Megiddo 113, 114, 118
Melos 42
Mencius 180
Menes (Narmer) 67
Menhirs 70
Menkaure (Mycerinus) 88, *95*
Menthuhotep II 114
Merchants 93
Mersin 68
Mesoamerica 23, 97
Mesolithic 11, 23, 54
Mesopotamia 43, 44, 62, *86*,
  87, 89, 93, 114, 144-5, 148
  architecture 29, *29*, 30, *30*,
    51, *51*, 52, *52*, 77, *77*, 78,
    78, 103, *103*, 104, *104*,
    129, *129*, 130, *130*, 156,
    156, 158, *158*, 221, *221*
  art 55, *55*, 56, *56*, 64, 81,
    81, 82, *82*, 107, *107*, 108,
    108, 133, *133*, 134, *134*,
    161, *161*, 162, *162*, 193,
    193, 194, *194*, 225, *225*,
    226, *226*
  technology 25, *25*, 26, *26*,
    47, *47*, 48, 73, *73*, 74,
    98, 99, *99*, 100, *100*,
    125, *125*, 126, *126*, 153,
    153, 154, *154*, 185, *185*,
    186, *186*, 217, *217*, 218,
    218
Messallina 204

Metallurgy 63, *65*, 75, *75*, 89,
  94, 96, 113, 184, 216
Metates 45, 127, *127*
Mexico 45, 71, 97
Microliths 23, *27*, *27*, 44, 46
Midas 151
Middle Formative Period 141
Middle Kingdom (Egypt) 114
Middle Minoan period 116
Millet 65
Mining 71
  in Sinai 88
Minoans 113, 116, 118, *132*
  architecture 130, *130-1*
  art 114, *114*, *115*, *134*, 135
Mitanni 118, 119, 148
Mithras 208
Moabites 148
Mochica 183, 201, *201*, 227,
  227
Mogollons 183
Mohenjo-Daro 93, 105, *105*,
  109, *109*, 131, *131*
Mona 203
Mongolians 96
Mongolization of Japan 182
Mons Badonicus 214
Montezuma 202
Monte Albán 141, 200
Mortar *26*
Mosaics 194
Moses 120
Mother goddess 41, 42, 43,
  54, 69, 93, 97, *97*
Motzu 180
Mound of the Dancers 180
Mount Gilboa 121
Mount Sinai 120
Mudbrick 50, 93
Murex shells 120
Mursilis I 117
Mycenae 116, *121*, 132
Mycenaeans 116, 121, 132
Mycerinus (Menkaure)

N

Nabataean Arabs 206
Nabonidas 151
Nabopalassar 150, 151
Naram-Sin *90*, 92
Narmer 62, 67
Narmer palette 62
Narratives of the States 144
Natufians 23, 26, *30*, 39, 40,
  43
Natural History 206
Naveta tombs 121, 131, *131*
Nazca 183, 201
Neanderthals 18, *18*, 19, 22,
  32
Neanderthaloids 18, 20
Near East 116
Nebuchadnezzar 145, 150,
  151, 156, *162*
Necho 150
Needles 21, 27, *27*, 44
Nefertiti 119, *120*, 132, 134,
  134
Nekhbet 66
Neolithic Revolution 39, 40,
  42, 44, 46, 61

Nero 204, *204*, 205, 206,
  209
New Grange 70, 71, 80, 83,
  83
New Kingdom (Egypt) 114,
  117, 120, 128, 129, 132
New Palaces (Crete) 114
Nile delta 66
Nile river 43, 66, 67, 208
Nile valley 43
Nimrud *1*, *150*, 168
Nineveh 44
Nippur 90
Nomes 67, 68
North America 45, 71, 122,
  141
Nubians 117, 150
Nuraghi 121, 147, 156, 159,
  159
Nutcracker Man 17

O

Obelisks 114, 130, *130*, 150
Obsidian 40, 42
Ochre 22, 142
Octavian (Augustus) 173-4,
  174
Odoacer 213
Old Kingdom (Egypt) 88-9,
  96, 106
Old Palace period (Crete) 116
Old Testament 144, 147
Olduvai Gorge *12*, 17
Olives, cultivation of 96
Olmecs 113, 141, 182, 184
  art 141, 147, 160, 163, *163*,
    183
  "big-heads" 122, 141, 160
  ceremonial centres 141, 156
Olympic games 139
Oppida 140, 145, 175, 177
Oracle 151
Oracle bones 122, 127, *127*
Origen 210
Osiris 119
Ostrogoths 212, 213, 214
Outcasts 178
Ovens *48*
Oxus 169, 178

P

Palaeolithic 11, 16, 19
Palestine 43, 67, 68
Pan P'o Ts'un 79, *79*
Pantheon 206, 220, 222, *223*
Paper making 216
Papyrus 63
Paracas Necropolis 183
Paracas textiles *182*, 183,
  195, *195*
Parisii 177
Parthenon 168, 190, *190*
Parthians 169, 172, 173, *173*,
  174, 178, 203, 204, 206,

  227, *227*
Pasargadae 145
Passage grave 70, *79*, 96
Passover 203
Paula 212
Pax Romana 174, 206, 209
Pazyryk 178, *179*, *180*, 195,
  195
Peanuts 122
Peking man 17
Peloponnese 42, 176
Peloponnesian War 168
Penteconters 152
Peoples of the Sea 120, 121,
  176
Pepi I 88, *108*
Pepi II 88
Pergamum 170, 172, 206
Pericles 168, *168*
Persepolis 146, 156, 178,
  188, 190, *190*, 194, *194*
Persia 145, 151
  architecture 156, 190, *190*,
    221, *221*, 222, *222*
  art 146, 193, *193*, 194,
    194, 225, *225*, 226, *226*
  technology 185, *185*, 186,
    217, *217*, 218, *218*
Persian empire 167, 177
Peru 97, 122, *131*
Petra 206
Phaistos *114*, 116
Pharaohs 62, 66, 87, 114,
  118
  Ahmose 117-18
  Akhenaten 119, *120*, 132
  Amenhotep III 119
  Hahremnab 120
  Hatshepsut 116, 118, *120*
  Khafra (Chephren) 88, *94*
  Khufu (Cheops) 88
  Menkaure (Mycerinus)
    88, *95*
  Menthuhotep 114
  Necho 150
  Pepi I 88, *108*
  Pepi II 88, 114
  Ptolemy II *170*
  Ramesses II 120, *121*
  Ramesses III 120, 121
  Seti I 120
  Shoshenk 149
  Snefru 88
  Thutmose I 118
  Thutmose III 116, *117*
  Tutankhamun *6*, 119, *119*,
    120, *126*, 128, 132, 134,
    134
  Zoser 88, *94*, 97
Pharos 170, 190, *190*
Phidias 168
Philip 169
Philippi 173
Philo 184
Philistines 121
Phoenicians 114, 120, 129,
  140, *141*, 142, 147, 170
  architecture 156
  art *114*, 160
  technology *141*, 152
Phrygians 148, 151
Pictograms 62
Picts 213
Pigs 70, 94
Pillars of Hercules 140
Pi-Ramesse 120
Pithecanthropus erectus 17
Pithoi 126, *126*

251

Plato 140, 168, 169
Pleistocene 16
Pliny the Elder 206
Pliny the Younger 208
Polybus 172
Pompeii *190, 206, 206*
Pompey 172
Pontic steppes 178
Popcorn 71
Poppaea 204
Portugal 96, 97
Potter's wheel 62, 72, 94
Pottery *65*, 80, 94, *114, 162, 218*
  fired 40
  in America 71, 97, 122, 142
  in Eastern Mediterranean 42, 147
  painted *40, 44*, 122
Potting 40, 44, 122
Praetorian guard 203
Praxiteles *2, 194*
Pre-Classic Age 97, 122
Pre-Classic period 141, 182
Pre-Dynastic (Egypt) 43, 66-7
Pre-projectile sites 23
Priesthood, in Egypt 88
Prince Rama 148
Projectile points 23, 26, *75*
  Clovis 23, *26*
  Folsom 23, *26*
  Sandia 23
  Scottsbluff *48*
Propylaea 168
Protoliterate Age 62, 64, 90
Psammetichus 150
Ptolemaic Dynasty 169
Ptolemies 169, 170, 173, 178
Ptolemy 209
Ptolemy II *170*
Ptolemy of Alexandria 209, 230, *230*
Pul (Tiglath-Pileser) 149
Punic Wars 170, 172, 180
Punjab 177, 178
Punt 118
Puranas 219
Pyramids
  American 200, 201
  Egyptian 88, 90, 104, *104*
  Moon and Sun 200, *201*
Pyrrhus 170
Pythagoras 141

Q

Quamran 205, 208-9

R

Radiocarbon dating 9, 20, 61, 65, 70, 71, 121
Ramayana 178
Ramesses II 120, *121*
Ramesses III 120, 121
Ramesseum 120

Ravenna 213, *214-15*
Re 118
Religious cults
  bulls 41, 93
  death 41
  fertility 41
  funerary 42
  tree 93
  veneration of animals 93
Republican Rome 167, 174, 194
Retreat of the Ten Thousand 168
Rice 93
Rigveda 140
Rillation cup 135, *135*
Rock engravings 45, 135, *135*
Rock paintings 43
Romans 170-4, 180, 202-14
  architecture 220, *220-1, 222-3, 222-3*
  art 202, 224, 225, *225, 226, 226*
  baths 210
  citizenship 210, 212
  Empire 199, *200*, 202
  emperors
    Antoninus Pius 209
    Augustus 174, *174*, 202, 203, 204, *226*
    Aurelius, Marcus 208, 209
    Caesar, Julius 172-3, *174*, 176, 177, 203
    Caligula 203, 204, 208
    Caracalla 210
    Claudius 177, 203, 204
    Constantine 178, *209*, 212, *212*
    Decius 210
    Diocletian 210-12, *210*
    Domitian 206
    Hadrian 208-9
    Honorius 213
    Julian the Apostate 212
    Leo 213
    Nero 204, *204*, 205, 206, 209
    Romulus Augustus 213
    Severus, Septimus 209-10, *209*
    Theodosius 212, 213
    Tiberius 203, 208
    Titus 205, 206
    Trajan 206-8
    Valens 213
    Varus 203
    Vespasian 204, 205-6
  roads 218, *218*
  Senate 205, 206
  technology 216, *216-17*, 218-19, *218-19*
Rome 139
  sacking of 176, 212, 213
Romulus Augustus 213
Roquepertuse 176
Roxane *171*
Rubicon 173
Rumania *42, 64*, 65

S

Sabines 170
St Augustine 202, 213
St Clement 210
St Helen 212
St Jerome 212
St Luke 206
St Mark 205
St Matthew 206
St Paul 203, 204, 205, 208
St Peter 205
Sais 150
Saite Dynasty 150, *162*
Saka 178
Samarra 43
Samarrans 43, 56, *56*
Samnites 170
San Agustín 183
San Lorenzo 141
Sanskrit 177
Sappho 144, 148
Sardinia 97
Sardis 148
Sargon 88, *90*, 92, 93
Sargon II *149*, 150, *162*
Sarmatians 178, *179*, 180, 206
Sassanids 210
Saul 121
Saxons 213, 214
Scandinavia 45, 54, 177
Schliemanns 96
Scipio Africanus 172
Scythians 145, 148, 150, 175, 178, 180, 195, *195*
  art *163, 178, 179*
Seals 63, 67
  Indus valley 93, 99, *101*
  Indus valley 93, 99, 101, *101*
  stamp *48, 75, 75*
Second Semitic Empire 114
Seismograph 216, 219, *219*
Seleucia 209
Seleucids 169, 170, 172
Semites 64, 90-2, 93, 96
Seneca 204
Sennacherib 150
Seti I 120
Severus, Septimus 209-10, *209*
Shaduf *100*
Shaft graves 116
Shalmaneser II 149
Shalmaneser III *1*
Shang Dynasty 113, 122, 140, 181
  architecture 128, 131, *131*
  art 133, 135, *135*
  technology 127, *127*
Sheep 40, 44, 65, 66, 70, 94, 97
Ships 72, *126, 141*, 142, 153, *153*, 186, *186*
Shoshenk 149
Shrines 41, *52*
Siberia 94
Sickle *26*
Sidon 119, 139, 147
Siege engines 142
  Assyrian 142, 154, *154*
  Roman *218*
Silk Road 180
Sind 65
Siva 93

Siyalk 44
Smelting 41, 61
"Snake" Goddess *114*, 116
Snaketown 183
Snefru 88
Soghun Valley 65
Solomon 121, 147, 149, *159*
Solon 151
Sophocles 168
South America 71, 97, 122, 141, 201
Spain *57*, 96, 97, 140, 177
Sparta 168
Spartacus 173
Spindles 40
Spinning 40
Squash 97
Ssu-ma 180
Standard of Ur *86*
Stelae *90*, 132, 141, 160
Step pyramid 88, 89
Stilicho 213
Stock-breeding 40, 43
Stoics 209
Stone Age
  Late 97
  Middle 23
  New 11, 23, 42, 43, 44, 69
  Old 11, 17, 18, 20, 21, 23
Stonehenge 97, 119, 121, 123, *123*, 131, *131*
Stone tools *17, 27*, 43, 65, 70, 71
Stone vessels 43
Story of Sinuhe 114
Strait of Magellan 23
Strand looping 44
Strettweg cart 163, *163*
Stupas 178, 188, 191, *191*
Sudras 178
Suetonius 206
Sumeria 43, 44, 64-5, 92, 93
Sumerian language 62, 93, 114
Sumerians 64, 93
Sunda Shelf 16
Sunflowers 141
Suppiluliumas 119, 120
Susa 65, 93

T

Tacitus 203, 205
Talayots 121
Tale of the Eloquent Peasant 114
Taoism 141
Tarquin kings 139
Tarsus 203
Tartessians 140, 177
Tartessus 140
Tarxien 96, 105, *105*
Tauret *194*
Taxila 178
Technology 24-7, 46-9, 72-5, 98-101, 124-7, 152-5, 184-7, 216-9
Tehuacán Valley 45, 71, 122
Telamon, battle of 176
Tell es-Sawwan 56, *56*
Temples 68, 71, 76, *78*, 90,

97, 102, 105, *105*, 178, 191, *191*, 223, *223*
Tenochtitlán 202
Tents 53
Teotihuacán 183, 200, 220
Tepe Yahya 93
Terracing 216
Tertullian 210
Tetrarchs 205, *205*
Textiles 42
   Paracas 182
Thales 141, 151, 153
Thebes 117, 118, 119
Theodoric 213
Theodosius 212, 213
Thera 116
Thermopylae 169
Thessaly 42
Third Dynasty 93
Tholos *78*
Thracians 148
Thucydides 168
Thutmose I 118
Thutmose III *117*, 118
Thong-softener 21
Thracians 148, 151
Tiahuanaco 183, 201, 220
Tiberius 203, *208*
Tiglath-Pileser 121, 149
Tiglath-Pileser III 149-50
Tigris-Euphrates 43, 44, 96
Tikal 182, 201
Timber 92, 96
Titus 205, 206
Tobacco 142
Tollund Man 177, *177*
Tombs 76, 78, *78*, 79, *79*, 96-7, *104*, *105*, 121, *130*, 131, *190*
Tools 43, 44
Torre 121
Tou Wan 182, 195, *195*
Tower of Babel 145
Trade 40, 41, 42, 70, 89, 93, 94, 142
Trajan 206-8
Transcaucasia 44
Transport 72
Tres Zapotes 141
Trireme 186, *186*
Triumvirate 173
Trojan War 116, 120
Troy 96, 105, *105*
True Cross 212
Trundholm sun chariot 122, *122*
Tso-ch'iu Ming 144
Turoe Stone *175*
Tutankhamun *6*, 119, *119*, 120, *126*, 128, 132, 134, *134*
"Two Lands" 66
Tyre 119, 120, 139, 147

U

Uaxactún 201
Ubaidans 63, 64
Ugarit 114, *114*, 116
Ulysses *206*
"Umbrella" lands 39, 40, 42, 43

Umma 90, 92
Upanishads 140, 144
Ur 63, 87, 90, 93
   destruction of 93
   Royal cemetery of 90, 97, 102, 106, 122
Urartu 145, 148, 150
Ur-Nammu 93
Urnfield cultures 140, 147
Uruk 62, 64, 71, 90

V

Valens 213
Valley of the Kings 118, 128, *134*
Valley of Mexico 45, 135, *135*, 141, *159*
Vandals 213
Varus 203
Veii 170
Venus of Laussel 22, *22*
Venus figurines 28, *34*, 35
   Cycladic *96*
Vercingetorix 172
Vergil 174, *174*, 206
Verica 203
Vespasian 204, 205-6
Vesuvius 206
Villanovans 155, *155*
Vinca 69
Vines 96
Virú Valley 97
Visigoths 212, 213
Vision of Nahum 150
Vortigern 213
Votive bronzes 122, *122*
Vulca 194
Vulture cult 41-2, *43*

W

Wadis 66
Wadjet 66
Wall reliefs 41
Walled towns 96
Warring States 180, 182
Watermill 216
Weaving 40, 44, 97, 98
Wessex 121
Western Mediterranean 43, 44, 69, 71, 96-7, 116, 121, 139, 140, 147
   architecture 28, *28*, 30, 50, *50*, 53, 76, *76*, 79, *79*, 102, *102*, 105, *105*, 128, 131, *131*, 156, *156*, 159, *159*, 190, *190*, 220, 220-1, 222, *222-3*
   art 32, *32*, 34, *34*, 54, *54*, 57, *57*, 80, *80*, 83, *83*, 106, *106*, 109, *109*, 132, *132*, 134, *134*, 160, *160*, 163, *163*, 192, *192*, 194, *194*, 225, *225*, 226, *226*
   technology 24, *24*, 26, *26*,

46, *46*, 48, 72, *72*, 75, 98, *98*, 101, *101*, 124, *124*, 127, *127*, 152, *152*, 155, *155*, 184, 185, 186, *186*, 216, 216-7, 218, *218-9*
Wheat 65, 70, 93, 97
   Einkorn 40, 42
   Emmer 40, 42
Wheel 62, 72, *74*, 98
Whetstone *26*
Woodland mound-builders 183
Woodworkers 41, 72, 124
Woolley 63
Writing 62, 72, 89, *114*, 116, 124, 152
   alphabetic 113-14, 142
   glyphic 201
Wulfila 212
Wu-ti 180

X

Xenophon 168
Xerxes 167

Y

Yahweh 120, 149, 150, 170
Yakshi 195, *195*
Yang Shao 65-6, 80, 94
Yayoi 182
Yueh Chi 178, 199
Yugoslavia 42

Z

Zab River 43
Zagros 39, 40, 44, 65, 92
Zakro 116, 118
Zapotecs 182, 200
Zealots 205
Zeus 170
Ziggurat 102, 104, *104*, 130, *130*, 144, 145, *158*
Zoroaster 141
Zoser 88, 89, *94*, 97

Acknowledgments

Photographic Sources
The photographs appearing in the book are identified below as follows:–
page number (in bold type); subject; museum or gallery (in italics); photographer or photographic source (in parentheses).

Jacket: Stone Circle, Castlerigg (Picturepoint Ltd) Back jacket: Head of Brutus (Alinari) Back jacket: Nefertiti; *Staatliche Museum, Berlin* (Bildarchir Preussicher Kulturbesitz) Inside back flap: The Good Shepherd (Sonia Halliday) Inside back flap: Photograph of Jacquetta Hawkes (Mark Gerson)
1 Ivory relief of warrior from Palace of Shalmaneser III; *Iraq Museum, Baghdad* (Picturepoint Ltd) **2** Bronze head of Aphrodite; *British Museum* (Michael Holford) **6** Back of Tutankhamun's throne; *Cairo Musuem* (Roger Wood) **8** Sphinx at Giza (Michael Holford) **10** Laconian kylix; *Bibliothèque Nationale, Paris* (Hirmer Fotoarchiv) **12** Olduvai Gorge, Tanzania, (Bruce Coleman Ltd) **14** The Hall of Bulls, Lascaux (Colorphoto Hinz) **31** Danger Cave, Utah (Werner Forman Archive) **34** Deer, Altamira, Spain (Picturepoint Ltd); Bison Altamira (Michael Holford); Stags and fish plaque, Lortet, France; *National Museum, St. Germain-en-Laye* (Photoresources) **35** Venus of Laussel; *Musée d'Aquitaine, Bordeaux* (Photographie, Giraudon); "Chinese Horse," Lascaux (Colorphoto Hinz); Venus of Willendorf; *Naturhistorisches Museum, Vienna* (Photoresources); Two horses, Pech-Merle (Jean Vertut) **38** Stag's head, Çatal Hùyùk; *Archaeological Museum, Ankara* (Mrs M. A. Mellaart) **52** Tower at Jericho (George Gerster/Rapho) **56** Halaf plate, Arpachiyah (Hirmer Fotoarchiv); The Hunter, Çatal Hùyùk; *Archaeological Museum, Ankara* (Mrs M. A. Mellaart); Hasan Dag, Çatal Hùyùk; *Archaeological Museum, Ankara* (Mrs M. A. Mellaart) **57** Amber carved animals; *National Museum, Copenhagen* (Museum photograph) **60** Head from Uruk, Mesopotamia; *Iraq Museum, Baghdad* (Hirmer Fotoarchiv) **64** Clay figurine of man, "The Thinker,"; *National Museum, Bucharest* (Photoresources) **66** Hunter's Palette from Egypt; *Ashmolean Museum* (Museum photograph); Ivory label of King Den; *British Museum* (Michael Holford) **68** Terracotta Idol, Eridu; *Iraq Museum, Baghdad* (Hirmer Fotoarchiv) **70** Painted beaker from Susa; *Iraq Museum, Baghdad* (Josephine Powell); Bronze hoard from Engedi (Ronald Sheridan) **71** Kerbstone, New Grange (Photoresources) **74** Clay tablet; *British Museum* (Photoresources) **78** Cone mosaics, Uruk; *Iraq Museum, Baghdad* (E. Bohm, Mainz) **82** Uruk vase; *Iraq Museum, Baghdad* (Holle Verlag); Narmer Palette; *Cairo Museum* (Werner Forman Archive); Flint knife with ivory handle from Gebel-el-Arak; *Louvre* (Ronald Sheridan) **83** Dimini pot; *National Museum, Athens* (Josephine Powell); Siyalk III beaker; *Archaeological Museum, Teheran* (Josephine Powell); Spiral decoration, New Grange (Photoresources); Amber horse; *Museen fur Vor-und Fruhgeschichte, Berlin* (Bildarchiv Preussischer Kulturbesitz); Yang Shao funerary pot; *Museum of Far Eastern Antiquities, Stockholm* (Museum photograph) **86** Standard of Ur, War; *British Museum* (Michael Holford) **89** Figure of Gilgamesh, Khorsabad; *Louvre* (Michael Holford) **90** Akkadian head of Sargon; *Iraq Museum, Baghdad* (Hirmer Fotoarchiv);

Stele of Naram Sin; *Louvre* (Michael Holford) **91** Goat in a Wepemnofret Stele; *Lowie Museum of Anthropology, University of California, Berkeley* (Museum photograph) **101** Gold jug; *Ankara Museum* (Josephine Powell); Flint Thicket, Ur; *British Museum* (Michael Holford); Gold helmet of Mes-Kalamshar; *Iraq Museum, Baghdad* (Hirmer Fotoarchiv) **92** Model of wooden plough; *British Museum* (Michael Holford) **94** Statue of Khafra; *Cairo Museum* (Robert Harding Assocs.); Statue of Zoser; *Cairo Museum* (Werner Forman Archive) **95** Geese from Meidum; *Cairo Museum* (Werner Forman Archive); Dwarf Seneb & Family; *Cairo Museum* (Robert Harding Assocs.); Pair Statue of King Menkaure and his Queen; *Museum of Fine Arts, Boston* (Peter Clayton) **96** Cycladic venus; *British Museum* (Michael Holford) **100** Copper Goddess; *British Museum* (Museum photograph); dagger; *National Museum, Copenhagen* (Museum photograph); Mohenjo-Daro seals; *National Museum of Pakistan, Karachi* (Robert Harding Assocs.) **104** Pyramids at Giza (Hirmer Fotoarchiv) **105** West Kennet Barrow (Michael Holford); Great Bath, Mohenjo-Daro (Josephine Powell); Temple at Tarxien, Malta (Robert Estall) **108** Votive statuette, Tell Asmar; *Iraq Museum, Baghdad* (Picturepoint Ltd); Boy with oxen from Tomb of Ti (Roger Wood); Seated scribe; *Cairo Museum* (Roger Wood); The great singer, Uranshe; *Damascus Museum* (Hirmer Fotoarchiv); Statuette of Pepi II and his mother; *Brooklyn Museum* (Museum photograph); Bull harp, Ur (Picturepoint Ltd.); Harp player; *National Museum, Athens* (Photoresources) **109** Sleeping lady from Hypogeum; *National Museum, Valletta, Malta* (Photoresources); Priest King; *National Museum of Pakistan, Karachi* (Josephine Powell); Beaker pot; *British Museum* (Photoresources); Grimes Graves goddess; *British Museum* (Photoresources) **112** Wedded couple, tomb of Ramose at Thebes (Hirmer Fotoarchiv) **114** Phaistos Disc; *Heraklion Museum, Crete* (Picturepoint Ltd); Phoenician ivory relief from Ugarit; *Louvre* (Photographie Giraudon); Minoan libation jug; *Heraklion Museum, Crete* (Photoresources) **115** Wall painting of Bluebird; *Heraklion Museum, Crete* (Photoresources); Sarcophagus from Hagia Triada; *Heraklion Museum, Crete* (Hirmer Fotoarchiv) **116** Hammurabi of Babylon; *Louvre* (Ronald Sheridan); Code of Hammurabi; *Louvre* (Mansell Collection) **117** Thutmose III; *Cairo Museum* (Bildarchiv Foto Marburg.) **118** Scene from "Book of the Dead"; *British Museum* (Michael Holford); Musicians and Dancers, Thebes (Michael Holford); Colossi of Memnon (Picturepoint Ltd) **119** Water offering to the Mummy; *British Museum* (Michael Holford); Nefertiti's daughters; *Ashmolean Museum* (Michael Holford); Tutankhamun's casket; *Cairo Museum* (Hirmer Fotoarchiv) **120** Queen Hatshepsut, Karnak (Peter Clayton); Akhenaten and Nefertiti (Peter Clayton) **121** Ramesses II, Karnak (Michael Holford); Lion Gate, Mycenae (Ronald Sheridan) **122** Shang spearhead; *British Museum* (Michael Holford); Shang Vessel (Robert Harding) **123** Stonehenge (Michael Holford); Chariot of the Sun; *National Museum, Copenhagen* (Museum photograph) **126** Tutankhamun's throne; *Cairo Museum* (F. L. Kennet/ George Rainbird Ltd) **127** Bronze ritual food vessel (Robert Harding Assocs.) **130** Deir-el-Bahari (Hirmer Fotoarchiv); Naveta es Tudons, Minorca (Photoresources) **130** Tombs Cala Coves (David Trump) **131** Street in Mohenjo-Daro (Robert Harding Assocs.); Stonehenge (Photoresources) **134** Sacrifice scene, Mari *Louvre* (Bulloz);

Head of Nefertiti; *Staatliche Museen, Berlin* (Bildarchiv Preussischer Kulturbesitz); Tutankhamun's pectoral; *Cairo Museum* (F. L. Kennet/George Rainbird Ltd) 134-5 Bull leaping fresco; *Heraklion Museum, Crete* (Photoresources) 135 King Tudhalias IV, Yazilikaya (Josephine Powell); "The Mask of Agamemnon"; *National Museum, Athens* (Photoresources); Ritual vessel; *Musée Cernuschi, Paris* (Michael Holford); Rillaton gold cup; *British Museum* (Eileen Tweedy) 138 Etruscan sarcophagus; *Museo di Villa Giulia, Rome* (Leonard von Matt) 141 Phoenician ship; *British Museum* (Michael Holford) 142 Hallstatt plate; *British Museum* (Museum photograph); Tiger's head; *Ostasiatische Museen, Cologne* (Michael Holford) 143 Theseus killing Minotaur; *British Museum* (Michael Holford) 144 Homer; *Louvre* (Ronald Sheridan); Winged lion of Sargon; *British Museum* (Ronald Sheridan) 145 Assurnasirpal enthroned; *British Museum* (Michael Holford); Audience scene, Persepolis (Oriental Institute, University of Chicago) 146 Olmec seated figure; *National Museum of Anthropology, Mexico* (Werner Forman Archive); Colossal head, La Venta, Mexico (Werner Forman Archive) 147 Strangford Apollo; *British Museum* (Photoresources); Apollo of Veii; *Museo di Villa Giulia, Rome* (Michael Holford) 149 Sargon II; *Museo Egizio, Turin* (Fotocolor G. Rampazzi, Turin) 150 Nimrud ivory; *Metropolitan Museum of Art, New York; Rogers Fund* (Museum photograph) 151 Calf bearer; *Acropolis Museum, Athens* (Hirmer Fotoarchiv) 154 Assurbanipal hunting wild asses; *British Museum* (Museum photograph) 162 Woodland hunting scene; *British Museum* (Michael Holford); Nebuchadnezzar II's Royal Chamber; *Staatliche Museen, Berlin* (Bildarchiv Preussischer Kulturbesitz); Geometric vase; *Antikensammlung, Munich* (Hirmer Fotoarchiv) 163 Etruscan warrior; *British Museum* (Michael Holford); Sardinian warrior; *National Museum, Copenhagen* (Museum photograph); Scythian panther; *Hermitage, Leningrad* (Photoresources); Mongolian girl; *Museum of Fine Arts, Boston* (Museum photograph); Jade ceremonial adze; *British Museum* (Werner Forman Archive) 166 Charioteer of Delphi; *Delphi Museum* (Hirmer Fotoarchiv) 168 Pericles; *British Museum* (Michael Holford); Darius; *Naples Museum* (Photoresources) 169 Head of Alexander (Photoresources); Alexander on horseback; *Archaeological Museum, Istanbul* (Photoresources) 170 Ptolemy and wife; *Hermitage, Leningrad* (Photoresources) 170 Alexander and Roxane; *Kunsthistorisches Museen, Vienna* (Museum photograph) 172 Dying warrior (Hirmer Fotoarchiv) 173 Parthian shot; *Teheran Museum* (William MacQuitty); Head of Cleopatra; *British Museum* (Michael Holford) 174 Julius Caesar (coin); *British Museum* (Michael Holford); Augustus (Photoresources); Vergil, Sousse, Tunisia (Photoresources) 175 Turoe stone, Galway, Eire (Photoresources); Gundestrup cauldron; *National Museum, Copenhagen* (Museum photograph) 178 Scythian plaque "blood brothers"; *Hermitage, Leningrad* (Photoresources) 179 Scythian stag; *Hermitage, Leningrad* (Photoresources); Samaritan plaque; *Hermitage, Leningrad* (Photoresources); Pazyryk saddle-cover; *Hermitage, Leningrad* (Photoresources) 180 Pazyryk silk phoenix; *Hermitage, Leningrad* (Photoresources) 181 Jade horse; *Victoria and Albert Museum* (Michael Holford); Han vessel; *Volkerkunde Museum* (Michael Holford); Han figure (Werner Forman Archive) 182 Paracas textile (Ferdinand Anton) 183 Olmec baby; *Private collection*

(Werner Forman Archive) 186 Camel, Persepolis (William MacQuitty) 187 Dejbjerg wagon; *National Museum, Copenhagen* (Museum photograph) 190 Naksh-i-Rustam (William MacQuitty); The Parthenon, Athens (Sonia Halliday); Persepolis (Oriental Institute, University of Chicago); Theatre at Epidaurus (Sonia Halliday); The First Pylon, Edfou (Michael Holford) 191 The Great Wall, China (William MacQuitty); Sanchi Stupa (Bury Peerless); West Gate of Sanchi (A. F. Kersting) 194 Gold rhyton; *Teheran Museum* (Josephine Powell); Statue of Hermes; *Olympia Museum* (Sonia Halliday); Persian and Mede, Persepolis (William MacQuitty); Etruscan head; *Vatican, Museo Gregoriano Etrusco, Rome* (Scala); Tauret; *British Museum* Michael Holford); Musicians' fresco, Tarquinia (Scala) 195 Battersea Shield; *British Museum* (Photoresources); Chinese leopard (Robert Harding Assocs.); Basse-Yutz flagon; *British Museum* (Museum photograph); Pazyryk wall-hanging; *Hermitage, Leningrad* (Photoresources); Paracas textile; *Private collection* (Michael Holford) 198 Ceiling, Baptistry of the Orthodox, Ravenna (Hirmer Fotoarchiv) 200 Han flying horse, *Peking Museum* (Robert Harding Assocs.) 201 Mochica figurine; *British Museum* (Museum photograph); Pyramid of the Sun, Teotihuacán (Werner Forman Archive) 202 Glass jug; *British Museum* (Michael Holford); Desborough mirror; *British Museum* (Museum photograph) 204 Coin of Nero; *British Museum* (Michael Holford); Augustus di Prima Porta; *Vatican Museum* (Scala) 205 The Tetrarchs, St Mark's, Venice (Scala) 207 Roman Fresco; *British Museum* (Michael Holroyd) 208 Head of Tiberius; Istanbul (Photoresources); Head of Julia; *Museum of Fine Arts, Budapest* (Photoresources); Head of Marcus Aurelius, Antalya, Turkey (Photoresources); Head of Caligula; *Cyprus Museum* (Photoresources); Head of Arcadius, Istanbul (Photoresources) 209 Septimus Severus; *Staatliche Museen, Berlin* (Bildarchiv Preussischer Kulturbesitz); Head of Constantine, Basilica Nova (Werner Forman Archive) 210 Coin of Diocletian (Photoresources) 211 Roman Forum (Werner Forman Archive) 212 Coin of Constantine (Photoresources) 214 Mosaic, S. Pudenziana, Rome (Scala); Mosaic, Arian Baptistry, Ravenna (Sonia Halliday); Mosaic, Galla Placidia, Ravenna (Sonia Halliday) 218 Roman road, Blackstone Edge (Picturepoint Ltd) 219 Roman hypocaust (A. F. Kersting) 222 Pont du Gard, Nîmes (A. F. Kersting); Temple of Ed Deir, Petra (A. F. Kersting); Roman Ampitheatre at Ed Djem (A. F. Kersting); Hadrian's Wall, Cawfield Crags (A. F. Kersting) 223 Maison Carrée, Nimes (A. F. Kersting); Roman theatre at Aspendos (Sonia Halliday); Interior of the Pantheon, Rome (Scala) 226 Parthian dish; *British Museum* (Michael Holford); Gravestone of a girl; *Staatliche Museen, Berlin* (Bildarchiv Preussische Kulturbesitz); Seated figure of young girl; *Museo nuovo nel Palazzo dei Conservatori, Rome* (Mansell Collection); Augustus cameo; *British Museum* (Photoresources); Anubis and Osiris; *Louvre* (Bulloz); Girl with stylus; *Museo Nazionale, Naples* (Scala); Sarcophagus of Junius Bassus; *Vatican* (Hirmer Fotoarchiv) 227 "Gloucester" head; *Gloucester City and Folk Museums* (Photoresources); Ajanta fresco (Victor Kennett); Horse and carriage (Robert Harding Assocs.); Buddha preaching; *Archaeological Museum, Sarnath* (Bury Peerless); Pottery incense burner (Eileen Tweedy); Mochica stirrup jar; *Museum of Archaeology and Ethnology, Cambridge* (Museum photograph) 230 Map (Michael Holford)

The Atlas of Early Man
was edited and designed by
DORLING KINDERSLEY
LIMITED

Managing Editor
Christopher Davis
Editor
Amy Carroll
Art Editors
Stephanie Todd
Julian Holland
Picture Researcher
Caroline Lucas

Dorling Kindersley Limited would like to thank James Mellaart and David Kindersley for their special assistance.

Artists
David Baird
Michael Craig
Vana Haggerty
Richard Jacobs
Sarah Kensington
David Nash
Linda Nash
Osborne/Marks
Ann Savage
Michael Woods

Cartography
Arka Graphics

Typesetting by Diagraphic
Typesetters Ltd., London

Reproduction by F. E.
Burman Ltd., London

Printing by Alabaster
Passmore and Sons Ltd.,
Maidstone